FOM-Edition

International Series

Series Editor
FOM Hochschule für Oekonomie & Management, Essen, Germany

In the course of its development, the FOM University of Applied Sciences founded a scientific publication series, the *FOM-Edition*, which is specifically dedicated to the publication projects of its lecturers. The *FOM-Edition* is divided into the following categories: textbooks, case study books, specialist books, and an international subseries *(International Series)*. This contribution is part of the *International Series*, which accompanies the FOM strategy of internationalization and enables a unique representation of the productive outcome of international research collaboration and partnership. Through this subseries, FOM University offers its lecturers, researchers, and cooperation partners a platform to share joint projects, methods, and insights internationally.

More information about this subseries at https://link.springer.com/bookseries/15755

Manfred Cassens · Zsófia Kollányi ·
Aleksandar Tsenov
Editors

Transdisciplinary Perspectives on Public Health in Europe

Anthology on the Occasion of the Arteria
Danubia Project

Editors
Manfred Cassens
ifgs, FOM University of Applied Sciences
Munich, Germany

Zsófia Kollányi
Eötvös Loránd University
Budapest, Hungary

Aleksandar Tsenov
FDIBA, Technical University Sofia
Sofia, Bulgaria

ISSN 2625-7114   ISSN 2625-7122   (electronic)
FOM-Edition
ISSN 2524-6739   ISSN 2524-6747   (electronic)
International Series
ISBN 978-3-658-33739-1   ISBN 978-3-658-33740-7   (eBook)
https://doi.org/10.1007/978-3-658-33740-7

Responsible Editor: Margit Schlomski
This Springer Gabler imprint is published by the registered company Springer Fachmedien Wiesbaden GmbH part of Springer Nature.
The registered company address is: Abraham-Lincoln-Str. 46, 65189 Wiesbaden, Germany

Foreword

Public health focuses on health promotion as well as primary and tertiary prevention. Thus, it accounts for the majority of public, non-medical health care. The meaning of this can only be vaguely guessed in the European context in times of the SARS 2 Covid-19 pandemic. Virologists around the world have been searching for an effective vaccine against SARS 1 and 2 for more than a decade, which has become more urgent in the present than ever before. Thus, traditional, and at the same time unpopular, public health measures intervene in every human life in a primary preventive and restrictive way. In addition to the current omnipresence of public health in Europe and even worldwide, due to Covid-19, public health has been dealing with another phenomenon of Western civilization, namely the epidemiological transition, at least since the Ottawa Charter. In short, it is about the change in the incidence of disease and mortality: away from infectious diseases and towards lifestyle-related diseases. The first WHO conference on health promotion in Ottawa, Canada, ended with a charter comprising five action fields. The Charter has been revised twice in the past 30 years, but has retained its essential core:

- Building healthy public policy
- Creating supportive environments
- Strengthening community action
- Developing personal skills
- Re-orienting health care services towards prevention of illness and promotion of health.

The implementation of the five action fields leads—via the central guiding concept of "individual health literacy"—to the three supporting pillars of healthy exercise, balanced and sustainable nutrition and resilience.

The implementation of the action areas requires structures that are as innovative as those of the Covid-19 pandemic. It is simply about the reorientation of health care services. Reflecting on such a reorientation was the content of the research initiation project "Arteria Danubia—Analysis and discussion on the implementation of model health regions in the upper and lower reaches of the Danube", which was funded by the German

Federal Ministry of Education and Research for the period from 2017 to 2019 (funding code 01DS17019). The project focused on the question, whether the concept of health regions—regional networks of local actors with the aim of improving the health care of the population—can be generally transferred to Hungary and Bulgaria. In appreciation of the successful completion of the project, the present book was produced with contributions from the participating partner universities and other associated, mostly university-based, organizations.

The thematic focus is on "Public Health" in all its implicit wealth of facets: The first of the three chapters begins with health policy ("Missing health political opportunities due to lack of nutritional behaviour acceptance") and extends to health education ("The Importance of Research-Based Learning as a Didactic Necessity in German Public Health Degree Programs"). This chapter also contains information on health regions. Public health-relevant topics are also dealt with under the focus of medicine. Two oncological-social medical topics focus on one of the main lifestyle-related mortalities in the Western Hemisphere: oncological diseases. The third article in this chapter deals with medical portals on the Internet and their use with a strong public health relation. The three contributions in the third chapter deal even more closely with one of the central topics of public health: the use of eHealth solutions. A contribution points to possible further solutions in the continuation of the Arteria Danubia-project (ComHeNet, Erasmus+) by developing digital solutions for health regions. The other two additional contributions deal with the "commercial value of health-related data" in terms of health economics and a topic which is becoming increasingly important for public health: geriatric care in the context of eHealth.

The editors would like to express their special thanks to Ms. Andrea Lakasz, Ms. Christine Prasch and Prof. Dr. Robert Dengler, who have contributed a great deal of work to the realisation of the project.

Prof. Dr. Manfred Cassens
Dr. Zsófia Kollányi
Prof. Dr. Aleksandar Tsenov

Contents

Part I Focus Public Health

**1 Missing Health Political Opportunities Due to a Lack
of Behavior Acceptance** 3
Thomas Breisach

**2 The Importance of Research-Based Learning as a Didactic
Necessity in German Public Health Degree Programs** 19
Manfred Cassens

**3 Community-Based Health Promotion for Senior Citizens—
What We Can Learn from South Korean Model of Senior Centers** 41
Yong-Seun Chang-Gusko, Ellen Meissner and Kai Kühne

4 The Impact of Health Literacy on the Healthcare System 59
Laura Eichhorn

**5 Tertiary Prevention and After-Care for Cancer Patients in
a Hotel Setting** 77
Kai Illing

6 Health Conferences in Germany, Austria and France—An Overview 85
Alfons Hollederer and Till Beiwinkel

**7 Vaccination Attitudes in Combatting Measles Along the Danube—
Ethical Aspects as Challenges** 101
Andrea Lakasz

**8 Lessons from the Creation and Failure of Two Regional Cooperation
Models in the Hungarian Health System** 121
Eva Orosz

**9 Occupational Health Management as Potential Element
in Combating Social and Regional Inequalities** 141
Manfred Cassens, Andrea Lakasz and Janusz Surzykiewicz

Part II   Focus Medicine

10   **Use and Significance of Expert Medical Advice on the Internet:
     Results of an Online Survey Among Users of German-Language
     Health Portals**   177
     Julian Wangler and Michael Jansky

11   **A Source Data Verification-Based Data Quality Analysis Within the
     Network of a German Comprehensive Cancer Center**   189
     Martina Borner, Diana Schweizer, Theres Fey, Daniel Nasseh
     and Robert Dengler

12   **The National Decade Against Cancer 2019–2029: Contents
     of the Initiative and Some Critical Thoughts**   201
     Robert Dengler

Part III   Focus Digitalization

13   **A Comprehensive Method for Multi-Criteria Evaluation of Health
     Regions**   217
     Aleksandar Tsenov, Velko Iltchev and Hristomir Yordanov

14   **The Commercial Value of Health-Related Data—An Empirical Study**   227
     Klemens Waldhör

15   **Health Apps in the Area of Conflict Between State Regulation
     and IT Architectures**   245
     Dominik Schrahe and Thomas Städter

16   **Acceptance Analysis and ELSI-Aspects of Sensor-Based
     Care-Management: Certain Results from a Qualitative Study
     Addressing Dehydration Management**   271
     Christian Heidl, Sebastian Müller and Jürgen Zerth

About the Editors

Manfred Cassens, Prof. Dr. habil. was appointed Professor for Health Management at the FOM University of Applied Sciences in January 2015. He is also director of the FOM Institute of Health & Social Affairs. In August 2017, he was granted teaching authorization for health education at the Faculty of Education and Philosophy of the Catholic University of Eichstätt-Ingolstadt. His main research interests focus equal opportunities in health and social epidemiology.

Zsófia Kollányi, PhD is a senior lecturer at the Faculty of Social Sciences, Eötvös Loránd University (Budapest). Her main field of research interest are health inequalities, and their social and economic roots and consequences, as well as the possibilities of health care and especially public health systems in improving health status and mitigating health inequalities. She teaches health policy and economics.

Aleksandar Tsenov, Prof. Dr. habil. is an Assoc. Professor, PhD at the Faculty of Telecommunications, Chair of Communications Networks, Technical University of Sofia, Bulgaria. After his degree in Telecommunications, he worked as a constructing engineer and later as a chief of telecommunications network operations team. He is Dean of the Faculty of German Engineering and Economics Education (FDIBA). Scientific interests: Management of information and communication systems, Process management of information systems and services.

List of Contributors

Till Beiwinkel, Dr. is a research associate at the Bavarian Health and Food Safety Authority (LGL) in Nuremberg, Germany. He is a trained sociologist and was awarded a PhD in the field of psychology and health. His professional activity focuses on the state-wide coordination of the Bavarian health regions[plus] including regional prevention and health promotion, health care and nursing care.

Martina Borner, M.Sc. is a consultant at WMC Healthcare GmbH in Munich, Germany. Previously, she worked as head of medical documentation at Ludwig-Maximilians-University in Munich. She graduated with a Master of Science in Public Health from FOM University of Applied Sciences.

Thomas Breisach, Prof. Dr. is Professor of Health and Social Management at the FOM University of Applied Sciences at the university center Munich. His main research focus is on strategy, marketing and communication as well as international health and nutrition policy with a focus on ingredients such as micronutrients and pharmaceuticals. He is inter alia a member of the Society for Applied Vitamin Research (GVF) and the German Society for Public Health (DGPH). Thomas Breisach, who can look back on many years of management expertise at the international group level as well as on the consulting side, works as a strategic consultant for international companies in the life science sector.

Yong-Seun Chang-Gusko, Prof. Dr. has been a full-time professor for Health & Social Affairs at the FOM University of Applied Sciences since 2015 and is also member of the Institute of Health & Social affairs (ifgs).

Since 2018 she is also project manager for the international cooperation between South Korea and Germany. Since 2019 she is visiting professor at the Korean Maritime and Ocean University and Kosin University in Busan/Korea. Her work focuses on the areas of corporate health management, health promotion and intercultural competence.

Robert Dengler, Prof. Dr. is physician with the focus in hematology and oncology.

Professional activity: A current focus is translational care research, especially in transsectoral settings. In this respect, he is currently working in a third party fund to evaluate a guideline of a national care system. Another focus is parmocoeconomics, with emphasis tumor treatment in the outpatient setting.

Beside that, he is a consultant for hospitals and private practices in oncology to support their engagement and involvement in selective contracting with the statutary health insurance.

Laura Eichhorn, B.Sc. studied Therapeutic Sciences and finished her master's degree in public health at the FOM University of Applied Sciences at the university center Munich. As examined physiotherapist she is head of the paediatric team of a private practice in Munich. Parallel to this she carries out consulting activities for a healthcare company as project manager in the areas of quality management and sustainable healthcare systems.

Theres Fey, Dr. has been coordinator of the Comprehensive Cancer Center in Munich (LMU Hospital), Germany, since 2016. After graduating from the University of Leipzig with a degree in pharmaceutics in 2006, she worked as a research scientist at Ludwig-Maximilians-University in Munich, where she also obtained her PhD in 2010.

Christian Heidl, Dr. is a research assistant and lecturer at the Wilhelm Löhe University of Applied Sciences in Fürth. He teaches in the field of gerontology and health sciences. His work and research focuse on the digitalization of nursing and health care, integrated research (ELSI) as well as quality of life and satisfaction research in nursing and gerontological care contexts.

Alfons Hollederer, Prof. Dr. habil. is professor for "Theory and Empirics of Health" at the Faculty of Human Sciences of the University of Kassel. He studied public health and social welfare. He is a Doctor of Public Health and habilitated in Public Health. The professorship focuses on analyses at the health care system level (macro level), of institutions and actors in the health care system (meso level) and of the health of those affected human beings (micro level).

Kai Illing, Prof. Dr. is Associate Professor at the FH Joanneum Graz/Bad Gleichenberg (University of Applied Sciences) in the faculty of Health Management in Tourism. He is CEO of TDC (Tourism Development HealthCare), a consultancy that focuses on the development of medical hotels. He is Auditor/Assessor for the international quality seals ISO 9000:2015, EFQM, KTQ, RegioSana, European Health and Spa Award. He is study director at the Apollon University of Applied Science for Health Economy, Bremen (Germany).

Velko Iltchev, Prof. Dr.-Ing. habil. graduated at the Technical University Sofia, Bulgaria in 1986. In his doctoral thesis "Language Processors for Deductive Databases" he developed a new method for processing recursive sets of rules, written in first-order predicate calculus. Prof. Iltchev habilitated in 2014 in the scientific area of "Language Processors". Since 2017 he is Vice-Dean of the German faculty at TU Sofia. Currently he works in rule-based decision support systems and in e-learning systems with AI.

Michael Jansky, Prof. Dr. med. Department of General and Geriatric Medicine, University Medical Center, Mainz, Germany

Kai Kühne, B.A. completed his training as a registered nurse in 2012 and worked as such at the Martini-Klinik at the University Clinic Hamburg Eppendorf GmbH until 2019. After completing his Bachelor's degree in Health and Social Management at the FOM University of Applied Sciences, he has been working in relevant project management. Since September 2019 he has been studying part-time in the Master Public Health at the FOM University of Applied Sciences.

Andrea Lakasz, M.Sc., B.A., Dipl.-Transl. worked for a decade as a translator/interpreter in the field of international relations at a government office in Budapest. After moving to Munich (2000), her professional reorientation took place. She obtained her degrees in Health and Social Management (B.A.) and Medicine Management (M.Sc.) at the FOM University of Applied Sciences at the university center Munich. She is involved in international cooperation focusing on health education and healthcare due to her professional and linguistics skills.

Ellen Meissner, Prof. Dr. has been a professor of business psychology at FOM University of Applied Sciences in Hamburg, Germany, since 2017. Before, she worked as a lecturer, consultant and coach. She graduated from the University of Osnabrück and Griffith University and she received her PhD in Organisational Behaviour from the University of Queensland in 2013.

Sebastian Müller, M.A. is a sociologist and trained electrician. After completing his master's degree, he worked as a research assistant at the German Youth Institute (DJI). Since 2016 he has been working at the research institute IDC at the Wilhelm Löhe University of Applied Sciences. The focus of his work is currently acceptance analyses, ELSI, implementation conditions of technological systems in the health sector, health care research questions and methodological questions of empirical social research.

Daniel Nasseh, Dr. has been working as IT coordinator and team leader at the Comprehensive Cancer Center in Munich, Germany, since 2014. He graduated with a degree in bioinformatics from Ludwig-Maximilians-University in Munich, where he also got his PhD in medical informatics.

Éva Orosz, Prof. Dr. Professor and Head of Doctoral Programme in Social Policy at the Faculty of Social Sciences, Eötvös Loránd University, Budapest. Her main areas of research are comparative studies on health systems performance; inequalities in health and health care; Hungarian health care reforms; health expenditure and financing. She has provided consultancy services several times for the OECD, WHO, World Bank since the early 1990s.

Dominik Schrahe, M.Sc. is lecturer at the FOM University of Applied Sciences at the university center in Munich. He is also research fellow at the FOM Institute of Health & Social Affairs (ifgs). His research focus is on IT-Security, information security management and data protection management especially in healthcare. Above that he is employed as IT Security Architect in an insurance company.

Diana Schweizer, M.Sc. is a data scienctist and business analyst at HanseMerkur in Hamburg, Germany. She previously worked at the Comprehensive Cancer Center at University Hospital (Ludwig-Maximilians-University), Munich.

Thomas Städter, Prof. Dr. is professor for Information Technology at the FOM University of Applied Sciences at the university center in Munich. His main focus is on IT-Management, IT-Architecture & Security Management and IT Project Management. His engagement as a lecturer is associated by activities where he acts as a subject matter expert for companies in the life sciences area. In addition, he offers consulting services for IT Security Management and Data Privacy.

Janusz Surzykiewicz, Prof. Dr. habil. is habilitated in Pedagogy and has doctoral degrees in pedagogy and theology. Since 2015, he holds the faculty chair for social pedagogy at the Catholic University of Eichstätt-Ingolstadt. His research focuses on resource-oriented prevention in the context of social and health behavior, with special emphasis on religious psychological issues. As a certified teaching trainer and coach, he is a member of the International Association of Coaching Institutes (ICI) and European Association for Supervision and Coaching (EASC).

Klemens Waldhör, Prof. Dr. has been a full-time teacher at the FOM University of Applied Sciences at the university center of Nuremberg since 2010, and in the same year he was appointed professor for business information technology ('Wirtschaftsinformatik'). His scientific interests and research deal with the topics of smartwatches and wearables in the field of AAL, data mining, artificial intelligence, project management and translation support.

Julian Wangler, Dr. Phil. is a research associate in the Department of General and Geriatric Medicine of the University Medical Centre Mainz (Universitätsmedizin Mainz). His research focus lies in the field of empirical healthcare services research with special emphasis on primary care and the impact of eHealth and mHealth on general practice and the healthcare system.

Hristomir Yordanov, Dr. has graduated BSc. in Radiocommunications from TU Sofia, Bulgaria in 2002 and MSc. and PhD from TU Munich, Germany, in 2006 and 2010 respectively. He is currently with the Faculty of German Engineering and Economics Education (FDIBA) at TU Sofia, where he serves as Vice-dean of research. His scientific work is in the field of medical sensor systems and remote telemetry.

Jürgen Zerth, Prof. Dr. habil. is Professor for Economics, especially Health Economics, at Wilhelm Löhe University of Applied Science in Fürth. He is also head of research institute IDC. Jürgen Zerth studied economics and health economics. After finishing doctorate in 2004 his research interests compasses different fields of health care management und health economics. During his postdoctoral period he also had lectures at University of Jena, at SISU-University Shanghai, FAU Erlangen Nuremberg and Bayreuth University.

Part I
Focus Public Health

Missing Health Political Opportunities Due to a Lack of Behavior Acceptance

Thomas Breisach

Contents

1.1 Background 4
1.2 Double Burden of Malnutrition—The Global Health (Economic) Challenge. 5
    1.2.1 The Global Health (Economic) Challenge. 5
    1.2.2 Focus on Analysis-Based Facts and Ideology-Free Strategies. 8
    1.2.3 Rethinking Existing Prevention Approaches 11
    1.2.4 Tolerating Health and Nutrition Behavior of Target Group is Key to Success 14
1.3 Conclusion 15
References. 16

Abstract

The Double Burden of Malnutrition is one of the biggest health political challenges in the world. There is not a single country not affected by it. Amongst other aspects the so-called supermarket revolution has reached all states and traditional diets are disappearing all over the world. For many people highly processed food is the basis of their daily diet. In 2016, the United Nations proclaimed the Decade of Nutrition in response to the importance of nutrition for the performance of national economies and the health of their population. In the past, well-intentioned health prevention

T. Breisach (✉)
FOM University of Applied Sciences, Munich, Germany
e-mail: thomas.breisach@fom.de

M. Cassens et al. (eds.), *Transdisciplinary Perspectives on Public Health in Europe*, FOM-Edition, https://doi.org/10.1007/978-3-658-33740-7_1

approaches often failed because they were driven by wishful thinking as well as ignoring the real world and health and nutritional behavior of the target groups for several reasons. For approaches to become relevant to health economies, they have to rely on a fact-based, reality tolerating analysis and be approached with ideology-free and operationalizable strategies. This also applies to the implementation of the strategies. A clearly differentiated approach must be taken, e.g. regarding the reduction of harmful ingredients or the enrichment of food. If activities would focus on change of behavior without respecting the taste of the population, they would result in a switch to other highly processed food with all its consequences on health only. Therefore, seen from a health political point of view, this would be counterproductive and modern civilization diseases could become an even bigger global health problem as expected by international experts.

1.1 Background

"No car, no meat, no plastic bags, no lemonade, no first-class train, no cigarettes, no commercials, no Nutella…Anything that doesn't fit into their world view should be forbidden" (Focus, 2018). With this tweet from July, 18th 2018, Nicola Beer, the former Secretary General of the German liberal Free Democratic Party (FDP), addressed a widespread problem with health or sustainability issues: namely that in many cases the focus is on bans and dogmatism, instead of striving for promising pragmatic solutions that are oriented towards people's living environments. The very well-known German TV chef Tim Mälzer also takes the same line with a statement that cannot be misunderstood in terms of clarity: "The well-meant advice from the lighthouse of the sublime and intellectuals as to what the supposedly perfect diet should look like simply does not help most consumers. On the contrary: In case of doubt, these statements only unsettle the reader even more" (Mälzer, 2018). The affluent societies in which food is always and at any time available and "absolutely de-emotionalized", have as a consequence that most people simply don't care about it at all (Mälzer, 2018). The consumption of highly processed foods has been identified as one of the key drivers for the rapidly increasing prevalence of obesity and its associated non-communicable diseases and costs. In Germany, 11% of health expenditure until 2050 will be spent on overweight and related conditions (OECD, 2019).

Obesity-related diseases will cause more than 90 million deaths in the 36 OECD member states over the next 30 years, reducing life expectancy by almost three years. Within the next 30 years, obesity and related diseases will also reduce the GDP of OECD countries by 3.3% (Fig. 1.1) and, according to OECD, will cause a household burden of yearly USD 360 per capita (OECD, 2019). According to the World Health Organization (WHO), the fight against malnutrition in its various forms is one of the greatest global health challenges, as many diseases are directly or indirectly linked to an unhealthy diet. The focus on malnutrition includes overweight, obesity and nutritional

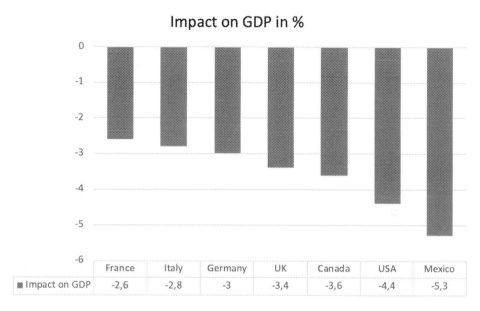

Fig. 1.1 The economic impact of obesity in selected countries until 2050. (own figure, based on OECD, 2019)

noncommunicable diseases (NCD) such as diabetes, heart disease and stroke. These diet-related NCDs are increasing in all age groups, especially in urban populations (WHO, 2017a). Unhealthy diet is the top risk factor for the global burden of disease (GBD) having a major effect on health. Thus, some are even calling for global action to help countries become more effective, e.g. in their fight against increasing obesity, since no country has a track record in this field (Ng et al., 2014).

1.2   Double Burden of Malnutrition—The Global Health (Economic) Challenge

1.2.1   The Global Health (Economic) Challenge

In 2016 the United Nations launched a decade of nutrition which is not only focusing on all forms of malnutrition and its health outcomes. Two of the goals of this UN decade are the reduction of anemia in women of reproductive age and the prevention of an increase in childhood overweight. Currently, 264 million women of reproductive age are affected by iron-amenable anemia and 42 million children are obese (WHO, 2018). Led by the Food and Agriculture Organization (FAO) and WHO, the UN, who asks the governments to take responsibility and to engage and work with all stakeholders (UN, 2016), named six fields of activities of the decade: The creation of sustainable, resilient food systems for healthy diets, the provision of social protection and nutrition-related education for everyone, the alignment of health systems to nutrition needs, the provision of universal coverage of essential nutrition interventions, the ensuring of trade and investment policies improving nutrition, the building of safe and supportive environments for nutrition at all ages and the strengthening and promotion of nutrition governance and accountability (WHO, 2016). Nutrition is directly addressed by the UN Sustainable Development Goals (SDG) through target number 2.2 "ending all forms of malnutrition by 2030" and it is seen as an enabler e.g. for the health-related SDG number 3 "good health and wellbeing" focusing on women, children and NCDs. Diet related NCD goals are a 30% relative reduction in mean population intake of salt, a 25% relative reduction in the prevalence of raised blood pressure or the containment of the prevalence of raised blood pressure according to national circumstances and a halt in the rise in diabetes and obesity (WHO, 2018).

At the 4th International Hidden Hunger Congress in Stuttgart, Francesco Branca, Director of the Nutrition Department of the WHO, stressed that an unhealthy diet is a wicked problem that is more challenging than air pollution (Branca, 2019). Due to income growth, urbanization and globalization, a significant change in the quality and quantity of food is now omnipresent (WHO, 2016). The countries are experiencing a rapid development regarding the double burden of malnutrition and there is no country in the world that is not affected by the globalization of nutrition and the disappearance of traditional diets. The Göttingen agricultural economist Martin Qaim, for example, has been talking about the so-called supermarket revolution for some years now (Qaim et al., 2014), which in the meantime has reached all countries and their eating habits. He also stresses that there are significant differences in the nutritional and health status of the populations, depending on whether a local food supply through supermarkets is available or not (Qaim, 2019). Qaim underlines "that supermarkets influence nutrition in multiple ways and directions" (Qaim et al., 2014). This is due, among other reasons, to the fact that supermarkets influence consumers' nutrition and eating habits not only by price but also by the shopping atmosphere, package sizes and the type of food offered. Increasing obesity rates are a result of changes in people's diets, their lifestyles, growing incomes and urbanization. The spread of supermarkets affects consumer food choices and the nutritional outcome all over the world. Shopping in supermarkets contributes to higher consumption of processed food and lower consumption of unprocessed foods. Beginning by the promotion of breast-milk substitutes (BMS) there is a significant daily influence of food marketing which has a strong impact on daily diet. Therefore, there is a real need to promote the WHO recommended low-cost fortified complementary food products. The first three years of life are already critical for good nutrition and healthy diet. With a broad availability of highly processed foods and beverages and growing evidence that children are consuming commercial snacks, attention has to be focused on increasing consumption of nutrient-rich food in early childhood and strategies have to be developed to limit consumption of unhealthy food and beverages (Zehner et al., 2019). This is one reason why in addition to undernutrition in infants and young children overweight is an emerging health issue. Small-scale studies in different countries have shown a higher consumption of sweet snack foods and soft drinks by young children (Huffman et al., 2014). It is not surprising, that a study on urban Kenya showed that the type of food offered in retailer affects people's food choices and nutrition and in consequence leads to a significantly higher BMI and obesity rate in the population (Demmler et al., 2018).

Thus, this form of food supply contributes, among other things, to the fact that EU countries are increasingly affected by obesity (see Fig. 1.2) and globally 1.9 billion adults have overweight, 600 million of these are obese (WHO, 2018). Therefore, a policy stimulating the sale of healthier food in supermarkets or a change of recipes of processed food could be promising to achieve positive nutritional effects. Retail food environment is increasingly considered in relation to obesity. Zeng investigated the impact of the access to supermarkets in the United States, e.g. the variations of supermarket openings and closings, showing that there "is little overall impact… on the BMI scores of low-income children. Therefore, improvement in healthy food access could at least help reduce childhood obesity rates among certain population groups" (Zeng et al., 2019). Another option to reduce the increase of obesity could be a higher taxation of highly processed food compared to less-processed food. A study on Sub-Saharan Africa (SSA) examined the possible impact of this approach on the prevalence of obesity and underweight in the adult population. The different taxing has shown significant and substantial

Country	2016	2012	2008	2004	2000
Austria	20.1	18.4	16.9	15.4	14.0
Belgium	22.1	20.7	19.5	18.2	17.0
Bulgaria	25.0	23.2	21.6	20.0	18.6
Croatia	24.4	22.5	20.7	19.0	17.5
Cyprus	21.8	20.4	19.1	17.8	16.4
Czechia	26.0	24.5	23.2	22.0	21.0
Denmark	19.7	18.1	16.7	15.3	14.0
Estonia	21.2	20.1	19.1	18.2	17.4
Finland	22.2	20.7	19.3	17.8	16.4
France	21.6	20.1	18.6	17.2	15.8
Germany	22.3	20.7	19.2	17.7	16.3
Greece	24.9	23.2	21.6	20.0	18.5
Hungary	26.4	24.5	22.6	20.9	19.6
Ireland	25.3	22.8	20.4	18.1	16.0
Italy	19.9	18.7	17.5	16.2	15.0
Latvia	23.6	22.4	21.3	20.2	19.3
Lithuania	26.3	25.0	23.8	22.6	21.6
Luxembourg	22.6	20.9	19.2	17.5	15.8
Malta	28.9	27.5	26.1	24.6	23.1
Netherlands	20.4	18.6	16.8	14.9	13.0
Poland	23.1	21.5	20.1	18.8	17.5
Portugal	20.8	19.0	17.2	15.4	13.7
Romania	22.5	20.7	19.0	17.5	16.2
Slovakia	20.5	19.1	17.8	16.6	15.5
Slovenia	20.2	18.8	17.5	16.2	15.1
Spain	23.8	22.4	21.0	19.7	18.3
Sweden	20.6	19.0	17.4	16.0	14.6
United Kingdom	27.8	25.4	23.1	20.8	18.6

Fig. 1.2 Development of prevalence of obesity among adults in EU-countries 2000–2016. (own visualization based on WHO Global Health Observatory data repository)

effects depending on the national income level or the gender. Boysen concluded that policies that result in different consumer price levels for the two food groups could affect eating behavior (Boysen et al., 2019).

Considering the fact that there is no health system in the world that is not affected by the consequences of the Double Burden of Malnutrition, from a health economic or political point of view it is negligent, that promising overall approaches such as food fortification and reduction of harmful ingredients still do not receive the attention or support needed for a successful implementation and thus exploitation of their possible public health potential. Linked with one fifth of deaths worldwide, unhealthy eating habits cause global health costs up to USD 2 trillion per year (FAO, 2019). The WHO defines the Double Burden of Malnutrition (DBM) as the "coexistence of undernutrition along with overweight, obesity or diet-related non-communicable diseases, within individuals, households and populations, and across the life-course" (WHO, 2016).

1.2.2 Focus on Analysis-Based Facts and Ideology-Free Strategies

Very often focus of public health organizations or heath enthusiasts is on behavior change only by neglecting daily diet, and consumer or health behavior of the population. This is actually an approach that completely ignores reality. In most countries it is still much more common to focus on informing consumers than involving processed food producers and changing food environments, e.g. by reformulation of processed foods or trans-fat banning (WHO, 2018). The other leading UN agency of the decade on nutrition, the FAO, focusses on overweight and obesity as well due soaring rates worldwide. Therefore, the World Food Day 2019 called for action to make healthy and sustainable diets available and affordable to everyone. The FAO wants to make the people aware of what they are eating, and it relies in its activities on countries, decision makers, companies, civil society and individuals to achieve healthy diets (FAO, 2019). For the leaders of FAO a multi stakeholder approach is the key for success in this global fight. Seen from a health political point of view, it is a great communication and advocacy challenge to close this gap so that societies e.g. will benefit from the advantages of food fortification and reduction of health risks by recipe change of convenience food and beverages. However, for being successful it is key to stay focused and to identify the barriers that could harm the benefit of this process. To have a better reach out of its activities e.g. in the field of behavior change the Swiss based nutrition think tank Sight and Life has already rightly added the health aspect to his strategic environment analysis (see Fig. 1.3). The Think Tank is using the PESTLHE analysis to gather and to systematically analyze the broader context and information on the interests of the relevant stakeholders, the barriers and the issues that are relevant in this context (Sight & Life, 2018). Taking in account that health and education are seen as key drivers for economies, both addressed by the World Bank in its Human Capital Project (HCI), it is astonishing that this segment of the macro analysis has not been addressed more prominent e.g. by business schools

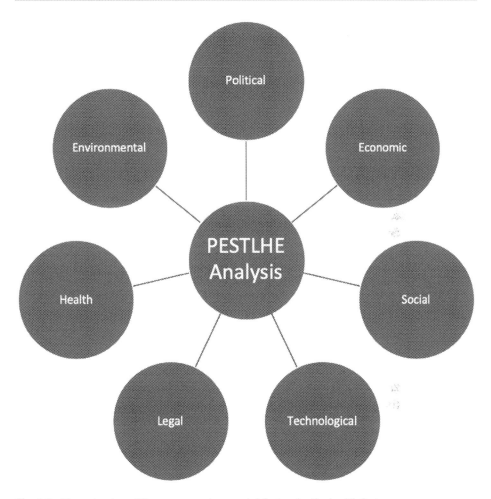

Fig. 1.3 The extension of the macro-environmental factors by the health factor

so far. The World Bank Group uses for its Human Capital Index (HCI) two indicators for the countries' overall health environment: The stunting rate of children under the age of 5 and the adult survival rate, which is defined as the proportion of 15-year-olds who will survive until age of 60. The first indicator reflects the health environment experienced during prenatal, infant, and early childhood development. The second one focusses on the health outcomes that a newborn child may experience as an adult. In its HCI, the World Bank combines the health and education components in a way reflecting their contribution to productivity, based on evidence from empirical studies (World Bank Group, 2018).

Apart from including macro health aspects, there has to be also a clear commitment to the involvement of all relevant stakeholders in the (behavior) change process for being successful. Seen from a strategic point of view without the involvement of industry and/

or population and the acceptance of its health and nutrition behavior no approach will have sustainable reach out on the specific health situation. The key for success is the question whether health workers or activists are willing respectively able to do this strategic analysis before starting their activities. Many players in the field of public health are not used to follow a strategic approach to reach the result they would like to have and therefore, seen from a strategic management point of view a lot of opportunities are missed. The completed analysis must be the basis for the strategy to be defined to be successful and achieve the defined health policy objectives. This is also valid for the fight against the health economic effects of the Double Burden of Malnutrition. An analysis as part of a holistic approach must be orientated towards the health policy objectives. The concept resulting from the planning has to comply with the requirements of the normative-political level and to contribute to the fulfilment of the mission. The task of strategic planning is to identify long-term opportunities and to develop them for society. In order to achieve this, it is important not only to analyze specific areas in a fact-based way, but also to critically question existing relevant processes, organizational structures, existing resources and especially attitudes and to examine them in a comprehensive analysis of the current situation in order to achieve the health policy objective. The opportunities and threats identified for the goal of fighting DBM, which result from the PESTHLE and specific environment, are subsequently compared with the own strengths and weaknesses relevant for achieving the health political goal. Thus, information from both a "market-based" and competence-based point of view becomes fundamental in a future-oriented strategic analysis of the current situation for the further derivation of goals and the strategies required to achieve them. At the strategic level, every decision therefore depends on an individual situation, individual resources and competencies and the assessment of the special situation. This strategic, precise, ideology-free analysis and the forecasts based on it must be the starting point of any strategic planning to be successful.

In this context, a strategic pragmatism is needed. Complexities must be reduced to create manageable simplicity to focus on the relevant facts and to avoid e.g. endless searches for further detailed information that is partly irrelevant for the overall objective. This complexity management and simplification necessary for success applies for the PESTLHE environment as well as to the rapidly changing micro-environment of the health market. Following this strategic pragmatism, ideological blinkers must be removed, and strategies must be implemented that are based on realities and, based on the analysis, have the greatest health political potential to combat DBM in the targeted region or country. Following James Müller's reasoning, measures for the prevention of overweight and obesity based on a detailed analysis of the condition factors and leading to the elimination of all changeable factors could lead to a significant reduction of the prevalence of overweight and obesity in children and adolescents (Müller et al., 2013).

To avoid misinterpretations, the strategy must be a binding behavioral plan oriented towards the realities of the living conditions to achieve the integrable goals of the individual activities, which must be strictly oriented towards the results of the analysis and not towards a wishful thinking, although well-meant. Unless a clear, fact-based goal orientation in planning, there may be uncertainties that lead to misunderstandings and uncoordinated, inconsistent action, which must be avoided in order not to jeopardize overall success. The precisely defined goals are therefore not only a binding orientation aid, but also have an important steering function for those involved in the fight against double burden, whether they are leaders of Intergovernmental Organizations (IGO), Non-Governmental Organizations (NGO), governmental bodies, industry or health workers. It is therefore essential that these strategic goals can be operationalized and are realistic. The defined goals are thus the basis for further strategy and operational planning and the basis for future success controlling. The strategic decisions made are therefore always dependent on the respective, specific challenges. It is important to focus on the relevant target countries, to focus on priorities and to define the framework for action as well as the general direction of the approach. Thereby it is important to make sure at this point of time not to get lost in operative measures, but to try to think in strategies and not to think about strategies. Choosing the form of strategy that is best for the respective health policy goal is always goal individual. In any case, following Clausewitz' strategic approach it is important to think in alternatives and to have a plan B even after the actual decision, which can be pursued further. These principles of a strategic approach must also form the basis of health policy activities within the framework of the Decade of Nutrition.

1.2.3 Rethinking Existing Prevention Approaches

In the area of behavioral prevention of obesity, for example James Müller was able to prove in an evaluation of 37 studies and data sets of 27,946 children that the classical, repeatedly demanded and promoted prevention approaches are not particularly sustainable and thus successful. A meta-analysis showed a high heterogeneity of interventions and study quality as well as the success of prevention. Success is more likely to be achieved among children of slim parents and among children from more educated families and more among girls than among boys (Müller, 2013). Consequently, the goal of all health policy approaches must therefore be to strengthen health-promoting everyday structures in the area of nutrition, e.g. through public private partnerships in food fortification, and at the same time to promote the self-responsibility of the population in terms of communication and to motivate them in the long term to eat healthier. To achieve this a clear commitment and an increased involvement of governments and all relevant groups will be needed to achieve this.

Most health-promoting measures, for example in corporate health management, mainly reach the same group: people who are mostly female, who are concerned with their health, have a healthy lifestyle and exercise sufficiently. Hence, it has to be asked to what extent these measures, as long as they are voluntary, can be useful in fighting the consequences of the DBM. Many men are not reached by healthy nutrition and behavior topics thematically. They find preventive courses boring and ignore the topic of health until they drop dead. However, for classical approaches to prevention and communication it is an obstacle that illness is perceived as a weakness that conflicts with men's self-image and that men therefore do not participate very much in health courses. For avoidable reasons, men die much earlier than women. Every second man suffers from cancer during his life, men smoke more often, are on average more obese and behave riskier overall. The paradox, however, is that in surveys men are subjectively much more satisfied with their own health than women. If public health politics want to reach this group and to be successful in this target group, they have to consider other approaches, because the majority of health communication and health and nutrition offers are too strongly focused on women. This means prevention that is suitable for men, if it should be successful, must look differently and be oriented towards their living environments. Thus, not only leisure behavior, but also the world of work has a strong influence on the nutritional behavior of people. Two more reasons why men are less concerned with prevention and health than women (Büssow, 2012). Men in lower paid jobs complaining more frequently about health problems caused by their profession normally are much less interested in prevention and in most societies, men work more often full-time than women.

For this reason, many countries rely not only on behavioral and relationship interventions but also on a reformulation of processed foods. For example, in the European Union (EU) most member states can present a reformulation measure for salt. Some 20 European countries are also relying on reformulation measures for trans-fat, total fat and added sugar. In Germany the National Strategy for the Reduction of Sugar, Fats and Salt in Finished Products is focusing on processed foods. The strategy defines finished products as processed products consisting of one or more foodstuffs to which at least sugars and/or fats and/or salt have been added. They are part of a modern lifestyle and often contain high levels of sugar, fats and salt. These processed foods can account for a high proportion of daily nutrition; some studies speak of up to 50% (Bundesministerium für Ernährung und Landwirtschaft, 2019). The strategy focuses on reducing the total number of calories in highly processed foods, reducing harmful ingredients such as trans fats, salt, sugar and improving nutrient composition by 2025. The German government expects the strategy to result in a double-digit reduction in sugar content. Germany's strategy came shortly after German physicians, in an open letter signed by more than 2000 professionals, called on the government to take concrete measures to fight malnutrition in Germany. Unhealthy lifestyles and obesity frequently occur in the German population. To fight the double burden, the doctors had called for four strategic approaches: Understandable food labelling, such as the traffic light system, restricting food advertising for children, tax incentives for the food industry to develop healthier recipes, and binding nutrition standards, e.g. for schools. Already as strategy paper the German approach has been criticized by some specialist associations, advocacy groups like Foodwatch and public health insurances, as the strategy paper would only be based on voluntary agreements by the industry. The associated reduction in unconscious sugar consumption would therefore not be sufficient and binding legal regulations would therefore be necessary. Other challenges for many successful solutions are often differences in the opinion between ministries of health and ministries of nutrition, even though it is common sense that the increasing prevalence of noncommunicable diseases, such as cardiovascular diseases or diabetes mellitus type 2, are enormous challenges for all health systems worldwide. Already since 2004 the WHO is targeting the main risk factors for these diseases (WHO, 2004). They all are associated with poor nutrition and lack of physical activity. The number of obese children and adolescents has globally risen tenfold over the past four decades. If this trend cannot be stopped and the obesity rates in children and adolescents continue soaring in industrialized countries and equally in low- and middle-income countries, in 2022 more children and adolescents will be obese than moderately or severely underweight (Imperial College London & WHO, 2017). In some European countries front pack labelling and taxing sugar, as requested by the German physicians in their letter are already gaining ground.

Following the WHO strategy, in 2007 the European Commission published an European strategy in its White Paper on a Strategy for Europe on Nutrition, Overweight and Obesity related health issues, to contribute to reducing e.g. overweight and obesity due to poor nutrition, because in the EU population levels of overweight and obesity have increased dramatically, particularly among children (European Commission, 2007). In line with the WHO for this coordinated approach, involving as many stakeholders as possible is planned. Strategies to tackle obesity have to avoid an increase of the risk of undernourishment. In some countries the problem of stunting coincides with, "and might in part contribute to, the rising prevalence of obesity in these countries." (Lobstein et al., 2015). To avoid this coincidence Lobstein et al. ask for a so-called healthy growth strategy. One approach within this strategy, which is already being pursued in many EU member states, is front pack labelling in its various variants such as NutriScore or traffic lights. The NutriScore label provides an overview of the health aspect of the processed product and takes positive and negative aspects into account. The system developed in France is also used in Spain and Belgium. Unhealthy ingredients have a negative impact on the score, while fruits, proteins or fibers have a positive one. The traffic light, indicating how much fat, sugar and salt is present in processed food, is used in the UK and Ireland on a voluntary basis. However, the British government is implementing a stricter regulation to halve UK child obesity rate of 20 per cent because the costs caused by obesity are too significant for the National Health System and for the personal life of the children. By all its legal restrictions planned e.g. on advertising, the British Government expects that it will force the food companies to reformulate their unhealthy products (Askew, 2018). On a voluntary basis, some European food producers, such as Danone and, in the future, Nestlé, are already using NutriScore labelling in some countries to give consumers greater transparency and better insight into the nutritional quality of food products (Handelsblatt, 2019). Another promising approach, which some of those in charge of public health are hoping for, is the taxation of sweetened beverages. There are numerous different approaches and the rules vary from market to market. Using best practices, this variant is ideal for lateral learning from other countries. In general, most health policy approaches dealing with the taxation of foods containing sugar, focus on beverages. However, in some countries there are already calls for a tax on sugar-containing snacks and foods. For many key opinion leaders, however, combating malnutrition by taxing foods containing sugar, which would lead to a significant increase in the price of soft drinks, would appear to be a way of reducing carbohydrate consumption, encouraging industry to develop healthier alternatives and generating a new source of revenue for public health. The United Kingdom introduced its Soft Drinks Industry Levy (SDIL) in 2018, which provides two tax rates for beverages containing sugar, one of 8 pence for beverages containing more than 5 g of sugar per 100 ml and another of 24 pence for those containing 8 g or more. In the same year, France introduced a differentiated tax rate for beverages according to their sugar content. In the same year France has introduced a tiered-tax rate for beverages according to their sugar content. The tax progressively increases up to 20 cents per liter for products with more than 11 g added sugar per 100 ml.

1.2.4 Tolerating Health and Nutrition Behavior of Target Group is Key to Success

A very promising approach to fight double burden is the reformulation of food with the aim of reducing sugar, fat and salt consumption and thus promoting a healthier diet by respecting the taste of the consumers. This is key, if public health leaders want to have a significant impact on the health system and its costs. Numerous scientific studies indicate that the current excessive consumption of processed food containing sugar, fat, saturated fats and salt increases the risk of noncommunicable diseases. An uncontrolled energy intake increases not only the risk of developing obesity. Reducing the intake of saturated fatty acids reduces the risk of coronary heart disease. The scientific evidence for a reduction of blood pressure through a reduced salt intake is proven too. In some countries, e.g. Germany, the salt intake in the adult population is significantly exceeding the WHO recommendations by 5 to 6 g per day. One reason for this is a high consumption of processed food. As a relatively preventive component of a holistic approach, the reformulation of food can contribute to facilitating a healthy diet, especially for those population groups that cannot or only poorly be reached with behavioral preventive measures and classic health communication approaches. Therefore, some countries started their reformulation initiatives already ten years ago. To achieve the respective reformulation goals, the countries rely on various methods such as laws, agreements initiated by the government and voluntary commitments on the part of food producers. In contrast to many other EU member states, Germany has not yet come up with any mandatory reformulation measures for total fat, saturated fatty acids, salt, sugar, energy content, portion sizes and whole grains.

However, to be successful, harmful ingredients reduction needs an understandable explanation to be accepted due?? a potential change in taste. Without respecting the willingness to switch of the consumer the new products will not be consumed and therefore, approaches will not have the impact needed. For this reason, it is important to iden-tify the information status of the population on harmful ingredients content. However, to equate this information status with consumer interest would be the next mistake that could be made. It is mandatory to determine whether the information status about the ingredients content is also behaviorally relevant and result in a rejection of products due to a "too high" salt, sugar or fat content, which seems rather unlikely among the public without appropriate communication. According to a recent German study, this was the case for sugar at 45%, fat at 38% and salt at 14%; A conscious decision for reduced foodstuffs showed similar differences (DLG, 2018). This suggests that the communi-cation activities, which are strongly focused on the harmfulness of sugar, are already having a clear impact on the public's awareness. For most consumers, the topic of salt has therefore not yet reached the population. However, the decisive factor for success regarding the widespread consumption of convenience products is the acceptance of the products with reduced contents. A 15% reduction in sugar is possible for consumers but should not be too much discussed. A reduction of the salt quantity by 10% is possible and can also be discussed without any problems. On the other hand, acceptance of the reduction of the fat content is not possible without loss of acceptance values, regardless of whether the reduction is discussed or not. However, in addition to consumer accept-ance, technological feasibility by manufacturers is crucial for successful implementation in this context. A study of Holger Buxel in 2017 has shown that experts estimate that fat and salt reduction is possible in many product groups in the range between 20 and 30%; a significant reduction of up to 50% is possible for sugar only (DLG, 2018).

1.3   Conclusion

If decision makers in health politics want to have a strong social impact in their coun-tries, they have to reflect their past and current activities and their personal attitudes, to rethink their behavior regarding prevention and become more strategic in their thinking. Success is guaranteed only if the decisions are based on a broad, fact driven analysis, e.g. the PESTHLE analysis.

Approaches are much more promising if the taste and the nutritional behavior of the population is accepted and schoolmasterly behavior is avoided. Seen from an undog-matic public health point of view promising approaches in this context are food fortifica-tion as well as reformulation of processed foods by reducing harmful ingredients. If this reformulation of recipes is not achieved on a voluntary basis, taxing unhealthy food and beverages can force producers to develop healthier products and to fight Double Burden of Malnutrition and its consequences.

To achieve this it is a long way to go because many health activists have to learn to accept that they have to be open to co-operate with other stakeholder groups, that there are different ways to achieve relevant health goals and that former communication and project concepts have to be rethought. If there is no willingness to accept these facts, activities will fail, and modern civilization diseases will become an even bigger problem to the world as expected by some experts.

References

Askew, K. (2018). Deep disquiet in the food and drink sector': Industry unhappy at regulation to halve UK childhood obesity. https://www.foodnavigator.com/Article/2018/06/25/UK-aims-to-halve-childhood-obesity-by-2030. Accessed 25 June 2018.

Boysen, O., Boysen-Urban, K., Bradford, H., & Balié, J. (2019). Taxing highly processed foods: What could be the impacts on obesity and underweight in sub-Saharan Africa? *World Development, 119*, 55–67.

Branca, F. (2019). *Making smart commitments to achieve global nutrition targets in the Decade of Nutrition*. Presentation at the 4th International Congress Hidden Hunger, Stuttgart. Unpublished presentation.

Bundesministerium für Ernährung und Landwirtschaft. (2019). *Nationale Reduktions- und Innovationsstrategie für Zucker, Fette und Salz in Fertigprodukten*. Bundesministerium für Ernährung und Landwirtschaft (BMEL), Bonn.

Büssow, R. (2012). Gesunde Ernährung und Bewegung - das ist für viele Männer Weiberkram. *Ärzte Zeitung, 96*, 5.

Commission of the European Communities. (2007). White paper on a strategy for Europe on nutrition, overweight and obesity related health issues, Brussels. Retrieved from Commission of the European Communities (2007). White Paper on a Strategy for Europe on Nutrition, Overweight and Obesity related health issues, Brussels. Accessed 25 Jun 2018.

Demmler K, Ecker O, & Qaim M (2018). Supermarket shopping and nutritional outcomes: A panel data analysis for urban Kenya. *World Development*, 102, February 2018, 292–303.

DLG. (2018). *DLG-Studie Reduktion von Zucker, Fett und Salz in Lebensmitteln – Zwischen Machbarkeit und Verbrauchererwartung*. DLG e.V. Fachzentrum Lebensmittel, Frankfurt.

FAO. (2019). World food day 2019, our actions are our future. http://www.fao.org/world-food-day/en/?utm_source=twitter&utm_medium=social+media&utm_campaign=fao. Accessed 30 Sept. 2019.

Focus. (2018). Der verzückend süße Dickmacher: Nutella-Frage spaltet – nicht nur die Grünen. https://www.focus.de/politik/deutschland/ex-ministerin-beschwerte-sich-beim-werberat-der-verzueckend-suesse-dickmacher-nutella-frage-spaltet-nicht-nur-die-gruenen_id_9281547.html. Accessed 30 Sept. 2019.

Handelsblatt. (2019). Nestlé führt Nährwert-Ampel „Nutri Score" ein. https://www.handelsblatt.com/unternehmen/handel-konsumgueter/nahrungsmittelkonzern-nestle-fuehrt-naehrwert-ampel-nutri-score-ein/24494312.html?ticket=ST-1152773-SMagf9EgfFvWyXbKkiCF-ap1. Accessed 30 Sept. 2019.

Huffman, S., Piwoz, E., Vosti, S., & Dewey, K. (2014). Babies, soft drinks and snacks: A concern in low- and middle-income countries? *Maternal and Child Nutrition, 2014*(10), 562–574.

Lobstein, T., Jackson-Leach, R., Moodie, M., Hall, K., Gortmaker, S., Swinburn, B., James, P., Wang, Y., & McPherson, K. (2015). Child and adolescent obesity: Part of a bigger picture. *The Lancet, 385*, 2510–2520.

Mälzer, T. (2018). Hört endlich auf, andere belehren zu wollen. https://www.focus.de/gesundheit/experten/ernaehrung-hoert-endlich-auf-andere-belehren-zu-wollen_id_9304006.html. Accessed 30 Sept. 2019.

Müller, J. (2013). Prävention von Übergewicht und Adipositas, 11. Deutsche Konferenz für Tabakkontrolle, 05.12.2013, Heidelberg. https://www.dkfz.de/de/tabakkontrolle/download/

Deutsche_Konferenzen_fuer_Tabakkontrolle/11_Deutsche_Konferenz_fuer_Tabakkontrolle/ Manfred_James_Mueller_2103.pdf?m=1421897700. Accessed 30 Sept. 2019.

Müller, J., Landsberg, B., & Plachta-Danielzik, S. (2013). Prävention von Übergewicht und Adipositas bei Kindern und Jugendlichen – Wie effektiv kann sie sein? *Ernährung & Medizin, 28*(1), 17–20.

Ng, M., Fleming, T., Robinson, M., Thomson, B., Graetz, N., & Bennett, D. (2014). Global, regional, and national prevalence of overweight and obesity in children and adults during 1980–2013: A systematic analysis for the Global Burden of Disease Study. *The Lancet, 384*, 766–781.

OECD Health Policy Studies. (2019). The heavy burden of obesity. The economics of prevention, Paris. https://www.oecd-ilibrary.org/docserver/67450d67-en.pdf?expires=1624984773&id=id& accname=guest&checksum=80996E8A951E27BF55C7157247BE5569. Accessed 29 Jun. 2021.

Qaim, M. et al. (2014). *Nutrition effects of the supermarket revolution on urban consumers and smallholder farmers in Kenya*, GlobalFood Discussion Papers, No. 40, Georg-August-Universität Göttingen, Research Training Group (RTG) 1666 - GlobalFood, Göttingen.

Qaim, M. (2019). Transformation of food value chains and the double burden of malnutrition. In *Presentation at the 4th International Congress Hidden Hunger*, Stuttgart. Unpublished presentation.

Sight and Life. (2018). Behavior change communication, Webinar 2 assessing the situation, Kaiseraugst. https://sightandlife.org/resources/#videos-podcasts&id=4380&f=all. Accessed 26 May 2018.

United Nations. (2016). 71st Session of the United Nations General Assembly - The UN decade of action on nutrition working together to implement the outcomes of the Second International Conference on Nutrition, New York. https://www.who.int/nutrition/events/2016_UNGA71_ side-event_finalreport_20sept.pdf?ua=1. Accessed 25 June 2018.

World Bank Group. (2018). The human capital project, Washington. https://openknowledge.world-bank.org/bitstream/handle/10986/30498/33252.pdf?sequence=5&isAllowed=y. Accessed 28 May 2020.

World Health Organization. (2004). Global strategy on diet, physical activity and health (2004), Geneva. https://www.who.int/dietphysicalactivity/strategy/eb11344/strategy_english_web.pdf?ua=1. Accessed 25 Jun 2018.

World Health Organization. (2016). The double burden of malnutrition brief, New York, Geneva. file:///C:/Users/Anwender/AppData/Local/Packages/Microsoft.MicrosoftEdge_8wekyb3d8bbwe/ TempState/Downloads/WHO-NMH-NHD-17.3-eng%20(1).pdf. Accessed 25 June 2018.

World Health Organization. (2017a). Global nutrition policy review 2016–2017. Geneva. https:// www.who.int/publications-detail/9789241514873. Accessed 30 Sept. 2019.

World Health Organization. (2017b) Tenfold increase in childhood and adolescent obesity in four decades: New study by Imperial College London and WHO. https://www.who.int/en/news-room/detail/11-10-2017-tenfold-increase-in-childhood-and-adolescent-obesity-in-four-decades-new-study-by-imperial-college-london-and-who. Accessed 25 June 2018.

World Health Organization, Food and Agriculture Organization of the United Nations. (2018). Driving commitment for nutrition within the UN decade of action on nutrition, Geneva. file:///C:/ Users/Anwender/AppData/Local/Packages/Microsoft.MicrosoftEdge_8wekyb3d8bbwe/ TempState/Downloads/WHO-NMH-NHD-17.11-eng%20(1).pdf. Accessed 30 Sept. 2019.

Zehner, E., Champeny, M., & Huffman, S. (2019.). Marketing and infant and young child feeding in rapidly evolving food environments. *Maternal and Child Nutrition, 15*, Supplement 4: Marketing and Consumption of Commercial Foods Fed to Young Children in Low and Middle-income Countries, Editorial.

Zeng, D., Thomsen, M., Nayga, R., & Bennette, J. (2019). Supermarket access and childhood bodyweight: Evidence from store openings and closings. *Economics & Human Biology, 33*, 78–88.

The Importance of Research-Based Learning as a Didactic Necessity in German Public Health Degree Programs

2

Manfred Cassens

Contents

2.1 Classic Frontal Teaching Formats Are in the Past—The Future Belongs to Research-Based Learning 20
    2.1.1 Understanding Oneself as a University of Applied Sciences................. 20
    2.1.2 Research Learning Under the Paradigm of Applied Sciences 23
2.2 Social Epidemiology and Social Space Analyses as Decisive Thematic Anchors........ 26
    2.2.1 Social Epidemiology Interests Public Health-Students,.... 27
    2.2.2 ...but Also Social Space Analyses 29
2.3 Students Gain Experience as Young Social Epidemiologists....................... 31
    2.3.1 Let's go—The Social Space Calls! 32
    2.3.2 First Results of the Action Field and Findings Regarding Didactics............ 36
    2.3.3 And Finally: Perspectives for Health Regions............................. 38
References.. 39

Abstract

Research-based learning is an outstanding and very demanding form of university education. Established teaching/learning formats have to be overcome, which begins with time-consuming didactic considerations of course planning, continues during the supervision of students during the semester and leads to a completely

M. Cassens (✉)
FOM University of Applied Sciences, Munich, Germany
e-mail: manfred.cassens@fom.de

M. Cassens
Catholic University of Eichstätt-Ingolstadt, Germany

M. Cassens et al. (eds.), *Transdisciplinary Perspectives on Public Health in Europe*, FOM-Edition, https://doi.org/10.1007/978-3-658-33740-7_2

different interpretation of the role of teachers. On the basis of necessary didactic pre-liminary considerations for the realization of research-based learning in a higher edu-cation context, the article introduces the concrete thematic implementation in the case study of the module "Introduction to Scientific Work". In order to be able to reflect research-based learning under the paradigms of self-regulated and self-organized learning again and again in team meetings at the horizontal level of the students, it proved to be useful to have a common topic to be worked on during the conception of the module. Due to the fact that all participants in the yet unfinished pilot project are studying one of the variants in the field of public health, initial experiences in a social science methodologically qualitative social space analysis appeared to be manage-able. On the basis of some target group-oriented comments on social epidemiology, the contribution describes the scientific significance of social space. On this basis, the implementation of the didactics of research-based learning in six courses, each consisting of four teaching units of 45 min, is presented. Concluding: This procedure was, of course, not in contradiction to the modular framework.

2.1   Classic Frontal Teaching Formats Are in the Past—The Future Belongs to Research-Based Learning

2.1.1   Understanding Oneself as a University of Applied Sciences

The following discussion focuses on "research-based learning" as a contribution to a par-adigm shift in the higher education context of teaching–learning relationships between students and their teachers that currently appears to be significant. Not only the degree programs associated with the Bologna Process change in comparison to the diploma degree programs. On the contrary, the demands on higher education pedagogy associ-ated with digitization are also changing. In the narrower context of one of the key terms, didactics (gr.: δ ι δ ά σ κ ε ι ν), people have dealt with it ever since advanced civilizations have existed—in other words, for at least six thousand years. The ancient Greek term didactics integrates both the side of the teachers (teach, instruct) and that of the learners (learn, be taught). As a core discipline of pedagogy, it deals with the theory of teaching at the metalevel and, as an applied science, with the creative transition of the same. The introductory part will now develop a didactic concept for the university's introductory module "Introduction to Scientific Work". At the end of the module, a seminar paper has to be written in the concrete case as proof of achievement in addition to a written exam. This often presents students of the first semester a (very) big challenge, it is usually the first contact with the scientific structure of a work, the world of scientific publishing and above all with scientific methods. It should also be noted that the term "methodology" (gr: μ ε θ ο δ ο λ ο γ ί α) already refers to a more fundamental character in its episte-miological context than the term "methods": "The reflection of scientific methods and the research process in general is called methodology" (Döring & Bortz, 2016). This is much more complex and multidimensional in the interdisciplinary health sciences than it is in the classical humanities and natural sciences. Radiological, biochemical, biophysical findings are just as implicit as the methods of empirical social sciences selected for the present context. Because this selection process is not self-evident in an interdisciplinary context, Klafki's important "Studies on Educational Theory and Didactics" (1974) was used for the selection process. Kron (2008) summarized the very comprehensive explanations in tabular form (Table 2.1).

The empirical social sciences have an immense importance in health sciences in the form of epidemiology. Against the background of the didactic analysis (here in particular point 2.III "Future significance", Table 2.1) this was already integrated in the revision of the subject "Introduction to scientific work" and with the inclusion of "Researchers learning" within the framework of an experimental project in the first semester. Epidemiological studies increasingly no longer refer exclusively to morbidity and mortality trends - and thus to the primarily descriptive statistical evaluation of routine data. Since a purely quantitative approach no longer seems to be sufficient, epidemiology increasingly has the task, in the context of epidemiological transition (Siegrist, 2005), of recording questions and answers on health promotion, subjectively perceived quality of life, individual health competence, individual behaviour and relationship prevention, and dealing with chronic disease progressions (Schaeffer et al. 2018) using alternative, interdisciplinary methods. For graduates of public health degree programs, this means that they will be able to apply methods independently and reflectively in the field of action after completing their studies in order to be able to use important decision-making bases for interventions.

While it was almost unthinkable until the 1970s to integrate quantitative and qualitative methods from the social sciences in terms of decision-making—e.g. within the framework of small-scale social space analyses—, public health today presents epidemiology with tasks that exceed classical social science methods by far in the context of epidemiology: two examples are given here: The socio-scientifically empirical evaluation of the relevant construct for health reporting, "stress perception" as a conventional self-declaration questionnaire, now faces a biophysiological equivalent: biofeedback, which

Table 2.1 Scheme of didactic analysis and structural planning model (Kron, 2008)

1. General Part	1. Historicality?
	2. Individual self-image?
	3. General sense?
	4. Structure of contents?
2. Special Part	I. Exemplary significance of educational content?
	II. present importance?
	III. future significance?
	IV. educational goals?
	V. Favourable teaching and learning conditions?

has been established since the 1980s. A second example: If wearables are activated with corresponding sensors to measure body values, these are much more valid than retrospectively oriented memory questionnaires, which are currently still being used. So, one thing quickly becomes clear: traditional questionnaires and oral survey methods can, depending on the chosen sample and measurement method, be accompanied by risks of sometimes considerable errors. However, they can be implemented relatively cheaply in comparison to the alternatives mentioned here and, if carefully examined, do not contain any potential for ethical conflict. However, this is the case with the digital solutions mentioned. In addition to the significantly higher costs, they very quickly reach ethical and data protection limits. This results in a conflict of objectives for which students should be prepared by an appropriate degree of methodological diversity within the framework of their studies. These didactic introductory reflections on research-based learning, guided by methodology, show one thing very clearly: the choice of methods must be made consciously; they represent a decision-making space in which students must be consciously involved. In the context of "learning to learn", the Canadian social psychologist Albert Bandura (*1923) can therefore be supported, who formulates the following goal for the course of study:

> "A main objective of formal education is to equip the student with intellectual tools, self-confidence and self-regulatory skills so that he can continue learning independently throughout his life. The rapid pace of technological innovation and the ever-increasing demand for knowledge make self-directed learning indispensable" (Bandura, 2007).

Since this should also apply to teaching in epidemiology, it is worth taking a first closer look at the didactics of research-based learning, which is closely linked to the concepts of self-directed and self-oriented learning (Herold & Herold, 2011; Konrad & Traub, 2010; Schunk, 2012).

At this point, a preliminary note on the integration of research-based learning: Particularly with regard to the introduction of bachelor's and master's degree programs, no fewer critics in the German-speaking world accused the new study format of "schooling" (Mieg, 2017). Whether this criticism is justified, cannot yet be conclusively assessed. In an upcoming evaluation, however, it seems considerable how the ECTS system (ECTS = European Credit Transfer System) is structured: The basis for the calculation is that one ECTS point is compared to an equivalent of 30 working hours. While the study regulations for diploma degree programs provided for a review of academic performance exclusively by means of certifications, master's and bachelor's degree programs contain at least one further dimension: a proportion of structured self-study which supplements the attendance hours at the university—and which is also charged within the framework of the ECTS system. Here a large temporal dispositive can be recognized, which often remains relatively unused by lecturers and thus without consequences. As a rule, structured self-study means that the reception of compulsory and supplementary literature is reviewed only in written exams. Tasks in the context of research-based learning, however, remain largely unnoticed. This insight is by no means profane marginalia, but in the overall context of this contribution rather a sad interim conclusion after about 10 years. To make it even clearer: With ECTS, the often misunderstood Bologna Process does indeed provide framework conditions which should not only enable but even promote research-based learning! On the contrary, however, the higher education landscape often lacks clever didactic approaches to using structured self-study in the sense of research-based learning within the individual modules, or even across modules. This is an important finding as a framework condition for the solution to be presented, since self-directed and self-organized learning should be introduced as the basis for innovation.

First of all, it should be noted that research-based learning is not specifically assigned to any of the traditional pedagogical-psychological theory schools, the behaviorist, constructivist or even the social-cognitive perspective. Rather, it is the case that research-based learning can be placed in the context of many relevant schools of thought. In the higher education learning context, it must be emphasized that students experience research processes in their various phases, which must systematically build on one another.

In this context, universities of applied sciences should perhaps demonstrate an even stronger commitment to applied research in order to transfer this philosophy into teaching using their own examples. For these educational institutions, this means a self-confessed "yes" to empirical regularities and to applied demand research. This should not necessarily be equated with prejudiced downgrading, a much-discussed process in academic circles, as opposed to basic research universities. But what do students usually get from this elementary characteristic "research" in the setting of a University of Applied Sciences during the course of their studies? Little to much too little—this could be the provocative answer. Studying at a University of Applied Sciences is one of the demands of this article, which should in principle imply a focus on practical relevance, on the above-mentioned empirical regularities and on research needs; research-based learning should or must even be used in all modules in free interpretation of the above-mentioned Bandura quote, where this is possible.

2.1.2 Research Learning Under the Paradigm of Applied Sciences

Research-based learning has its roots among other things in social psychology, in particular in the early phase of the American Kurt Lewin (1890–1947). The socio-psychological assumption generally focuses on interpersonal interaction. Lewin, as a pioneer of his "Action Research" approach, was concerned with promoting democratic decision-making and the participation of practitioners in the research process. He himself succeeded in implementing the action research approach in cooperation with the Columbus University's Teachers College, but no role-out took place. With the establishment of the social-cognitive learning theory, shaped by the already mentioned Canadian social psychologist Albert Bandura, it was possible to inspire further university and school circles for research-based learning. In Germany, this alternative teaching and learning format established itself from the 1960s onwards and was linked to the founding of several universities (including TU Dortmund and Bielefeld University). Of course, the thinking of the "1968 generation" also influenced this pressure to innovate. During the 1970s and 1980s, however, there were also deficits, which Mieg has clearly outlined (2017). According to this author, on the one hand, many lecturers used the phases of research-based learning of their students during courses to their own advantage. On the other hand, it was recognised that there was often a lack of clear process structures for research-based learning. Fig. 2.1 gives an idea in graphic form of how complex the procedural prerequisites for research-based learning are.

However, "Stations of teaching–learning process oriented towards research knowledge" and "Stations of teaching–learning process oriented towards the research process" are two parallel process paths that need to be integrated. This is generally a challenging task for the didactic conception of a course and even more for the module "Introduction to Scientific Work" in the first semester. Following Langemeyer (2017), the starting points for Process 1 are "Learning as comprehension" and for Process 2 "Learning as Development". The central goal of the first process path is "Knowledge as Reflection", that of the second is "Knowledge as Anticipation". As far as this process-based listing

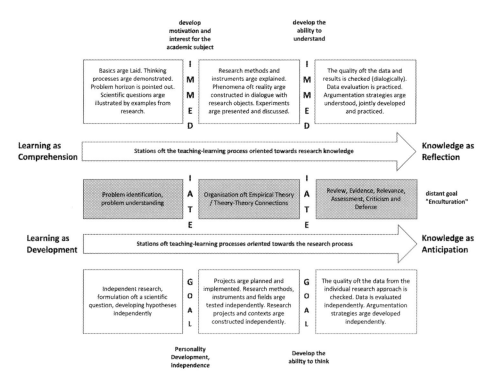

Fig. 2.1 Research oriented university courses as a process of enculturation (Langemeyer, 2017, p. 93)

of terms at the metalevel, in the direction of further didactic operationalization in the university context is concerned, which is presented in Fig. 2.2, van der Donk, (2014) show in their Research Learning Cycle very successfully how this can be achieved. The module to be developed further in the course of this article has six lectures including four teaching units of 45 min each as a framework condition.

In the monographic publication, the authors use their Research Learning Cycle to develop a system of milestones and sub goals that can be operationalized in a highly didactic way, consisting of six fields of work. Ideally, this can be supplemented by an Innovation Cycle in an inter-semester project. In the present case of the six lectures, each one is assigned to one of the main topics from the Research Learning Cycle.

In the context of research-based learning, it is now also worth taking a look at the smaller units of university didactic. In the present case, this concerns the structure of the four coupled teaching units. The question is how the structure of research-based learning differs from conventional courses. An answer to this question can be found by observing the ARIPE scheme (Fig. 2.3). In addition, this structure reveals the extent to which the role interpretation and the self-image of the teachers change at the lowest didactic conceptual level (university teaching unit with 45 min). While this was and still is the case, which is oriented in very narrow interpretation to the Latin term docēns (lat. for docēre: teach, teach), in research-based learning there is a need for situational arrangers with very deep and broad-based expertise in the object of research.

In the free interpretation of the phases "Aligning", "Reactivating" and "Evaluation", a rather heavily culled interpretation of didactic concepts can be affiliated. At the latest, however, the phase "Informing/Processing" implies a possibly repetitive cycle of individual work, followed by a phase of work in small groups. This "heart" of research-based learning, conceived according to the ARIPE scheme, is concluded with a presentation of

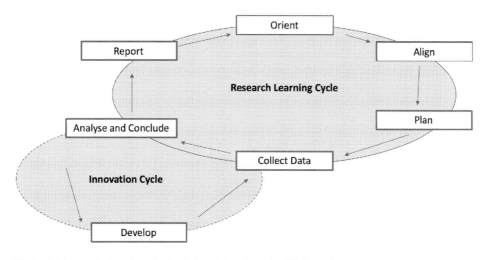

Fig. 2.2 Research Learning Cycle (c.f.: v.d. Donk et al., 2014, p. 39)

Fig. 2.3 The ARIPE scheme to illustrate a university lesson unit (two times 45 min. in a row)

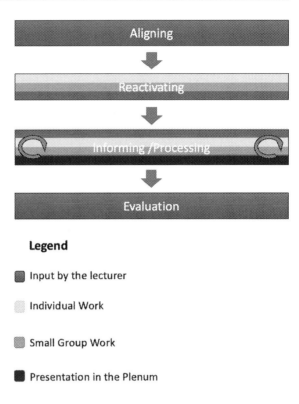

all results in the plenum. How varied and interesting the "Informing/Processing" phase can be designed, is documented in numerous didactic manuals available in German (Groß, 2014; Groß et al., 2012; Knoll, 2003; Rummer, 2014). From the didactic perspective, a well-estimated measure of innovative methods should be used during the "Informing/Processing" phase, which means that students should be able to positively evaluate the emotional sensations of manageability, comprehensibility, and meaningfulness. This means, above all, an average learning speed in this phase, frequent direct contacts between teachers and the small groups, as well as the highest possible consistency within the learning groups over the total number of courses.

2.2 Social Epidemiology and Social Space Analyses as Decisive Thematic Anchors

Based on the didactic remarks on the "Why?" and "How?" of research-based learning, the second section of this article deals with the core question of "What? In the course of several years, the authors of this article have reduced numerous aspects of the social-scientific-methodological requirement profile resulting from the module requirements in the sense of social-cognitive theory. In this context, also, it is again possible to refer seamlessly to the German didactician Wolfgang Klafki (1927–2016) (1974), who distinguishes between the exemplary and the elementary in the context of categorical education: The module "Introduction to Scientific Work" is about understanding the principle of creating a scientific paper, applying it for the first time, and being able to transfer it to subsequent academic achievements. As an example, this is done in the module on the basis of a jointly developed main topic of social epidemiology. Epidemiology can generally be defined as "a branch of science [interpreted, n. f. a.] dealing with the distribution of diseases and their physical, chemical, psychological and social determinants and consequences in the population" (Brüggemann et al., 2014). In addition, the authors narrow down social epidemiology as follows:

> "A branch of science that combines questions and methods from the social sciences and medical epidemiology. Goal: Clarification of health and disease-relevant questions, whereby beyond the biomedical model of traditional epidemiology, the relationships between society and health in particular are investigated" (ibid.).

Traditionally, social epidemiology uses empirical social research methods on the basis of a set of indicators too. Usually, these are not yet mastered by first-semester students and cannot be assumed either.

2.2.1 Social Epidemiology Interests Public Health-Students,…

As far as the interests of public health students are concerned, surveys on their motivation to study alone show that it is above all topics and tasks that deal with social epidemiology. The interaction of social inequality, which has an effect on health, should be mentioned above all (Lampert et al., 2016). The current generation of students seems to be aware of this connection due to the currently worsening situation (Hurrelmann & Albrecht 2014). Many public health students consider it likely that their current comfortable living situation will change in the future, given the demographic development they consciously perceive. With regard to the healthcare system, they therefore assume that care will deteriorate. The perspective assessment leads to a different individual precautionary behavior than which these students perceive in their personal environment. These impressions of peers in their own peer groups in turn coincide with the findings of two current studies: Firstly, the third "population-related health survey for children and adolescents ("KiGGS-Wave 2")" (Poethko-Müller et al., 2018). On the other hand, it deals with the results of the current DKV Health Report (German Health Insurance 2018). According to both surveys, the current generation of students and pupils in compulsory education will suffer from chronic illness earlier due to their lifestyle—with a further increase in lifetime prognosis. Prior to this contemporary experience of one's own peer group, social inequality and the resulting rise in inequality are of concern to public health students, which means that a high degree of intrinsically motivated interest in knowledge can be reinforced with the first major topic area of social epidemiology.

The same applies to the assessment of environmental issues that students perceive on a daily basis in their everyday lives. The current generation of students and pupils is very ambivalent. While a majority of young people still seem to behave according to the principles of a throwaway society, the proportion of those who are worried about the future is increasing. The currently world-famous initiator of the "Fridays for Future" wave, Greta Thunberg (* 2003) expresses these fears: "Why should I be studying for a future that soon may be no more, when no one is doing anything to save that future?" (fridaysforfuture 2019). In the course of their studies, public health students deal with environmental diseases if they are not already familiar with such pathogenic reactions to increased stress due to frequent previous professional experience. Since the consequences of global climate change, emissions gas scandals and the use of toxic substances in agriculture are almost ubiquitous, and escape is hardly feasible, it can be assumed that a great interest in dealing with related issues is intrinsically motivated.

A third and final point in this article, which speaks in favour of integrating social epidemiology into the module "Introduction to Scientific Work", is that public health has a political claim. This was not only underlined with the action field "health in all policies" of the WHO Ottawa Charta for health promotion. Recent literature sources also emphasise this demand (see above Kickbusch & Buckett, 2010). At the local level, students experience health and social policy as "parliaments of the elderly" (Hurrelmann & Albrecht 2014), as many reports by students in the course of the project on research-based learning show. In this respect, a supplementary look at the data handbook of the German Parliament (2018) reveals that the average age of members of parliament is permanently over 49 years since 1994. Furthermore, the peak average age in the 4th parliamentary term (1961) was 52.3 years. In contrast to Austria, a country where the voting age is 16 and running for the office of a MP is also possible from that age, 2,367,951 voters* from the age cohort of Greta Thunberg are completely disregarded in Germany (Statistisches Bundesamt, 2018). A side note: The youngest member of the current 19th parliamentary term of the German parliament was 24 years old at its constituent session. This impression is also confirmed at the local and regional level—the lifeworld of still strongly self-referentially oriented beginners—at the political level and at the implementation level of research-based learning at the reference location of Munich. Zick (2016) explains that the average age of the 33,000 people employed by the city administration is 45, with the addition that one third of these people will retire by 2025. According to the attributions of Hurrelmann and Albrecht (2014) to the generation of current students, who are involved in research-based learning have hitherto been municipal institutions of health promotion and prevention: Students often report in the context of "health in all policies" about limited enthusiasm, inside-the-box-thinking between health and social policy and a low degree of dynamism on the part of a large number of municipal employees. According to the reports, it is rather the voluntary civic commitment which develops innovative and cross-border solutions in the sense of "health in all policies" within the project framework. Poor spatial accessibility is often recognised in the context of primary prevention in order to describe the lack of "health in all policies" as a deficit.

In the overall context of this contribution, it should be noted, with regard to social epidemiology, that it can be didactically skillfully used and incorporated as a deflection roller. Classic social-epidemiological problems on a cognitive metalevel lead to the identification of deficits in one's own world on the basis of high intrinsic motivation, to describe these and to develop solutions. The fact that this takes place in relation to one's own urban district serves as additional motivation. At the scientific level, it is thus possible to develop an interest in research-based learning.

2.2.2 …but Also Social Space Analyses

The term "social space", which has just been mentioned for the first time, is another elementary characteristic of the didactic implementation concept still to be presented in the module "Introduction to Scientific Work". The social space became relevant to German sociology for the first time in the context of the "Marienthal Study", which was carried out in 1932. Lazarsfeld (2014) identified here an important "intersection" of several sociological currents, but above all the summary of statistics and the "introductory description of individual cases". Thus, at the latest, with this study on unemployment, the combination of quantitative and qualitative methods in the social space can be documented. This approach is now described as "mixed methods" and is established in the health sciences (Niederberger, 2018; Schilling et al. 2015). At latest, since the WHO Charter of Ottawa (1986), the social space has become outstanding relevance in the context of the setting approach. 23 years after the ratification of this basic document, the Hamburg-based social physician Alf Trojan (2009) will aptly call the district as the "mother of all settings". All five action fields of the Ottawa Charter for Health Promotion can be easily combined with this variant of social space:

- Development of a health-promoting overall policy,
- Create health-promoting living environments,
- Promote health-related community action,
- Develop personal competencies and
- Reorienting health services.

If students explore their own social space on this basis, they also carry out structured, systematic and transparent scientific steps in their seminar paper for the first time. Concerning the part "Discussion" they reflect implementation concepts and refer the Charter's action strategies from the aspect of their district. These are as follows:

- Health advocacy,
- Enable and
- Mediation and networking (mediate).

In the period after the Ottawa Charter, the "rediscovery of the social space" (Riege & Schubert, 2014) was only due to its implementation in public health. The authors cite further reasons in a more sociological context: social urban renewal, youth welfare planning and the reorganization of social services. Furthermore, they complain that "recent publications on qualitative social research contain few or no contributions on empirical analyses of social spaces" (ibid.). Based on one of the most influential sociologists and social philosophers of the twentieth century, Pierre F. Bourdieu (1930–2002), the didactic pre-consideration of the authors of this article was to build up according cognitive knowledge through the discovery of one's own social space through emotional knowledge. The definitely relevant steps of structuring, systematic and transparent procedure are to be linked this way via one's own life world. The so called "silent curriculum" of the module "Introduction to Scientific Work" includes "grasping the essence of what is experienced and seen on the spot, that is, the most astonishing insights and most surprising experiences, their core". These can have their content "quite elsewhere" than it is expressed, e.g. by publicly available statistics (cf. Bordieu 1979). In this context Table 2.2 shows how diverse the levels of investigation and objectives of a mixed method analysis are, with which the complex social structure of a district or a rural residential area should be recorded in contrast to conventional epidemiological reporting.

The social science methods being derived from this can also be found in Table 2.3. Many of the methods presented here are mentioned in the following subsection; these are applied by the students in the field test. This also implies that 24 teaching units of 45 min each represent a very narrow time window, in order to do exemplary work on such an elementary topic as the preparation of a first seminar paper.

The quantitative survey methods listed in Table 2.3 cannot be generated in their entirety in the form of primary data within the framework of the given time range. In the present case, this represents a possibility of interlocking with the second semester,

Table 2.2 Levels of investigation and objectives of a social space analysis that differentiating subspaces inwardly (Riege & Schubert, 2014)

Levels of investigation		Aims
1	Space delimitation and space definition	Differentiation of significant social/physical subspaces of the urban area
2	Structural profiling	Determination of patterns of socio-structural/socio-economic structures by sub-areas
3	Inventory description	Identification of existing problems/resources/potentials
4	Exploration of habitats and areas of use	In-depth field recording of subjectively and collectively constructed (perceptual) spaces

Table 2.3 Methodological approaches to social space analysis (Riege & Schubert, 2014)

Survey context	Methods
Physical space delimitation and spatial definition	Zoning, mapping, urban image analysis, district history
Structural analyses by administration rooms	Statistical structural analyses, social indicators
Surveys in the use room	Narrative interviews, focused guideline discussions, group discussions, passers-by surveys
Systemic observations and surveys in the usage space	Participating observation, Burano-method, semiotic analysis (street reading), media document analysis, stakeholder analysis, network analysis, action research/activating survey, ethnographic-method
Survey of subjective usage aspects of the social space	Urban district exploration / inspection, action area analysis, life world analysis / needle method

in which the module "Quantitative Methods and Evaluation Research" is taught. This seems to be a special attraction, but also a challenge, since modular studies often run the risk of the content being patched together.

2.3   Students Gain Experience as Young Social Epidemiologists

What is the pilot project about? First-semester students are to learn the elementary skills of scientific work in six courses of four teaching units each. The basic condition for this is that FOM students study part-time at a university of applied sciences: This can mean that students study either from Monday to Thursday on several evenings per week, or on two consecutive days of the week, alternating between these two time models on Friday evening and Saturday. These three study time models attract above all those who have already completed an apprenticeship/a placement and have initial work experience. In the present case, these are in bachelor's degree programs in

- Health and Social management,
- Health Psychology & Medical Education and
- Social Work.

Most of them have previous professional experience in nursing (children, adult and geriatric) as social security employees, physiotherapists or social workers. A minority of them have a general matriculation standard, which means that there is a lack of prior experience regarding the work necessary for this level of education. For the majority of the students, the module "Introduction to Scientific Work" represents the first contact with the topic "Preparing an independent scientific document"; moreover, they shall do it at a significantly higher age than which is the norm for students starting at the European qualification level 4 (general higher education entrance qualification). Many of them have an emotional connection of respect with the module right from the start, which in some cases even leads to fears of failure. This assessment is based on an initial survey of the authors in the context of each kick-off event (two to three courses during the current 11 semesters). As the first author left the topic of the seminar paper open for a total of eight semesters and taught the entire spectrum of quantitative and qualitative social science research in the form of frontal teaching according to the modular overall guidelines, the concept of research-based learning presented here has been practiced for three semesters now. This paradigm shift was induced, because it had become quite clear in the last four years that students had already verbalized fears on an emotional level at the beginning of the course; partly with strong atmospheric effects on the further lectures of the module. In addition, the seminar papers were not prepared at a minimum level of what was academically acceptable and required because of the overburdened content of the courses; thus the general output quality before the switch to research-based learning left much to be desired. The consequence of this general constellation was that narrative texts on unscientific topics were produced over a period of four years on the basis of the topics chosen by the students themselves; the social science methods were not applied to any extent in the majority of the papers submitted. The goal of developing the elementary through the exemplary could—this must be clearly stated—not be achieved in this constellation.

After the last three semesters, the didactic and content-related paradigm shift is to be described, which led both to a significantly increased output quality and to a more than significant reduction in the emotional attitude of the students. On the basis of the didactic change of concept, all effects of self-regulated and self-directed learning can be seen. The dynamic concept, which is still undergoing further development, has already been presented several times at scientific conferences and congresses.

2.3.1 Let's go—The Social Space Calls!

The switch to research-based learning was accompanied by a considerable reduction in the descriptive thematization of social science methods. On the other hand, the adaptation and integration of research learning cycles into the six courses was becoming more and more common. Figure 2.4 shows how this took place: The didactic planning of the module was based on the structure diagram of small-scale social space analyses by Urban and Weiser (2006).

Within the framework of the opening event, which now has the title "Orientation", the first two teaching units provide an introduction to the module "Introduction to Scientific Work". On the one hand, examination modalities and teaching contents are reflected here, and on the other hand expectations of the course and self-requirements are

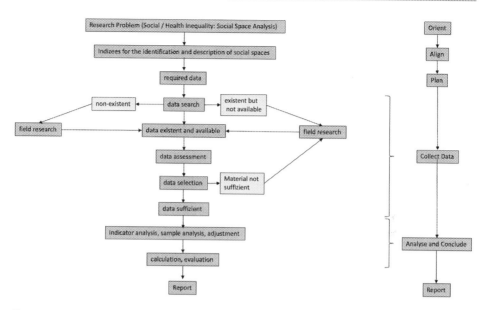

Fig. 2.4 Process of a small-scale social space analysis that considers the Research learning cycle one-dimensionally

reflected. In addition, a first theoretical orientation regarding the social space takes place. In order to develop awareness for public health courses, the teaching impulse in the third teaching unit is fundamentally concerned with social and health inequality on the basis of Mielck's theory model (2006) (Fig. in the book contribution Cassens, Lakasz, Surzykiewicz).

In the present case, the Bavarian capital Munich consists of 25 regulatory city districts, some of which are very different, even contradictory, as far as the facts described here are concerned. This is particularly noticeable in Munich's urban district 18 Untergiesing-Harlaching. As long as Untergiesing is still "characterized above all by its still recognizable character as a formerly typical working-class suburb with a simple and dense housing stock" (Landeshauptstadt München 2019), the district part "Harlaching/ Menterschweige aus der garden city idea of the second-to-last turn of the century as a representative villa district" (ibid.). This introductory description alone makes it clear that it is a demanding but motivating challenge for the students to grasp their own social space in all its contrasts within the framework of a seminar paper. Within the framework of the first course, the following aspects will be dealt with in terms of scientific work and thus on the metalevel: To select a research object (social space), to limit it thematically according to given criteria (factors of inequality relevant to social epidemiology), to link it with a general literature search for the first time and, as a result of this process, to present it to a small group. In the context of self-directed and self-organized learning, the homework is to work through the "Munich District Study" (Landeshauptstadt München,

2016) as basic secondary data material, and to extract and adequately secure the data necessary for one's own social space.

The subsequent course, entitled "Aligning", focuses on three main areas. It starts with a small group work, in which the probable range of the own investigation is presented on the basis of the past research results. The results of self-directed learning must therefore be presented; experience has shown that not developing these tasks increases group-dynamic expectations such as: "Hey, you should do that until next time". The results are presented to the plenum as an overview. It is essential in this section that the own results are linked to the model of social-health inequality. The second teaching unit, in the form of a teaching–learning discussion, consists of working out basic elements of a research goal and a research question and then deriving this in an exemplary way and in the same way for all students. Since it turned out to be too difficult from the point of view of the degree of abstraction, both are specified in the module by the lecturer: "The research objective is to analyze the health inequality resulting from social inequality on the basis of three categories (preventive health care, health care and quality of life) in the form of five guideline interviews each with six questions in one's own district". The research question derived is: "To what extent can the health inequality in Munich's district XY be proven by the triangulation of data sources and interviews?" The last two teaching units of this course consist of searching digital search engines and specialist databases for relevant data sets on the basis of impulses from the teacher. It is essential to get acquainted with the differences between the two research instruments in order to be able to use them adequately in the future and to learn to document the hits accordingly. As homework for the second course, a first social room inspection must take place. The aim of these systemic observations and social-scientifically methodologically guided surveys in the district is to carry out participatory observation, semiotic analyses (street reading), media document analyses, stakeholder analyses, network analyses and, if necessary, ethnographic methods.

At the beginning of the third course "Planning", the results of the self-directed learning package are presented in small groups, compared and then presented to the plenum. The first lecturer impulse of the event refers to the selected model of social and health inequality. On the basis of this case study, the qualitative principles of the theories or theoretical models must have a novel character. In this model, the dimensions "differences in health burdens", "differences in personal coping resources" and "differences in health care" are replaced by "health care prevention", "health care in the district" and "subjective quality of life". On the basis of introductory explanations about the structure of guideline interviews, the learning groups are given supplementary keywords on the three dimensions so that they can continue working independently resp. on their own: The essential part of the second section of this course consists of developing two central questions to each of the three dimensions in the small learning groups across districts. These will be written on cards and attached to pin boards later. Finally, the students select a total of six questions for the guideline interview. The voting also takes place in small groups. On the metalevel of scientific work, the students learned in the third course to select and justify methods of data collection in order to draw up a theory-based research plan. The homework is about a further essential learning step, which has to be worked out self-oriented. The homework consists of writing a first, highly simplified research plan, containing the following four aspects, which must be reflected descriptively in writing:

- General requirements (reason for investigation, context, general conditions, integration of one's own social space analysis into other investigations identified within the research framework).
- Description of identified conflict potentials in the social space (results of literature research, conflict potentials, justification of the selected social-scientifically qualitative methods, reference of the social space to the model of social-health inequality).
- Transfer of research goal and research question to the selected social space.
- Specific planning of the "Survey" phase (Who should be questioned why?).

The fourth course "Survey" focuses on first practical field research experiences. Before this, the results of the homework (research plans) are discussed in small groups. In the sense of openness to results, the lecturer visits the learning groups and answers questions, but the results will be not collected and corrected due to self-orientation and control. Subsequently, the students go outside in order to find interview partners who will answer them to the questions. Since many students gain experience as interviewers for the first time in their lives, tandem or board interviews have proven to be constructive. In addition, the content of the key questions with regard to qualitative method-specific quality criteria (Mayring, 2016) can be reviewed once again in the wake of this small field research. The practical field research comprises two teaching units, which are always followed by a very active, dynamic and positive emotional compilation of the results, including their evaluation. At the end of the course, the students will have their guideline-supported questionnaire at their disposal and be able to carry out the five guideline-interviews required within the framework of the seminar work as a homework assignment in a self-organized manner and then transcribe them until the fifth course.

The fifth and at the same time penultimate event of the module focuses on qualitative content analysis as an exemplary analytical instrument of empirical social research (Helfferich, 2011; Gläser & Laudel, 2010) under the title "Analyzing and drawing conclusions". This very important step in the implementation of the present didactic concept can only be carried out on the basis of the already transcribed and thus electronically available data. For this reason, a strongly shortened meeting of the small groups will take place in this event. What characterizes this teaching/learning unit, on the other hand, is the work on one's own text, the systematic and structured qualitative content analysis. They thus learn the compression of self-generated text material. This step takes up the first half of the course. The second half is then designed in a small group framework: The aim here is to discursively draw conclusions from the compressed material. In specific terms, this means firstly: Which statements can be condensed in relation to the three dimensions "health care", "preventive health care" and "subjective quality of life"? And secondly: In what connection can the self-generated data be evaluated and interpreted with the otherwise researched data sources (e.g. Munich District Study, Health Reporting Bavaria)? Thirdly, based on the triangulated results, which are being discussed in the small groups, a reference will be made by each student to the theoretical model of social-health inequality. The homework in this course is to begin with the systematic and structured writing of the results. This is done on the basis of a predefined template that indirectly reflects the research learning cycle. In the main part it includes the following subchapters:

- Detailed description of the research object and state of research
- Plausibility check of the research and investigation plan
- Results of literature research and original data
- Discussion
- Conclusion

The last course includes the preparation for the exam. This is a multiple choice exam with a total of 30 closed items, each with four possible answers, which is written about two weeks after the last course. The second part of the course consists of a workshop in the small groups, during which the results of the writing process will be presented and discussed.

2.3.2 First Results of the Action Field and Findings Regarding Didactics

The evaluation of the findings is based on two different principles. The first is the transcripts of the second author, who simultaneously is lecturer of the respective module within the framework of research-based learning. This will be supplemented by written and verbal comments of the students. the second principle is quality output; hereby particularly the seminar papers and not the second module achievement, the examinations should be considered.

It could have been seen during the courses that have been held so far in accordance with the research-based learning concept that the small group work led to intensive discussions via a clearly perceptible increase in dynamics. Especially the courses three (Development of key questions) and four (Field test) led to changes in attitudes towards the module. For all six cohorts, this led to a degree of identification with the chosen research topic that could not be established previously. The exchange about one's own interview experiences as a homework assignment in the fourth course contributed to this at the beginning of the fifth course; it was not only about self-directed learning, but almost even experiential learning. The students also welcomed the fact that their partial results will be used within the framework of research at the FOM Institute for Health &

Social Affairs. They feel appreciated and perceive their tasks with significantly increased awareness. However, it must also be noted that research-based learning entails an additional workload that should not be underestimated. During their practical experience, students seek the advice of their lecturers more frequently than in case of frontal didactics. Ultimately, it should also be mentioned that during all three semesters until now, experience has been gained leading to conceptual changes in the structure of the courses and will probably continue to do so.

In order to guarantee the objectivity of the evaluation process, an external evaluation and marking of the seminar papers has been carried out by one and the same person for three years (six semesters). On the basis of a comprehensive set of documents, she was asked to set up a comparative list of "Summary of expert findings before and after the shift to research-based learning". The results are as follows:

Before the Shift

- Almost exclusively descriptive, mostly narrative works were submitted.
- Many documents resembled experience essays.
- There was little interest and effort on the part of the reviewer to penetrate a subject scientifically. On the contrary, the seminar papers gave the impression that the seminar paper is a great burden and its meaningfulness is not comprehensible. The assumption often arose that "something had to be sketched out quickly" in order to get rid of the unpleasant task as quickly as possible.
- This resulted in a partly massive problem for the expert with regard to marking: Since the seminar papers often did not meet the minimum requirements for a scientific paper, it was not only difficult to formulate at least some positive statements regarding a free commentary, rather, the marking of the work was generally difficult due to the overall performance.
- With regard to the dimensions "comprehensibility" and "manageability", the evaluator emphasized that the seminar papers conveyed the impression of great uncertainty. The students seemed to have dealt with the questions "What must I do at all?" and "How must I solve my tasks?"
- Ultimately, this led to the fact that this deficient quality of the results influenced the reviewer motivationally.

After the shift

- In none of the three semesters was a descriptive narrative work submitted, but only original works.
- The writing style of the submitted works indicates that they were created with much more commitment and effort.
- An interest in the topic "social space analysis of one's own district", and "social epidemiology" can also be recognized.

- The recognizable interest, commitment and effort are traceable from an expert's perspective to the fact that the seminar papers
  - by choosing the topic "social space analysis", students are given a sense of meaning that implies a high affinity to the chosen studies.
  - be perceived as a manageable task because the guideline interviews are developed together and the qualitative content analyses are developed in group work on the basis of the own case studies. In addition, the template provided in the framework of the research-based learning approach makes the orientation much easier and is used in almost all cases.
  - the students, as the results show, seem to know what is important in the seminar work in terms of comprehensibility.
- All this ultimately led to a significant increase in the quality of the results. The evaluator emphasises that she, too, feels significantly more pleasure in taking on this responsible activity.

2.3.3   And Finally: Perspectives for Health Regions

This contribution, together with others, is part of the research initiation project "Arteria Danubia", dealing with the optional introduction of health regions. The Bavarian health regions ^{plus} have a certain outstanding character, which is described in this book by Hollederer & Beiwinkel. In a broader context, the current Bavarian Prevention Plan (2015) calls for the further development of health reporting. Two problems are implicit in this regard at least. Together with the health monitoring of the federal government, the format seems to be an outdated and reader-unfriendly one to many of those who surveyed personally (especially students and doctors). Qualitatively generated statements would be a stylistic element to innovate the established structures. A second problem is that the offices of the 50 Bavarian health regions ^{plus} have usually only one office space. In this way, if the regions are to make their own contribution to Bavaria's health reporting, as it is required by the prevention plan, new structures must be created from the perspective of organizing personnel alone, which have not existed previously. It would be conceivable, for example, to link the research-based learning approach presented here to school projects or even to social science topics (social studies, sociology). Even a connection to the technical work necessary for the general higher education entrance qualification as a preliminary stage of a scientific seminar work, could be considered. On the other hand, cost-intensive contracts with sociological institutes are ruled out because of the very limited budget of the health regions ^{plus}. On the other hand, in addition to schools, civil commitment, people who frequently come together in senior citizens', youth or open district meetings, may be considered. There are some risks involved in incorporating them, but from the author's point of view it undoubtedly represents a realistic way of generating important data. Research-based learning seems to be the only immaterial format for volunteer involvement, because participants have fun and pleasure with generating data.

References

Bandura, A. (2007). Albert Bandura. In A. Woolfolk (Hrsg.), *Pädagogische Psychologie* (12. überarb. Aufl. Übersetzt u. bearb. v. Schönpflug, U). Pearson.

Bayerisches Staatsministerium für Gesundheit und Pflege. (2015). *Bayerischer Präventionsplan.* Tiefenbach: Schmerbeck.

Bourdieu, B. (1979). *La distinction. Critique sociale du jugement.* Paris: Les Editions de Minuit.

Brüggemann, S., Niehues, C., Rose, A. D., & Schwöbel, B. (Eds.). (2014). *Pschyrembel – Sozialmedizin und Public Health* (2 aktual). De Gruyter.

Deutsche Krankenversicherung (Ed.) (2018). DKV-Report 2018 – Wie gesund lebt Deutschland? https://www.ergo-com/-/media/ergocom/pdf.../dkv-report-2018/dkv-report-2018pdf. Accessed: 4 July 2019.

Deutscher Bundestag. (2018). Durchschnittsalter des Deutschen Bundestages. https://www.bundestag.de/resource/blob/272474/4a216913aff5f5c25c41572257a57e4a/Kapitel_03_02_Durchschnittsalter-pdf-data.pdf. Accessed: 4 July 2019.

Döring, N., & Bortz, J. (2016). *Forschungsmethoden und Evaluation in den Sozial- und Humanwissenschaften* (5. kompl. überarb., aktual. und erw. Aufl. Berlin u.). Springer.

Donk, C. vd., Lanen, B. v., & Wright, M.T. (2014). *Praxisforschung im Sozial- und Gesundheitswesen.* Huber.

Fridays for Future. (2019). We are the future. http://www.fridaysforfuture.org. Accessed 04 July 2019.

Gläser, J., & Laudel, G. (2010). *Experteninterviews und qualitative Inhaltsanalyse* (4. überarb. Aufl.). VS.

Groß, H. (2014). *Munterrichtsmethoden – 22 weitere aktivierende Lehrmethoden für die Seminarpraxis* (Vol. 2). Schelling.

Groß, H., Boden, B., & Boden, N. (2012). *Munterrichtsmethoden – 22 aktivierende Lehrmethoden für die Seminarpraxis* (Bd. 1. 3. kompl. überarb. Aufl). Schelling.

Hellferich, C. (2011). *Die Qualität qualitativer Daten – Manual für die Durchführung qualitativer Interviews* (4th ed.). VS.

Herold, C., & Herold, M. (2011). *Selbstorganisiertes Lernen in Schule und Beruf.* Beltz.

Hurrelmann, K., & Albrech, E. (2014). *Die heimlichen Revolutionäre – Wie die Generation Y unsere Welt verändert.* Beltz.

Kickbusch, I., & Buckett, K. (2010). Implementing health in all policies. Adelaide 2010. http://www.whogis.com/sdhconference/resources/implementinghiapadel-sahealth-100622.pdf. Accessed 30 June 2019.

Klafki, W. (1974). *Studien zur Bildungstheorie und Didaktik.* Beltz.

Knoll, J. (2003). *Kurs- und Seminarmethoden – Ein Trainingsbuch zur Gestaltung von Kursen und Seminaren, Arbeits- und Gesprächskreisen* (10. neu ausgest. Aufl.). Beltz.

Konrad, K., & Traub, S. (2010). *Selbstgesteuertes Lernen: Grundwissen und Tipps für die Praxis.* Schneider.

Kron, F. W. (2008). *Grundwissen Didaktik.* Reinhardt.

Lampert, T., Richter, M., Schneider, S., Spallek, J., & Dragano, N. (2016). Soziale Ungleichheit und Gesundheit – Stand und Perspektiven der sozialepidemiologischen Forschung in

Deutschland. *Bundesgesundheitsblatt – Gesundheitsforschung – Gesundheitsschutz,* 59 (2), 153–165.

Landeshauptstadt München. (2016). *Münchener Stadtteilstudie – Fortschreibung 2015.* dm.

Langemeyer, I. (2017). Das forschungsbezogene Studium als Enkulturation in Wissenschaft. In H. Mieg & J. Lehmann (Hrsg.), *Forschendes Lernen – Wie die Lehre in Universität und Fachhochschule erneuert werden kann* (S. 91–100). Campus.

Lazarsfeld, P. (2014). Die soziographische Methode in der Marienthalstudie – Auszüge aus Vorspruch und Einleitung (Original 1932). In M. Miege & H. Schubert (Hrsg.), *Sozialraumanalyse: Grundlagen – Methoden – Praxis* (4. unveränd. Aufl., S. 64–73). FH Köln - In-house printing shop.

Mayring, P. (2016). *Einführung in die qualitative Sozialforschung* (6. überarb. Aufl.). Beltz.

Mieg, H. (2017). Forschendes Lernen – Erste Bilanz. In H. Mieg & J. Lehmann, J. (Hrsg.), *Forschendes Lernen – Wie die Lehre in Universität und Fachhochschule erneuert werden kann* (S. 15–31). Campus.

Mielck, A. (2006). *Soziale Ungleichheit und Gesundheit – Einführung in die aktuelle Diskussion.* Huber.

Niederberger, M. (2018). Mixed-Methods-Studien in der Gesundheitsförderung – Studie über junge Menschen mit Fluchterfahrung. *Prävention & Gesundheitsförderung, 13*(1), 85–90.

Poethko-Müller, C., Kuntz, B., Lampert, T., & Neuhauser, H. (2018). Die allgemeine Gesundheit von Kindern und Jugendlichen in Deutschland – Querschnittergebnisse aus KiGGS Welle 2 und Trends. *Journal of Health Monitoring, 3*(1), 8–14.

Riege, M., & Schubert, H. (2014). Zur Analyse sozialer Räume – Ein interdisziplinärer Integrationsversuch. In M. Riege & H. Schubert (Eds.), *Sozialraumanalyse: Grundlagen – Methoden – Praxis.* (4. unveränd. Aufl.). FH Köln - In-house printing shop.

Rummer, M. (Hrsg.) (2014). *Vorlesungen innovativ gestalten – Neue Lernformen für große Lerngruppen.* Beltz.

Schaeffer, D., Hurrelmann, K., Bauer, U., & Kolpatzik, K., (2018). Nationaler Aktionsplan Gesundheitskompetenz – Die Gesundheitskompetenz in Deutschland stärken. http://www.nap-gesundheitskompetenz.de. Accessed 16 Jun 2019.

Schilling, R., Hoebel, J., Müters, S., & Lange, C. (2015). Pilotstudie zur Durchführung von Mixed-Mode-Gesundheitsbefragungen in der Erwachsenenbevölkerung (Pilotstudie GEDA 2.0). In Robert Koch-Institut (Hrsg.), *Beiträge zur Gesundheitsberichterstattung des Bundes.* Robert Koch-Institut In-house printing shop.

Siegrist, J. (2005). *Medizinische Soziologie* (6. Aufl. München u.). Urban und Fischer.

Schunk, D. (2012). *Learning Theories – An Educational Perspective.* Pearson.

Statistisches Bundesamt. (2018). Anzahl der Geburten in Deutschland von 1991 bis 2017. https://de. statista.com/statistik/daten/studie/235/umfrage/anzahl-der-geburten-seit-1993.pdf. Accessed: 2 July 2019.

Trojan, A. (2009). Prävention und Gesundheitsförderung in Städten und Gemeinden. In K. Hurrelmann, T. Klotz, & J. Haisch (Hrsg.), *Lehrbuch Prävention und Gesundheitsförderung* (2. überarb. Aufl. S. 307–317). Huber.

Urban, M., & Weiser, U. (2006). *Kleinräumige Sozialraumanalysen – Theoretische Grundlagen und praktische Durchführung.* Saxonia.

Zick, F. (2016). 33.000 Mitarbeiter: Das Rathaus wird immer größer. *Münchener Abendzeitung.* 16.01.2015.

Community-Based Health Promotion for Senior Citizens—What We Can Learn from South Korean Model of Senior Centers

3

Yong-Seun Chang-Gusko, Ellen Meissner and Kai Kühne

Contents

3.1 Introduction 43
3.2 Goal of the Study 44
3.3 Best Practice Case Study 44
    3.3.1 Findings of the Evaluation 47
3.4 Situation in Germany 48
    3.4.1 Demographic Change in Germany 48
    3.4.2 Situation of Seniors 49
3.5 Conceptualizing German Senior Centre 51
    3.5.1 Aim of the Project 51
    3.5.2 Description of the Model 52
    3.5.3 Process 54
3.6 Conclusion/Outlook 55
References 56

Y.-S. Chang-Gusko (✉)
Kosin University, Busan, South Korea, Max und Ingeburg Herz Stiftung, Hamburg, Germany
e-mail: yc@meinlido.de

E. Meissner
FOM University of Applied Sciences, Hamburg, Germany
e-mail: ellen.meissner@fom.de

K. Kühne
Max und Ingeburg Herz Stiftung, Hamburg, Germany
e-mail: kk@meinlido.de

M. Cassens et al. (eds.), *Transdisciplinary Perspectives on Public Health in Europe*,
FOM-Edition, https://doi.org/10.1007/978-3-658-33740-7_3

Abstract

The rapid increase of an ageing population poses great challenges, specifically those related to older peoples' health. Therefore, most societies will need to promote healthy behaviour, prevent diseases, and develop impactful yet cost-effective strategies. There is ample evidence that social bonds, social activities, and maintaining a social network are essential for healthy aging. Consequently, health promotion focusses on the active inclusion of seniors into social activities of the community. Based on the experience of senior centres in Korea, this project conceptualizes senior centres in Germany. Korean senior centres are widely known in the community and work in collaborative partnerships on the regional and supra-regional level. These centres offer senior citizens a wide variety of leisure and social activities, as well as programs and services that promote health and prevent diseases. The Seoul Government found that senior centres have a positive effect on physical health. Social networking was shown to be one of the main benefits resulting in increased life satisfaction. An evaluation study at the University of Bielefeld (Germany) generated a synopsis of existing quarter development projects in NRW. The study concludes that there is currently no common understanding or concept for senior-appropriate quarter development, which is reflected in the great heterogeneity of concepts. Experiences and findings from previous projects are also not yet sufficiently documented and generally accessible. Previous projects are quarter-focused, where the neighbourhood serves as a reference, but only few projects directly address the needs and requirements of people in this neighbourhood. The project Lido has the goal of addressing the above-mentioned challenges. It will create centres for activities, discussions, encounters and information—a space offering seniors a variety of useful services and facilities. Senior citizens can access information on governmental affairs or ask fellow seniors or other community members. Motivated and active seniors are given the opportunity to initiate their own activities and projects. New relationships can be developed and maintained through participation and just meeting in the common spaces. The emphasis lies in networking and combining online and offline resources and facilities and encouraging active involvement of the elderly. This alternative approach in empowering community interest groups can benefit the elderly with a variety of social activities, but also reduces the financial burden on the centre. The aim of Lido is to support and facilitate social participation of individuals and the wider community. It also seeks to connect all stakeholders in the community in order to boost social support and community engagement which will ultimately benefit all.

3.1   Introduction

Societies worldwide are facing a significant increase in their ageing population. According to a report from the American Census Bureau from 2015, 8.5% of people worldwide (617 million) are aged 65 and over. This percentage is projected to increase to nearly 17% of the world's population by 2050 (1.6 billion). For the USA the year 2030 will mark an important demographic turning point when all 'Baby Boomers' will be older than 65 years of age. At this point they will outnumber the younger generation for the first time in US history (He et al., 2015). Since the 1970s mortality at ages 80 years and older has continued to fall and so the gains in record life expectancies were fuelled by progress at older ages. In 1950 the probability of survival beyond the age of 80 years to 90 years was on average 15–16% for women and 12% for men in most developed countries. In 2002 the rate had already increased to 37% and 25%, respectively. In Japan, the country with the best chances of a long life, the probability is currently over 50% for women. The remarkable gain of about 30 years in life expectancy in these countries stands out as one of the most important accomplishments of the twentieth century (Rau et al., 2008). Given better health care, this trend will see most babies born since 2000 in France, Italy, UK, USA, Canada, Japan and Germany will celebrate their 100th birthday (Christensen et al., 2009).

However, the rapid increase of an ageing population poses great challenges, specifically to older peoples' health. The most rapidly growing segment of the population in developed countries over the past decades is the group aged over 85 years and this is also the group most susceptible to disability. The prevalence of diseases in the elderly population might partly be caused by improved medical knowledge and health services for elderly people. It is assumed that diseases such as type 2 diabetes, hypertension and some cancers now get diagnosed earlier and receive better treatment. On the other hand, these improvements lead to longer periods of morbidity, which usually means a decline in physical functioning and a rise in prevalence of chronic diseases in this age group (Jeune & Brønnum-Hansen, 2008). Development of disease and disability among elderly people will therefore have a fundamental impact on society and pose severe challenges for the traditional social welfare state (Engberg et al., 2009). Therefore, most societies will need to develop impactful yet cost-effective strategies to manage the health burdens associated with an ageing population.

In this context the term "successful aging" has captured the attention of researchers for decades. Rowe and Kahn (1998) defined successful aging as "avoidance of diseases and disability; maintenance of high physical and cognitive function; and sustained engagement in social and productive activities". According to this definition, social bonds, social activities, and maintaining a social network are essential for healthy aging. In reality though, elderly people are more likely to suffer from loneliness and social isolation. Consequently, health promotion strategies for the elderly generation should have three aims: maintaining and increasing physical and mental capacity, self-care and maintaining one's social network. Inclusion of seniors in the social activities of the community do not always have to be formal or require a lot of financing. However, they very often require an appropriate social infrastructure (Golinowska et al., 2016).

3.2   Goal of the Study

The goal of this study is to develop and plan the project ‚Lido' (German acronym for zest for life, innovation, digital and locally) which aims to ensure participation, independence and a self-determined life for older people who still live in their own homes. This is to counteract loneliness and social isolation often feared by older people in our society. In this study, a secondary data analysis of the situation in Germany, combined with stakeholder analysis and a best-case example from South Korea, is used to develop a concept of how to provide seniors not just with offline but also online participation.

3.3   Best Practice Case Study

Korean society is rapidly progressing towards the 'Centennial Society', experiencing both, sharp declines in fertility and substantial gains in longevity. South Korea has become a super-aged society 10 years earlier than Japan. According to an official prediction based on the population dynamics of fertility and mortality,14.5% of Koreans will be over the age of 65 in 2018, increasing to 20.8% by 2026 (Kang et al., 2012). A forecasting model of national age-specific mortality and life expectancy predict a 90% probability of life expectancy higher than 86.7 years for south Korean women born in 2030. This means a number one ranking of longevity for Korean women followed by France, Spain, and Japan. Men's life expectancy at birth in South Korea will surpass 80 years in 2030 with a probability of over 95% (Kontis et al., 2017).

Chronic diseases dominate the morbidity pattern of the elderly and the presence of multiple chronic conditions which are quite common in older people in South Korea, increase their risk of developing disability and dependency (Kang et al., 2012). Elderly people account for a large share of health expenditure and admissions for social care needs. Medical costs in health insurance for this age group for example have continued to rise as the population ages, increasing from 2 trillion won (approx. 1.6 billion Euro) in 1999 to around 12 trillion won (approx. 10 billion Euro) in 2009 resulting in 30.5% of the total medical costs (Yi & Hwang, 2015). Given the rapid increase in the Korean elderly population, the economic and psycho-social burden imposed on older adults and their caregivers is therefore being increasingly recognized as a major social problem with wide political implications.

In order to address these challenges caused by an ageing society, Korean government implemented a long-term care insurance system (LTCI) in 2008. This policy was developed to promote long-term health of the elderly through prevention whilst reducing national medical expenditures and stabilizing fiscal insurance costs (Choi & McDougall, 2007). Everyone who contributes to health insurance simultaneously contributes to LTCI. The long-term care insurance was designed as a separate scheme from the national health insurance based on functional impairment, benefits, coverage of community-based and institutional care, and a financing structure through multi-party contributions (Kang et al., 2012). LTCI funding is separate from National Health Insurance System (NHIS), but is administered by NHIS to reduce administrative costs. 6.55% of health insurance premium contributes to LTCI and the financing mix is composed of contributions (60–65%), tax subsidies (20%) and co-payment by service users (20% for institutional services and 15% for home- based services). The difference in payments for institutional care compared to home-based services was introduced to promote community-based care, i.e. keep the elderly looked after in their own homes for longer (Jeon & Kwon, 2017). In contrast to Long Term Care (LTC) in other countries like Germany, where an LTC system has been developed for people with disabilities, including older people, LTCI in Korea was introduced specifically in the context of an ageing society. It aims at prevention as one of the key measures to address the complexity of such a society. As part of the implementation of home- and community-based preventive long-term care programs, support for existing 'senior centres' was favoured over new large-scale infrastructure projects (Kwon, 2009).

Korean senior centres are widely known and visited community centres for elder citizen. 83.7% of senior citizens are aware of senior centres which serve as local gathering and communication centres. Today, older Koreans have access to more than 64,000 senior or elderly community centres throughout South Korea. Between 30 and 40% of the elderly visit these centres. They represent a uniquely Korean way of taking care of the elderly that is rarely seen in other countries (Hankyoreh, 2016a). The senior centres in Korea are similar to the better-known YMCA community centres in the United States and act as a social welfare institution in order to support seniors to socialize. In contrast to the YMCA's paid membership and program-oriented activities, the Korean senior centres are financially supported by the government and have strong welfare characteristics, offering places to get together for seniors, independent of their income. These centres offer senior citizens a wide variety of leisure and social activities, as well as programs and services that promote health and prevent diseases (Fig. 3.1). In Korea different forms of 'senior centres' coexist. The municipal managed 'senior welfare centres' act as a unified access point for individuals with diverse needs including community-health care, home visiting stations, social welfare councils. Many of these centres combine the mentioned health focus with offerings of leisure activities, educational and health promotion programs. These centres offer elderly people the freedom to pursue friendships, exchange information, learn and work on projects together. The "senior community centres" on the other hand are more numerous and smaller in scale and provide places for social and leisure activities. To help improve the operations of these often self-organized senior community centres, the municipality assigns one government official to

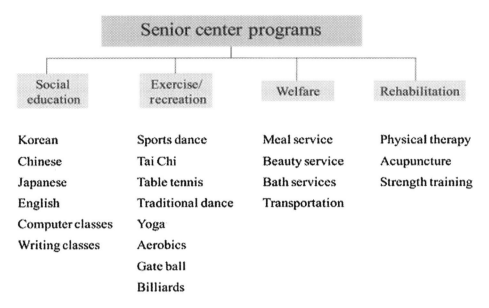

Fig. 3.1 Typical activity programs offered by the senior centre (Kim et al., 2012)

each centre to offer advice on how to improve or develop programs for older adults and to serve as an intermediary for the government to identify and address community needs. To promote healthy lifestyles among older adults, the Korean government launched a national program called the Elderly Health Promotion Project in 2008. Ever since local governments and public organizations provide health-related courses and services for seniors at a number of community centres (ARC-Report, n. d).

The Korean seniors themselves are quite a homogeneous group. They have devoted their lives to their children and as a consequence have not been adequately prepared for their post retirement years. Due to different circumstances, e.g. the Korean War in the fifties, these seniors have relatively low levels of education and only a few of them have had access to digital devices until reaching their senior years. Through lack of access to relevant information, low digital literacy contributes further to socio-economic inequality, obstruction of social participation and integration (Kim & Choi, 2014). According to research on factors influencing the information-seeking activities about health, hobbies and entertainment programs, the main source of information for the elderly have been their fellow seniors. Studies have demonstrated, that these interactions with other seniors enhance the interpersonal relationships and self-satisfaction (Kim et al., 2011). Through document analysis Yi and Hwang (2015) studied social isolation and interpersonal relationship and its impact on social isolation of the elderly in Korea alongside other changes in the South Korean society, such as changes of family relationship, social structure, economic structure and culture. They define social isolation as cut-off from the society, meaning that the microsystem surrounding people has become hollow and the social support serving as a buffer zone is weak with little resources that can be mobilized when needed. Of the six million senior citizens over 65 in South Korea 1.19 million live alone; 2.2 times the number compared to a decade ago (Yi & Hwang, 2015). Studies on social isolation of older people show a rate of social isolation of 25 to 35% (Hawthorne, 2008) and a positive correlation between quality of life, satisfaction levels with life and social connectedness of the elderly. Despite these facts, old people are more and more likely in wanting to reduce their dependency on other to not burden them. However, by willingly avoiding interactions with others, their social integration is disappearing and they are driven even further into loneliness (Yi & Hwang, 2015).

Accordingly, the Korean government has increased the senior welfare budget from 6.2% of GDP in 2005 to 9.33% in 2013 (Hankyoreh, 2016b). A Senior Welfare Department was implemented in 2014 consisting of Senior Policy Team, Social Participation Support Team, Community Care Team, Facilities Management Team, Funeral Culture Team and Baby Boomer Policy Team and the second life Supporting Department was established in 2015. This department aims to support Korean Baby-Boomers, born after the Korean War, between 1955 and 1962 by addressing their specific needs and challenges. Furthermore, the Healthy City Paradigm announced in 1984 by the World Health Organization to promote healthy cities and communities in order to improve mortality and quality of life was first introduced in South Korea in 1996. Since 2018, 93 full member cities and 11 associate member cities actively promote health, linking city's living conditions with the citizens' health and consider health promotion as basic measurement of the community according to supporting results of studies that older adults' happiness is strongly related to the quality of services provided within a city that enable residents to age in place (Hogan et al., 2016).

3.3.1 Findings of the Evaluation

An evaluation study by the Seoul Government in 2012 (Seoul Government, 2012) based on data of 2083 senior centers in Seoul (out of 3198 in total) and 1243 individual interviews from 25 districts revealed that 75.8% of the users were satisfied with the center. The most named reason for the visit of the center was relationship with other visitor (83.5%), sharing lunch (78.4%) and participating in the programs offered (67.2%). When asked about changes in daily life since visiting the center, 86.5% of the interview partner named the positive impact on their social relationships, mostly an increased number of friends. Also mentioned was an increased joy of life (84.6%) (see Fig. 3.2 upper table). Of the people interviewed, 80.3% mentioned improvement in mental health and in 73.3% in physical health since participating in the senior centers (see Fig. 3.2 lower table).

Confirming the results of the evaluation of Seoul Government studies in advanced countries, including Korea, additional studies support the expected positive effects of senior centres on physical health (fall prevention, resistance exercise, and walking

Change in daily life

Visit to the center (All information in percent: %)

Increase	Total	Gender		Age		
		Male	Female	60y	70y	80y
Friends	85,5	78,8	88	62,7	84,2	88,8
Joy of Life	84,6	71,9	89,4	68,6	82,7	88
Health	78,1	69,2	81,4	58,8	78,7	79,2

Changes after Program Attendance (All information in percent: %)

Incease	Total	Gender		Age		
		Male	Female	60y	70y	80y
Psych. Health	80,3	69,4	83,4	48	78,6	83,9
Phys. Health	73,3	58,5	77,5	34,6	73,9	75,1
Leisure life diversity	56,2	50,5	57,7	45,8	54,4	58,6
Learning motivation	33,3	46,2	29,5	38,5	36,4	29,6
Job offer	32,1	38,5	30,2	42,3	38	25,6

Fig. 3.2 Senior Centre program monitoring

distance) and psychological health (depressive symptoms, friendships, and stress-related distress) (Kim et al., 2012). Results of controlled studies revealed that users of senior centres, more than non-users achieved higher scores in physical functioning and vitality assuming that seniors benefiting not only physically but mentally as well (Kim et al., 2011). Another outcome of the evaluation by the Seoul Government was that social networking was one of the main benefits, resulting in increased numbers of friends and life satisfaction. Studies in other countries have resumed that the use of senior centres can improve psychological wellbeing, help alleviate depression, foster friendships and social interactions and reduce stress levels (Aday et al., 2006; Choi & McDougall, 2007; Farone, et al., 2005). Elderly women who live alone and are considered at greater risk for loneliness and depression were able to form new supportive friendships resulting in positive mental and physical outcomes (Aday et al., 2006).

3.4 Situation in Germany

3.4.1 Demographic Change in Germany

Compared to the end of the nineteenth century, life expectancy in Germany has doubled. Estimates of the Federal Statistical Office in Germany predict that the demographic ageing will continue over the next decades (Statistisches Bundesamt, 2016). According to Eurostat the median age of the EU-28's population was highest in Germany and Italy with half of the population being older than 42.8 years compared to the youngest median age of 31.4 years in Turkey in 2017. According to the World Economic Forum there will be fewer Germans under the age of 30 than there are Germans older than 60 by 2019 (Desjardins, n. d.).

Compared to the global population average of 24.4% being under 14 and only 12.3% older than 60 years, this ratio is extreme considering the fact of progressive ageing of the older population itself. The group of very old is growing faster than any other age segment of the EU's population with the share of 80 years and above projected to more than double between 2017 and 2080 from 5.5 to 12.7%. Already every forth citizen in Germany is 60 years or older. As the 'Baby Boomers' are reaching retirement age over the next few years, this will further increase to one in three in the next three decades (Heible, 2015).

3.4.2 Situation of Seniors

The dramatic increase in the proportion of the elderly has sparked extensive geronto-logical and medical research in many different fields. One of the key factors driving the growing interest in scientific inquiry is the concern regarding the consequences of popu-lation ageing, particularly increased spending on health and social care services. These policy concerns have prompted a search for ways to enable older people to maintain their mobility and independence in order to avoid costly and dependency-promoting institu-tional care (Walker, 2005). Understanding the relationship between health and subjective well-being at old age is of great socio-political importance.

Generally, it is assumed and expected that life satisfaction declines in older age, but in reality, a large body of gerontological literature on relationship between age and life sat-isfaction shows that there is no simple age-related decline in life satisfaction. Many stud-ies have found a U-shaped relationship between age and life satisfaction, with the lowest satisfaction between mid-30s and mid-40s. This result was confirmed by data from the first 14 waves of the British Household Panel Study (BHPS) even after controlling for individual heterogeneity (Clark, 2007). In contrast, other international data indicate that age has an inconsistent relationship with happiness and the U-shaped relationship is only found in rich English-speaking countries (Deaton, 2008) and that overall life satisfac-tion remains remarkably constant across life within cohorts, once adjusted for several explanatory variables e.g. World War II in Germany for individuals born between 1930 and 1960. One issue of particular interest in this discussion is the fact that objective, as opposed to subjective health has no strong effect on life satisfaction. A possible expla-nation for this surprising correlation is provided by a number of gerontological study results that indicate that subjective well-being is strongly influenced by social participa-tion. Physical health as measured by objective health measures might only indirectly and with a time lag affect functional health, which in turn then influences social participation (Gwozdz & Sousa-Poza, 2010). The Survey of Health and Living Status of the Elderly in Taiwan concludes that the cohort experience has an important impact on life satisfac-tion and supports the importance of social participation (Chen, 2001). Berg et al., (2006) explain the rather weak correlation between objective health and subjective well-being with the fact that life satisfaction in old age may become more dependent on what really matters in old age. Factors determining quality of life in old age have been found to be maintenance of independence, control over one's life, social role functioning and social participation (Walker, 2005).

In this context, international research recognizes the importance of the quarter, the place of residence and neighbourhood for health and well-being in old age. A cohort study with a sample of 1157 senior citizens aged 69–78 in the UK examined the relationship between neighbourhood and mental well-being. The results of the study showed that people show a higher level of well-being when they have a sense of attachment to their neighbourhood and report only few problems in the neighbourhood. This relationship was found independently of income, social class, limitations such as illness or disability, mobility limitations or perceived social support (Gale et al., 2011).

The level of mental well-being further depends on the cooperation of all actors and the communication between them and how openly the people in need of care are approached and how accessible they are (Kümpers & Falk, 2013). Activation and participation of all involved in the neighbourhood and the cooperation of the municipality and civil society was pointed out as an important prerequisite for a sustainable age-appropriate and generation-friendly quarter development (Hollbach-Grömig & Seidel-Schulze, 2007).

An evaluation study at the University of Bielefeld generated a synopsis of existing quarter development projects in NRW.

The study concludes that:

- there is currently **no common understanding or concept** for senior-appropriate quarter development, which is reflected in the great heterogeneity of concepts. Experiences and findings from previous projects are also **not yet sufficiently documented** and **generally accessible**
- there are **different municipal frameworks**, requiring different strategies for quarter development and
- previous projects are quarter-focused, where the neighbourhood serves as a reference, but only few projects directly address the **needs and requirements of people in this neighbourhood** (Hämel et al., 2012).

Community engagement (CE), activation and participation of all involved in the neighbourhood is considered a key component of new collaborative models of care. CE has the potential to bring together a wider range of services e.g. including schools and local businesses with a view to tailor the approach to the needs of the communities themselves. Many studies suggest that, when citizens get more involved and engaged to shape their local service it leads to more tailored and integrated services. This has a positive impact on the management of their own health and well-being and results in improved community health and well-being (Milton et al., 2011).

An international review study points in the same direction and confirms that community engagement is crucial for high quality and efficient care, calling out the following key contributing factors among others for successful community engagement (De Weger et al., 2018):

- Foster a *safe and trusting environment*, enabling citizens to provide input;
- Ensure citizens' *early involvement and share decision-making* and governance with citizens; and
- Consider both *citizens' and organizations' motivations.*

3.5 Conceptualizing German Senior Centre

Back in the 1980s, concepts such as "Home First", "Ageing at Home" and "Outpatient over Inpatient" were established. They had the goal of supporting people to live as long and as independently as possible in their own home, even if care or other assistance is needed. These concepts shifted the focus to the home, the household and the family and projects such as "Age-friendly Cities" developed by the WHO and "Dementia-friendly; Municipality" by Aktion Dementia e.V.. Quarter in this context means a spatial expansion that is manageable, socially constructible, not necessarily delimited administratively and is related to everyday life and social interactions, thus providing an interactive environment (Schnur, 2008). The aspect of identification is especially important and quarters offer potential for at least partial local identification, i.e. the quarter must be experienced as a relational space by its inhabitants. Local community and their neighbourhood have significant impact on the quality of life and health of elderly. Social relationships are positively associated with health status across the life span and the decline of social networks may be one key challenge for older people contributing to decrease in subjective well-being and life satisfaction (Chang et al., 2014).

3.5.1 Aim of the Project

Welfare facilities for elderly adequately operated within a local community, like senior centres could foster social exchanges and counteract the social isolation of the elderly (Yi & Hwang, 2015). The Korean model of easily accessible, affordable and well known senior centres has shown positive influence on life satisfaction, social relationship and subjective well-being (Seoul Government, 2012).

The project Lido has the goal of creating a centre for activities, discussions, encounters and information—a space offering seniors a variety of useful services and facilities. Senior citizens can access information on governmental affairs or ask fellow seniors or other community members. Motivated and active seniors are given the opportunity to initiate their own activities and projects. New relationships can be developed and maintained through participation and just meeting in at the common spaces. The project focuses on supporting seniors to continue their daily routines in a self-determined way. None of the offered activities are compulsory. There are also input and resources for the seniors to establish and carry out their own activities. Thus, one example of engaging the elderly in the activities is a planned training project called 'Silversurfer Train Peers'. Seniors who are active users of the internet and online resources train less experienced seniors sharing their experience and knowledge. This way, various levels of digital literacy can be catered for. Again, this emphasises the uniqueness of the planned approach combining various online and offline resources and facilities and encouraging active involvement of the elderly.

3.5.2   Description of the Model

The project Lido aims to gather the results and experiences of research and practice example from South Korea and translate them into German context. This is achieved through the following:

- **Early involvement, shared decision-making and governance with citizens:** The local parish was won as initial partner and was from the start involved in all steps. In collaboration with the parish council it was possible to identify all relevant stakeholders and discuss the project with them and interested citizens during an information event and in many personal meetings before the start of the project.
- **Foster safe and trusting environment:** The local parish represented through the reverent was the organizer of the interviews for the needs analysis with citizens to ensure a safe and trusting environment. The interviews were conducted by students of a cooperating university which also increased the confidence. Questionnaires were distributed via a local civic association to their members and via local care-service to their patients.
- **Population—and community-oriented needs and resource assessment** (De Weger et al., 2018): Qualitative Interviews with seniors, focus group with care takers and discussions with all relevant stakeholders in the community covering the following areas: needs, motivations, difficulties, barriers, hopes. Questionnaires via local stakeholders to ensure input from less active and mobile seniors.
- **Acknowledge different municipal frameworks** (Hämel et al., 2012)**:** Identifying relevant local stakeholders, their role, needs and motivation through open communication and discussion.
- **No common understanding or concept, not yet sufficiently documented** and **generally accessible:** Lido aims to address the above-mentioned gap of common understanding and concept of senior-appropriate quarter development. A collaboration of local stakeholders, group of university students and professors in charge of needs and resource analysis and evaluation supported by a foundation working in the aged-care

sector will be in charge of documentation, modelling and on—and offline communication of the concept to not only local, but also regional and national audiences.

The following model (Fig. 3.3) depicts elements of a systematic quartier focussed on- and offline offering for seniors.

At the centre of the model is the individual with his/her needs and wishes to independently plan their day to day life. This is embedded in the collective needs of the target group, the resources of the community and the support from the wider society as well as close relatives, friends and neighbours. From an offline perspective, the planned services, activities and gatherings tailored to the elderly according to the results of a needs and resource analysis will be offered in a senior citizen centre, where a vast network of information to help seniors to navigate everyday life will also be provided. There will be an on-site contact person from the parish responsible for the senior centre to whom seniors can turn with confidence for questions concerning official, local and organizational matters. This creates a one-stop service for the target group, where they can clarify all questions and issues with a single point of contact. Activities in the senior centre will be complemented by different offers from other local players like local civic association,

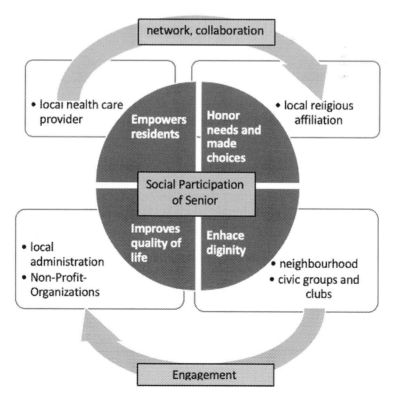

Fig. 3.3 Model Lido—Empowering community to enhance social participation of elderly

assisted living and local sporting clubs to combine and utilize community resources. The centre itself, but also all the other cooperating institutions should be easily accessible by foot or a short ride on public transport for local citizens.

Online, the network will provide a barrier free platform, where all relevant activities, news and information for the elderly in the district will be presented in an easy mainly 'read only' manner in order to increase accessibility for elderly with limited digital experiences. In addition, more competent seniors are given a means of communication which also allows them to stay in contact with like-minded people in case of immobility or other challenges.

3.5.3 Process

To implement project Lido, a quarter with an average population mix was chosen. Seniors 65 years and older were chosen as target group and it was considered which institution would be suitable as first point of contact. The requirements on this institution where awareness in the target group, social engagement, particularly in aged care work, free or low-cost offerings, a national presence (to ensure possibility of national expansion) and a trusted image. These requirements are most likely met by the church. As a result, the St. Simeon congregation in Osdorf became the first point of contact. This was timely as St. Simeon was in the process of launching an initiative for senior work activities themselves. Furthermore, the location of Osdorf was ideal as a number of potential cooperation partners are based in close proximity.

To support the project scientifically, the University of Economics and Management (FOM) and a foundation active in the field of aged-care joined the project. The foundation took the responsibility for facilitating and funding the project Lido. As part of this partnership, the following topics emerged for study projects:

- Stakeholder analysis with 2 groups of elderly 65–69 and 70+ aiming to find out the needs and wants
- Investigating of e-participation of older people; it will be distinguished between older people who are online on a regular basis and older people who are offline
- Collecting experiences of relatives of the elderly (some with caring responsibilities) through focus groups; questions to be raised are around possibilities and future developments
- Analysis of resources already existing in the communities; one analysis is focusing on the particular suburb that was chosen for the trial of a senior centre, the other analysis is more general on all of Hamburg; questions to be answered are which resources are already accessible for the elderly and can those be further developed
- Another study works on creating a digital platform to connect stakeholders on one side and the user (elderly) on the other. Here, the focus is on barrier free access, an

Table 3.1   Project Plan

02/2019—Mid 2020	ToDo	3rd quarter 2020–2021	2022
Project Preparation: – cooperation partners – consider practice models – resource stocktaking (care provider, cost units, authorities) – science (needs analysis, literature recherche)	Identification: – IT Partner – pilot community Research: – Start in march 2019 (FOM)	Pilot Project: – district-offer, demand, coordinated, participatory – Online-Platform: health information and education, individual functions like chat, search, login, newsfeed and filter, simplified	Rollout: – one senior centre in every district
Approach/Attempt: – dismantling of barriers (intrinsically/ extrinsically) – low threshold access, local and digital	Foundation: – Networking for project partners – project coordination	Evaluation: – recommendations for action – modelling	Evaluation: – model differentiation

individually customisable user level and a gatekeeper-controlled access for partners to protect the elderly.

Project plan

Based on the results of the research, a pilot project tailored to the target group will be kicked off, planned for Q3 of 2020. Following, an evaluation is planned in Q3/Q4 of 2021 and a review of the initial concept will be conducted. The second phase of the project is to introduce and evaluate the revised concept in several communities in Hamburg with different social composition. The third phase of the project will be the final conceptualization of a senior centre to enhance social participation of senior citizen by boosting engagement of local community, which then could be rollout to other parts of the city of Hamburg (see table Table 3.1).

3.6   Conclusion/Outlook

It is evident that the demographic change will continue to significantly increase the average age of the population. While the German government has already begun to develop legal drafts, regulations and directives in response to this, it is up to the municipalities and communities to act now. As mentioned above, various studies have shown the importance and impact of social networks and meaningful relationships on health, well-being and life satisfaction not just for individuals but also entire populations. Meaningful social interaction and developing and maintaining friendships are one of the most important activities in human life. Some countries, such as Korea, have started to establish sustainable concepts much earlier and can serve as examples for German projects such as Lido. This alternative approach is empowering community interest groups and can benefit the elderly with a variety of social activities, but also reduces the financial burden on the centre. The aim of Lido is to support and facilitate social participation of individuals and the wider community. It also seeks to connect all stakeholders in the community in order to boost social support and community engagement which will ultimately benefit all.

References

Aday, R. H., Kehoe, G. C., & Farney, L. A. (2006). Impact of senior center friendships on aging women who live alone. *Journal of Women & Aging, 18*(57–73), 2006. https://doi.org/10.1300/J074v18n01_05

AARP International & FP Analysis (n. d.) ARC-Report: The Aging Readiness & Competitiveness Report Korea. https://arc.aarpinternational.org/File%20Library/Full%20Reports/ARC-Report---Korea.pdf Assessed 18 Jun 2019.

Berg, A. I., Hassing, L. B., McClearn, G. E., & Johansson, B. (2006). What matters for life satisfaction in the oldest-old? *Aging and Mental Health, 10*, 257–264. https://doi.org/10.1080/13607860500409435

Chang, P.-J., Wray, L., & Lin, Y. (2014). Social relationships, leisure activity, and health in older adults. *Health Psychology, 33*(6), 516–523. https://doi.org/10.1037/hea0000051

Chen, C. (2001). Aging and life satisfaction. *Social Indicators Research, 54*, 57–79. https://doi.org/10.1023/A:1007260728792

Choi, N. G., & McDougall, G. J. (2007). Comparison of depressive symptoms between homebound older adults and ambulatory older adults. *Aging and Mental Health, 11*, 310–322. https://doi.org/10.1080/13607860600844614

Christensen, K., Doblhammer, G., Rau, R., & Vaupel, J. W. (2009). Ageing populations: The challenges ahead. *Lancet, 374*, 1196–1208. https://doi.org/10.1016/S0140-6736(09)61460-4

Clark, A. E. (2007). Born to be mild? Cohort effects don't (fully) explain why well-being is U-Shaped in age. Forschungsinstitut Zur Zuk. Arb. IZA DP No. 3170, 1–29.

Deaton, A. (2008). Income, health and wellbeing around the world: Evidence from the Gallup world poll. *Journal of Economic Perspectives, 22*, 53–72. https://doi.org/10.1257/jep.22.2.53

Desjardins, J. (n. d.). Germany will hit a significant demographic milestone over the next year [WWW Document]. The World Economic Forum. https://www.weforum.org/agenda/2018/01/germany-will-hit-a-significant-demographic-milestone-over-the-next-year/. Accessed 6 June 2019.

De Weger, E., Van Vooren, N., Luijkx, K. G., Baan, C. A., & Drewes, H. W. (2018). Achieving successful community engagement: A rapid realist review. *BMC Health Services Research, 18*(1), 285. https://doi.org/10.1186/s12913-018-3090-1

Destatis, Statistisches Bundesamt. (2016). *Ältere Menschen in Deutschland und der EU.*

Engberg, H., Oksuzyan, A., Jeune, B., Vaupel, J. W., & Christensen, K. (2009). Centenarians—A useful model for healthy aging? A 29-year follow-up of hospitalizations among 40 000 Danes born in 1905. *Aging Cell, 8*, 270–276. https://doi.org/10.1111/j.1474-9726.2009.00474.x

Farone, D. W., Fitzpatrick, T. R., & Tran, T. V. (2005). Use of senior centers as a moderator of stress related distress among Latino elders. *The Hournal of Gerontological Social Work, 46*, 65–83. https://doi.org/10.1300/J083v46n01_05

Gale, C. R., Dennison, E. M., Cooper, C., & Sayer, A. A. (2011). Neighbourhood environment and positive mental health in older people: The Hertfordshire Cohort Study. *Health & Place, 17*(4), 867–874.

Golinowska, S., Groot, W., Baji, P., & Pavlova, M. (2016). Health promotion targeting older people. *BMC Health Services Research, 16*(5), 345. https://doi.org/10.1186/s12913-016-1514-3

Gwozdz, W., & Sousa-Poza, A. (2010). Ageing, Health and life satisfaction of the oldest old: An analysis for Germany. *Social Indicators Research, 97,* 397–417. https://doi.org/10.1007/s11205-009-9508-8

Hankyoreh. (2016a). [Reportage] Elderly community centers a place to ease loneliness on remote islands. http://english.hani.co.kr/arti/english_edition/e_national/776258.html. Accessed 27 May 2019.

Hankyoreh. (2016b). Elderly community centers a place to ease loneliness on remote islands. http://english.hani.co.kr/arti/english_edition/e_national/776258.html. Accessed 27 May 2019.

Hämel, K., Vogt, D., Düllmann, D., Olbermann, E., & Barth, C. (2012). Synopse - Altersgerechte Quartiersentwicklung und quartiersnahe Versorgung Hilfe- und Pflegebedürftiger: Eine qualitative Bestandsaufnahme von Quartiersprojekten und Unterstützungsangeboten zur Quartiersentwicklung. Institution für Pflegewissenschaft an der Universität Bielefeld, IPW und Forschungsgesellschaft für Gerontologie e.V., FFG, Bielefeld. https://www.uni-bielefeld.de/(de)/gesundhw/ag6/downloads/quartier.pdf. Accessed 27 May, 2019.

Hawthorne, G. (2008). Perceived social isolation in a community sample: Its prevalence and correlates with aspects of peoples' lives. *Social Psychiatry and Psychiatric Epidemiology, 43*(2), 140–150.

He, W., Goodkind, D., & Kowal, P. (2015). An aging world: 2015. *International Population Reports, 175.*

Heible, C. (2015). *Langfristige Perspektiven der Gesundheitswirtschaft: Eine CGE-Analyse demografischer und technologischer Wachstumseffekte.* Springer Gabler.

Hogan, M. J., Leyden, K. M., Conway, R., Goldberg, A., Walsh, D., & McKenna-Plumley, P. E. (2016). Happiness and health across the lifespan in five major cities: The impact of place and government performance. *Social Science and Medicine, 162,*168–176. https://doi.org/10.1016/j.socscimed.2016.06.030. Accessed 27 May 2019.

Hollbach-Grömig, B., & Seidel-Schulze, A. (2007). *Seniorenbezogene Gesundheitsförderung und Prävention auf kommunaler Ebene: Eine Bestandsaufnahme* (2. Aufl.). Bundeszentrale für gesundheitliche Aufklärung (BZgA).

Jeon, B., & Kwon, S. (2017). Health and long-term care systems for older people in the republic of Korea: Policy challenges and lessons. *Health System Reform, 3,* 214–223. https://doi.org/10.1080/23288604.2017.1345052

Jeune, B., & Brønnum-Hansen, H. (2008). Trends in health expectancy at age 65 for various health indicators, 1987–2005 Denmark. *European Journal of Ageing, 5,* 279. https://doi.org/10.1007/s10433-008-0100-x

Kang, I.-O., Park, C. Y., & Lee, Y. (2012). Role of healthcare in Korean long-term care insurance. *Journal of Korean Medical Science, 27,* 41–46. https://doi.org/10.3346/jkms.2012.27.

Kim, H.-S., Harada, K., Miyashita, M., Lee, E.-A., Park, J.-K., & Nakamura, Y. (2011). Use of senior center and the health-related quality of life in Korean older adults. *Journal of Preventive Medicine and Public Health, 44,* 149–156. https://doi.org/10.3961/jpmph.2011.44.4.149

Kim, H.-S., Miyashita, M., Harada, K., Park, J.-H., So, J.-M., & Nakamura, Y. (2012). Psychological, social, and environmental factors associated with utilization of senior centers among older adults *Korea. Journal of Preventive Medicine and Public Health, 45,* 244–250. https://doi.org/10.3961/jpmph.2012.45.4.244

Kim, S., & Cho, H. (2014). Still hungry for information: Information seeking behavior of senior citizens in South Korea.Semanticscholar.org. https://pdfs.semanticscholar.org/788e/e2519ba2d-3cbc2fcfa57f63596e66fad2784.pdf. Accessed 27 May 2019.

Kontis, V., Bennett, J. E., Mathers, C. D., Li, G., Foreman, K., & Ezzati, M. (2017). Future life expectancy in 35 industrialised countries: Projections with a Bayesian model ensemble. *The Lancet, 389*, 1323–1335. https://doi.org/10.1016/S0140-6736(16)32381-9

Kümpers, S., & Falk, K. (2013). Zur Bedeutung des Sozialraums für Gesundheitschancen und autonome Lebensgestaltung sozial benachteiligter Älterer: Befunde aus Berlin und Brandenburg. In C. Vogel, A. Motel-Klingebiel (Hrsg.), *Altern im sozialen Wandel: Die Rückkehr der Altersarmut?*, 81–97. https://doi.org/10.1007/978-3-531-18714-3_4.

Kwon, S. (2009). The introduction of long-term care insurance in South Korea. *Eurohealth, 15*, 28–29.

Milton, K., Bull, F. C., & Bauman, A. (2011). Reliability and validity testing of a single-item physical activity measure. *British Journal of Sports Medicine, 45*(3), 203–208. https://doi.org/10.1136/bjsm.2009.068395

Rau, R., Soroko, E., Jasilionis, D., & Vaupel, J. W. (2008). Continued reductions in mortality. Advanced ages. *Population and Development Review, 34*, 747–768. https://doi.org/10.1111/j.1728-4457.2008.00249.x

Rowe, J. W., & Kahn, R. L. (1998). Successful aging. *Aging Milan Italy, 10*, 142–144.

Schnur, O. (2008). *Quartiersforschung - Zwischen Theorie und Praxis*. VS Verlag/VS Research.

Walker, A. (2005). A European perspective on quality of life in old age. *European Journal of Ageing, 2*(2–12), 2005. https://doi.org/10.1007/s10433-005-0500-0

Yi, E.-S., & Hwang, H.-J. (2015). A study on the social behavior and social isolation of the elderly Korea. *The Journal of Exercise Rehabilitation, 11*, 125–132. https://doi.org/10.12965/jer.150215.

The Impact of Health Literacy on the Healthcare System

4

Laura Eichhorn

Contents

4.1   Health Literacy in Context.   60
    4.1.1   Definition of the Term   60
    4.1.2   The Relationship between Health Literacy and Health   61
    4.1.3   Health Literacy in a Disease Management Context.   62
    4.1.4   Health Literacy in a Health Promotion Context.   63
4.2   Measure Health Literacy   65
    4.2.1   The European Health Literacy Survey Questionnaire   65
    4.2.2   The Health Literacy Questionnaire   67
4.3   Actual Health Literacy Status   68
4.4   Improving Health Literacy.   70
    4.4.1   Health Literacy at a Patient Level   71
    4.4.2   Health Literacy at a Level of Healthcare Personnel & Small Organizations.   71
    4.4.3   Health Literacy at an Organizational & Population Level.   72
4.5   Health Literacy and the Future.   72
References.   74

L. Eichhorn (✉)
Former Research Fellow, FOM University of Applied Sciences, Munich, Germany
e-mail: eichhorn.laura@freenet.de

© The Author(s), under exclusive license to Springer Fachmedien Wiesbaden GmbH,   59
part of Springer Nature 2022
M. Cassens et al. (eds.), *Transdisciplinary Perspectives on Public Health in Europe*,
FOM-Edition, https://doi.org/10.1007/978-3-658-33740-7_4

Abstract

Health literacy can be understood as a decision-making competency, it describes the ability to find sufficient information, to understand, to asses and apply them in order to obtain health and alleviate disease. The healthcare industry of the twenty-first century is facing many changes. The aging society, fast-evolving government regulations, the shortage of skilled professionals, technological innovations and the role change in relationship between health-care workers and patients, creating an environment in which health literacy is considered as an essential requirement for consumers of the healthcare system (Schaeffer et al., 2017). This is mirrored by the fact that health literacy has been on the agenda of the World Health Organization (WHO) throughout the last two centuries. It has first been mentioned in the global conference on health promotion in Jakarta in 1997 (WHO, 1997), later named as a "key action" in the WHO Bangkok Charter for Health promotion in a Globalized World (WHO, 2005) and recently positioned as one of three key pillars for achieving sustainable development in the Shanghai Declaration on health promotion (WHO, 2016). This article will discuss the purpose of health literacy for the healthcare system and provides the actual state of the international scientific discussion.

4.1 Health Literacy in Context

4.1.1 Definition of the Term

Originating from the Anglo-American language area, the meaning of health literacy has been discussed in scientific literature for a number of years. The term health literacy was first mentioned in 1974 in a paper accusing the need of minimum health education standards for all school levels in the USA (National Library of Medicine, 2000). In 1992 a study funded by the Robert Wood Johnson Foundation (Williams, et al., 1995) defined health literacy as the ability to perform health related tasks requiring reading and computational skills. The authors developed the "Test of Functional Health Literacy in Adults" (TOFHLA) and firstly measured health literacy skills in English- and Spanish-speaking adults. Following this work, numerous studies related to health literacy can be found in the literature. These studies define health literacy based on a disease or disease management theme. Focusing on the Term "Literacy", it had been understood as a metaphor for different competences like: food literacy, physical literacy, financial literacy, etc. Health literacy was mostly related to the functional understanding of literacy, like reading and writing skills which are essentially for a patient to participate in treatment and therapy. The change in discussing about health literacy in a public health or health communication context, was opened by an article of Don Nutbeam (1998). He first described health literacy in the meaning of health competence, and discusses its importance for self-determined and qualified health decisions. In 1998 the WHO published the nowadays most cited definition of health literacy (WHO, 1998). In the "Health Promotion Glossary" it is defined as:

> "Health Literacy represents the cognitive and social skills, that determine the motivation and ability of individuals to gain access to, understand and use information in ways which promote and maintain good health. Health Literacy means more than being able to read pamphlets and successfully take appointment. By improving people's access to health information, and their capacity to use it effectively, health literacy is critical to empowerment." (WHO, 1998)

According to this definition, based on a public health view, health literacy expresses cognitive and social skills which are necessary to access information and to utilize them for maintaining good health. The meaning of health literacy in this context exceeds the functional understanding and is considered as a precondition for health maintenance. The chances to execute successful health promotion programs without a competent use of medical or health related information are very restricted.

Nutbeam (Nutbeam, 1998) differentiates three types of health literacy: functional literacy, communicative/interactive literacy and critical literacy. Communicative or interactive literacy describes the consumer's ability to "extract information and derive meaning from different forms of communications" (Nutbeam, 2008). Critical literacy applies on the ability to analyze information to gain control over health-related decisions. These skills enable the consumer to improve control over his or her health and to take better responsibility for health decisions. Health literacy is an important capability talking about informed choices and empowered patients (Nutbeam, 1998).

In Europe the definition of health literacy is strongly influenced by the European Health Literacy Survey Questionnaire (Sorensen et al., 2013). It defines health literacy as a prerequisite for making qualified decisions to manage health challenges in everyday life, picturing health literacy with all its determinants and consequences on the healthcare system.

That health literacy is a fundamental part of empowered patients can also be seen in the American literature. The Healthy People 2010 defines it as "the degree to which individuals have the capacity to obtain, process, and understand basic health information and services needed to make appropriate health decisions" (National Library of Medicine, 2000).

4.1.2 The Relationship between Health Literacy and Health

These new approaches on health literacy proof the international importance of the discussion. Some research actually goes beyond and suggests, that health literacy is a stronger predictor of health status than socioeconomic status, age or ethnic background could be (Schillinger et al., 2002).

Research determines the causes and consequences of health literacy, the outcome shown is diverse and multifaceted. General literacy, income, race, socio-economic status, social support and cultural background effect health literacy (Paasche-Orlow & Wolf, 2007). A connection between patients with low health literacy and health stands out. It offers itself in a poorer health status, including measures of morbidity, intermediate disease markers, use of health resources and a lack of knowledge (Schillinger et al., 2002). Furthermore, low literacy is associated with decreased comprehension, lower compliance rates, poorer self-reported health, increased hospitalizations and health costs (Schaeffer et al., 2017). Focusing on specific health conditions and health behavior, studies show that low health literacy competences are related to limited knowledge of the patient's particular disease and its capabilities in disease prevention, resulting in a less healthy behavior, increased use of health care services like hospitalization and poorer health status (Bjornsen et al., 2017). One of the reasons is the fact that low literate patients have difficulties understanding patient education materials such as written instructions or prescription labels (Paasche-Orlow, 2007).

In summary low literacy competence is associated directly and indirectly with poor health outcomes (Parker, 2000). It is observable in the use of prevention services, self-management of disease and relation to responsiveness to health education. By improving people's access and ability to read and utilize health information the barriers created by the increasing complexity of the health care system can be overcome.

4.1.3   Health Literacy in a Disease Management Context

Nutbeam developed a model to illustrate the challenges in the disease management progress and the health care system resulting from low health literacy. In this context low health literacy compliance is seen as a potential risk factor that needs to be managed to enable patients to take part in the clinical care system as an informed patient (Fig. 4.1). High health literacy shows an improvement in the compliance of the patient especially in decision making, medication use, self-management in chronic disease and a reduced duration in hospitalization (Bjornsen et al., 2017). The Model of Paasche-Orlow and Wolf (2007) is connecting health literacy and health outcomes to three key issues: access to health care, the interaction between patients and professionals and selfcare. These key points can be found in the conceptual model of Nutbeam (2008) who modified the "Institute of Medicine Model of Health Literacy" by the comments of Baker (Baker et al., 2002). The model involves all participants in the health care progress: the patient, the health care provider and the professionals with the objective of an improved clinical outcome. At first the prior knowledge or health related numeracy is assessed by a tool like REALM or TOFHLA, referred to this outcome the sensitivity for individuals with low literacy increases, this sensitivity improves the access to health care services and the interaction between the patient and the health care providers. This leaves a clinician better placed to provide patient education that is adjusted to individual needs and

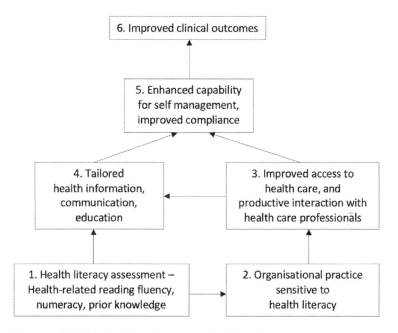

Fig. 4.1 Conceptual Model of Health Literacy as a Risk (Nutbeam, 2008)

capacities. Like discussed before a more tailored health care and an empowered patient does improve the clinical outcome and reduce the hospitalization.

The Conceptual model of health literacy as a risk is a common model to conceptualize interventions for improving condition-specific health literacies.

4.1.4 Health Literacy in a Health Promotion Context

The second conceptual model illustrates health literacy in a health promotion context. It determines the causes of high health literacy and reflects on the consequences. Health promotion considers health literacy skills as an opportunity enabling individuals to improve greater control over their health and the range of personal, social and environmental determinants of health. From the public health perspective, health literacy is seen as an asset to be built, that supports greater empowerment in health decision-making (Nutbeam, 2008). A model which displays the necessary steps to improve health literacy is shown in Fig. 4.2. It is impacted by concepts of adult learning and health promotion.

The model can be divided in two parts: Steps 1 to 5 which represent the sources of health literacy skills, and 7 to 10 which describe the results of improved health literacy competences.

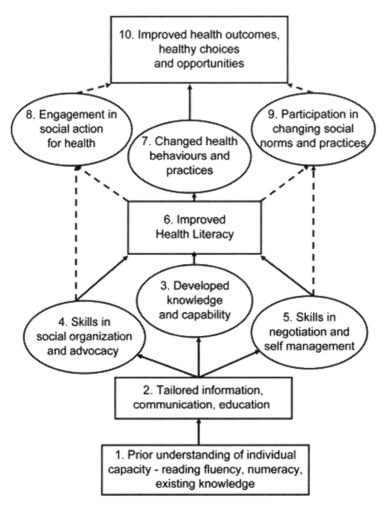

Fig. 4.2 Conceptual Model of Health Literacy as an Asset (Nutbeam, 2008)

The conceptual models of Nutbeam (2008) show a close connection between health literacy, compliance of a patient and its health behavior. The health behavior and needs of a patient influence his position in therapy and treatment. Since the 1990 the paternalistic relationship between provider and client has turned to a more levelled relationship. The concept of empowerment was described as a "process by which people gain mastery over their lives" (Rappaport, 1981). In patients with chronic disease the ideal of a patient centered health care decision making is considered by programs like the Arthritis Self-Management Preparation (ASMP) and the expert patient (Barlow, 2007). Shared decision making is described as a process that involves patients in the choice of therapy as much as possible. To achieve this, it is indispensable to ensure a grade of health literacy skills. Schulz & Hartung describe the concept of the expert patient as "a health care consumer who will compile knowledge about his condition, not quite leveling with physicians, but becoming more and more like it." (Schulz & Hartung, 2017). Patient empowerment is meant to lead to an increased responsibility to personal health behavior in social situations and in organizations. Within an improved health literacy, the empowerment of the patient will grow and lead to a more self-determined participation of the patient in the disease management process.

4.2   Measure Health Literacy

Health literacy can not only be measured by the health status but also by the monetary results for the health care system. Currently a number of studies consider the impact of low literacy competences on the health care system (Schaeffer et al., 2017). According to this proven relationship, it became necessary to measure health literacy competences of the population and significant patient groups.

There are various instruments for health literacy, all focusing on different aspects. Most of them reflect basic literacy and numeric skills, also called functional literacy. This is the focus of the widely used tools—"Test of Functional Health Literacy in Adults" (TOFLHA, Parker et al. 2000) and "Rapid Estimate of Adult Literacy in Medicine" (Davis et al., 1991). But these tests are not sufficient for measuring health literacy beyond the functional level (U.S. Institute of Medicine, 2009). Another way to evaluate health literacy are health knowledge tests. These tests are validated for special clinical settings mainly for chronical diseases. Some of them are the "Asthma Self-Management Questionnaire" (Mancuso et al., 2009) or the "Diabetes Knowledge Test" (Fitzgerald et al., 1998). The growing complexity of the healthcare system and the differing health information being promoted, led to health literacy being a key consideration for health promotion and improving the quality of health services (Nutbeam, 1998; Sorensen et al., 2013). For health literacy as a key consideration, competences like to navigate the health system, to communicate and engage with healthcare providers, to advocate for one's right to health services and engage in critical appraisal of health information, need to be considered as well (HLS-EU Consortium, 2012). Two health literacy tools exist including this perspective of health literacy: "The Health Literacy Questionnaire" (Osborne et al., 2013) and the "European Health Literacy Survey Questionnaire" (HLS-EU Consortium, 2012).

4.2.1   The European Health Literacy Survey Questionnaire

The aim of the "European Health Literacy Survey Questionnaire" (HLS-EU-Q47) was to assess the health literacy competences of the population at a country level. It was developed based on a review of the extant literature (Pelikan & Gnahal, 2017; Sorensen et al.,

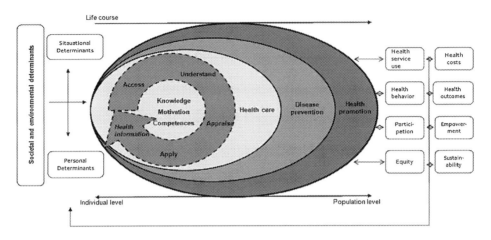

Fig. 4.3 Integrated Model of Health Literacy (HLS-EU Consortium, 2012)

2013). Health literacy is defined as the ability to access, understand, appraise and apply literature in order to improve personal health behavior, clinical outcome and health status (Fig. 4.3). To analyze this ability four key points of health information processing were defined:

1. To access/find health information
2. To understand health information
3. To appraise/analyze health information
4. To apply/utilize health information

The 47 questions of the HLS-EU were created by a matrix (cf. Fig. 4.4) from the three health related divisions and the four steps of the health information cycle. For a precise evaluation and comparison, the answer options of the questionnaire were transformed into numerical values. A number of European countries started own national population surveys using the HLS-EU-Q47. Germany (Schaeffer et al., 2017), Hungary (Koltai & Kun, 2016), Czech Republic (Kucera et al., 2016), Italy (Palumbo et al., 2016) Portugal (Espanha & Avila, 2016) and Switzerland (Bieri et al., 2016) completed a national Health literacy survey. Outside Europe the HLS-EU was used by a number of Asian countries adding further questions (HLS-EU-Q86) (Duong et al., 2015).

	access/find/obtain information relevant to health	Understand information relevant to health	Appraise/judge/evaluate information relevant to health	Apply/use information relevant to health
Healthcare	Ability to access information on medical and clinical issues	Ability to understand medical information and derive meaning	Ability to interpret and evaluate medical information	Ability to make informed decisions on medical issues
Disease prevention	Ability to access information on risk factors for health	Ability to understand information on risk factors and derive meaning	Ability to interpret and evaluate information on risk factors for health	Ability to make informed decisions on risk factors for health
Health promotion	Ability to update oneself on determinants of health in the social and physical environment	Ability to understand information on determinants of health in the social and physical environment and derive meaning	Ability to interpret and evaluate information on health determinants in the social and physical environment	Ability to make informed decisions on health determinants in the social and physical environment

Fig. 4.4 HLS-EU health literacy matrix (HLS-EU Consortium, 2012)

4.2.2   The Health Literacy Questionnaire

Contrary to the HLS-EU, the Health Literacy Questionnaire (HLQ) does not create an overall rating of health literacy (Osborne et al., 2013). Developed by a strong person-, practitioner- and organization-centered approach, the HLQ contains nine dimensions of health literacy measured with 44 questions.

1. Feeling understood and supported by health care providers
2. Having sufficient information to manage my health
3. Actively managing my health
4. Social support for health
5. Approach of health information
6. Ability to actively engage with health care providers
7. Navigating the health care system
8. Ability to find good health information
9. Reading and understanding health information well enough to know what to do

The authors of the HLQ decided to forego a single score of health literacy as the nine scales measure conceptually different aspects and it would be inappropriate to unite the answers into one score (HLS-EU Consotium, 2012). Furthermore, they argue that the concept of health literacy is multidimensional, the independent nine scales demonstrate this. To clearly assess the abilities of a person´s health literacy the elements of health literacy need to be scored separately in order to prevent an invalid measure. The intent

a person from the community...	Problems seen as...	Health literacy filters	Other filters
approaches service	• Large numbers of eligible people in community who do not access service	• Knowledge of services and their roles • Confident approaching services • Trust • Know entitlements	• Openness of organisation • Physical barriers • Time barriers
is accepted into service	• Large numbers of people who approach the service but decline or are declined entry	• Knowledge of health service and how they work including entry steps • Ability to explain needs • Trust (through assessment processes)	• Eligibility criteria • Organisational priorities and performance targets
receives services	• Large numbers of drop-outs or failures to attend (FTA) • Demographic or health status groups don't participate	• Difficulty understanding health service processes • Difficulty negotiating with health providers	• Lack of flexibility in service types and times • Personal difficulties with staff
participates in relevant programs and/or services	• Difficulty recruiting to particular programs or services (e.g. prevention) • Drop-outs and FTA	• Able to discriminate what might be useful from a range of options • Feel more comfortable 'just doing what the doctor says' • Health is a low priority (relatively)	• Lack of service variety and time options • Pressure of performance indicators and funding models
services respond to needs	• Drop-outs and FTA for particular service • Failure to achieve desired outcomes	• Ability to engage providers to explain needs, ask questions and negotiate • Unrealistic expectations • Services fail to accommodate learning needs and styles	• Financial and staff constraints
fully understanding engagement with providers	• Failure to establish rapport or fully participate • Disappointment in experience and outcomes	• Ability to adapt knowledge for application in personal life situations • Failure to recognise client needs for general vs practical information	• Dissimilar demographic to health providers

Fig. 4.5 Filters that determine a person's participation and inclusion in healthcare (Batterham et al., 2014)

of the HLQ is to fully picture the needs and abilities of health literacy in individuals and groups. Therefore, a single score would not offer the possibility to enable practitioners to see which aspects should be in focus to improve health literacy in their intervention.

In a project called Ophelia (Batterham et al., 2014), a structured workshop was used to analyze the HLQ data and generate a broad range of ideas about what is necessary to meet the needs of clients, and support the organization. The results are represented in so called "filters" that determine a person's participation and inclusion in healthcare based on the dates of the HLQ (Fig. 4.5).

4.3 Actual Health Literacy Status

For many European countries the "European Health Literacy Questionnaire" in 2011 was the first to measure health literacy at a country level (HLS-EU Consotium, 2012).

In Germany more than half of the population has difficulties dealing with health information and exhibit a "limited" health literacy competence (cf. Fig. 4.6. Limited describes the combination of the factor "inadequate" and "problematic"). Compared to Ireland with 40% of "limited" health literacy or Poland (44,6%) and Greece (44,8%) the competences in health literacy are considerably higher than in Germany. With only a third of the measured population, the Netherlands show the highest health literacy competences in Europe (HLS-EU Consortium, 2012).

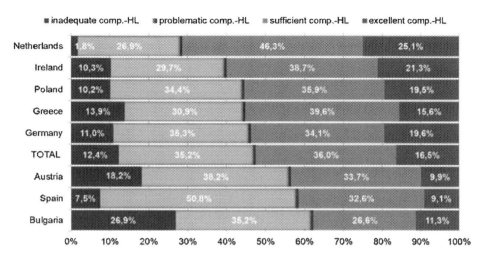

Fig. 4.6 Levels of general Health Literacy Index by Country and for the total sample (HLS-Consortium, 2012)

Austria revised the measurement in the following years specified to special population groups (Dietscher & Pelikan, 2017). In 2012 58% of the adolescents showed "limited" health literacy. The response pattern of the adolescents was similar to those of the adults. Germany remeasured the health literacy skills of the whole of Germany in 2013 (HLS-EU-Q47 in 2011 measured only one state, NRW, of Germany), with an outcome of 31,9% "problematic" and 12,3% "inadequate health literacy competences", the health literacy score decreased.

The outcome of the 2015 measuring in Switzerland showed similar data to the European Health Literacy Questionnaire from 2011 (HLS-EU Consortium, 2012). 9% of the swiss population had an "inadequate" competence and at 45% a "problematic" competence in health literacy.

The United States measured health literacy with a comparable tool. The prevalence of "limited" health literacy competences in 1993 was 48% (23% Level "inadequate" and 25% Level "problematic"). In 2003 the percent of "limited" health literacy was 36% (14% Level "inadequate" 22% Level "problematic") (US Institute of Medicine, 2009).

Kazuhiro Nakayama (Nakayama et al., 2015) carried out the HLS-EU-47 in Japan in 2015. The results showed a lower rate in health literacy skills than in Europe. The percentages of "inadequate" ranged from 40,9 to 60,1% in Japan, for comparison in Europe the range was 12,1 to 20,1%. Combined responses of "inadequate" and "problematic" which indicates the factor "limited" states at 47,9% in Europe and 85,4% in Japan.

Fig. 4.6 shows the results for eight countries.

4.4   Improving Health Literacy

The Outcome shows that low literacy is a mayor health challenge in the twenty-first century. It is a growing consensus that research should focus more on the development and testing of interventions to improve health literacy competences. This acquires intervention models to conceptualize how to achieve better health literacy. By reviewing current literature, 23 models could be found. Most of these models focus on the association of health literacy and its determinants and consequences. Like the Conceptual model of health literacy" by Nutbeam (2008) shown before. Only five models could be found that briefly described possible implications for intervention. Health literacy interventions can be divided into the levels they address to improve the competence:

1. Patient level
2. Healthcare personnel level
3. Organizational/Population level

4.4.1   Health Literacy at a Patient Level

Von Wagner (2009) relates his model of health literacy to psychological models of behavioral change following the "Rubicon Model of Action Phases". It pictures the determines of health literacy and adds socio-cognitive determinants structured into a motivational and volitional phase (Fig. 4.7). This model clearly differs from the two other models described and focuses on the individuum and its learning behavior. It can be used in three domains of health actions: access and use of health services, patient-provider interactions and management of health and illness.

4.4.2   Health Literacy at a Level of Healthcare Personnel & Small Organizations

The "Health Literacy Model" understands itself as the first real intervention model. It was developed by a multimethod approach, consisting of a literature review, an online consultation of health literacy experts and two consensus meetings with members studying health literacy among aged adults in Europe. The model focuses on improving health literacy in elderly adults. It was designed focusing on a prevention context. The model effects two types of interventions to improve health literacy "by empowering people by affecting individual or population-based determinants", and "by improving the communication used in the healthcare systems" (Geboers et al., 2018) (Fig. 4.8).

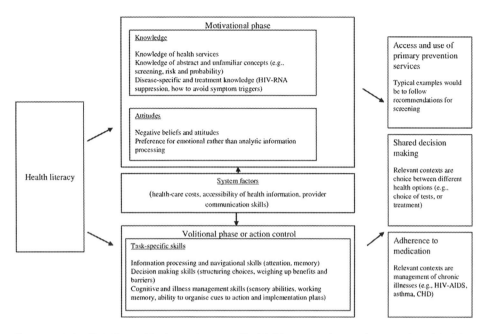

Fig. 4.7 A detailed View of Pathways between Health Literacy and screening use, shared desicion making and medication adherence (Von Wagner, 2009)

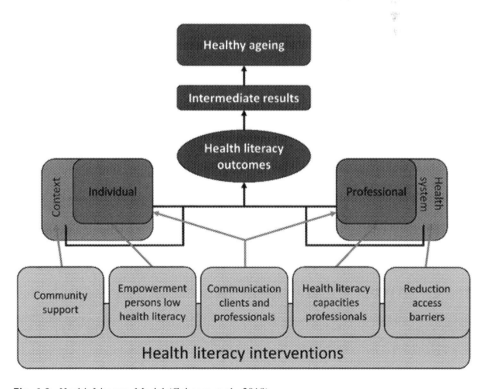

Fig. 4.8 Health Literacy Model (Geboers et al., 2018)

The model can be used as a schedule to improve health literacy competences. Osborne and Beauchamp (2017) accuse that without improved health literacy in the initial situation, the opportunity to establish a sustainable health promotion program is not given in place. Especially if health should be considered from the public health perspective, this model is imperative to improve health literacy in the general population.

4.4.3   Health Literacy at an Organizational & Population Level

The Ophelia project was developed to implicate a health literacy thinking into patient care, service design and population surveys (Batterham et al., 2014). Three conceptual models were specified as base of the project: intervention mapping, quality improvement collaboratives and realist synthesis (Fig. 4.9).

Ophelia includes six steps divided into three main phases: first phase is a needs assessment using the HLQ, second phase creates intervention plans by utilizing the PDCA cycle involving the frontline staff and management, third phase tests the intervention to determine if the intervention can improve the identified limitations (Batterham et al., 2014).

4.5   Health Literacy and the Future

Since the European Health Literacy Survey in 2011, health literacy has gained importance and many interventions have been developed to improve the competencies. The majority of interventions focus on the patients' health literacy competencies. Especially for chronical diseases multiple studies could be identified. The development of measures and health literacy programs for specific medical conditions, like various types of cancer, diabetes, cardiovascular disease, HIV and AIDS, arthritis, asthma, sleeping problems and mental health, as well as in clinical dental care can be found in the current literature (Bjornsen et al., 2017; Osborne et al., 2013). Some studies are defined by the target groups like care-depended people, in parenting, adolescents or pregnant women, others aim at specific treatments (Osborne et al., 2017).

Even mostly unconsidered parts of health, like nursing are affected by health literacy as a key competence to patients. Care-dependent people in particular rely on health information and health literacy, but exhibit merely low competences (HLS Consortium, 2012). The "Teach more, do less" approach focuses on health education and self-determinacy of care-dependent people. In the hospital care context, interventions like the "Health Literacy Friendly Hospital" or the "Health Literate Organization" have been initiated to educate patients and improve disease-oriented competences (Dietscher & Pelikan, 2017).

1.   Needs assessment

The HLQ and semi-structured interviews assess health literacy needs, and organisational assessments determine contextual enablers and barriers.

2.   Identify performance objectives, determinants and change objectives

Use a structured workshop format to engage key stakeholders from participating sites in interpretation of HLQ data, and generate a broad range of ideas about what is needed locally to meet the needs of clients, and to support the organisation to meet the needs of clients.

3.   Selection of interventions, methods, and strategies

The project management team at each site considers needs assessment data, intervention ideas, develops program logic models and selects appropriate interventions to test. Promotion of communities of practice.

4.   Detailed design and planning of interventions

The research team will work with the sites to co-create and pre-test interventions, resources, and specify evaluation activities in Plan-Do-Study-Act (PDSA) cycles.

5.   Adoption and implementation of interventions.

PDSA cycles are implemented and results considered by project management group.

6.   Implementation trial

For those pilot interventions demonstrating potential to improve health literacy and health outcomes, implementation and evaluation plans are determined and trials are conducted.

Fig. 4.9 Steps of Ophelia Process for Development of Health Literacy Interventions. (Batterham et al., 2014)

Health literacy in e-Health interventions is a common tool to improve health literacy skills in health promotion and processing health information (Schaeffer et al., 2017).

A political perspective health literacy gained importance. Nearly all countries introduced the improvement of health literacy in their action plans (Trezona et al., 2018). Some countries focus on periodical monitoring and evaluation like New Zealand, Austria and China.

In summary health literacy is a mainstay when it comes to the challenges of the health care system in the twenty-first century. Challenges like an aging population, hospitalization, skills shortage, migration, digitalization, globalization and increasing complexity of the healthcare system can be positively affected by health literacy (HLS Consortium, 2012). Improvement of health literacy competences is already taking part in most of the challenges mentioned. Nevertheless, the topic requires particular attention. If we want to overcome these challenges successfully, we need to pursue a change in paradigm, from disease management to health-maintenance. Health literacy is an important step to fulfill this change considering the point of view we have on our health.

References

Baker, D. W., Gazmararian, J. A., Williams, M. V., Scott, Y., Parker, R. M., Green, D., Ren, J., & Peel, J. (2002). Functional health literacy and the risk of hospital admission among Medicare managed care enrollees. *American Journal of Public Health, 92*, 1278–1283.

Barlow, J. (2007). Das "Expert-Patient" Programm aus Großbritanien. *Managed Care, 2*, 20–23.

Batterham, R. W., Buchbinder, R., Beauchamp, A., Dodson, S., Elsworth, G. R., & Osborne, R. H. (2014). The OPtimising HEalth LIterAcy (Ophelia) process: Study protocol for using health literacy profiling and community engagement to create and implement health reform. *BMC Public Health, 14*, 694.

Bieri, U., Kocher, J.P., Gauch, C., Tschoepe, S., Venetz, A., & Hagemann, M. (2016). *Bevölkerungsumfrage "Erhebung Gesundheitskompetenz 2015". Schlussbericht. Studie im Auftrag des Bundesamts für Gesundheit BAG, Abteilung Gesundheitsstrategien*. Bundesamt für Gesundheit, Abteilung Gesundheitsstrategien 2016. gfs.

Bjornsen, H. N., Espnes, G. A., Eilertsen, M. E., Ringdal, R., & Moksnes, U. K. (2017). The Relationship between positive mental health literacy and mental well-being among adolescents: Implications for School health services. *J School Nursing, 35*(2), 96–106.

Davis, T. C., Crouch, M. A., Long, S. W., Jackson, R. H., Bates, P., George, R. B., & Bairnsfthather, L. E. (1991). Rapid assessment of literacy levels of adult primary care patients. *Family Med, 23*, 433–435.

Dietscher, C., & Pelikan, J. M. (2017). Healthliterate Hospitals and Health Organisations - Results from an Austrian Feasibility Study on the Self-assessment of organizing Health Literacy in Hospitals. In D. Schaeffer, J. M. Pelikan (Eds.), *Health Literacy Forschungsstand und Perspektiven* (pp. 303–314). Hogrefe.

Duong, V. T., Lin, I. F., Sorensen, K., Pelikan, J. M., van den Broucke, S., Lin, Y. C., & Chang, P. W. (2015). Health literacy in Taiwan: A population-based study. *Asia-Pacific Journal of Public Health, 27*(8), 871–880. https://doi.org/10.1177/1010539515607962

Espanha, R., & Avila, P. (2016). Health literacy survey Portugal: A contribution for the knowledge on health and communications. *Procedia Computer Science, 100*, 1033–1041.

Fitzgerald, J. T., Funnel, M. M., Hess, G. E., Barr, P. A., Anderson, R. M., Hiss, R. G., & Davis, W. K. (1998). The reliability and validity of a brief diabetes knowledge test. *Diabetes Care, 21*, 706–710.

Geboers, B., Reijneveld, A., Koot, J., & de Winter, A. (2018). Moving towards a comprehensive approach for health literacy interventions: The develop of a health literacy intervention model. *International Journal of Environmental Research and Public Health, 15*, 1268. https://doi.org/10.3390/ijerph15061268

HLS-EU Consortium. (2012). Comparative report on health literacy in eight EU member states: The European Health Literacy Survey (HLS-EU). Maastricht: http:// www.health-literacy.eu. Accessed 14 Apr 2019.

Kucera, Z., Pelikan, J. M., & Steflova, A. (2016). Health literacy in Czech population results of the comparative representation research. *Casopis Lekaru Ceskych, 155*(5), 233–241.

Mancuso, C. A., Sayles, W., & Allegrante, J. P. (2009). Development and testing of the asthma selfmade questionnaire. *Ann Allergy Asthma Immunology, 102*, 294–302.

Nakayama, K., Osaka, W., Togari, T., Ishikawa, H., Yonekura, Y., Sekido, A., & Matsumoto, M. (2015). Comprehensive health literacy in Japan is lower than in Europe: A validated Japanese-language assessment of health literacy. *BMC Public Health, 15*, 505. https://doi.org/10.1186/s12889-015-1835-x

National Library of Medicine. (2000). *Current bibliographies in medicine: Health literacy national institutes of health, US department of health and human services, Bethesda, MD.* National Academy Press.

Nutbeam, D. (1998). Health promotion glossary. *Health Promotion International, 13*(4), 349–364. https://doi.org/10.1093/heapro/13.4.349

Nutbeam, D. (2008). The evolving concept of health literacy. *Social Science and Medicine, 67*, 2072–2078.

Osborne, R. H., Batterham, R. W., Elsworth, G. R., Hawkins, M., & Buchbinder, R. (2013). The grounded psychometric development and initial validation of the Health Literacy Questionnaire (HLQ). *BMC Public Health, 13*, 658. https://doi.org/10.1186/1471-2458-13-658

Osborne, R. H., & Beauchamp, A. (2017). Optimising health literacy, equity and access (Ophelia). In D. Schaeffer & Pelikan J. M. (Eds.), *Health Literacy Forschungsstand und Perspektiven.* Hogrefe.

Paasche-Orlow, M. K., & Wolf, M. S. (2007). The causal pathway linking health literacy to health outcomes. *American Journal of Health Behaviour, 31*, 19–26.

Palumbo, R., Annarumma, C., Adinolfi, P., Musella, M., & Piscopo, G. (2016). The Italian heath literacy project: Insights from assessment of health literacy skills in italy. *Health Policy, 120*(9), 1087–1094. https://doi.org/10.1016/j.healthpol.2016.08.007

Parker, R. M. (2000). Health literacy: A challenge for American patients and their health care providers. *Health Promotion International, 15*, 277–291.

Pelikan, J. M., & Gnahal, K. (2017). Die europäische Gesundheitskompetenz Studie: Konzept, Instrument und ausgewählte Ergebisse. In D. Schaeffer & J. M. Pelikan (Eds.), *Health Literacy. Forschungsstand und Perspektiven* (pp.93–126). Hogrefe.

Rappaport, J. (1981). In praise of paradox: A social policy of empowerment over prevention. *American Journal of Community Psychology, 9*, 1–25.

Schaeffer, D., Vogt, E. M., Berens, E. M., Messer, M., Quenzel G, & Hurrelmann, K (2017). Health literacy Deutschland. In D. Schaeffer & J. M. Pelikan (Eds.), *Health Literacy Forschungsstand und Perspektiven* (pp. 129–143). Hogrefe.

Schillinger, D., Grumbach, K., Piette, J., Wang, F., Osmond, D., Daher, C., Palacios, J., Sullivan, G. D., & Bindman, A. B. (2002). Association of health literacy with diabetes outcomes. *JAMA, 288*, 475–482.

Schulz, P. J., & Hartung, U. (2017). The future of health literacy. In D. Schaeffer & J. M. Pelikan (Eds.), *Health Literacy Forschungsstand und Perspektiven* (pp.79–92). Hogrefe.

Sorensen, K., Van den Broucke, S., Pelikan, J. M., Fullam, J., Doyle, G., Slonska, Z., Kondilis, B., Stoffels, V., Osborne, R. H., & Brand, H. (2013). Measuring health literacy in populations: Illuminating the design and development process of the European Health Literacy Survey Questionnaire (HLS-EU-Q). *BMC Public Health, 13*, 948.

Trezona, A., Rowlands, G., & Nutbeam, D. (2018). Progress in Implementing national policies and strategies for health literacy—What have we learned so far? *International Journal of Environmental Research Public Health, 15*, 1554. https://doi.org/10.3390/ijerph15071554

US Institute of Medicine. (2009). *Measures of health literacy: Workshop summary*. The National Academies Press.

Von Wagner, C., Steptoe, A., Wolf, M. S., & Wardle, J. (2009). Health literacy and health actions: A review and a framework from health psychology. *Health Education & Behavior, 36*, 860–877.

Williams, M. V., Parker, R. M., Baker, D. W., Parikh, N. S., Pitkin, K., Coates, W. C., & Nurss, J. R. (1995). Inadequate functional health literacy among patients at two public hospitals. *Journal of the American Medical Association, 274*, 1677–1682.

World Health Organization (WHO) (1997). The Jakarta declaration on leading health promotion into the 21st century. In *Proceedings of the Fourth International Conference on Health Promotion, Jakarta, Indonesia, 21–25 July 1997*. World Health Organization. https://www.who.int/healthpromotion/conferences/previous/jakarta/en/hpr_jakarta_declaration_german.pdf?ua=1. Accessed 20 Apr 2019.

World Health Organisation (WHO). (1998). *Health promotion glossary*. WHO. https://www.who.int/healthpromotion/about/HPR%20Glossary%201998.pdf?ua=1. Accessed 20 Apr 2019.

World Health Organization (WHO). (2005). The Bangkok charter for health promotion in a globalized world. In *Proceedings of the Sixth Global Conference on Health Promotion, Bangkok, Thailand, 7–11 August 2005*. World Health Organization. https://www.who.int/healthpromotion/conferences/6gchp/BCHP_German_version.pdf?ua=1. Accessed 20 Apr 2019.

World Health Organization (WHO). (2016). Shanghai declaration on promoting health in the 2030 agenda for sustainable development. In *Proceedings of the 9th Global Conference on Health Promotion, Shanghai, China, 21–24 November 2016*. World Health Organization. https://www.who.int/healthpromotion/conferences/9gchp/shanghai-declaration.pdf. Accessed 20 Apr 2019.

Tertiary Prevention and After-Care for Cancer Patients in a Hotel Setting

5

Kai Illing

Contents

5.1   Tourism for the Sick, Tourism for the Healthy 78
5.2   Is Cancer an Indication That Motivates People to Keep on Traveling?............... 79
5.3   From a Clinical Setting to a Tourist Setting...................................... 80
5.4   What Type of Services can be Offered for Cancer Patients in a Hotel Setting 80
5.5   Services for Relatives and Fellow-Travelers and Family Members, Respectively 83
5.6   Co-operations... 84
5.7   Summary 84
References... 84

Abstract

We assume that holiday taking is generally representing a positive activity. It is normally recognized as opportunity for enjoyment, escapism, relaxation and outdoor activities. There are healthy tourists who use their holidays without having any motivation to improve their health status, whereas other groups suffering from a moderate health-related problem use their time for preventive or curative activities. But what about those who suffer from a severe disease such as cancer? Those people have had their treatments in a hospital and they probably had an after-care stay in a rehabilitation clinic. The phase after the abovementioned treatments often leaves patients alone regarding further possibilities for therapy and/or invigorating and health-promoting

K. Illing (✉)
Health Management in Tourism, FH Joanneum, Bad Gleichenberg, Austria
e-mail: kai.illing@fh-joanneum.at

© The Author(s), under exclusive license to Springer Fachmedien Wiesbaden GmbH, part of Springer Nature 2022
M. Cassens et al. (eds.), *Transdisciplinary Perspectives on Public Health in Europe*, FOM-Edition, https://doi.org/10.1007/978-3-658-33740-7_5

pastimes. The subject of this essay is to investigate whether a tourist setting is a suitable location for offering services for people suffering from cancer. Strengths and weaknesses of a medical hotel in comparison to specialized clinics are going to be assessed and the preferences of cancer patients regarding holiday taking, respectively. All in all, a new business model is being discussed here and the idea to achieve a better overview about target group identification in medical tourism.

5.1 Tourism for the Sick, Tourism for the Healthy

Tourism is rich in types of establishments that care for the health of their guests. The so called Medical-Wellness-Continuum, or as others call it the Illness-Wellness-Continuum (Miller, 2005), indicates, that the focus of a health tourist establishment can be more on the medical side or more on the pampering and wellness side. Table 5.1 tries to give an overview about the many hotel types and spa types, respectively, that are located somewhere between medicine, wellness and pampering, respectively.

So, simplifying greatly, it can be said that patients and guests are the healthier the further down they are placed in the table mentioned above. The hotel type being discussed

Table 5.1 Different Hotel types and spa types in the Medical-Wellness-Continuum (Illing, 2019b)

1	Decreasing medical experience	Only hospital (acute care, surgery, invasive treatments)
2		Special clinics for prevention and after care (e.g. rehabilitation)
3		Private clinic offering elective care focusing on specialized interventions, hotel-like facilities to a certain extent
4		Hotel offering medical care and supplementary treatments on a non-medical level for clearly defined illnesses (e.g. cancer, burnout), hotel does not have the status as private clinic, instead often run as Ltd
5		Often called Medical Hotel, hotel-like facilities, medical department may have the status as private clinic, low invasive care or non-invasive care, focus on preventive procedures
6		Hotel disposes of a spa that tries to implement some medical quality with aid of medical doctors who show up irregularly, no daily medical services
7		Hotel offers pampering services and indulging spa facilities without any medical background
8		Only Hotel without any spa facilities (food and lodging)

in this paper belongs to line no. 4. Its guests are characterized by a certain disease with the access to the hotel being restricted to those suffering from this disease and their accompanying family members (relatives).

A medical hotel is characterized by certain features that can normally not be applied to clinical establishments such as legal forms that are typical for hotels as for example a limited liability company (Ltd.), guests who show up as self-payers, a medical concept that focuses on non-invasive and often preventive treatments sometimes even in the outdoors (Mutz & Müller, 2016), a service-oriented attitude towards the guests, and facilities that win over with luxurious rooms including elaborate spa and fitness areas.

5.2   Is Cancer an Indication That Motivates People to Keep on Traveling?

Hunter-Jones (2005) published two articles about holiday taking of cancer patients. According to her publication, there are patients who avoid travelling due to their disease whereas others keep on travelling. Regarding the latter one benefits to health and well-being were identified (Hunter-Jones, 2003). Such benefits impact upon "personal health, social effectiveness, personal identity, self-image, independence, future career prospects, and personal behavior". Hunter Jones (2003, p. 174) presents core statements from sick cancer patients regarding reasons for holiday taking such as:

> "Change of scene, to be with family, to feel better in myself, to have a break from the treatment regime, to be somebody else even if only for a short time, to relax, to travel to a warmer and sunnier climate, to have something to look forward to, to draw a line under illness and start again, to recharge batteries, to be happy again, to be normal again, to escape from being perceived as a sick person, to make the most of life, to rebuild confidence, to rebuild self-esteem, to fight depression, to overcome social isolation and make new friends, to relieve stress, to spend time with relatives, to rebuild strength, to reduce anxiety, to provide a means of escapism, to improve mental wellbeing, to enable physical relaxation, and to provide a goal to work toward".

These statements were reordered to create synonymous groups of meaning such as a) new targets/motivation, b) social embedding, c) fight sequela, d) feeling good again, and e) relaxation/wellbeing altogether showing the outcome as can be seen in Fig. 5.1.

Interestingly, the fight against resulting diseases from cancer therapy ("fight sequela") does not seem to be the core motivation to take a holiday, instead the motivated begin of a new life seems to be more important. So, holidays obviously help to regain pace regarding a new start. In that respect, holiday services for cancer patients in a hotel setting should not concentrate on the patient's medical history only but on all those activities that help to start anew and forget their clinical past (Illing 2009, p. 87).

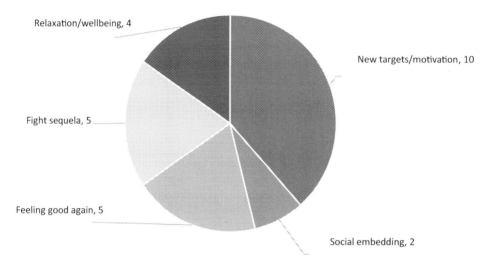

Reasons for participating in holiday taking

Relaxation/wellbeing, 4

New targets/motivation, 10

Fight sequela, 5

Feeling good again, 5

Social embedding, 2

Fig. 5.1 Reasons of cancer patients for participating in holiday taking

5.3 From a Clinical Setting to a Tourist Setting

Table 5.2 tries to merge the clinical approach to cancer with the tourist one. The upper part of the table outlines the "aims of rehabilitation", leading to the "areas of intervention" and finally to the role a medical hotel can play (Illing, 2019b).

Since a hotel normally does not dispose of high-end medical devices that can relieve or even heal severe consequences of a tumor or even the tumor itself, all things that are connected to "functional factors" can probably not be covered in a tourist setting. The more it is about emotional factors the more a tourist setting can contribute. "Physical factors" can be covered by a hotel, too, if related treatments focus on non-invasive ones.

5.4 What Type of Services can be Offered for Cancer Patients in a Hotel Setting

Figure 5.2 offers an overview about services that are offered by public ambulatory cancer counseling centers in Austria (Illing, 2019a). It seems that the provision of information plays a major role to contribute to the health literacy of sick persons. Other aspects such as therapy, prevention, and treatments play an important role, too.

Obviously, the public ambulatory cancer counseling centers in Austria do not rely on medical interventions, instead they offer preventive care of all kind. Remarks:

Table 5.2 The aims of rehabilitation, areas of interventions and the role of a medical hotel

	Aims of Rehabilitation			
R E H A B I L I T A T I O N	1. To influence the basic disease	2. To relieve the consequences of a cancer disease	3. to heal/relieve secondary diseases	4. to improve life quality
	Examples: Tumor (malignant neoplasm)	Examples: Immobility, loss of organ, hair loss, being bedridden	Example: Atherosclerosis	Examples: depression, fatigue
	Hardly be realized in a hotel setting	Partly be realized in a hotel setting	Partly be realized in a hotel setting	Realizable in a hotel setting

	Areas of Intervention		
M E D I C A L	1. Functional Factors	2. Physical Factors	Emotional Factors
	Examples: Less muscular strength, malfunction of organs	Examples: Pain, scars, hair loss, weight loss, wound healing disorder	Examples: Fear, dolefulness, dispiritedness, despair
	Needs profound medical expertise, hardly realizable in a tourist setting	Cosmetic procedures with dermatologic background, all types of sport and fitness (indoor, outdoor) with special trainers, nutrition counseling, rest and relaxation	All kinds of interventions presented by MACSIM (see subchapter 1.4)

H O T E L

Increasing strengths of a medical hotel

→ → → → → → → → → →

"Prevention" in this context means services comprising early diagnosis such as early detection of breast cancer.

Figure 5.3 presents a different structure and uses the example of cancer patients to show how core interventions and supplementary ones can be distinguished. This illustration leads to a possible approach for tourist providers that are less likely to rely on medical treatments for cure or relief than on those interventions that are presented here as supplementary. All interventions called supplementary require less medical expertise and can be offered easily in a tourist setting.

One of the most important intervention in almost all stages of a cancer disease is movement-oriented activity (active exercise therapy) that can take place indoor and in

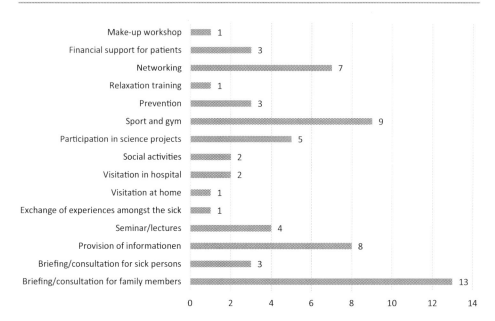

Fig. 5.2 Number of services of public ambulatory cancer counseling centers in Austria

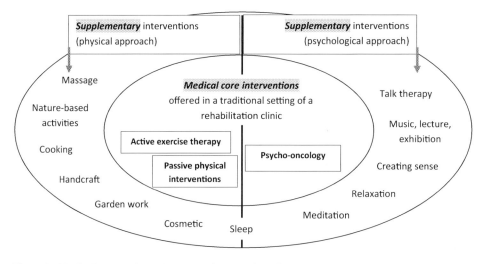

Fig. 5.3 Medical core and supplementary interventions for cancer patients

the outdoors. That's why the location of the hotel is of great importance. The access to a sport-minded surrounding such as lakes or rolling hills offering hiking paths and cycle tracks are of great help.

Table 5.3 MACSIM as acronym for non-medical interventions in a hotel-setting for cancer patients

More medical	less medical
Therapy and ...	**...MACSIM**
Selected interventions from the rehabilitative medicine and medical prevention	motoric/physical → Learn normality with handicraft and motoric activities (e.g. dancing)
	affective → Wellbeing and relaxation with aid of empathic staff, pampering services, and cozy rooms
	cognitive → health literacy (learning about diseases and coping-strategies)
	spiritual → to find meaning, truth, and awareness in supernatural dimensions
	inspirational → to get ideas and inspiration
	motivational → enhancing stamina, setting motivational goals for the future

MACSIM is an acronym that should be understood as an umbrella term for all hotel-related services which are a useful supplement to medical interventions for cancer patients. Services associated with MACSIM can have a medical foundation, but it focuses primarily on supplementary interventions that do not necessarily have a medical background (see Table 5.3).

All activities covered by the term MACSIM can be offered to a great or lesser extent in a medical way. Example: All "motoric/physical" activities can be offered by occupational therapists or just by persons who know how to do pottery, painting, weaving, outdoor-sport, and the like. Whatever the hotel is going to offer in the Medical-Wellness-Continuum, it is essential to understand the patient's existential orientation and therefore to take account of their disease-related physical and psychological limitations. So, at least the leading therapist should be well trained even if the hotel does not offer medical services.

5.5 Services for Relatives and Fellow-Travelers and Family Members, Respectively

It can be assumed that the strain (emotional and physical pressure) of caring family members is so severe that they are prepared to take courses in order to facilitate their own life and the one of those affected by cancer. This point was mentioned most often when it comes to the services offered by Austrian public ambulatory cancer counseling centers (Illing, 2019a). The need for "Briefing/consultation for family members" leads to the conclusion that there is a demand in creating seminars with the following issues mentioned most often by them: a) daily care for cancer patients in all different health statuses, b) nutrition (healthy food), c) psychological services, and d) palliative care.

Another opportunity for the medical cancer hotel is a professional outreach-service that sends therapists from the hotel to visit patients at home delivering services that are requested.

5.6   Co-operations

The type of hotel that is being discussed in this paper offers many chances for co-operation with other establishments: a) In case guests are suffering from deteriorating health conditions, they should be quickly able to be sent to co-operating specialists offering acute care due to a prearranged agreement. b) When guests feel better, other tourist companies can be recommended that offer holidays in a protected environment, too. c) When guests return home, contacts to ambulatory and public cancer counseling centers can be given or to other specialists. d) Another area of co-operation is the supplying industry (food and beverage, medical devices, wellness, and spa supply such as massage oils or cosmetic products).

5.7   Summary

Cancer patients who avoid travelling due to their disease might be attracted by a medical hotel if it offers medical services tailor-made for certain cancer diseases. Others, who are still mobile and targeting optimistically a better future might be attracted by a less medical hotel that focuses on real holidays and a greater psychological distance to the clinical past of the patients. In any case, the medical hotel can be more than just a hotel for cancer patients. It can be the platform for all needs that come up in the phase of post clinical treatments.

References

Hunter-Jones, P. (2003). Managing cancer: The role of holiday-taking. *Journal of Travel Medicine, 10*(3), 170–176.

Hunter-Jones, P. (2005). Cancer and tourism. *Annals of Tourism Research, 32*(1), 70–92.

Illing, K. (2009). *Gesundheitstourismus und Spa-Management*. Oldenbourg.

Illing, K. (2019a). Systematic review of homepages of public cancer counseling centers in Austria. Unpublished document.

Illing, K. (2019b). Das "Krankenhotel", eine Alternative zur Reha-Klinik? Tourismus Wissen – quarterly. http://tourismuswissen.tai.at/?page_id_524. Accessed 3 June 2020.

Miller, J. (2005). Wellness: The history and development of a concept. *Spektrum Freizeit, 1*, 84–102.

Mutz, M., & Müller, J. (2016). Mental health benefits of outdoor adventures: Results from two pilot studies. *Journal of Adolescence, 49*, 105–114.

Health Conferences in Germany, Austria and France—An Overview

6

Alfons Hollederer and Till Beiwinkel

Contents

6.1 Introduction 86
6.2 Methods 87
6.3 Results 87
    6.3.1 Topics, Goals and Stakeholders 87
    6.3.2 Distribution of Health Conferences in Germany, Austria and France 90
    6.3.3 Evaluation Results of Health Conferences 93
6.4 Discussion 95
References 97

Abstract

Purpose: Structured health conferences have the function of "round tables" for setting priorities in healthcare and health promotion, for regional health planning, cooperation and participation. They are a problem-solving approach in the health policy of France, Austria and Germany. Methods: The literature review describes and explores health conferences. It is based on a search in Cochrane Library, MEDPILOT/LIVIVO, PubMed and the "Health for All"-database of WHO Europe. Results: The literature

A. Hollederer
Faculty of Human Sciences, University of Kassel, Kassel, Germany
e-mail: alfons.hollederer@uni-kassel.de

T. Beiwinkel (✉)
Bavarian Health and Food Safety Authority (LGL), Nuremberg, Germany
e-mail: Till.Beiwinkel@lgl.bayern.de

© The Author(s), under exclusive license to Springer Fachmedien Wiesbaden GmbH,
part of Springer Nature 2022
M. Cassens et al. (eds.), *Transdisciplinary Perspectives on Public Health in Europe*,
FOM-Edition, https://doi.org/10.1007/978-3-658-33740-7_6

review shows that health conferences are widespread and identifies numerous health conferences in Germany, Austria and France at the country, federal state, regional and community levels. The conceptual basis varies. The implementation strategies ranged from solely communal activities to efforts by federal states up to a nationwide establishment of regional health and autonomy conferences in France. Health conferences are carried out in five federal states in Austria and in 14 federal states in Germany. In Germany, there are about 190 regional health conferences, and health regions[plus] can be found in approx. half of the country and city districts. The few existing evaluation studies claim positive effects of health conferences on cooperation and networking but also contain critical reflections regarding their limited options. Conclusions: There is a need for formative and summative evaluation. Health conferences may be helpful in countries with federal structure or in health systems based on a social insurance system. More exchange between the different health conferences could foster their conceptual basis and help to develop innovative approaches.

6.1   Introduction

Demographic and social change present a challenge to the European health systems. According to the health reports of the World Health Organization (WHO, 2015) and of the Organization for Economic Co-operation and Development (OECD, 2015) the health status in Europe has improved, however, health inequalities remain between and within countries, e.g. in terms of live expectancy. Most of the inequalities are caused by social determinants, including political, socioeconomic and environmental factors (WHO, 2013a). "Health 2020" is a new European framework with strategic goals, requirements and priorities for the European Region of the WHO (2013b). This framework aims to improve health for all and reduce the health inequalities as well as to strengthen leadership and participatory governance for health. The "whole-of-government approach" (WHO, 2013a) includes multilevel activities from local to global government actions.

The WHO Regions for Health Network (WHO, 2008) points out that regions are active promoters for better health. Good health is a responsibility of the regions, and quality and innovation in health services need a regional basis (WHO, 2008). Increased networking, cooperation building and coordination between the relevant local representatives of the health care system are needed to tackle regional public health problems. In this context, structured health conferences offer the opportunity to take greater responsibility regarding local health planning and therefore have the potential to be used as an appropriate instrument for health management. Following the definition of Meier (1995), health conferences are "round tables" involving all representatives of relevant groups and institutions of the health system and targeting information, understanding, cooperation and participation. Their work is based on the principle of consensus. A further discussion is being conducted about the potential of health conferences to strengthen intersectoral governance for health in all policies beyond health care (Brand & Michelsen, 2012).

Although health conferences have been existing in Europe for a long time, there is a lack of knowledge concerning their characteristics, structural and process quality, effects as well as promoting factors. Therefore, the authors describe and analyze health conferences in the following overview.

6.2   Methods

This literature review is based on a search in specialist databases Cochrane Library, MEDPILOT/LIVIVO and PubMed and the "Health for All"-Database (HFA_DB) of WHO Europe. "health conferences" was the main search term and additionally, the authors (AH) searched for the terms "health dialog", "health forum", "health region" and "round table" in the title or abstract. The intervention region is part of Germany, Austria or France. Furthermore, articles published in the time from 1995 to 2016 and written in English or German language were looked for. The literature search was performed by the authors. 31 articles were included and numerous articles were excluded, because they describe health conferences in terms of congresses or symposia.

6.3   Results

6.3.1   Topics, Goals and Stakeholders

The approaches are rather heterogeneous, however certain characteristics are common in all identified health conferences. The literature review presents an overview of priority issues, organizational structures, methods, activities as well as outputs of health conferences. The methodology of the conferences follows the "Public Health Action Cycle" (Rosenbrock, 1995) explicitly in Austria (Hofmarcher & Quentin, 2013) as well as the German federal states North Rhine-Westphalia (NRW) (Knesebeck et al., 2002; Zamora, 2002; Murza et al., 2005), Baden-Württemberg (Roller & Wuthe, 2014), Bavaria (Hollederer et al., 2015), and Berlin (BSGUV, 2010). According to that, the action cycle of an exemplary health conference begins with the assessment and the identification of a health problem. The next steps comprise the development of strategies, their implementation and evaluation. The results of the evaluation are then integrated in the health monitoring systems.

Health conferences focus on a wide range of topics e.g. health problems at population level, challenges regarding health care and health promotion as well as health issues related to vulnerable groups (Table 6.1). The selection of certain topics depends on the conceptual setup of the health conference, legal regulations, political priority of specific topics, local problem constellations, and expected benefits of cooperation. The priority setting of health conferences is evident from the setup of working groups or

Table 6.1 Characteristics of health conferences

Priority issues	Organizational structure and activities	Outputs
a) Health care – local health care problems – innovative health care concepts – interface outpatient-impatient care – common diseases (depression, cancer, cardiovascular disease, diabetes, etc.) – nursing care (infrastructure) – palliative and hospice care – community psychiatry, mental health – support of addicted people – hygiene, infectious diseases, HIV – environmental health, urban planning – health-related self-help groups – patient education and orientation – health care economy – quality development – health expenditures *b) Prevention of illness, promotion of health and physical activity, prevention of addiction* *c) Health in specific periods of the life course* – infant mortality – health of children and adolescents – medical and social care of the elderly (multiple morbidity, dementia, etc.) *d) Health of target groups* – women's and men's health – people with migration background – socially disadvantaged, long-term unemployed, homeless, poor people – social or regional health inequities	– health conferences (generally once a year) – chairperson – agency – preparatory committee for agenda-setting – working groups – cooperation projects – symposiums – health days, etc – health planning	– transfer of knowledge and information – resolutions on priority health issues Recommendations – Statements on hospital planning or (regional) needs planning – formulation of strategies concerning health policy – health targets – initiation of projects and activities – networking and cooperation – support of health monitoring – transfer between federal state and local authority

commissions, which are able to concentrate on a specific health problem in the long-term. Recurrent topics include joint tasks such as prevention, which require coordination and organization at the local level. The effectiveness of health conferences depends overwhelmingly on the members' willingness to participate as well as their influence, because membership is predominantly based on cooperative practices and methods. Within their own sector, members generally implement projects and interventions on a voluntary basis.

Health conferences usually support politics by providing advice and moreover, create transparency or publicity. In many places, they contribute to health monitoring and initiate health reports on specific topics. They can also improve the mutual interchange between federal states and local authorities. Health conferences may be used to devolve national strategies for the regional level, as in France, or to provide the federal level with statements regarding hospital planning (ARS, 2017), as in the German federal State Northrhine-Westfalia (Murza et al., 2005). In France and Austria, they may also participate in political decisions on health expenditures.

Furthermore, health conferences offer the opportunity to define regional health targets at population level. National and regional health targets are frequently used to adapt the global "Health for All" (HFA) policy of the WHO to specific needs and priorities of individual regions (Wismar et al., 2008). For the German federal states Baden-Württemberg, Berlin, Brandenburg, Mecklenburg-West-Pomerania, Saxony-Anhalt and Thuringia, health targets build an explicit part of the conceptual frameworks for health conferences. In some cases, local health conferences formulate health targets independent of higher levels, e.g. the city of Bielefeld (2011), Ennepe-Ruhrkreis (Boschek & Kügler, 2002) or Hamburg-Altona (2011). In Austria, the national health conference provided a platform for a dialogue leading to ten nationwide health targets in 2012 (Hofmarcher & Quentin, 2013). With the first federal conference on health, the process of agreeing on national health goals for the next 20 years started. These health targets were also adopted by the health conferences of Upper Austria and Styria. In France, strategic health targets are included in the regional health planning processes, involving the health conferences (Chevreul et al., 2010).

The choice of the members for a health conference is a fundamental selection decision. On the one hand, all relevant representatives of health-related organizations should take part, while on the other hand, the conference should not be too large in order to assure its functioning. The French health conferences also put emphasis on a democratic involvement of the public. This is a reason why they also organize local health conferences.

In many cases, an office or agency is set up alongside the establishment of a health conference. In Germany and Austria, the majority of such agencies were integrated in neutral institutions like the local health authority, the county council or the public health service. The agency organizes the health conference, prepares the meetings, supports the transfer of information, documents the results and assists the working groups. In the German federal states Baden-Württemberg, Bavaria and Northrhine-Westfalia, the federal state health authorities support these processes based on their expertise. They advise the heads of the agencies, organize exchange of experiences and symposiums, and provide coordination support. The integration of the agencies of health conferences add new tasks to the public health service, i.e. in the field of coordination and management.

6.3.2   Distribution of Health Conferences in Germany, Austria and France

Figure 6.1 shows the identified health conferences for Germany, Austria and France as well as for the border region Meuse-Rhine. The distribution of health conferences across Europe is regionally diverse. Implementation strategies within the various countries started in different phases and ranged from isolated activities to a nationwide implementation as in France.

France

France was the first country that has systematically developed Regional Conferences (RC) with a focus on population health and public health priorities. Initially, 20 regions participated in 1995 and 1996, accompanied by a National Health Conference (Verpillat & Demeulemeester, 1997). During the process of generating regional public health plans, the regional conferences were consulted. Later, the Public Health Bill established the more elaborated regional health and autonomy conferences ("Conférence Régionale de

Fig. 6.1 Overview of health conferences in Germany, Austria and France

Santé et de l´Autonomie", CRSA) in all of its 27 regions as well as a national health conference. The aim is to manage health care at the regional level (Chevreul et al., 2010; Cecchi, 2010; Devictor, 2010). The CRSA comprise all relevant stakeholders of the health care system, i.e. representatives of local authorities, local conferences, employers and trade unions, patients, organizations responsible for prevention, health service providers and health professions (ARS, 2017). The health conferences participate in the regional health planning and their outcomes flow into the regional planning process. They offer the opportunity to share information, make proposals and create transparency, and their statements are available for the public. The health conferences are also used to democratically debate certain health issues at the regional level. They build commissions and working groups for the fields of prevention, organization of the health care system, prices and fees as well as patients' rights. They set health policy targets for the respective region. In addition, health conferences contribute to the regional strategic health plan and the regional health care policy. The health conferences also assess the region's health situation as well as social or regional inequalities in terms of access to the health care system. They inform the national health conference and the Ministry of Health. The health conferences set priorities for public health, e.g. ten regions have identified care for underserved populations with limited access to health care and initiated the establishment of about 300 centers providing 24-h access to care (Ettelt et al., 2008).

Germany

The developments in France triggered discussions about appropriate solutions for regional health planning in Germany and its federal states. In contrast to France, there are currently no nationwide efforts for implementing health conferences in Germany. Structured health conferences in Germany were established on initiatives of several health ministries of the federal states or activities of local authorities in different periods. Health conferences are often established at the level of the federal states and regional levels (Fig. 6.1). Resulting from the German Federalism, federal states have a major responsibility for health policy. Fig. 6.1 presents approx. 190 regional conferences in more than about the half of the German counties in 14 federal states. According to the respective ambitions, the implementation strategies ranged from isolated activities to an implementation in the whole federal state. At the local level, the variety of terms used for the concept of health conferences indicates the conceptual heterogeneity and the different spatial scales.

The federal states assisted health conferences by providing political, professional and financial support as well as legislation to establish health conferences. The most health conferences are located in West Germany. Due to the ambitions of the federal states, the distribution of health conferences across Germany is regionally quite different.

Health conferences were most consistently established by NRW as part of a new public health service strategy which made health conferences compulsory. At the end of 2001, all 54 counties had implemented health conferences in NRW. For a period of three years, they received resources and coordination aids as support by the federal state.

According to the Public Health Service Act, local health conferences aim to improve the coordination of health care at the local level. If required, they give recommendations which should be implemented on the basis of the commitment of its stakeholders. The hospital law of NRW also authorizes health conferences to make statements concerning issues of regional planning. The local health conferences of NRW were used as a model by other German federal states. Districts in Berlin and Hamburg established health conferences as well (BSGUV, 2010).

In 2010, the federal state of Baden-Wuerttemberg began implementing local health conferences based on a top-down approach. Participation of the local level is voluntary while the federal level provides initial, one-time investment and offers financial support for projects (Roller & Wuthe, 2014). All 44 counties established health conferences by law.

The federal state of Hesse established a state-wide structure by transforming the existing hospital conferences of its six hospital regions, which were based on the hospital law of Hesse, into health conferences in 2010.

After the project "future region" in three model regions, Lower Saxony initiated the follow-up project "health region". From the beginning of 2014, the experiences of this preliminary project spread to 20 counties in Lower Saxony (Brandes et al., 2014).

Bavaria started a pilot project for regional health conferences comprising three regions in 2013 (Hollederer & Stühler, 2017). The main goal of it is the improvement of local health care as well as the identification and elimination of local health care deficits. In 2015, the intervention approach was developed further to the concept of the "health regions[plus]", and conducted activities in the fields of health care, prevention and health promotion, as well as other regional issues. The health regions[plus] are funded by the state ministry and coordinated by a central office on the state level. In 2015, 24 regions took part in the comprehensive community-wide approach and in 2019, this number has grown to currently 50 health regions[plus], covering about two thirds of the state of Bavaria.

Austria
The developments in Austria are influenced by the WHO "Health for All"-strategy and the European experiences. There are similarities between the Austrian health care system, as well as links to strategic health targets, financing systems and federal state health funds (Hofmarcher & Quentin, 2013). The national health conference involves all relevant stakeholders of the health care system. If required, the health minister convenes the national health conference to advice the national health agency. The federal states may also implement health conferences to advice federal state health funds. Currently, health conferences exist in five of the nine federal states, i.e. Carinthia, Lower Austria, Upper Austria, Styria and Tirol. Since 2006, they regularly organize conferences on priority issues regarding health care and federal state health policy. In 2012, the 10 national health targets were rolled forward to the state level and from there to each municipality (Cassens et al., 2014). In addition, there is a local health conference in Rudolfheim-Fünfhaus, which is a district of the capital of Vienna.

Euregio Meuse-Rhine

The Euregio Meuse-Rhine in the border region of Germany, Belgium and the Netherlands has already organized a health conference. This demonstrates that a health conference can function as a cross-border management instrument of health management for border regions in the European Union. The Euregio Meuse-Rhine between Aachen, Liège and Maastricht is considered a model-type region. The Euregio has already been testing cooperation models in the health sector and between university hospitals. Based on the cross-border cooperation, citizens living near the border of the Netherlands, Germany and Belgium have easy access to comprehensive medical care.

6.3.3   Evaluation Results of Health Conferences

Results of Health Conferences in Germany

There are only few evaluation studies concerning health conferences in Germany. Controlled trials including intervention group and control group regions or pre-post-studies do not exist.

A positive exception is the comprehensive accompanying research related to the local health conferences in the German federal state of NRW. The systematic accompanying research was part of the preliminary project "Local coordination of Health and Social Care" in 28 counties of NRW from 1995 to 1998 (Ministry of Women, Youth, Family and Health of NRW, 2000; Knesebeck et al., 2002; Zamora, 2002). Results show that the involved stakeholders were largely positive in their rating concerning the interactions in the conferences and working groups, the degree of participation, the working atmosphere, and the cooperation across organizations and professions. Aspects related to the financing of the activities as well as competition were considered as negative. Important promoting factors of health conferences were the level of expertise and integration in terms of leadership and moderation. About 40% of the recommendations were implemented during the project. The majority of the activities aimed at the provision of information and knowledge transfer. The probability of implementation was higher for activities concerning the improvement of coordination at local level and the management of interfaces than for the expansion or restructuring of health care. The quality of process and outcome of a given activity depended largely on the selected topics.

In 2003, another analysis was conducted regarding the evaluation of the public health service law (Murza et al., 2005). During the study period, 178 recommendations for activities were passed and 192 working groups had been established. About two third of the interviewed members assessed health conferences as a useful tool to improve cooperation and coordination. The work within the local health conferences was also seen as successful.

Based on two surveys, the delegates of the Association of Statutory Health Insurance Physicians and the Medical Association Westphalia-Lippe made mixed judgements about the success of health conferences (Wüstenbecker, 2003). The process of coming to recommendations was rated rather positive while their implementation was criticized. However, health conferences are less successful in realizing the "health in all policies" approach of the WHO, which aims at prioritizing health issues in all political fields and not only the field of health policy (Ziemer & Grunow-Lutter, 2007).

In addition to this overall picture, there are two regional surveys from Herne and Heinsberg (Ziemer & Grunow-Lutter, 2007; Brandenburg et al., 1998; Brandenburg et al., 1999). The authors observed a continuous and active participation in the health conferences and a relatively high proportion of implemented recommendations. About one fourth of the participants stated that they were disappointed due to the fact that planned collaborative actions were not realized. The survey of the council Heinsberg included 44 high-level officers of county administrations and showed that networking across different county departments on health matters as well as the integration of political decision-makers was hardly achieved (Ziemer & Grunow-Lutter, 2007). The further development of health conferences in the German federal state of NRW including the output, was very heterogeneous (Werse, 2010).

Beyond NRW, there were only few accompanying studies about health conferences in Germany. A study on the health conferences of Berlin concluded that they are a well-established instrument for health policy dialogue, inform the public about health-related issues, promote the discussion of different approaches and support the networking of the stakeholders (BSGUV, 2010). Six out of eight health conferences implemented activities and projects following their previous recommendations and goals.

A formative evaluation study explores structures, processes and results of health conferences in three model regions in Bavaria (Hollederer & Stühler, 2017). In a survey of 80 participants, almost everyone agreed that health conferences are suited to improve health care and cooperation after approx. 18 months. Nearly all of the respondents agreed that the previous work was successful. Most interviewees were satisfied or rather satisfied with the processes but the level of satisfaction varied among the member groups. According to a large part of the respondents, the majority actively took part in the health conferences. Nearly all of the interviewees would also take part in the future. Similarly, the preliminary evaluation of the new health regions[plus] implemented in Bavaria since 2015 indicate positive results in terms of structural- and process quality (Hollederer, 2017). Within a short time period, the health regions[plus] were able to implement structured health conferences with high engagement of local actors, followed by regional health reports and projects in the two areas of activity, namely health promotion and health care (Bödeker et al., 2016). Another preliminary design study in Lower Saxony confirmed the importance of structure quality and the positive influence of management (Brandes et al., 2014). The commitment of the participants is essential for the impact of health conferences.

Single reports provide good examples for the implementation of activites, e.g. the report on health targets by the health conference of Altona in Hamburg (2011) and the report on the project "Transition of Patients in Essen" by the Health and Nursing Care Conference of Essen in NRW (Pieper et al., 2008).

Results of Health Conferences in France and Austria

In France, the evaluation of the first phase of the French health conferences was carried out in 1996. 175 members of the regional conferences (conferences regionals, CR) were interviewed by telephone on state of health and public health priorities (Verpillat & Demeulemeester, 1997). The results revealed an overall very high satisfaction; over 90% of the participants were either very satisfied or rather satisfied. More than 80% of the participants perceived the priority setting based on consensus as adequate. About half of the participants stated that the scheduled time for public discussion was too short. The majority was in favor of continuing health conferences. Mixed evaluation results of the operational regional health programs led to a further development of the health care policy on the national level: 100 national public health objectives were set and 5 strategic national plans for were announced for the period 2004–2008 (Wismar et al., 2008).

Any evaluation studies for Austrian health conferences could not be found in the literature database.

6.4   Discussion

The review shows that numerous health conferences exist as a result of government intervention in France, Germany and Austria. For all health systems based on a social insurance system (Germany, Austria and France) and countries with a federal structure (Germany) could have been found that the establishment of health conferences seems to be helpful. How, in the case of Austria, few published reports on the results of health conferences exist and thus no conclusion can be drawn. There is a greater need for coordination between the different levels of government and at their interfaces. Health conferences work for rural as well as metropolitan areas. The regional size of a health conference seems to be no determinant for its success. For the assurance of process quality and the quality of the results, specific recommendations will be made based on the experiences of "round tables" in the context of local health conferences or health regions[plus], which may serve as guidance for the future development of health conferences in the international context (Tab. 6.2).

The regional scale of health conferences is mainly based on administrative boundaries of counties, cities and federal states. Successful urban health conferences exist both at the level of districts, e.g. in Hamburg, Berlin or Vienna and at the level of whole cities, e.g. Düsseldorf. In France, health conferences are nationwide. In Austria, seven of nine States conduct health conferences. In Germany, conferences are established in more about the half of the German counties. Compared to other European countries, the German health care system is characterized by self-government and corporatism as well as its strong sectoral separation of inpatient and outpatient care. The complexity and the many sectoral interfaces in particular require communication, shared responsibilities and cooperation.

Tab. 6.2 Recommendations for „round tables" in the context of local health conferences or health regions^plus (Hollederer, 2016)

A. Assurance of Process Quality

Include all relevant local representatives of health care providers, financial providers and health policy while maintaining the work ability by an average size, as far as possible

Strengthening of patient and citizen orientation, self-help and empowerment as well as integration of selected representatives as members

Using existing local strengths in health care by including other member organizations (e.g. universities)

Transparent selection of topics according to criteria such as problem relevance, population reference, options for intervention, own responsibilities, additional value of cooperation etc

Focusing the contents on the improvement of local health care and the implementation of prevention and health promotion. In case of a consensus body, there should be a stronger focus on undersupply and coordinating activities

Build working groups, involving local health care experts, for the intensive perennial work on problems. Give the possibility of affiliation for existing other working groups and structures

Plan starter-projects for the development of cooperative structures (e.g. preparation of health guides or information material)

Initiate appropriate cooperation and coordination projects (characteristics as e.g. interdisciplinary, multi-professional, cross-sectoral as well as across policy areas and organizations)

Ensure professional moderation in all committees and community work

Adopt and publish statements and resolutions about local health policies, regional health planning and questions of the health care system

B. Assurance of the Quality of the Results

1. Identify local public health problems with an own needs-assessment and comparative analyses as well as expert interviews

2. Link the activities with local health reporting and build up monitoring of health care

3. Identify "Models of best practice", evaluate the state of research, reflect assumption of effectiveness and effect sizes

4. Set realistic local health targets and assure connection to framework programs

5. Ensure the concept and planning quality of the projects systematically, enable early participation of target groups, and take into account regional specifics

6. Ensure the sustainability of the projects or activities from the outset (e.g. potential transfer into standard care)

7. Initiate accompanying process evaluation about structure building, cooperation, working groups, projects, etc

8. Commission summative evaluation studies in case of promising routine and big projects

9. Structured discussion of the main results for development of intervention approaches

10. Publish results and problem-solving approaches, and provide intervention materials that are suited for other regions (e.g. on the homepage). Organize exchange of information and experiences with other municipalities

Health conferences have the potential for municipal and regional health management while they are also at risk of low effectiveness. Due to their limited regulatory power, they cannot resolve conflicts of interests and allocation as well as existing systemic problems, but they may mitigate them through their consensual approach. Sufficient funding, resources and a supportive environment are "hard" factors for the success of health conferences while leadership, moderation, agency and agenda setting are important "soft" factors.

According to surveys of members of health conferences, the positive aspects of cooperation and networking clearly outbalance critical statements about limited policy options, few activities and restricted budgets. Health conferences carry the potential to increase health policy options in the region and to create synergies, primarily through networking of the stakeholders and increased cooperation. Systematic evaluation of the functioning of health conferences is missing, e.g. effects of recommendations on hospital planning and resource allocation as well as regarding policy advice. A publication bias cannot be excluded. The output of health conferences can be measured by the established working groups, recommendations, statements or implemented activities and cooperation projects. The actual outcome of health conferences, i.e. population health indicators, is difficult to measure, especially in the short term. However, in terms of an outcome evaluation it is possible to focus on the selected priority issues or on the set health targets on their accomplishment. This would require the evaluation of single projects or health targets that are part of the health conference. The few existing evaluations focus on the delivered output instead of population-level outcomes so that the question of sustainable impact of health conferences remains unanswered.

This overview reveals the strong heterogeneity of health conferences both between and within countries, which provides an opportunity for the identification of best practice models and a diversification of the present approach. Systematic comparisons of the different countries, types of health conferences and regional scales as well as the development of a typology still need to be examined. An intensified exchange of experiences between the protagonists of health conferences might advance the conceptual development and harmonization of the health care sector in European regions. It is interesting in context of the European Union harmonization that health conferences may help to organize cross-border health services.

Structured health conferences need a long-term perspective and the commitment of all relevant actors in health care and politics. When this is given, health conferences offer new opportunities for the organization of local health services, regional health policy and health planning, and the implementation of public health programs.

References

Agence Régionale de Santé. (ARS). (2017). Conférence Régionale de la Santé et de l´Autonomie. https://www.iledefrance.ars.sante.fr/conference-regionale-de-sante-et-de-lautonomie-1. Accessed 24 Nov 2019.

Bezirksamt Altona. (Hrsg.). (2011). *Evaluation der Umsetzung der Altonaer Gesundheitsziele 2008–2010*. Bezirksamt Altona. Dezernat Soziales, Jugend und Gesundheit. Fachamt Gesundheit.

Bödeker, M., Deiters, T., Eicher, A., Hollederer, A., Pfister, F., & Wildner, M. (2016). Wie können die Gesundheitsversorgung, -förderung und Prävention regional optimiert werden? – Die Entwicklung der Gesundheitsregionen[plus] in Bayern. *Public Health Forum, 24*(4), 290–293.

Boschek, H. J., & Kügler, K. J. (2002). Kommunale Gesundheitsziele aus Sicht von Bürgern und Experten – Ergebnisse zweier Befragungen im Ennepe-Ruhr-Kreis. *Das Gesundheitswesen, 64*, 633–638.

Brand, H., & Michelsen, K. (2012). Collaborative governance: The example of health conferences. In D. V. McQueen, M. Wismar, V. Lin, C. M. Jones, & M. Davies (Eds.), *Intersectoral governance for health in all policies* (pp. 165–184). WHO Regional Office for Europe.

Brandenburg, A., Renner, A., v. Ferber, C., & Winkler, K. (1998). Chancen und Risiken von Gesundheitskonferenzen. Eine empirische Analyse kommunaler Gesundheitspolitik. http://haberbosch-reisen.eu. Accessed 24 Nov 2019.

Brandenburg, A., v. Ferber, C., Renner, A., & Winkler, K. (1999). Gesundheitskonferenzen als kommunaler Handlungsprozess. In Deutsche Gesellschaft für Public Health (Ed.), *Public-Health-Forschung in Deutschland* (pp. 1–13). Huber.

Brandes, S., Bregulla, I., & Altgeld, T. (2014). Zukunftsregionen Gesundheit. Kommunale Gesundheitslandschaften. Bericht zur Abschlussevaluation. Hannover. Landesvereinigung für Gesundheit und Akademie für Sozialmedizin Niedersachsen e. V. Arbeitsbereich Evaluation und Praxisforschung.

Cassens, M., Zeller, C., Wieser, A., Meyer; W., Schneider, K., & Tuite, A. (2014). Community as a setting for future oriented health promotion in Austria: "Living Healthy in the Olympia Region Seefeld" as an Example for Health Learning in a Scientific Context". In Y. B. Larock & D. C. Gustave (Ed.), *Health education – Parental and educators` perspectives and needs assessment* (pp. 107–137). Nova publishers.

Cecchi, C. (2010). Les conferences regionals de santé: Bilan, constats risques, défis et perspectives. *Santé Publique, 22*(1), 113–120.

Chevreul, K., Durand-Zaleski, I., Bahrami, S., Hernández-Quevedo, C., & Mladovsky, P. (2010). France health system review. *Health Systems in Transition, 12*(6), 1–291.

Devictor, B. (2010). Les conferences regionals de santé et de l´autonomie (CRSA): Qu´en sera-t-il de la démocratie sanitaire en region? *Santé Publique, 22*(1), 121–129.

Ettelt, S., Nolte, E., Thomson, S., & Mays, N. (2008). Capacity planning in health care: A review of the international experience. Policy Brief. World Health Organization. European Observatory on Health Systems and Policies.

Hofmarcher, M., & Quentin, W. (2013). Austria: Health system review. Health systems in translation. World Health Organization Regional Office for Europe.

Hollederer, A. (2016). Regionale Gesundheitskonferenzen und Gesundheitsregionen[plus] in Deutschland: Struktur-, Prozess- Und Ergebnisqualitäten. *Public Health Forum, 24*(1), 22–25.

Hollederer, A. (2017). Struktur- und Prozessqualität am Beispiel der neuen Gesundheitsregionen[plus] in Bayern. *Das Gesundheitswesen., 79*(04), 299–374. https://doi.org/10.1055/s-0037-1602061

Hollederer, A., & Stühler, K. (2017). Kooperation im Gesundheitswesen: Formative Evaluation des Modellprojektes Regionale Gesundheitskonferenzen in Bayern. *Gesundheitswesen, 79*(08/09), 605–612. https://doi.org/10.1055/s-0041-110673

Hollederer, A., Eicher, A., Pfister, F., Stühler, K., & Wildner, M. (2015). Vernetzung, Koordination und Verantwortung durch Gesundheitsregionen[plus]: Neue gesundheitspolitische Ansätze und Entwicklungen in Bayern. *Das Gesundheitswesen*. https://doi.org/10.1055/s-0035-1555892.

Knesebeck, O., Joksimovic, L., Badura, B., & Siegrist, J. (2002). Evaluation of a community-level policy intervention. *Health Policy, 61*, 111–122.

Meier, B. (1995). Gesundheitskonferenzen – Instrumente der Kooperation zwischen Anspruch und Wirklichkeit. *Das Gesundheitswesen, 57*, 645–651.

Murza, G., Werse, B., & Brand, H. (2005). Ortsnahe Koordinierung der gesundheitlichen Versorgung in Nordrhein-Westfalen. Zwischenbilanz Des Nordrhein-Westfälischen Modells. *Bundesgesundheitsblatt, 10*, 1162–1169.

OECD. (2015). Health at a glance 2015: OECD indicators, OECD Publishing, Paris, France. https://doi.org/10.1787/health_glance-2015-1-en. Accessed 2 May 2017.

Pieper, C., Kolankowska I., Weiland, D., & Daul, T. (2008). Abschlussbericht Evaluation des Modells „Patientenüberleitung in Essen". Institut für Medizinische Informatik, Biometrie und Epidemiologie. https://media.essen.de/media/wwwessende/aemter/53/gesundheitskonferenz/ evaluationsberichtpatientenberleitung.pdf. Accessed 24 Nov 2019.

Roller, G., & Wuthe, J. (2014). Runde Tische, Gesundheitskonferenzen, Gesundheitsregionen – Evolutionsgeschichte eines Projektes des Öffentlichen Gesundheitsdienstes. *Public Health Forum, 12*(4), 13–15.

Rosenbrock, R. (1995). Public Health als soziale Intervention. *Das Gesundheitswesen, 57*(3), 140–144.

Stadt Bielefeld. (Ed.). (2011). Bielefelder Gesundheitsziele 2015. Dezernat Umwelt und Klimaschutz- Gesundheits-, Veterinär- und Lebensmittelüberwachungsamt. https://www.bielefeld. de/ftp/dokumente/Abschlussbericht_Gesundheitsziele2010-2015.pdf. Accessed 24 Nov 2019.

Senate Administration of Berlin. (BSGUV). (2010). Schlussbericht Projekt: Umsetzung des Gesundheitsdienst-Gesetzes (GDG). Referat: Öffentlicher Gesundheitsdienst, Prävention und Gesundheitsförderung (I E), Projektgruppe. https://digital.zlb.de/viewer/metadata/33404329/1/ LOG_0003/ Accessed 24 Nov 2019.

Verpillat, P., & Demeulemeester, R. (1997). Evaluation of regional conferences on health status and the priorities of public health. *Santé Publique, 9*(1), 91–103.

Werse, W. (2010). Kommunale Gesundheitskonferenzen in Nordrhein-Westfalen. Erfahrungen Und Perspektiven. *Das Gesundheitswesen, 72*(3), 146–149.

Wismar, M., McKee, M., Ernst, K., Srivastava, D., & Busse, R. (2008). Health targets in Europe. Learning from experience. European Observatory on Health Systems and Policies. Observatory Studies Series No 13. https://apps.who.int/iris/handle/10665/107909. Accessed 24 Nov 2019.

World Health Organization. (Ed.). (2008). Ten theses on regional health and wealth: regions invest in health - and it pays off for both people and the economy! WHO Regional Office for Europe. https://apps.who.int/iris/handle/10665/107896

World Health Organization. (Ed.). (2013a). Health 2020. A European policy framework and strategy for the 21st century. http://www.euro.who.int/__data/assets/pdf_file/0011/199532/ Health2020-Long.pdf?ua=1. Accessed 24 Nov 2019.

World Health Organization. (Ed.). (2013b). Review of social determinants and the health divide in the WHO European Region: final report. ISBN: 978 92 890 0030 7. http://www.euro.who. int/en/publications/abstracts/review-of-social-determinants-and-the-health-divide-in-the-who-european-region.-final-report. Accessed 24 Nov 2019.

World Health Organization. (Ed.). (2015). The European health report 2015. Targets and beyond – Reaching new frontiers in evidence. ISBN 978 92 890 1431 1.https://www.euro.who.int/en/ data-and-evidence/european-health-report/european-health-report-2015/european-health-report-2015-the.-targets-and-beyond-reachingnew-frontiers-in-evidence.-highlights. Accessed 07 July 2021.

Wüstenbecker, M. (2003). Kommunale Gesundheitskonferenzen im Urteil ärztlicher Delegierter. *Westfälisches Ärzteblatt, 8*, 11.

Zamona, P. (2002). Möglichkeiten, Grenzen und Perspektiven einer Optimierung der gesundheitlichen Versorgung durch Kommunalisierung von gesundheitsbezogenen Steuerungs- und Managementprozessen. Unpubl. PhD-Thesis, Bielefeld: University of Bielefeld.

Ziemer, B., & Grunow-Lutter, V. (2007). Lokale Gesundheitspolitik und Gesundheitsplanung aus der Sicht der EntscheidungsträgerInnen des kommunalen politisch-administrativen Systems. *Das Gesundheitswesen, 69*(10), 534–540.

Vaccination Attitudes in Combatting Measles Along the Danube—Ethical Aspects as Challenges

Andrea Lakasz

Contents

7.1   Different Approaches to a Constant Challenge 102
    7.1.1   Measles—An Example of Vaccination Behavior. 102
    7.1.2   General Vaccination Situation in the Danube Riverine States 103
7.2   What do Employees in a Clinical Setting Think?—A Case Study 107
    7.2.1   Results 107
    7.2.2   Discussion 108
    7.2.3   Why People Hesitate About Immunization 109
7.3   Ethical Aspects. 112
    7.3.1   Why do People Decline Immunization? 113
    7.3.2   What Should be Done?—No Clear Recommendations Regarding
           Immunization are Possible. 114
References. 116

Abstract

Measles, once regarded as a childhood disease, has become a disease of adults due to vaccination gaps that have developed in the past decades. Society is divided, vaccination refusers insist on the basic right of personal liberty. On the contrary, vaccine advocates argue with social responsibility and the introduction of mandatory vaccination. Advantages of mandatory vaccination for society, and the hesitation of individuals, especially parents, as a disadvantage, conflict. Ethical aspects have

A. Lakasz (✉)
Former Research Fellow, FOM University of Applied Sciences, Munich, Germany

M. Cassens et al. (eds.), *Transdisciplinary Perspectives on Public Health in Europe*, FOM-Edition, https://doi.org/10.1007/978-3-658-33740-7_7

come into focus and led to public health challenges regarding sub-optimal vaccina-tion coverage. How could ethics help individuals to decide in favor of vaccination and act responsibly? Immunization issues in the three cooperation countries of the Arteria Danubia (ArDa) project are discussed with special focus on Germany, sup-ported by a single case study about vaccination attitudes. The results of the study indicate that the assumed anti-vaccination attitude was not supported in the clinical setting. Nevertheless, on the level of society, more education and information work are needed to improve vaccination coverage.

7.1   Different Approaches to a Constant Challenge

The cooperation countries of the Arteria Danubia (ArDa) project have made the elimi-nation of measles a priority (WHO, 2012). However, the three countries Bulgaria, Germany, and Hungary as part of the European Region of the WHO, have different approaches to vaccination prophylaxis, immunization, and prevention measures. In this context, a kind of immunization skepticism has emerged in Germany in recent decades. As a result, outbreaks have repeatedly occurred, highlighting the discussion about vac-cination (Robert Koch-Institut, 2015). Respective regulations and the current situa-tion in each country as well as ethical aspects, which have been proven to be obstacles especially in Germany, will be discussed. In addition, the results of a single case study conducted in clinical setting will be presented to underline vaccination attitudes—to illustrate the importance of immunization in healthcare facilities.

7.1.1   Measles—An Example of Vaccination Behavior

Measles is a highly contagious disease associated with serious complications. Nevertheless, it is vaccine-preventable: two applications of the combined vaccine are enough for lifelong immunity. From a public health point of view, vaccination cover-age should be increased steadily, and any existing vaccination gaps should be closed. To combat the disease, a vaccination rate of at least 95% should be achieved to pre-vent the transmission of the pathogens and guarantee the immunity of the population. Furthermore, vaccination uptake and catch-up by adolescents and adults with missing or uncertain vaccination status, should be raised (WHO, 2018c).

Vaccination side effects usually fade away without severe complications. According to the Standing Committee on Vaccination (STIKO) in Germany, serious complications rarely occur (Robert Koch-Institut, 2015). Data of the Paul Ehrlich-Institut (PEI) show that 1696 suspected cases, with side effects after immunization against measles, were reported in Germany from January 2001 until the end of December 2012. Only 3.4% of these cases were identified suffering from permanent damage, and 0.9% ($n = 15$) died. Nonetheless, the PEI could not identify a confirmed, probable or possible causality for vaccination in any of the death cases, i.e. the probability of a serious complication after immunization against measles is very low (Paul Ehrlich-Institut, 2017). Adults have a higher rate of side effects leading to an increased rate of hospital admissions. The distribution of the age groups in the reported cases shows that measles is no longer exclusively a childhood disease (ibid.).

The success of public health interventions to eliminate the disease correlates with the attitude of the population. Outbreaks are catalyzed by unvaccinated individuals; at the same time, they benefit from herd immunity (CBHS Health Fund, 2017). To achieve a better vaccination coverage, and the goal of eliminating measles, the attitude of the population should be influenced towards immunization. This means that individuals should reconcile their attitude—which is often influenced by external factors such as the media—with their willingness, i.e. social responsibility—the consequences of non-vaccination for other members of the society—to behave positively and vaccinate. However, there is no information available about the outcome of the immunization or eventual complications at the time of inoculation. The main goal is to increase vaccination coverage and to eliminate measles (ECDC, 2018). To improve vaccination coverage, mandatory vaccination against measles has already been introduced in nine countries of the European Union, including France and Italy (Bozzola et al., 2018).

7.1.2 General Vaccination Situation in the Danube Riverine States

Vaccination status was defined as a health indicator by the WHO. This indicator makes it possible to measure any progress or deterioration regarding vaccination status. In addition, vaccination was determined as one of the Sustainable Development Goals (SDGs) in the European Region of the WHO (WHO, 2017).

The WHO promotes the involvement of everyone, the population, parents, doctors, and individuals in combatting measles. The interventions also include that immunized individuals inform others about the fact that vaccination saves lives. Only by means of immunization will it be possible to protect those who can't be immunized for medical reasons or are still too young to be vaccinated (< 12–14 months). Thus, the elimination of measles is a cross-social goal that can only be achieved together (WHO, 2018a). More than half of the countries in the European Region of the WHO managed to stop the transmission of the endemic disease by 2015 (Datta et al., 2018) and 21 of the 53 countries eliminated measles by 2017 (Hübschen et al., 2017). However, measles still causes problems in Germany because regional outbreaks occur. Reports on the increase of cases in Europe in the first months of 2018 indicate that prevention measures in countries, where vaccination is not mandatory, should be reconsidered or possibly intensified to avoid new outbreaks (WHO, 2014).

Data of the European Centre for Disease Prevention and Control (ECDC) show that there are vaccination gaps among young adults and adolescents, which must be closed to prevent the transmission of measles. The European Immunization Week conducted in spring 2018 aimed to raise public awareness about preventive measures, the risks of being unvaccinated, and non-vaccination in general. The suboptimal coverage in context of incidence should be improved too. Inoculation as the only preventive measure against measles could protect the population in case of an outbreak (ECDC, 2018).

To optimize measures and reduce incidence in the affected settings, the cooperation between stakeholders like authorities, doctors, and the population is necessary (Datta et al., 2018). In addition to political measures, technical capacities, and public awareness are needed to eliminate the disease (Biellik et al., 2016).

Immunization against measles is mandatory in most countries along the Danube. Apart from Austria, Germany, and Romania, all riverine countries including Slovakia, Hungary, Croatia, Serbia, and Bulgaria introduced the combined vaccine after World War II (Bozzola et al., 2018). Although, despite high vaccination coverage, outbreaks endanger the population and remind public health authorities of the importance of monitoring and surveillance (Seguliev et al., 2007). Anti-vaccination movements and campaigns lead to political debates and contribute in all of the countries to the spread of the disease (Holt, 2018).

Most recent WHO data show that 174 confirmed cases occurred in Bulgaria from 2017 to July 2018 (WHO, 2018b). There were 1378 infections in Germany and 49 in Hungary during the same period (ibid.). Most cases were identified in the age group of 15 years and older in Germany, suggesting that missing immunization in childhood resulted in a vaccination gap, which contributed to the transmission of measles. Only in 2017, about 50% of all patients were older than 14 years in Germany which pointed out that the disease can also infect adults (Robert Koch-Institut, 2018).

Bulgaria and Hungary are characterized by centralized health systems, low per capita health expenditure in comparison to the WHO European Region, high out-of-pocket payments (48% in Bulgaria and 29% in Hungary compared to the EU average of 15%), and a life expectancy, which is 5–6 years lower than the EU average (IHME, 2017a; b). Infectious diseases such as HIV, tuberculosis or hepatitis B are challenges for both countries. Regarding measles, the vaccination coverage for children under one year is about the same, 94% in Bulgaria, and higher, 99% in Hungary, than in the European Region of the WHO (95%) (OECD, 2017a, b).

High vaccination coverage has developed in Bulgaria and Hungary historically, because of mandatory immunization in childhood (ECDC, n. d.). However, surveillance should be continued to prevent the introduction of measles from neighboring countries. Education of and information for vulnerable lower social classes should be intensified to avoid the evolvement of vaccination gaps (Rigó et al., 2012).

Ethical discussions are intensifying because of media influence and anti-vaccine movements in Hungary and Bulgaria too. However, there aren't many alternatives because the central mandatory immunization applies to all parents (Botás, 2016). The view of the population should be switched into the direction of public health to accentuate social responsibility. Health authorities, and eventually the state, could intervene by introducing penalty fees for parents declining immunization (ProCon.org, 2018).

In addition to more education and information work, the raising of awareness for people with alternative worldviews should be targeted to increase vaccination coverage (Holt, 2018).

Bulgaria

Measles have already been eliminated in Bulgaria (WHO Regional Office for Europe, 2018a). Since the 1930s, cases must be reported and registered. The vaccine against measles was introduced in the early 1970s. The first dose is given at the age of 13 months, followed by the second one at the age of 12 years. The country has also drawn up a national action plan to combat the disease. Immunization against measles is mandatory. Children under 16 are covered by the state insurance and have full access to medical services, including vaccinations (Radosveta, 2011).

Although the vaccination coverage at national level was considered high, there was a nationwide outbreak between 2009 and 2011. Measles was "imported" to the country hence more than 20 thousand individuals—mostly children—were infected, mainly of the Roma population; 24 of them died. The authorities evaluated the data and acted consistently: the vaccine was administered free, communication activities in the country, and the cooperation with the WHO Regional Office were intensified. Suboptimal access to medical services and missing information were identified as causes of the transmission. For this reason, long-term cooperation and communication strategies were developed to close vaccination gaps and identify susceptible individuals (Muscat et al., 2016).

Between 2012 and 2016, 16 measles cases were identified, including one case of the genotype H1 in 2016, which was introduced to the country. The affected person was between 20–29 years old. A laboratory test was carried out in two cases in 2016, one of which was found positive. The immunity of the population is about 90%. Vaccination coverage has declined slightly since 2014; 92% of the children were immunized against measles in 2015 (ibid.).

The Roma population was predominantly affected during the outbreak in 2017 again, 41% of the sufferers were unvaccinated. Due to nosocomial transmission at the children's department, 24 individuals contracted the disease and one child died (< 1 year) (Kurchatova et al., 2017).

Vaccination programs will be promoted in the framework of the Bulgarian National Vaccination Program, especially among the Roma population (Radosveta, 2011).

Hungary

Measles is considered eradicated in Hungary (WHO Regional Office for Europe, 2018b). Although there is no national action plan for combatting the disease, the immunization against it is being regulated by law since 1954. In 1969, mandatory vaccination was introduced; the second dose of the vaccine is available since 1989 (Nemzeti Népegészségügyi Központ, n. d.). The doses are administered at the age of 15 months and 11 years as a combined vaccine. It can be given at the doctor's office or at school by a school doctor (Nemzeti Népegészségügyi Központ, 2018). Meanwhile, parents can be sanctioned or fined if they refuse to immunize their children (European Forum for Vaccine Vigilance, n. d.). Between 2012 and 2016, three confirmed cases of the genotype D4 were identified in Hungary. In 2016, three suspected cases were found, and 89 samples were examined in laboratories. The three cases reported in 2017 were introduced from Romania. In spite of vaccination campaigns, it is suspected that the reason for the transmission was the missing second dose (Orosz et al., 2018).

A study conducted among hospital personnel in 2017 showed that despite intensive immunization and high vaccination coverage, a vaccination gap evolved in the age group of 41–45 years. The results suggest that the control of protective antibodies is necessary to avoid a possible transmission of the disease in health facilities. Monitoring/surveillance is continuing strictly in the country to ensure the immunity of the population (Lengyel et al., 2018).

Germany

As part of the European Region of the WHO, the German government has also set the goal of eliminating measles by 2015 (Robert Koch-Institut, 2018). Despite a significant increase in immunization rates since 2001, regional outbreaks have still occurred (Robert Koch-Institut, 2015). Current evidence indicates that the number of cases among young adults born after 1970 has increased. 40% of the infected individuals were older than 20 years. A vaccination gap was identified as the cause of this phenomenon, which could have been traced back to philosophical, religious or spiritual reasons, lack of information, and inadequate access to medical care (Matysiak-Klose & Wicker, 2017).

The incidence of infectious diseases has fallen significantly in recent decades, which is the result of vaccination campaigns and increased information work. In comparison to Bulgaria and Hungary, there is no mandatory vaccination in Germany. For this reason, vaccinations are only recommended by pediatricians during routine examinations and later by general practitioners for adolescents and adults during a doctor's appointment (ECDC, 2017).

After the Prevention Act took into force in Germany on July 25, 2015, the German Academy for Child and Adolescent Medicine (DAKJ) called for the strengthening of the regulation about mandatory vaccination and counseling. They argued that there was an increased risk of transmission in community facilities such as day-care centers, because small children and infants cannot be injected with the live vaccine. On the one hand, older, unvaccinated siblings could possibly introduce the disease into the facility, and, on the other hand, be endangered or get infected themselves. For this reason, it is indispensable that parents are advised correctly, and children will be immunized completely. The DAKJ suggested the development of a standardized regulation to check the vaccination status of children before admission to a community facility. In addition, parents must be informed about their responsibility for the common good, and legal steps should be taken against doctors violating the medical duty of care and quality assurance (Deutsche Akademie für Kinder- und Jugendmedizin e. V., 2017).

In accordance with the Prevention Act, the immunization status must be checked at routine examinations during childhood. In case of admission to a kindergarden or a day-care center, the proof of vaccination advice given by a doctor must be presented. Should measles occur in kindergardens, schools or after-school care centers, unvaccinated children might be excluded temporarily.

Additionally, it is possible regarding personnel in health-care facilities that employers can make the employment of new personnel dependent on the vaccination status (ibid.).

The project of eliminating measles by 2015 failed in Germany. 929 individuals contracted the disease in 2017, 42% of them ranged 0 to 2 and 30% aged 10 to 19 (Robert Koch-Institut, 2018). The incidence was 0.4 per 100,000 inhabitants in 2016, and the highest incidence was identified among small children. The lack of herd immunity was identified as the reason of the outbreaks in 2016 (ibid.). Statistical data show that approx. 2,500 cases occurred in Germany in 2015, about half of them in Berlin.

Despite preventive initiatives and measures, many Germans are hesitant or skeptical and do not vaccinate their children, which leads to the evolvement of vaccination gaps triggering infection chains and outbreaks. The efforts of health authorities focus on epidemiological measures, which require interdisciplinary efforts (Eichner et al., 2017). The Prevention Act clarifies that the immunization against measles serves the aims of primary prevention. Discussions and evaluations of the data at state and federal level are progressing. The National Action Plan for the Elimination of Measles and Rubella for 2015–2020 summarizes the strategic goals and includes proposals for the implementation of interventions like the reduction of incidence, increasing vaccination coverage, and the improvement of epidemiological surveillance (Bundesministerium für Gesundheit, 2015).

7.2   What do Employees in a Clinical Setting Think?—A Case Study

Ethical aspects of vaccination attitudes in relation to measles were examined in the context of the ongoing social discussion by means of qualitative research design. The survey was linked to the theories of medical and public health ethics as well as the theory of utilitarianism. Document analysis served as data collection technique; the processing was carried out descriptively. The example in the clinical setting served the illustration of vaccination attitudes towards measles (Table 7.1).

7.2.1   Results

39 of 86 employees took part in the single case study which corresponds to a response rate of 45.3%. All questionnaires were evaluated, disregarded whether the questionnaire

Table 7.1 Key data of the case study

Period	Between April 15 and May 15, 2015
Participants	Employees of the Department of Radiation Oncology of the LMU Munich with patient contact
Instrument	Partially standardized online questionnaire with 12 close-ended and 2 open-ended questions
Response rate	45.3%

was completed to the end or it had been discontinued in the meantime (n=3, all female). 82.1% (n=32) of the respondents were female, the male proportion was 17.9% (n=7). 89.5% (n=34) of the participants were vaccinated against measles, four (10.5%) answered with no and one did not answer. 91.2% (n=32) of the respondents were vaccinated in childhood and 8.8% (n=3) as an adult. 23 (65.7%) of those who answered the question received the second dose of the vaccine. 97.4% (n=38) of the participants were not afraid of vaccinations and were aware of their immunization status. The vaccination titer (measuring the degree of the immunity of the body against a disease) was known to 42.1% (n=16) of those surveyed. To the question, if in case of missing immunization, a vaccination was foreseen in 2015, four participants answered with yes. 91.7% (n=37) of the respondents were not afraid of contracting measles. The risk of being infected by a patient in the workplace was estimated by 25.3% (n=10) as high, by 50% (n=20) as average and by 23.7% (n=9) as low. 94.7% (n=36) of those who responded to the question would agree with the introduction of mandatory vaccination (Table 7.2).

The data indicated that the assumed declination of mandatory vaccination by society could not have been confirmed in the clinical setting. The respondents of the closed cohort demanded the introduction of mandatory vaccination and more information.

7.2.2 Discussion

The data show in comparison to the objections to vaccinations published by the RKI that the employees in the clinical setting do not doubt the positive effects of vaccinations

Table 7.2 Results of the open-ended questions

Country of vaccination	Germany: n=29 Austria: n=3 Other: n=7
Proposals for desired measure	Mandatory vaccination: n=10 More education / information work: n=7 Free titer determination: n=1 No mandatory vaccination: n=2

(Robert Koch-Institut, 2016a). Both vaccination refusers referred to a measles infection in childhood. The objection of the ineffectiveness of the vaccine and that of the short-term protection as well as the need for the constant repetition of the vaccination can be disproved. The results suggest that the information work by physicians about the risks of declining the vaccination should be improved. Immunization in childhood indicates that early vaccination correlates with the avoidance of getting measles later positively. The objection that the vaccine causes the disease, can be excluded. 37% (n = 14) of the respondents demanded more information concerning vaccination. Statistical data imply that 60% of unvaccinated subjects did not let themselves vaccinated because no one pointed out the need for immunization (Robert Koch-Institut, 2017). Thus, the demand for more education and information work could be confirmed in the study. However, the assumed declination of mandatory vaccination at societal level couldn't be confirmed. By recognizing the importance and benefits of immunization, individuals working in the clinical setting can control their attitude in a way that an uptake or a catch-up will follow. Thus, positively contributing both to one's own well-being and to that of the community.

In relation to infectious diseases, there are increased risks in health care facilities because it is not possible to check the vaccination status of every patient before they meet medical personnel. During outbreaks with an increased number of cases, the risk of transmission increases for the employees too. Regarding the clinical setting, the vaccination status of the employees will be recorded by the occupational medical service. Furthermore, it is not possible to diagnose the disease during the incubation period in health facilities and prevent the transmission of the disease. The applicable hygiene measures cover only the procedures for diagnosed measles infection. The endangerment of other patients or visitors in the hospital by contagious patients can only be reduced with increased hygiene measures. The regulations applicable in hospitals and health-care facilities in accordance with § 36 Prevention Act and the guidelines of the Robert Koch-Institute for Hospital Hygiene and Infection Prevention determine the internal procedures for the prevention of nosocomial infections in hygiene plans. These documents are regarded as mandatory official instructions for all employees (Robert Koch-Institut, 2016b).

7.2.3 Why People Hesitate About Immunization

At the level of the individual, the discussion concerns the following questions: should people be vaccinated or not? If yes, what are the advantages and disadvantages of the immunization for the individual? If not, what risks can non-vaccination cause for the individual and for society? Does an unvaccinated individual act ethically? Should mandatory vaccination be introduced?

Further questions arise regarding ethical action on the part of the authorities and the state: Is it the task of a government or authority to ensure that as many individuals as possible are immunized to prevent diseases which could lead to death? Which interventions in the individual's self-determination are justified to generate health benefits for society? The examination of possible causes of the shift in the affected age groups brought up ethical questions too. The causes of vaccination gaps as well as the issues why some parents do not vaccinate their children, and which factors play a role in connection with the attitude of vaccination refusers will be disputed as well (Robert Koch-Institut, 2016a). From the ethical/moral point of view, a question arises for the individual: What should be done to act morally well and correctly regarding immunization? External factors, such as the media, have a controversial influence on the individual's opinion about vaccination. The need for immunization is more difficult to communicate because the development of vaccinations could mean that there is no longer any acute threat to the population. As a result, the risks of infection will be underestimated, and the risks of vaccination overestimated (The College of Physicians of Philadelphia, 2018b).

The question of justice will be considered too. An individual ignoring his social responsibility by not being vaccinated based on religious or spiritual beliefs and thereby increasing the risk of infection or the spread of measles to other members of the society, is treated in the same way as an individual who can't or may not be vaccinated because of immunodeficiency or chronic illness. An unvaccinated person has the same right to health-care financed by general funds as another person who cannot be vaccinated for medical reasons (ibid.). Different factors, like the political, the social and economic environment, and the health attitude of individuals create tensions too. These result in problems for public health measures, because the actions of the individuals related to their vaccination attitude cannot be measured or estimated in advance.

Vaccination Attitudes
The society is divided into two groups if it comes to the issue of immunization against an infectious disease such as measles.

Advocacy
One of the groups includes individuals, who do not doubt the need for vaccination, i.e. accept it and therefore vaccinate their children against measles as soon as possible and in accordance with the doctor's suggestion. Vaccine advocates do not tolerate vaccination gaps. They believe that vaccination is a task of society to prevent diseases and that vaccination prevents and/or eradicates dangerous diseases. Their attitude improves the health status of the population (Greenwood, 2014).

Declination
The other group includes those individuals, who consider vaccination unnecessary or even dangerous. The reasons for the negative attitude of this people can be philosophical, based on religion, may result from lack of information or insufficient access to medical care. Another reason, which was also identified for declination, is the fear of vaccination.

In their argumentation, refusers also refer to possible complications or side effects after being immunized (Robert Koch-Institut, 2016a).

Opponents decline the introduction of mandatory vaccination. They assess immunization as an infringement of their personal rights and development (The College of Physicians of Philadelphia, 2018a). However, they benefit from herd immunity and cannot be excluded from it, i.e. they benefit from the fact that other people are vaccinated (Fig. 7.1). Vaccination refusers will be accused of not fulfilling their social responsibility. Moreover, vaccination refusers believe that immunization is superfluous and causes more harm than good. They doubt the efficacy of vaccines and rate vaccination risks higher than infection risks and have different ideas about benefit and damage. This asymmetry is irresolvable for them, as the harm of immunization will be rated higher than the benefits of it. Some vaccination refusers reject immunization for religious reasons and point out that diseases are divine means of command or tests that they must accept. In this argumentation, the possible risks are not considered either for one's self or the community. Followers of alternative views also argue that vaccination is disruptive because it is contrary to their ideas of naturalness. In this view, vaccination does not fit into the inviolable rhythms of nature (ProCon.org, 2018). Additionally, opponents think that vaccination campaigns organized by health authorities serve profit interests. They point out the corruption in the pharmaceutical industry, although the costs of vaccination against measles are out of proportion to the costs of admissions to hospital (Schadwinkel & Stockrahm, 2015).

State Authorities
To protect the community from epidemics, the state has the right to introduce a general obligation to vaccinate. If epidemics lead to deaths, the individual autonomy can be restricted by force majeure. However, the individual decides about whether to be vaccinated. This freedom of choice should not be violated by a mandatory provision on

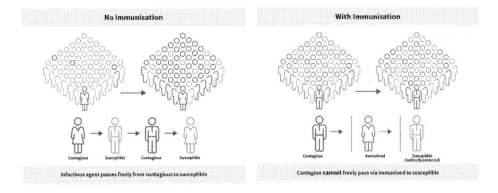

Fig. 7.1 Herd immunity protects the individual and the community (CBHS Health Fund, 2017)

vaccination issued by the state. Nonetheless, society requires individuals to take responsibility for their fellow human beings.

Historical experience has shown that vaccination has a significant effect in the fight against infectious diseases. Today's social, cultural, and economic status would not have evolved without vaccination (Greenwood, 2014). Consequently, the population should know that vaccines have a primary role in the field of prevention. Therefore, individuals should not neglect their own social responsibility in the form of declining immunization because their attitude would endanger other members of the society. A social optimum cannot be reached this way. It is of public interest to prevent the transmission of highly infectious pathogens or the possible spread of diseases which have already been classified as eliminated. Vaccination is necessary if it is effective, safe, and can prevent a communicable disease. It has advantages both for individuals and for society.

From an economic point of view, mandatory vaccination would reduce morbidity rate and thus lower costs.

7.3   Ethical Aspects

Immunization is associated with positive and negative effects. The individual faces tension between personal, social, and economic interests. It should be considered from the unvaccinated person's point of view whether and to what extent he could deal with possible complications if contracting the disease. The second consideration should relate to the own social responsibility, i.e. which consequences the actions could have for other members of society. First, considering medical ethics, the actions of individuals related to diseases and health are examined. In this regard, the fundamental values of medical actions are explained: the well-being of the individual, because high vaccination coverage results in the well-being of the community, the principle of no harm, meaning that vaccination prevents the transmission of the disease to other people, as well as the damage to one's own health, and moreover, the principles of patient autonomy, justice, and human dignity (Boyd, 2005). Detailed explanation and information should be given by doctors in a way that the patient decides in favor of immunization. The physician's action is mainly based on the principle of no harm. Concerning the principle of patient autonomy, the decision of the patient for non-vaccination must be respected by the doctor, although the doctor knows that a vaccinated patient would act according to the principle of care. The asymmetry of competence between the physician advising the patient and the patient seeking for advice should be resolved or optimally adjusted in the direction of symmetry. Immunization can only be carried out based on informed consent. As a guideline, the best possible information must be given by the doctor. This means that the efficacy, the side effects, and the possible harm must be examined and communicated to the patient adequately. It is the indispensable condition for immunization and the expression of respect for autonomy on behalf of physicians (Markose et al., 2016).

Second, regarding public health ethics, the relationship between individuals and governmental measures as well as institutions being active in the health sector, remains in focus. In this context, the actions of an individual have an impact on other individuals, at the same time, every individual is affected by the actions of other individuals. For this reason, interventions and measures should address the whole population (Thomas et al., 2002). Immunization against measles leads to controversial discussions, because it is uncertain whether and to what extent health authorities or the state may influence the attitude of individuals in the interest of public health. In this regard, the freedom of action and the self-determination of individuals are opposed to the protection of society and the public. On this basis, the question arises whether social interests can be placed above the interests of individuals. If the individual does not fulfill his social responsibility, i.e. vaccinate, society must consider several risk factors about a possible spread of the disease. Additionally, high treatment costs arise because of complications due to unvaccination, which are to be borne by other contributors based on the principle of solidarity (Coggon & AM Viens, 2017).

Third, the aspects of utilitarianism play a role which focus on the evaluation of the consequences of an action. In addition to the individual benefit, the benefit for the whole, i.e. the population, will be considered. In this context, the focus of action is the increase of general well-being (WHO, 2017). According to the principles of utilitarianism, an individual who does not vaccinate, will also consider the consequences of the declination of immunization. In this case, he will think about whether the decision leads to good or evil for himself and for others. The benefit for the individual would be lifelong immunity with low risks of vaccination complications or side effects if vaccinated. On the other hand, in case of non-vaccination, an infection cannot be excluded despite herd immunity - even as an adult. In this case, the costs of the complications (both health and material) could outweigh the benefits for the individual (Mack, 2004). The social discussion indicates that ethical issues regarding vaccination can only be answered by responsible individual and social action. On the basis of utilitarianism, benefits and costs should be weighed up and the consequences of one's own decision should be considered; both by the state in the case of the introduction of a mandatory vaccination and by the opponents with regard to causing damage to other members of the society (Mandal et al., 2016).

7.3.1 Why do People Decline Immunization?

The individual is confronted with the question of how he should behave or why one does not want to be vaccinated. One will be accused of irresponsible action when declining immunization, because non-vaccination contributes to the spread of the disease and prevents elimination. However, individual beliefs, the possible fear of vaccination or the side effects, i.e. vaccination risks, are important when deciding. In case of declining, the individual's attitude takes precedence over social responsibility. The balance between morally good and morally evil is subjective; the individual decides against vaccination to the best of his knowledge and conscience. At the same time, the question arises: what the individual should do in order to not contract measles or spread it if unvaccinated and contagious. The consequences should be considered in terms of moral standards, the individual himself is responsible for the consequences of non-vaccination. If deciding not to vaccinate, the own personal immunity against the disease as well as social responsibility will be ignored. In the intrapersonal conflict of action, the individual is confronted with the task of weighing up the advantages and disadvantages of his actions and the consequences of his final decision. With the decision for non-vaccination, the individual decides for accepting the risk of contracting the disease - probably with complications - in the future. These consequences are acceptable and mean that they do not let their freedom or self-determination out of their hands.

The dilemma of action related to non-vaccination will be generated in a field of tension between different information. The individual is informed about both the advantages and the disadvantages of immunization. Nonetheless, in the decision-making process, the individual relies on subjectively formal motives like virtues, intentions, previous experiences and conscience, and on laws and/or predominant norms which apply in the society at the objective material level. The individual weighs goods and evils sovereignly, both in the decision for the vaccination and the declination of it to the end that the decision turns out as morally good and correct as possible. The individual alone will be responsible for the consequences of his decision which can be predictable, meaning that there are no side effects on the day after vaccination; or unpredictable, i.e. contracting measles with severe complications sooner or later if unvaccinated. As a short-term consequence, avoiding rash and as a long-term one, no long-term or lifelong immunity against measles, and the risk of contracting the disease as an adult should be considered. Lifelong immunity after vaccination, herd immunity and social responsibility for fellow human beings are not relevant for people declining vaccination. They cannot reach a compromise, because the decision can only be made either/or.

7.3.2   What Should be Done?—No Clear Recommendations Regarding Immunization are Possible

Communicable diseases have decreased significantly during the last hundred years. As a result, vaccinations and hygiene measures lost importance for morbidity and mortality among the population. In previous times, interventions in the self-determination of individuals could have been justified with the protection of the public or the community. Nowadays, the situation is different. It is controversial whether health authorities may, can or should intervene in the private sphere or individual lifestyles to protect society. Public health and individual self-determination conflict regarding mandatory vaccination. In this context, ethics should provide individuals with criteria to make the best possible moral decision. However, the introduction of mandatory vaccination in Germany, which would be desirable from a public health perspective, could address the challenge and enable positive effects in the foreseeable future. Public interest should be put in the focus if new outbreaks divide society (Field, 2008). The arguments of opponents can only be rebutted by means of legal regulations in case of emergencies (e.g. endemics or epidemics). Media coverage of the risks and the complications after vaccination and that of non-vaccination should be influenced in a way that a higher vaccination coverage can be achieved on voluntary basis. Additionally, in the setting of health facilities, prophylactic measures should be reconsidered concerning both the vaccination status of employees and the dealing with contagious patients. Without exact data on the vaccination status of employees, a possible transmission of the disease to patients cannot be excluded in healthcare facilities and vice versa.

Contagious diseases like measles can be prevented by individual action. If no individual steps will be taken, the individual may die. Mandatory vaccination could prevent serious complications or deaths. However, the question arises whether the self-determination of individuals or the protection against infectious diseases has priority. The principles of no harm and patient autonomy compete in this regard. Moreover, the introduction of mandatory vaccination would violate the principle of freedom and autonomy. Mandatory vaccination should not be the first choice, but voluntary immunization through intensified information campaigns should be facilitated. Thus, vaccination refusers should be persuaded to comply with social responsibility and vaccinate. In the interest of public health, the decisions on vaccination recommendations and programs should be clarified further. Raising the awareness for the benefits of immunization and the need for closing vaccination gaps could lead to achieving the goal of eliminating measles as set by the WHO. Futhermore, vaccination coverage could be increased through proactive government action. Education, incentives and the promotion of immunization could have a positive impact on voluntary vaccination which facilitate ethical decision-making for individuals.

The elimination of measles will remain a challenge in countries where immunization is not mandatory, e.g. Germany. The cooperation between public health authorities, policymakers, doctors, and the population is inevitable to combat the disease in all cooperation countries of the ArDa project. In addition to the development of action plans and recommendations, measures will be needed to reduce prejudice and anti-vaccination attitudes triggering transmission in the case of outbreaks. Disparities indicate that there is a need for the improvement of measures to increase coverage and access, thus ensuring the benefit of vaccination for the population. A viral infection with complications, which can no longer be regarded merely as a childhood disease, could be eradicated as a problem of the health-care system through vaccination, which should be used as a main approach and primary preventive measure.

References

Biellik, R., Davidkin, I., Esposito, S., Lobanov, A., Kojouharova, M., Pfaff, G., Santos, J. I., Simpson, J., Mamou, M. B., Butler, R., Deshevoi, S., Huseynov, S., Jankovic, D., & Shefer, A. (2016). Slow progress. In finalizing measles and rubella elimination in the European region. *Health Aff (millwood), 35*, 322–326. https://doi.org/10.1377/hlthaff.2015.1055

Botás, E. (2016). Globális népirtás a kötelező védőoltások segítségével? - Interjú dr. Novák Hunorral. http://www.life.hu/csalad/20160630-interju-dr-novak-hunorral-a-kotelezo-vedooltasokrol-es-oltasellenessegrol.html. Accessed 25 Nov 2018.

Boyd, K. M. (2005). Medical ethics: Principles, persons, and perspectives: From controversy to conversation. *Journal of Medical Ethics, 31*, 481–486. https://doi.org/10.1136/jme.2003.005710

Bozzola, E., Spina, G., Russo, R., Bozzola, M., Corsello, G., & Villani, A. (2018). Mandatory vaccinations in European countries, undocumented information, false news and the impact on vaccination uptake: The position of the Italian pediatric society. *Italian Journal of Pediatrics, 44*,. https://doi.org/10.1186/s13052-018-0504-y

Bundesministerium für Gesundheit. (2015). Nationaler Aktionsplan 2015–2020 zur Elimination der Masern und Röteln in Deutschland: Hintergründe, Ziele und Strategien. https://www.gmkonline.de/documents/Aktionsplan_Masern_Roeteln_2.pdf. Accessed 2 Dec 2018.

CBHS Health Fund. (2017). Herd immunity | How vaccinations protect children and save lives. https://www.cbhs.com.au/health-well-being-blog/blog-article/2017/06/22/how-herd-immunity-works. Accessed 25 Nov 2018.

Coggon, J., & Viens, A. M. (2017). Public health ethics in practice: A background paper on public health ethics for the UK publich health skills and knowledge framework. https://assets.publishing.service.gov.uk/government/uploads/system/uploads/attachment_data/file/609620/PHSKF_public_health_ethics_in_practice.pdf. Accessed 25 Nov 2018.

Datta, S. S., O'Connor, P. M., Jankovic, D., Muscat, M., Ben Mamou, M. C., Singh, S., Kaloumenos, T., Reef, S., Papania, M., & Butler, R. (2018). Progress and challenges in measles and rubella elimination in the WHO European Region. *Vaccine, 36*, 5408–5415. https://doi.org/10.1016/j.vaccine.2017.06.042

Deutsche Akademie für Kinder- und Jugendmedizin e. V. (2017). Pressemitteilung "Pädiater warnen vor gefährlichen Masernerkrankungen". https://www.dakj.de/pressemitteilungen/pressemitteilung-paediater-warnen-vor-gefaehrlichen-masernerkrankungen/. Accessed 25 Nov 2018.

ECDC. (n. d.). Vaccine scheduler: Bulgaria and Hungary. https://vaccine-schedule.ecdc.europa.eu/Scheduler/ByCountries?SelectedCountry1Id=35&SelectedCountry2Id=95&IncludeChildAgeGroup=true&IncludeChildAgeGroup=false&IncludeAdultAgeGroup=true&IncludeAdultAgeGroup=false. Accessed 25 Nov 2018.

ECDC. (2017). Vaccine scheduler: Germany. https://vaccine-schedule.ecdc.europa.eu/Scheduler/ByCountry?SelectedCountryId=6&IncludeChildAgeGroup=true&IncludeChildAgeGroup=false&IncludeAdultAgeGroup=true&IncludeAdultAgeGroup=false. Accessed 25 Nov 2018.

ECDC. (2018). European immunization week. https://ecdc.europa.eu/en/news-events/european-immunization-week-2018. Accessed 10 Oct 2018.

Eichner, L., Wjst, S., Brockmann, S. O., Wolfers, K., & Eichner, M. (2017). Local measles vaccination gaps in Germany and the role of vaccination providers. *BMC Public Health, 17*, 656. https://doi.org/10.1186/s12889-017-4663-3

European Forum for Vaccine Vigilance. (n. d.). Hungary. https://www.efvv.eu/hungary-2-2/#bg. Accessed 10 October 2018.

Field, R. I. (2008). Vaccine declinations present new challenges for public health. *Pharmacy and Therapeutics, 33*, 542–543.

Greenwood, B. (2014). The contribution of vaccination to global health: Past, present and future. *Philosophical Transactions of the Royal Society of London. Series b, Biological Sciences, 369*, 20130433. https://doi.org/10.1098/rstb.2013.0433

Holt, E. (2018). 41 000 measles cases in Europe since the beginning of 2018. *The Lancet, 392*, 724. https://doi.org/10.1016/S0140-6736(18)32031-2

Hübschen, J. M., Bork, S. M., Brown, K. E., Mankertz, A., Santibanez, S., Mamou, M. B., Mulders, M. N., & Muller, C. P. (2017). Challenges of measles and rubella laboratory diagnostic in the era of elimination. *Clinical Microbiology & Infection, 23*, 511–515. https://doi.org/10.1016/j.cmi.2017.04.009

IHME. (2017a). Bulgaria. http://www.healthdata.org/bulgaria. Accessed 25 Nov 2018.

IHME. (2017b). Hungary. http://www.healthdata.org/hungary. Accessed 25 Nov 2018.

Kurchatova, A., Krumova, S., Vladimirova, N., Nikolaeva-Glomb, L., Stoyanova, A., Kantardjiev, T., & Gatcheva, N. (2017). Preliminary findings indicate nosocomial transmission and Roma population as most affected group in ongoing measles B3 genotype outbreak in Bulgaria, March to August 2017. *Eurosurveillance Weekly, 22*,. https://doi.org/10.2807/1560-7917.ES.2017.22.36.30611

Lengyel, G., Marossy, A., Ánosi, N., Farkas, S. L., Kele, B., Nemes-Nikodém, É., Szentgyörgyi, V., Kopcsó, I., & Mátyus, M. (2018). Screening of more than 2000 Hungarian healthcare workers' anti-measles antibody level: results and possible population-level consequences. *Epidemiol Infect*, 1–5. https://doi.org/10.1017/S0950268818002571.

Mack, P. (2004). Utilitarian ethics in healthcare. http://www.ijcim.th.org/past_editions/2004V12N3/ijcimv3n1_article6.pdf. Accessed 25 Nov 2018.

Mandal, J., Ponnambath, D. K., & Parija, S. C. (2016). Utilitarian and deontological ethics in medicine. *Tropical Parasitology, 6*, 5–7. https://doi.org/10.4103/2229-5070.175024

Markose, A., Krishnan, R., & Ramesh, M. (2016). Medical ethics. *Journal of Pharmacy and Bioallied Sciences, 8*, S1-4. https://doi.org/10.4103/0975-7406.191934

Matysiak-Klose, D., & Wicker, S. (2017). Masern in Deutschland – Epidemiologie und Management (Measles in Germany: An Epidemiological Analysis and First Measures for Containment). *Deutsche Medizinische Wochenschrift, 142*, 1767–1772. https://doi.org/10.1055/s-0043-117973

Muscat, M., Marinova, L., Mankertz, A., Gatcheva, N., Mihneva, Z., Santibanez, S., Kunchev, A., Filipova, R., & Kojouharova, M. (2016). The measles outbreak in Bulgaria, 2009–2011: An epidemiological assessment and lessons learnt. *Eurosurveillance Weekly, 21*, 30152. https://doi.org/10.2807/1560-7917.ES.2016.21.9.30152

Nemzeti Népegészségügyi Központ. (n. d.). Vacsatc - Oltásbiztonság | Lakossági oldalak | Védőoltások bevezetése és főbb változásai Magyarországon. http://www.vacsatc.hu/?V%C3%A9d%C3%B5olt%C3%A1sok-bevezet%C3%A9se-%C3%A9s-f%C3%B5bb-v%C3%A1ltoz%C3%A1sai-Magyarorsz%C3%A1gon&pid=121. Accessed 25 Nov 2018.

Nemzeti Népegészségügyi Központ. (2018). Vacsatc - Oltásbiztonság | Lakossági oldalak | Gyermekkori védőoltások. http://www.vacsatc.hu/?Gyermekkori-v%C3%A9d%C3%B5olt%C3%A1sok&pid=24. Accessed 25 Nov 2018.

OECD. (2017a). Bulgaria: Country health profile 2017. https://read.oecd-ilibrary.org/social-issues-migration-health/bulgaria-country-health-profile-2017_9789264283305-en#page1. Accessed 2 Dec 2018.

OECD. (2017b). Hungary: Country health profile 2017. https://www.oecd-ilibrary.org/docserver/9789264283411-en.pdf?expires=1539189265&id=id&accname=guest&checksum=4FEDB4AFE57D41A7A3254EB52F14678A. Accessed 10 Oct 2018.

Orosz, L., Gáspár, G., Rózsa, Á., Rákos, N., Sziveri, S., & Bosnyákovits, T. (2018). Epidemiological situation of measles in Romania, Italy, and Hungary: On what threats should we focus nowadays? *Acta Microbiologica Et Immunologica Hungarica, 65*, 127–134. https://doi.org/10.1556/030.65.2018.014

Paul-Ehrlich-Institut. (2017). Aktuelle Informationen zu Masernimpfstoffen. https://www.pei.de/DE/arzneimittel/impfstoff-impfstoffe-fuer-den-menschen/masern/aktuell/masern-impfstoffe-aktuell-node.html. Accessed 10 Oct 2018.

ProCon.org. (2018). Should any vaccines be required for children? https://vaccines.procon.org/. Accessed 11 Dec 2018.

Radosveta, F. (2011). Bulgarian national immunisation program. http://www.vhpb.org/files/html/Meetings_and_publications/Presentations/SOFS22.pdf. Accessed 10 Oct 2018.

Rigó, Z., Szomor, K. N., Nagy, O., & Takács, M. (2012). Are we protected? Imported measles - On the way to eradication. *Acta Microbiologica Et Immunologica Hungarica, 59*, 119–129. https://doi.org/10.1556/AMicr.59.2012.1.12

Robert Koch-Institut. (2015). Masern, Mumps, Röteln - Der Berliner Masernausbruch aus Sicht des Nationalen Referenzzentrums Masern, Mumps, Röteln. https://www.rki.de/DE/Content/Infekt/NRZ/MMR/Berliner_Masernausbruch_aus_Sicht_des_NRZ.ht. Accessed 10 Oct 2018.

Robert Koch-Institut. (2016a). Bedeutung von Impfungen - Antworten des Robert Koch-Instituts und des Paul-Ehrlich-Instituts zu den 20 häufigsten Einwänden gegen das Impfen. https://www.rki.de/DE/Content/Infekt/Impfen/Bedeutung/Schutzimpfungen_20_Einwaende.html#doc2378400bodyText14. Accessed 10 Oct 2018.

Robert Koch-Institut. (2016b). Ergänzende Informationen - Übersicht der Infektionserkrankungen und erforderliche Maßnahmen als Grundlage für Festlegungen im Hygieneplan. https://www.rki.de/DE/Content/Infekt/Krankenhaushygiene/Kommission/Ergaenzende_Informationen/Tabelle_Infketionserkr_Ma%C3%9Fnahm_Elsevier.html. Accessed 25 Nov 2018.

Robert Koch-Institut. (2017). Impfungen A - Z - Schutzimpfung gegen Masern. https://www.rki.de/DE/Content/Infekt/Impfen/ImpfungenAZ/MMR_Masern/Masern.html. Accessed 10 Oct 2018.

Robert Koch-Institut. (2018). Aktuelle Epidemiologie der Masern in Deutschland. *Krankenhaus-Hygiene + Infektionsverhütung, 325*–330. https://doi.org/10.1016/j.khinf.2018.09.001.

Schadwinkel, A., & Stockrahm, S. (2015). Masern: Schluss mit den Masern-Mythen! https://www.zeit.de/wissen/gesundheit/2015-02/masern-impfung-risiko. Accessed 10 Oct 2018.

Seguliev, Z., Duric, P., Petrovic, V., Stefanovic, S., Cosic, G., Hrnjakovic, I. C., Milosevic, V., Karagiannis, I., Boxall, N., & Jankovic, D. (2007). Current measles outbreak in Serbia: A preliminary report. *Eurosurveillance Weekly, 12*(E070315), 2.

The College of Physicians of Philadelphia (2018a). Ethical issues and vaccines | History of vaccines. https://www.historyofvaccines.org/content/articles/ethical-issues-and-vaccines. Accessed 13 Dec 2018.

The College of Physicians of Philadelphia (2018b). Misconceptions about vaccines | History of vaccines. https://www.historyofvaccines.org/content/articles/misconceptions-about-vaccines. Accessed 13 Dec 2018.

Thomas, J. C., Sage, M., Dillenberg, J., & Guillory, V. J. (2002). A code of ethics for public health. *American Journal of Public Health, 92*, 1057–1059.

WHO. (2012). Global measles & rubella strategic plan. http://apps.who.int/iris/bitstream/handle/10665/44855/9789241503396_eng.pdf;jsessionid=202CD8144B185003026C1E20A784F47F?sequence=1. Accessed 10 Oct 2018.

WHO. (2014). European vaccine action plan 2015–2020. http://www.euro.who.int/__data/assets/pdf_file/0007/255679/WHO_EVAP_UK_v30_WEBx.

pdf?ua=1&bcsi_scan_7c94624addd45e46=0&bcsi_scan_filename=WHO_EVAP_UK_v30_WEBx.pdf. Accessed 25 Nov 2018.

WHO. (2017). Core health indicators in the WHO European region 2017. http://www.euro.who.int/__data/assets/pdf_file/0005/346325/CHI_EN_WEB.pdf?ua=1. Accessed 10 Oct 2018.

WHO. (2018a). Assessment report of the Global vaccine action plan. http://www.who.int/immunization/en/. Accessed 25 Nov 2018.

WHO. (2018b). Country slides measles: Country slides measles. http://www.who.int/immunization/monitoring_surveillance/burden/vpd/surveillance_type/Country_slides_measles.pdf?ua=1. Accessed 10 Oct 2018.

WHO. (2018c). Measles. https://www.who.int/immunization/diseases/measles/en/. Accessed 25 Nov 2018.

WHO Regional Office for Europe. (2018a). Measles and rubella elimination country profile, Bulgaria. http://www.euro.who.int/__data/assets/pdf_file/0009/367731/mr-cp-bulgaria-eng.pdf?ua=1. Accessed 10 Oct 2018.

WHO Regional Office for Europe. (2018b). Measles and rubella elimination country profile, Hungary. http://www.euro.who.int/__data/assets/pdf_file/004/367753/mr-cp-hungary-eng.pdf?ua=1. Accessed 10 Oct 2018.

Lessons from the Creation and Failure of Two Regional Cooperation Models in the Hungarian Health System

8

Eva Orosz

Contents

8.1 Introduction 122
8.2 The Health Service Delivery Modernisation project 124
    8.2.1 Precedents: The Failure of Attempts to Restructure Health Care Delivery 124
    8.2.2 An Innovative Approach to Tackle the Problems of the Health Care Delivery 125
    8.2.3 Key Ideas and Implementation of the HSDM-Tender 126
    8.2.4 Most Important Results 128
8.3 The Managed Care Scheme 128
    8.3.1 Main Problems of the Family Physician Service in the mid-1990's 129
    8.3.2 Key Features of the MCS 130
    8.3.3 Experiences with the MCS Pilot 132
    8.3.4 Review by the State of Audit Office 133
8.4 Success and Failure Factors of the Attempts for Building New Institutional Structures. . . 133
    8.4.1 Success Factors 134
    8.4.2 Factors Having Led to the Failure of the HSDM Project[9] 135
    8.4.3 Factors Having Led to the Failure of MCS 136
8.5 Final remarks 138
References. 139

Abstract

The paper analyses on the one hand the factors outside and within the Hungarian health system that made possible the formation of the following cooperation models

E. Orosz (✉)
Faculty of Social Sciences, Eötvös Loránd University Budapest, Budapest, Hungary
e-mail: orosz.eva@tatk.elte.hu

M. Cassens et al. (eds.), *Transdisciplinary Perspectives on Public Health in Europe*,
FOM-Edition, https://doi.org/10.1007/978-3-658-33740-7_8

and on the other hand the factors resulting in their failure. The Managed Care Scheme (MSC) was introduced as a pilot project in 1999 with elements similar to the UK GP fundholding scheme. By 2015 eighteen provider groups operated under the scheme. Their mixed experiences, however, provided a pretext for attacks by the opposing interest groups. The MCS was eliminated in 2008. Under Health Service Delivery Modernization Program (HSDM) financed from a World Bank loan in 1997–98, a pilot region consisting of three or four counties was to be selected through a competition and substantial financial support was envisaged for service restructuring. Although five regional consortia covering the whole country were formed and applications were submitted and evaluated when the new government came to power in September 1998 it declared the tender null and void. The lessons from the story of both the HSDM and MCS are relevant even today not only from a historical point of view. Weak coordination among health care providers is still one of the major problems hindering the improvement in efficiency and quality. The management of patient pathways is still missing from the day-to-day operation of the Hungarian health care system. The lessons are, however, even more important from an institutional point of view—as they highlight weaknesses hindering the capacity of the Hungarian health care system to improve its performance.

8.1   Introduction

Care-coordination in health systems has been on the agenda of many OECD countries for the past decades. It seems obvious that care coordination can improve quality and efficiency. The experiences, however, show that implementation of effective coordination is hindered by several factors. "For almost all countries, there are systematic problems with co-ordination of care for patients with chronic illness." (OECD, 2010, p. 129). For several reasons, new institutions or regulations aimed at coordination among providers or care-coordination for given chronic diseases have not been among the key priorities of reform programs prepared by the governments in Hungary. The two experimental projects discussed in this paper came to the scene from outside.

The paper analyses the creation and failure of two regional cooperation models that were initiated in the Hungarian health care system at the end of the 1990s. As most of the back then structural problems of the health care system have been persisted or even worsened, the key ideas of these reform attempts can be also regarded relevant today. The Health Service Delivery Modernization Programme (HSDM) was a component of a health-specific loan provided by the World Bank in the second half of the 1990s: it intended to introduce strategic planning and cooperation at macro-regional level. The Managed Care Scheme (MCS) was introduced as a pilot project in 1999 with elements partly similar to the UK GP fundholding schemes, partly to the American Health

Maintenance Organizations (HMOs): it intended to introduce care-coordination at the micro-level.

In general terms, three major factors have influenced the transformation of the Hungarian health-care system: exogenous factors (i.e., socio-economic transition); path-dependency by the state-socialist health system; and health policy innovation. Both the MCS and HSDM can be regarded as health policy innovation. The long-lasting crisis of the state-socialist healthcare system was characterised by four fundamental problems, which together led to the poor performance of the sector: (i) the subordination of the health-care sector to economic production that led to decades of low growth of health expenditure; (ii) the exclusive role of the State in the formal system, and, as its 'flip-side', the 'second economy' of health care (i.e. under-the-table payments); (iii) command and control governance, and as its 'flip-side', the great role of informal bargaining; and (iv) a lack of personal choice and voice for the users of the formal system. Largely insep-arable from each other, these problems together accounted for most of the weaknesses of the system. Reforms started in 1989–90 in the health-care system can be understood as attempts for the destruction of old institutions and the creation of new ones compatible with the new political and economic regime. The cooperation models discussed in this paper can be regarded as such kind of new institutions.

The paper intends to go beyond the description of the professional ideas of the HSDM and MCS—it focuses, on the one hand, the factors outside and within the Hungarian health system that made possible the formation of the two regional cooperation mod-els and, on the other hand, the factors that resulted in their failure. The socio-economic and political circumstances forced and also hindered health care reforms at the same time. The Hungarian economy experienced prolonged stagnation and large fiscal deficit and public debt in the 1980s and the early 1990s (Bokros, 1998). It was exacerbated by the transitional crisis in the economy that accompanied the political transition of 1989–1990. The Gross Domestic Product (GDP) continuously decreased between 1988 and 1993. The real GDP in 1993 was lower by 18 percent than in 1988. As a consequence, Hungary`s public finances sharply deteriorated.[1] By the mid-1990s, it had become obvi-ous that the socio-economic transformation, including the reform of the health-care sys-tem, would involve a far longer and more painful process than had been expected. To avoid the fiscal crisis, the Government implemented a radical fiscal adjustment in 1995. The Government's radical economic stabilisation measures rather than the situation of the health sector determined that the key priorities for this period were to reduce pub-lic spending on health. There were no financial resources available for a comprehen-sive health care reform. Public expenditure on health decreased from 6.0% of GDP in

---

[1]The budget deficit reached 8.4 percent of the GDP in 1994, with the general government debt amounting to about 90 percent of the GDP (Barabás et al., 1998).

1992 to 4.9% in 1998.[2] The post-1997 economic growth—that followed the successful economic stabilization—generated increasing budgetary revenues, which could have provided financial resources for modernisation of the health care system. The governments (regardless the ruling political parties), however, failed to utilise the opportunity provided by the improving economy. The share of public resources devoted to the health sector (as percentage of the GDP) continued to decrease: from 4.9% in 1998 to 4.6% in 2001. Meanwhile day-to-day disturbances further intensified and the trust among health personnel and the population further eroded, modernisation of the health system had been at standstill since the mid-1990s.

8.2   The Health Service Delivery Modernisation project

8.2.1   Precedents: The Failure of Attempts to Restructure Health Care Delivery

Reforms in the health sector already started in 1988–89 and continued along similar concepts after the political transition. Private practice and enterprises were authorised; tax-based funding was switched to compulsory social health insurance; ownership of health facilities within the public sector was transferred to local governments; Family Physician Service (FPS) was created and capitation-based payment introduced; outpatient care remuneration based partly on a fee-for-service scheme, and hospital care remuneration based on DRG-type scheme were introduced. However, many underlying causes—often interdependent—of inadequate performance persisted or were created by the new reforms: an outdated and unbalanced hospital-network and structure of health care delivery (e.g. a dominant role of inpatient care, little use of day-surgery, a limited role for group-practice in primary care, etc.); perverse efficiency incentives for providers (e.g. provider payment methods and the system of under-the-table payment worked against the replacement of inpatient care by other forms of healthcare); uncoordinated service delivery (e.g. weak gatekeeping role of general practitioners (GPs); lack of co-ordination in the treatment of chronic diseases, etc.); lack of incentives and tools for the Health Insurance Fund Administration (HIFA) to act as an effective purchasing agent; lack of incentives and autonomy for hospital managers to improve efficiency (across the vertical spectrum of care); and overall, deficiencies in the governance of the healthcare system throughout the whole transition period (Orosz & Burns, 2000).

At the beginning of the 1990s, it was expected that the introduction of DRG-based financing would be able to mitigate the problems of the hospital sector. When the failure

---

[2]Per capita public spending on health was lower (in real value) by 6 percent in 1998 than it was in1992; and only by 2 percent higher in 2001 than it was in 1992. Source of data: OECD Health Data 2018.

of this concept was realised, a centrally planned bed reduction programme was initiated. At the beginning of 1994, the Ministry of Welfare (MoW) attempted to dictate the number of beds required in each hospital. After meeting with widespread opposition, this programme was replaced by a somewhat more flexible approach in 1996. However, the hospital restructuring process lost credibility and the persistence of excess capacity, particularly in acute hospital care continued to be a major cause of inefficiency and financial shortage.

8.2.2 An Innovative Approach to Tackle the Problems of the Health Care Delivery

Under the circumstances described above there was a need and an opportunity also for a new and innovative approach. As already mentioned, the HSDM was a sub-component of a health-sector modernization project financed by a loan from the World Bank—a model experiment for creating regional organisation of health care services (World Bank, 2001). The concept was developed by a project-team (a unit within the World Bank Project Office of the MoW). To select the model region, a public tender was launched in August 1997. Five regional consortia that consisted of the hospitals and main stakeholders of three or four counties and covered the whole country were formed. They prepared and submitted their HSDM proposal in March 1998. Evaluation was made and the winner regional consortia selected in April 1998. However, this coincided in time with the campaign period of the national election. The Minister of Health decided not to declare the results.[3] The government that came into power in 1998 June decided to stop the HSDM project and gave up this component of the WB loan. In the following the paper briefly summarises the concept and the implementation process of HSDM-tender focusing on the success factors and expectations. The factors having led to the failure of the project are summarized at the end of the paper.

Concept of the HSDM Project

The HSDM project intended to introduce two major functions at the regional level: strategic planning and co-ordination of service restructuring. These were new functions which had not been effectively addressed at county level. Furthermore, it was realized that economic and technological factors tended to make the regional level as most appropriate to fulfil these functions. International experience suggested that regions with 1–3 million population had the optimum size to develop a health care system providing the

---

[3]Between 1994 and 1998 the coalition of the Hungarian Socialist Party (MSZP) and the Free Democrats (SZDSZ) was in power. In 1998, the party of Young Democrats (FIDESZ) in coalition with the Hungarian Democratic Forum (MDF) and the Independent Smallholders Party (FKGP) came into power.

entire comprehensive package of services in a co-ordinated, efficient way. Priorities of the HSDM project were:

- replacement of hospitalisation (in professionally justified cases) with one day surgical treatment, ambulant care, family doctor's service, home care and social assistance, as well as nursing homes and social care institutions;
- elaboration of optimum "patient pathways" within the regions. Development of an attitude and practice for continuous and co-ordinated provision of health services— extending from prevention to rehabilitation- for the most important chronic illnesses;
- improvement of quality and efficiency in the hospital service delivery system of the region. Improvement of the distribution of activities between the hospitals in the region, and development of optimum activity structure within the hospitals.

The HSDM project intended to finance a regional project consisting of 4–6 specific service improvement programs aiming at the priorities mentioned above. It was also realized that the regional approach and organisation of the health service delivery required new financial incentives. The main incentives for the regional consortia was that savings resulting from the regional restructuring and coordination of health care delivery were declared to remain in the region and be used or reinvested there. The region implementing the project was to be given a regional sub-budget, separated within the national Health Insurance Fund budget, in order to ensure that savings generated by modernisation would be kept in the region. The regional budget was to be set according to the capitation method adjusted to the age-structure of the region.

8.2.3   Key Ideas and Implementation of the HSDM-Tender

The way of implementation envisaged had several innovative elements. The HSDM project was designed to apply a bottom up, grass root approach for modernisation of health service delivery, promoting a dialogue between the relevant stakeholders in the region. The project as a model experiment was to be implemented by a self-organised region which was to be selected through open competition. The declared plan was that—based on experience gained from this experiment -, the regional organisation of health care delivery would be initiated in other regions of Hungary too, ultimately covering the whole country. The World Bank was ready to provide additional loan in case of successful implementation of the experiment. Although the implementation of the model project did not start, it is worthwhile to analyse the key ideas and the implementation of the tender.

Following a short preparatory period, the implementation of the HSDM project started in August, 1997. A complex implementation and supervisory arrangement were established, a detailed tender documentation was prepared, issued and provided wide publicity (Ministry of Welfare, 1997). As a response to the tender invitation, five regional consortia were self-organised and submitted their proposals in March 1998.

The eligibility criteria for a Regional consortium were as follows: the region had to include a minimum of two counties, with a total population between 900.000 and 3 million. Budapest was considered as one county; the consortium had to include at least all the county public health authorities, county governments and medical universities/county hospitals, and county health insurance offices in the region. The following five regional consortia were formed by mid-September of 1997 and all of them submitted the required documents in March of 1998:

- Regional Health Consortium of Southern Trans-Danubia
- Regional Health Improvement Consortium of the Southern Great Plain
- „For Health" Regional Health Consortium of North-East Hungary
- Regional Health Consortium of Budapest and Pest, Heves and Nógrád Counties
- "Felso-Pannon" Health Improvement Consortium

The regional consortia elaborated two documents:

- (1) Regional Health Improvement Strategy (Strategic Plan) made up of:
  - a Health Plan that provided a comprehensive picture of the health status of the population of the region and of the major factors influencing it as well as containing a program of actions aimed to improve the health status of the population of the region which envisaged the participation of local governments, non-governmental organisations, health service personnel and the State Public Health Autority (ÁNTSZ); and
  - a Regional Health Service Restructuring Plan that analysed the situation of curative/preventive services and provided a medium-term program for the modernisation of health care services.

These documents were expected to ensure that the concrete programmes to be financed were in line with a long-term strategic plan for the region concerned.

(2) Specific Service Improvement Programs (IV-VI), to be financed by the project. These programs had to be in line with the Regional Restructuring Plan. The evaluation committee ranked the Consortium of the Southern Great Plain as the winner. This consortium planned the following service improvement programs:

I. Replacement of hospitalisation (in professionally justified cases) with one day surgical treatment, nursing homes and social institutions, ambulatory care, family doctor's service, home care and social assistance
II. Improvement of quality and efficiency in the hospital service delivery system of the region

III. Development of optimum „patient routes" in the case of mental health services within the region

IV. Development of optimum „patient routes" in the case of maternal and child care within the region

V. Development of optimum „patient routes" in the case of cardio-vascular diseases within the region

VI. Development of optimum „patient routes" in the case of cancer care within the region

8.2.4   Most Important Results

The objectives of the HSDM project were well-received by the local actors of the health care system. The establishment of the regional consortia covering the whole country showed the positive reception by the majority of the stakeholders. It was the first time in the history of the Hungarian health care system when three or more counties, their leading institutions and the medical universities had started a formal co-operation in the interests of developing joint health strategy.

The HSDM mobilized groups of experts and considerable intellectual energies in the regions who had knowledge and ideas concerning how to tackle the problems of health care delivery in their regions. Regional think tanks were formed during a few months. They were able to adapt the detailed guidelines (issued together with the call for tender) for preparing the regional strategic plans and service improvement programs to the specific circumstances in the given region. Neither before nor afterwards were such complex health programs prepared at regional level in Hungary. The HSDM programmes could have provided the starting points and the professional basis for a longer-term modernization process of the health care delivery system. In a wider sense, the HSDM project could have generated changes in the health care management culture and the decision-making mechanisms. However, it was stopped just one year after its start. The factors having led to its failure are discussed at the end of the paper.

8.3   The Managed Care Scheme

The initiative of the Managed Care Scheme (MCS) was an attempt to reform the health care system by focusing on primary care and changes at micro-level. It was inspired partly by the UK GP fundholding scheme and partly by the American HMOs, but it also had several elements developed by Hungarian experts (Gaál et al., 2011). Main goals were to provide financial incentives to health care providers to coordinate their activities across primary care, outpatient and inpatient care for a population living in a geographically defined area, and hence improve efficiency and quality of care. MCS could be considered as an innovative response to the serious problems in primary care. However, the needs for reformation would not have been enough for its implementation. MCS came on the health-policy agenda from outside. The driving force was one of the richest entrepreneurs of the early 1990s (Imre Somody) who had real commitment to initiate new solutions for the problems in the healthcare sector.[4] In 1996, he established a healthcare centre (Mission Health House) and 'healthy life-style park' in a village (Veresegyház[5]) nearby Budapest and invited a group of experts to work with him. This expert group developed the concept of MCS and due to the successful lobbying by the entrepreneur, who had good relationships with the then prime minister, the decision concerning the implementation was made by the government relatively quickly (and without a professional or public consultation). MCS was introduced as a pilot project in 1999—through an amendment to the Act XCI of 1998 on the Social Insurance Funds' Budget of 1999 (Gaál et al., 2011). In the mid-2000s, however, the mixed experiences of the MCS provided a pretext for attacks by the opposing interest groups. The MCS was eliminated by the then government in 2008. This section of the paper discusses the concept of and experiences with the MCS. The factors having led to its failure are discussed at the end of the paper.

8.3.1 Main Problems of the Family Physician Service in the mid-1990s

Since the creation of the Family Physician Service (FPS) in 1992, a major health policy goal has been to strengthen the GPs' gatekeeper role, to ensure that patients receive quality care when and where it is needed. But while the initial reform envisaged expanding prevention and developing quality assurance, the actual reform was limited to the functional privatisation of the GPs practice[6] and the introduction of the capitation payment[7] system. Doctors' practices did not change much. GPs continued to offer mainly prescription and referral services and exercised only a weak gate-keeping function. Economic, organisational and human resource obstacles hindered the strengthening of the role of GPs. The payment system provided no incentives to play a gatekeeper role. Most GPs

---

[4]Some of the statements in this section rest partly on the author's personal research notes on the given period and articles in some dailies. For example: https://www.napi.hu/magyar_vallalatok/osteremlo-lett-a-milliardosbol.670600.html.

[5]The selection of the village is explained by the fact that Imre Somody established his pharmaceutical company (Pharmavit) specialized in the production of vitamin effervescent tablets there in 1988.

[6]Functional privatization meant that GPs became self-employed, but their services remained publicly financed and local governments provided the facilities for them.

[7]Capitation payments to family physicians (based on the number and age-structure of the persons signed on the list of the GP) represented about 75 per cent of the revenues received by GPs from the HIFA,

worked in single practice and a proper system of supervision and quality assurance was lacking (Orosz & Burns, 2000).

The Government that came to power in 1998 dissolved the self-government of the health insurance, stopped the HSDM project, and declared that a competing insurance model would be introduced by 2000. The MCS was not on the health care agenda. The Government was, however, prevented from undertaking the insurance reform, by the power struggle within the public administration, and among fractions within the main governing party,[8] as well as by the inadequate administrative capacities of the MoW. By the mid-1999, the idea of a competing health insurance market was taken off the political agenda. This situation—in lack of any other reform idea within the government circle—helped the MCS to gain support.

8.3.2   Key Features of the MCS

The general goal of MCS was to improve efficiency and quality through care-coordination and new incentives. The MCS wanted to change the day-to-day practice of GPs, the attitude of both the doctors and patients, as well as the relationships between providers and the relationships between patients and doctors. The given MCS was expected to take responsibility for the care of the population group living in the area of MCS concerned. Patients were expected to take an active role in maintaining or restoring their health. The new organizational framework, the coordination processes and the new incentives were regarded as the main tools.

Leading Role of the Care-coordinator
The two main elements of the new organizational framework were: the care-coordinator organization and the contracts between the care-coordinator and the health care provider who joined the given MCS. A group of family doctors, an outpatient clinic or a hospital or a private company established for this purpose could act as a care-coordinator. The National Health Insurance Fund Administration (NHIFA) launched an application every year for which care coordinators could apply. The care-coordinator should have a contract with GPs in a geographically continuous area. Hence, family doctors and not individuals living in the area concerned chose whether to join the MCS.

Network of GP Practices, Outpatient Clinics and Hospitals
To establish a MCS required contracts between the care-coordinator and the GPs and other providers involved in the given MCS. These contracts served as a basis for the

---

[8]The idea of the competing insurance model put forward by the Office of the Prime Minister was strongly opposed by the Ministries of Health and Finance and certain circles within the governing political parties.

cooperation among the providers, as well as determined how the savings were distributed among them.

Influencing the Patients' Behaviour

No administrative changes concerning the patients' choice were introduced. Patients were allowed to choose GPs and specialists freely and to access health care outside their MCS (ie. at providers not contracted with the given MCS). However, the payments made to the providers outside the given MCS were also deducted from the virtual account of the care-coordinator. The MCS-pilot wanted to influence the behaviour of patients through the changes in the behaviour of GPs—they were expected to monitor the patient's pathway and influence the patient's choice by giving advice as well as by introduction of disease management methods. Furthermore, MCSs were expected to launch health promotion and prevention activities and use new tools of health promotion information.

Virtual Budget

The budgets of the MCSs were determined on the basis of capitation adjusted for sex and age. The budget was, however, only a technical account: the budget amount was not transferred to the bank account of the care-coordinator. The ways of payment by NHIFA to the providers did not change—the additional element was that the NHIFA also registered the relevant payments on the separated virtual accounts of the care coordinators. The NHIFA actually transferred only the amount set for prevention programmes and administration to the care-coordinators. At the end of the budgetary year, if savings occurred on the virtual account of a care-coordinator, they were transferred to him.

Incentives

In the traditional system, GPs did not receive any feedback if they prescribed unnecessary medical examinations (e.g. blood test, CT, MRI, etc.) or prescribed inappropriate medicines. As they received payments largely unrelated to their activity, GPs did not have incentives in cooperation with other GPs or specialists in order to enhance efficiency and quality of care. The MCS-pilot aimed to change these disincentives by ensuring that savings (i.e., the difference between the virtual budget and the actual spending on the group of population belonging to the given MCS) remained at the MCS. The savings could be used for reward-payments to doctors (or other health care providers), or to improve the facilities or other circumstances of the MCS.

However, as the capitation formula was rather rudimentary (adjusted only for the age and sex), inappropriate incentives also worked. Care-coordinators could produce savings by attracting GPs with populations healthier than the average.

Low Risk for the Population
If deficit occurred at a given MCS through some years, the contract between care-coordinator and NHIFA could be terminated by the NHIFA, without generating any risk for the population concerned.

Emphasis on Prevention and Management of Chronic Diseases
The application had to contain plans for prevention programmes and protocol development. The protocols could serve also as professional basis for the development of disease-management programmes. NHIFA provided a lump-sum money for the prevention programmes and also for the administration of MCSs. The care-coordinators were allowed to develop prevention programmes of their choice.

New Tools of Quality Improvement
The care-coordinators received the data from the NHIFA concerning health care utilization by the population concerned. These data provided good opportunity for analysing patient pathways at the level of individuals, and the GPs' practice patterns. This gave sound information to care-coordinators for discussion with GPs, if changes in their practices seemed desirable. The development of protocols also served quality improvement.

8.3.3   Experiences with the MCS Pilot

Due to incentives already discussed, the experiences were mixed. Many care-coordinator organizations were monitoring the patients' pathways, activity of GPs, developed and introduced protocols and certain elements of disease-management programmes (e.g. asthma), organized education for GPs, and provided wide-ranging information for the population. For example, the Mission Health Centre developed new methods for analysing the patients' pathways and involved not only the expert-group of the care-coordinator but GPs and specialists working in the practice of the analysis. The expert-group monitored the actual pathways of the patients, utilization of medicines, prescribing-pattern of GPs. The expert-group provided feedback to GPs and other providers (hospitals). This new way of operation started to influence the treatment behaviour of GPs and provided incentives for cooperation.

Development of protocols was also one of the obligatory activities of the MCSs and an important tool of quality development. At the beginning, there was no coordination among MCSs in this respect, later Health Services Management Training Centre of the Semmelweis University started to coordinate the protocol development.

According to a survey among the care-coordinators, the followings were, among others, emphasised as the most important results of the MCSs:

- the utilization of protocols reduced the variety in the treatment of patients with the same disease

- changes in the prescribing patters of GPs led to savings
- the development of common IT systems helped the management of patients' pathways and increased transparency concerning the GPs' practice (Bodnár & Vörös, 2008).

Some of the care-coordinators, however, only focused on producing savings—and the risk-selection was the easier way to achieve it.

8.3.4 Review by the State of Audit Office

The State Audit Office (SAO) conducted a review on the experiences of MCSs in 2005. This emphasised, among others, the following problems:

- "It is not clear whether the MCS serves as a pilot for restructuring health care delivery or a pilot for reforming the compulsory health insurance […]
- The professional and financial foundation of the model experiment is incomplete […]
- Although required by law, the expert group for the assessment of the experience of the model experiment was not established by the Minister of Health […]
- The calculation process of the capitation payment and the management of the virtual accounts are not transparent enough. […]
- It was not assessed by the NHIFA what kind of factors caused the savings on the accounts of MCSs. It cannot be proved to what extent the prevention, use of protocols and other measures taken by the care-coordinators contributed to the savings." (State Audit Office, 2005).

The Review of the SAO formulated several proposals for the Government, the Ministry of Health and the NHIA as well as the care-coordinators. It was proposed that the Government should prepare a proposal for a Parliamentary resolution on the evaluation of the MCS model experiment, with particular regards to the main purpose of the pilot and the results achieved, as well as the further fate of the MCS pilot. On the one hand, the Review by the SAO was very critical, but on the other hand, it left the door open both for the continuation and the dissolution of the MCS-pilot.

8.4 Success and Failure Factors of the Attempts for Building New Institutional Structures

The story of both the HSDM and MCS are relevant even today not only from a historical point of view. Weak coordination among health care providers is still one of the major problems hindering the improvement in efficiency and quality. The management of patient's pathways is still missing from the day-to-day operation of the Hungarian health care. The lessons from the story of HSDM and MCS are however even more important from an institutional point of view—as they highlight weaknesses hindering the capacity of the Hungarian health care system to improve its performance. In the following, first the success factors of the two projects are discussed jointly. Then, the factors having led to their failures are analysed separately in the case of the two projects.

8.4.1   Success Factors

Windows of Opportunity

Both pilot projects can be considered a case of 'windows of opportunity' (Hurst, 2010). On one hand, grave problems in the health care system and dissatisfaction of the public and health care professionals were visible and called for reforms; on the other hand—despite many sketchy ideas discussed during the years—no consensually agreed, feasible reform plans emerged. In this situation, new, feasible reform plans, offered by outside actors—having strong influence on the minister of health (HSDM) or the Prime Minister (MCS)—appeared on the scene. These circumstances led to quick and determined political decisions.

Meeting of Sound Reform Ideas and Strong Actors

Both the key ideas of these structural changes and the driving actors came from outside of the health care administration. In the case of HSDM, it was the Hungarian Office of the World Bank and the World Bank Office of the Ministry of Health. In the case of MCS it was an entrepreneur who had good relationships with the then prime minister. These driving actors invited a group of experts—from the academic sphere or the field of health care—to elaborate feasible reform plans for structural changes in the health care delivery system.

Technical Preconditions Were Created Outside of the Health Care Administration

In both cases, organizations already existed that could accommodate new units for the implementation of the pilot projects. In the case of HSDM, it was the World Bank Office of the Ministry of Health where a new unit was established for the management of the HSDM project. In the case of MCS it was the Mission Health Centre that served as a home for the development of the concepts of MCS. In both cases the managements of the projects were established outside the health care administration (Ministry of Health and Health Insurance Fund Administration). This was important, because the experience showed that if the tasks of the day-to-day operation and managing a reform project were placed in the same organization, the pressures of the first task pushed the second into the background. Some differences can also be highlighted. In the case of HSDM, the HSDM-unit at the World Bank Office was responsible for coordination at national level. In the case of MCS, the Mission Health Centre played an important role in the elaboration of the concept, and it acted as a care-coordinator, but it did not have a national-level coordinating role during the implementation.

Adequate Monetary and Non-monetary Incentives
Both projects had clear monetary and non-monetary incentives for the participants. In both cases clear connections between the efforts made by the implementing actors (participating health care providers) and the reward expected in the case of success were created. The tool for this was a separated budget based on capitation payment defined according to the population concerned (adjusted by sex and age). In the case of the HSDM, the region implementing the project was to be given a regional sub-budget to be set according to the capitation payment method—in order to ensure that savings generated by modernisation would be kept in the region. In the case of MCS, the MCS received a budget that was determined on the basis of capitation and the savings remained at the MCS concerned.

Capable Local Leaders Were Spontaneously Selected
Both projects were implemented through public tenders. The pressure to apply and elaborate proposals encouraged the selection of capable local leaders. These leaders could gain support from the medical profession. Furthermore, from the beginning the local medical professions were involved in the planning and implementation.

8.4.2 Factors Having Led to the Failure of the HSDM Project[9]

Conflicts with HISG and NHIFA
Problems in co-operation with the Health Insurance Self-government (HISG) and the National Health Insurance Fund Administration (NHIFA) emerged at the very beginning. The management of the HSDM project and the MoW attempted to involve the HISG and the NHIFA right from the beginning of the design and planning of the project. The NHIFA and the HISG, however, decided that the county health insurance offices would not take part in the regional consortia and the NHIFA and the HISG started a campaign in the press against the HSDM project. To the public, one of their objections was that the implementation would have violated the legislation concerning health financing. Their other objection was that it was unjust if only the winning region received all the resources. According to the NHIFA all the regions should have received some money from the resources available for the project.[10] The real reasons for the hostile attitude were different. It was obvious that if the HSDM project had been implemented, the decision-making role of HISG and NHIFA in resources allocation would have decreased

---

[9]The author was involved in the HSDM project. Some of the statements in this section rest on her personal experience.

[10]It should be noted that they were also aware of that the resources available for the HSDM were only enough to reach tangible changes in one region.

considerably. Therefore, the NHIFA and the HISG followed their short-term institutional interests instead of the long-term interest of the health care system and the population.

The Ministry of Welfare Supported the Project Only Half-heartedly
The support by the leading officials in the MoW was not unanimous. Some of them found the project too radical and considered harmful if regional strategic plans would have managed the modernization of the health care sector, instead of a national plan (even if the regional plans were developed along guidelines issued by the project). Furthermore, they did not believe that experts of the regions had enough professional and management capacity to manage the restructuring in the health care delivery.

The Decisive Factor: Changes in the Governing Parties
There is no doubt that the decisive factor of the failure of the HSDM project was the changes in the government. The leading party (FIDESZ) of the new government[11] that came into power in June 1998 opposed strongly the HSDM project—as they had a fundamentally different agenda for the health care reform. As already mentioned, the government stopped the HSDM project, and put forward the goal of the introduction of the competing insurance system by 2000. By mid-1999, however, the idea of a competing health insurance system was taken off the agenda.

8.4.3   Factors Having Led to the Failure of MCS

A considerable difference between the HSDM and the MCS is that the later one was in operation for 10 years—hence the experiences of the day-to-day operation could be seen. As in many other cases, the interpretations of the experiences by the main actors concerned differed to a great extent. The supporters acknowledged that the problems—mainly in the regulation concerning the MCS—revealed by the Review of the SAO existed, but their conclusion was that the government should have remedied these problems. The conclusion of the opponents—based on the Review of the SAO—was that the MCS had to be dissolved.

The Lack of Proper Implementation Strategy
It was obvious that at the launch of the MCS-pilot many details were not adequately elaborated. Several elements of the regulation concerning the pilot project would have required continuous development, as well as the implementation would have required adequate monitoring. The NHIFA had the responsibility to set the budget of the MCSs, define the methods of the capitation payment, as well as to monitor the professional

---

[11]This Government was formed by the conservative parties: the FIDESZ-MP (Young Democrats), the FKGP (Independent Smallholders Party) and the MDF (Hungarian Democratic Forum).

and financial performance of the MCSs. However, the NHIFA did not put effort into the monitoring and evaluation, nor in the improvement of the details of the regulation. It should also be emphasised that the lack of continuous development after the introduction of a new element into the health financing or delivery system has ever been a general feature of the Hungarian health care administration.

The Healthcare Administration Supported the MCS Only Half-heartedly

A part of the leading officials in the MoW preferred to continue the traditional model of single practice of self-employed GPs. Hence, they were reluctant in supporting the MCS. It is clearly reflected by the fact that, although required by law, the Minister of Health did not establish the expert group for the assessment of the experience of the MCS (SAO, 2005). A part of the leading officials in the NHIFA had similar attitude and this influenced the way in which the NHIFA fulfilled its obligations concerning the MCS.

A Parallel Agenda

All the factors mentioned previously were influenced by a deep-rooted reason: below the surface a parallel agenda existed. Since the early 1990s, the replacement of the single-payer, centralized compulsory health insurance (managed by the NHIFA) by a competing insurance model was a recurring theme from time to time. In spring of 2004, the Ministry of Health[12] attempted to turn the MCS into a competing insurance system. According to the proposal,[13] "care-manager" organisations were to be established and were required to put down in a separated bank account such huge amount of money that only commercial insurance companies were likely to be able to fulfil this requirement. The already existing MCSs would have been overtaken by the new "care-manager" organisations. It remained, however, an unrealized plan, as the proposal was opposed—for several and partly different reasons—by all the major actors of the health system and also by considerable groups within the Socialist Party. After the Socialist-Free Democrats coalition having won the national election in 2006, the Free Democrats gave the minister of health and they put forward an even more radical programme for the introduction of a competing insurance model. Obviously, the MCS was considered an obstacle. In December 2007, the Parliament passed a bill on Health Insurance Funds that envisaged to establish 22 health insurance funds (joint-stock companies) that would have replaced the centralized HIFA; as well as to introduce competition among them. However, a fierce political battle around the other reform step of the

---

[12]At that time the minister of health was given by the Socialist Party in the coalition government of the Socialist Party and the Party of Free Democrats.

[13]Some of the statements in this section rest partly on the author's personal research notes on the given period and articles in some dailies. For example: Jövőre országossá válik az irányított betegellátás rendszere.

https://hirkozpont.magyarorszag.hu/hirek/egeszsegugyireform20040415.html

government—namely the introduction of user charges for physician visits and hospital stays[14]—led to political circumstances under which the government decided to eliminate the user charges and also to repeal the act on competing insurance funds. The failure of the attempt to introduce a competing insurance system did not change the government attitude towards MCS and a Government Decree passed at the end of 2008 dissolved the managed care system. According to a Hungarian saying: "the baby was poured out with the bath water".

8.5   Final remarks

The paper analysed the creation and failure of two regional cooperation models in the Hungarian health care system. Their stories clearly show that the indisputable need for care-coordination and a sound and feasible professional program is not enough. Under the Hungarian circumstances, the establishment of institutional framework of cooperation and care-coordination intertwined with decentralization of the decision-making power within the health care sector. Most of the leading officials of health care authorities tended to support the professional goals of care-coordination but opposed the decentralization. This was in line with the general direction of recentralization in the Hungarian public administration since the mid-1990s.

Since the failure of HSDM and MCS there has not been any attempt for the development of coordination structures at regional level. In the primary care a small-scale experiment for introduction of group-practice of GPs was conducted (Papp, 2017)— but without considerable effect on the practice of health care delivery. The longstanding serious problems of the health system, such as outdated and unbalanced structure of healthcare delivery (e.g. an excessive hospital network with outdated technology and a shortage of staff, little use of day surgery, limited role of group practice in primary care etc.); increasing shortage of doctors and nurses; uncoordinated service delivery (e.g. lack of coordination in the treatment of chronic diseases); perverse efficiency incentives for providers (e.g. deficiencies of the provider payment methods and the widespread under-the-table payments) have not changed or even exacerbated since the late 1990s.

Coping effectively with the intertwined problems of the healthcare system have been demanding a well-conceived and long-ranging health-care sector reform strategy, with specific programmes, a clear governance framework, skilled and committed health-care

---

[14]In early 2008, the main opposition parties initiated a referendum on user charges for physician visits and hospital stays and on tuition fees in state-funded higher education. In March 2008, an overwhelming majority of voters (more than 80%) voted against the user charges and tuition fees. It was a shocking political failure that sealed the fate of the government at the next election. In fear of a similar shock in case of a referendum on the competing insurance funds, the Parliament repealed the act in May 2008.

management and administration, and support from health-care professionals and the public for the aims and goals of the reforms. Unfortunately, none or few of these elements could be assembled at any given time. There has never been consensus, even within the ruling political parties, on a vision and the basic reform alternatives. Lack of 'reform-oiling' resources, lack of consensus, weakness of public administration, and lack of political commitment have been interwoven and have reinforced each other. All these led to alarming problems of access to and quality of health care in Hungary. In the second half of the 2010s the grave situation of the healthcare system has become the No.1 concern for Hungarians.

References

Bodnár, M., & Vörös, L. (2008). Irányított betegellátás a mosonmagyaróvári kistérségben – Managed care system in the small-area of Mosonmagyaróvár. *Egészségügyi Gazdasági Szemle, 4,* 36–42.

Barabás, G., Hamecz, I., & Neményi, J. (1998). Fiscal deficit and public debt during the transition. In L. Bokros & J. Dethie (Eds.), *Public finance reform during the transition. The experience of Hungary* (pp. 59–94). The World Bank.

Bokros, L. (1998). The unfinished agenda. In L. Bokros & J. Dethier (Eds.), *Public finance reform during the transition – The experience of Hungary* (pp. 535–568). The World Bank.

Gaál, P., Szigeti, S., Csere, M., Gaskins, M., & Panteli, D. (2011). *Hungary. Health system review. Health systems in transition.* World Health Organization on behalf of the European Observatory on Health Systems and Policies.

Hurst, J. (2010). Effective ways to realise policy reforms in health systems. OECD Health Working papers No. 51. OECD, Paris. http://www.oecd.org/officialdocuments/publicdisplaydocumentpdf/?cote=DELSA/HEA/WD/HWP(2010)2&doclanguage=en. Accessed 25 May 2019.

Ministry of Welfare. (1997). Tender dossier of the health service delivery modernisation sub-component of the health services and management project. (available from Ministry of Welfare, 1055 Budapest).

OECD (2010). *Value for money in health spending. OECD health policy studies.* OECDpublishing. https://www.oecd-ilibrary.org/social-issues-migration-health/value-for-money-in-health-spending_9789264088818-en. Accessed 30 May 2020.

Orosz, E., & Burns, A. (2000). *The Healthcare System in Hungary.* Economics Department Working Papers. No. 241. OECD, Paris. p. 53 http://www.oecd.org/economy/public-finance/1883815.pdf Accessed 25 May 2019.

Papp, M. (2017). Az alapellátás-fejlesztés tapasztalatai, jövője – Experience and future of the development of primary health care. *Népegészségügy, 1,* 4–8.

State Audit Office. (2005). *JELENTÉS az irányított betegellátási modellkísérlet ellenőrzéséről] Review on the managed care model experiment].* Budapest: Állami Számvevőszék [State Audit Office]. https://era.aeek.hu/magyar-ASZjelentesek.php. Accessed 25 May 2019.

World Bank. (2001). Hungary – Health services and management project (English). World Bank. http://documents.worldbank.org/curated/en/299741468035042894/Hungary-Health-Services-and-Management-Project. Accessed 25 May 2019.

Occupational Health Management as Potential Element in Combating Social and Regional Inequalities

Manfred Cassens, Andrea Lakasz and Janusz Surzykiewicz

Contents

9.1   Introduction: 1996—Establishment of the German Act on the Implementation
      of Measures of Occupational Safety and Health to Encourage Improvements in the
      Safety and Health Protection of Workers at Work (ArbSchG) and Its Consequences. 143
9.2   Method and Science-Theoretical Embedding: Secondary Data Analysis Based on the
      Model of Social and Health Inequality 148
9.3   Results: Current Effects of Occupational Health Management on Social and
      Regional Inequality in Germany 153
      9.3.1   Prevention Guideline 153
      9.3.2   DAK and BKK Health Reports 155
      9.3.3   Reports of the Federal Agency for Occupational Safety and Health "Working
              World in Transition". 157
      9.3.4   Focus Reports of the Confederation of German Trade Unions "DGB-Index
              Good Work". 159
9.4   Discussion: Where Further Impulses Must Be Set 162
      9.4.1   Discussion of the Prevention Guideline. 162
      9.4.2   Discussion of the DAK and BKK Health Reports. 163

M. Cassens (✉)
FOM University of Applied Sciences, Munich, Germany
e-mail: manfred.cassens@fom.de

M. Cassens · J. Surzykiewicz
Catholic University of Eichstätt-Ingolstadt, Eichstatt, Germany

J. Surzykiewicz
Cardinal Stefan Wyszyński University, Warsaw, Poland

A. Lakasz
Former Research Fellow, FOM University of Applied Sciences, Munich, Germany

© The Author(s), under exclusive license to Springer Fachmedien Wiesbaden GmbH,
part of Springer Nature 2022
M. Cassens et al. (eds.), *Transdisciplinary Perspectives on Public Health in Europe*,
FOM-Edition, https://doi.org/10.1007/978-3-658-33740-7_9

    9.4.3   Discussion of the Reports of the Federal Agency for Occupational Safety
          and Health "Working World in Transition" 165

    9.4.4   Reflection of the Focus Reports "DGB-Index Good Work" 166

9.5   Conclusion: The Setting Workplace Has Only Very Limited Chances of Intervention. . . . 167

    9.5.1   Unfortunately, Health Insurance Remains Health Insurance—for the Time Being. . . 168

    9.5.2   The Company and Ethics. 168

    9.5.3   The Patient Should Care: Starting to Take Responsibility for Themselves
          as Early as Possible 169

References. 169

Abstract

Introduction: The epidemiological transition has been going along with demographic aging since the 1980s; its effects are becoming increasingly present. The legislator has addressed this issue with the introduction of the German Act on the Implementation of Measures of Occupational Safety and Health to Encourage Improvements in the Safety and Health Protection of Workers at Work (ArbSchG, 1996), however companies have reacted only hesitantly with the implementation of occupational health management. This impulse, contrarily, has only been a superficially decisive element in the implementation of the Ottawa Charter in the setting of workplaces in Germany. This process, which has been started slowly, was accelerated by projects and the follow-up legislation, not least by the Prevention Act (PrävG, 2015), which prompted a large number of major social partners to take joint action. Methods: The contribution is based on a total of four datasets for the years from 2015 to 2019, which were analysed and interpreted on the basis of the model of social and resulting health inequalities. The datasets include the prevention reports of the statutory health insurance funds, the annual individual reports of the umbrella association of the company health insurance funds and DAK-Gesundheit, the annual reports "Working World in Transition" of the Federal Institute for Occupational Safety and Health (BAUA), as well as the index of the German Trade Union Federation: "DGB-Index Gute Arbeit", which is also published annually. Results: It is assumed that there are clear inequalities in terms of sectors, regions, company size and gender. In addition, the prevention reports and the BAUA reports indicate the low level of epidemiological and practical effects regarding the implementation of the ArbSchG. Discussion: It will be reflected why the measures, taken by the social partners until now, are insufficient to provide decisive support in implementing or even maintaining occupational health management, particularly for micro and small enterprises, as they build the main group of employers. Moreover, it will also be examined, which consequences health inequalities resulting from a deficient occupational health management could have. Conclusion: It seems to be clear that health promotion of insured members cannot be the core task of health insurance companies. Despite the dazzling term of Corporate Social Responsibility, there are also ethical limits to be set for occupational health management. After all, employees can be encouraged as citizens, but cannot be obliged to behave in a health-promoting manner, as it is the case in some Asian countries. And whether the National Action Plan for the promotion of individual health literacy initiated in 2018 will lead to the urgently indicated behavioural changes at the personal level, remains to be seen.

9.1   Introduction: 1996—Establishment of the German Act on the Implementation of Measures of Occupational Safety and Health to Encourage Improvements in the Safety and Health Protection of Workers at Work (ArbSchG) and Its Consequences

As far as the form is concerned, a distinction should be made between the terms "occupational health management" and "occupational health promotion", because of its relevance for this article. In the first case, the understanding underlying this article assumes that the focus is on management processes which are based on key figures, which corresponds certainly with company management. At the operational level, health has the advantage that it can be connected and integrated with other—established—management systems. Faller (2017) identifies the justifiable danger of expert bias and the resulting top-down processes, which imply little room for participation in the sense of Wright et al. (2010). On the other hand, occupational health promotion in the sense of the WHO-Ottawa Charter for Health Promotion (1986) can be interpreted as enabling employees to actively participate in shaping the workplace environment. The active participation of employees and the associated potential for identification is countered by generally known disadvantages which can be associated with volunteers. In the further course of this contribution, the first mentioned version of occupational health management (OHM) is assumed.

The German ArbSchG, established in Germany in 1996, supplemented the Occupational Safety Law (ASiG), which was 23 years older, by substantial changes. It follows in its recognizable proactivity the credo "Precaution is better than aftercare" and was therefore tantamount to a paradigm shift at that time. In the same year, the law was connected with the implementation of the Federal Institute for Occupational Safety and Health (BAuA), having the following main tasks: "observation and analysis of occupational safety, the health situation, the working conditions and their effects on the health of workers in companies and administrations as well as the development of solutions" (cf. Brüggemann et al., 2015). The work of the BAuA, however, goes further: In addition to observation and analysis, direct and indirect implementation support with regard to the ArbSchG, it is concerned with the further development of primary and tertiary preventive working conditions, primarily on the basis of occupational medicine and epidemiological evidence. It goes without saying that this development (establishment of law and institution), based on a cautious retrospective assessment from a temporary distance of more than 20 years, may have led to clear emotional and social effects of uncertainty in the established process-based organisations. At the latest, if the timespan since the law was supplemented by the "Risk assessment of mental stress at work" (§ 5 (3) 6 ArbSchG) in 2013 is considered, it is currently clear that this law will be implemented only by about 59% of German companies (Wulf et al., 2017). In their contribution, Wulf et al. note what might have been valid twenty years before: "Despite the high economic relevance of mental health and the legal obligations of the employer to record mental stress in the context of risk assessment, it can be observed that many companies have implementation problems or do not meet their legal obligations" (ibid.).

If even large DAX-listed companies, but above all small and medium-sized enterprises—assuming a sincere effort a priori—have problems with the implementation and updating of the ArbSchG, the question should be investigated: which factors are identified as obstacles, since it is, after all, a matter of the implementation of legal requirements and by no means an optional task. A list of the reasons can be found in Fig. 9.1; although the respective decisive survey was conducted eleven years ago (2009), its timeliness does not seem to have changed (Bechmann et al., 2011).

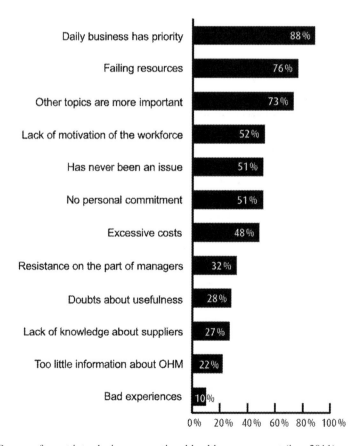

Fig. 9.1 Reasons for not introducing occupational health management (iga, 2011)

A recent study (Arps et al., 2019), in which 284 German and mostly medium-sized companies took part, identified the following additional obstacles (Fig. 9.1).

"- Offers of physical activities dominate OHM
- Digital tools do not yet play a major role in OHM
- Work intensification and poor management are a burden on health
- Mental hazard assessment is still not a compulsory programme
- The connection between digital transformation and OHM is insufficiently recognized
- OHM lacks an overall strategic orientation: activities are still too often "one-day flies".
- Lack of qualified OHM representatives
- And top management still knows too little about the health of the employees".

It is precisely for this reason that various state and public institutions systematically created third-party funding in the form of projects over several years, which were intended to enable a nationwide rollout. Without this important and mutually insightful phase, the high standard of OHM achieved in the medium term would not have been conceivable, despite all the deficits described above.

First of all, the "Cooperation Programme Work and Health" (KOPAG), which is still primarily oriented towards the pathogenic paradigm, should be mentioned, which covered the ratification of the ArbSchG (1996) during a timeframe from 1994 to 1997—the project was funded by the then Federal Ministry of Labour and Social Affairs (BMA). The aim of this basic project was to "develop methods for the health-conscious design of working on the basis of analyses of (work-related) stress and burden and to implement them in models" (DGUV, 1999). To achieve this goal, the Federal Association of Company Health Insurance Funds and the Federation of Institutions for Statutory Accident Insurance and Prevention supplemented the following data: Company personnel data, incapacity-to-work data from the company health insurance funds, accident data from the industrial employers' liability insurance associations, data on occupational illnesses from the industrial employers' liability insurance associations, occupational health data, exposure data from companies and the employers' liability insurance associations, results of the risk assessment, and, if applicable, the results of the company medical basic examination and the results of employee surveys. In order to prove the possible connections, the multiple Poisson regression analysis method was used (see Wollschläger, 2015). In addition to the results, which essentially showed a particularly massive risk exposure for the retail trade, KOPAG (Cooperation Programme Work and Health) was of central importance to the entire development process, because here "for the first time work incapacity data with hazard and stress profiles of homogeneous workplace types" (DGUV, 1999) were statistically combined and subsequently implemented in the form of specific design recommendations. These included both an extended profitability analysis and specific prevention proposals, which can be evaluated as the starting point for current OHM approaches for and in Germany. Based on KOPAG, a follow-up project was realized by the Federal Ministry of Labour and Health in 1999 and 2002 with the "Integration Programme Work and Health" (IPAG), in which the Federal

Association of Company Health Insurance Funds and the German Social Accident Insurance (DGUV) participated again. In addition, the AOK Federal Association, as the largest German health insurance company, the Federal Association of Guild Health Insurance Companies, the Association of Substitute Health Insurance Companies (vdek), and smaller insurance companies also participated. The aim was to develop a model cooperation between the statutory accident insurance and health insurance institutions in order to meet the requirements of the already established ArbSchG. The focus was on small and medium-sized companies, since large companies at that time often developed autonomous structures of occupational health management. For this purpose, IPAG focused on companies in the paint industry as well as inward care facilities (clinics) in order to not only correlate data related to incapacity to work, as was the case at KOPAG. By means of expert surveys, the already mentioned workplace types were classified in a more differentiated way for both sectors (Böhnke, 2005), e.g. for the setting clinic: chief physicians, senior physicians, senior consultants, residents, …, nursing and health care assistants as well as nursing trainees. The very heterogeneous requirements of the wards were also considered in the categorisation:

For example, the special features of palliative care or emergency rooms have been included. The same applies in the figurative sense to the paint industry. At IPAG, primary preventive interventions also made it possible for health insurance companies to offer services based on previously evaluated data and knowledge of workplace types for the first time. In this, and in the context of the period under review, the so-called Reform Act of 2000 ("GKV-Reformgesetz") regarding the statutory health insurances must be mentioned too. Incorporated in 1989 as § 20 in the fifth of a total of twelve German Social Code Books (SGB V, "Gesetzliche Krankenkassen"), this was amended for the first time. Services of primary prevention generated thereby to binding mandatory offers of the statutory health insurance funds, and occupational health promotion turned to an optional service (see Singer, 2010). The "Leitfaden Prävention" (Prevention Guideline), published by the German National Association of Statutory Health Insurance Funds (GKVS) and the German National Association of Medical Services (MDS), which was developed for the first time to implement this section, was also of great relevance for the further development of occupational health management. In this document, which has been revised for the third time, applicants can find basic information on financial support for their own projects in the context of occupational health promotion. The "Initiative for Health and Work" (iga) and the "Initiative for New Quality of Work" (INQA) subsequently (2002) provided impulses which still exist today. iga, which was initiated by the umbrella organisation of the company health insurance funds, the German Statutory Accident Insurance Fund, the Federal Association of the AOK, and the umbrella organisation of the substitute funds, pursues the goal of further developing prevention and intervention approaches involving providers, with a focus on occupational health and safety and health promotion. The initiative also sees itself as a platform for interdisciplinary cooperation between insurance organisations and companies, institutions, experts, and other bodies. INQA is a network led by the German Federal Ministry of Labour and Social Affairs in which the social partners (employers 'and employees' representatives), the Federal Employment Agency, the Federal Institute for Occupational Safety and Health and the Central Association of German Trade Unions cooperate. Well-interpreted "aim of the initiators is to find a balance between the interests of the employees in health-promoting working conditions and the economic interests of the companies" (Singer, 2010). In line with this goal, the initiative sees itself as a source of impetus, coach, and mediator in health-related topics of leadership, diversity, health, and competence (see Initiative Neue Qualität der Arbeit, 2020). As a result of the Accident Insurance Modernisation Act (UVMG), the National Occupational Health and Safety Conference was established in 2008. This conference is composed of three representatives each from the Federal Government, the federal states and the accident insurance institutions with voting rights, as well as advisory representatives of top-level organisations of the social partners. The establishment of this institution had to take place on the basis of international, and even more so, European requirements in order to implement the "Joint German Occupational Safety and Health Strategy" (GDA) adopted by the 84th Conference of Labour and Social Ministers of the federal states in the previous year. The following occupational safety and health objectives are currently being focused on in the 3rd GDA period:

- good work design for musculoskeletal strain,
- good work design for mental stress and
- safe handling of carcinogenic hazardous substances.

GDA's website points out with regard to the monitoring of the implementation of the ArbSchG that "the supervisory staff of the executing agencies carry out around 20,000 inspections in predominantly small and medium-sized companies (less than 250 employees) every year" (GDA, 2019). If we subtract from the total of 3,483,961 companies in Germany those having more than 250 employees, only 15,425 remain (Statista, 2020). In order to put the now rather relativising, if not frustrating number of controlled companies into an adequate ratio, the large number of companies with 0 to 9 employees (3,103,896) and those with 10 to 49 employees (still 298,874) is worth mentioning, which may never be inspected, and which therefore make up the majority of the 45% of companies mentioned at the beginning of this article, where the "risk assessment of mental stress" (§ 5, para. 3, sentence 6) regulated in the ArbSchG in 2013 is still not carried out. The German vernacular has a more than succinct answer to this question: "To be self-employed means to work oneself (alone) and constantly". The main reason for the criticism of the implementation of occupational health management in Germany, which is to be manifested here, is to be found in this sub-function of control, which is unfortunately plausible for personnel and thus cost reasons. For the large number of micro and small medium-sized companies, OHM is currently still taking place to a too limited extent or not at all. Even the implementation of legal requirements as a minimum target could not be achieved in 45% of the German companies by means of self-disclosure or maximum randomly controlled companies since the establishment of the ArbSchG. A small silver lining on the horizon is at best the Prevention Act of 2015, which raise the already mentioned § 20 of the Social Code Book V by a significantly increased network of participating funding organisations beyond the services of the statutory health insurances. Among other things, the Prevention Act aims to alleviate health inequalities, the existence of which is beyond doubt in Germany (Lampert et al., 2018; Mielck, 2005). In the context of the law, the current prevention report 2019, to be submitted annually by the statutory health insurers, can be referred to: the "estimated value" of the number of employees reached in the meantime has risen from 621,913 (2009) to 2,152,547 (2018); this applies to 61% of the above-mentioned company size of up to 249 employees. However, there may not be time to relax—especially since the most risk-exposed company size (1 to 9 employees) has only five percent of subsidized measures (GKV & MDS, 2019).

9.2 Method and Science-Theoretical Embedding: Secondary Data Analysis Based on the Model of Social and Health Inequality

Social epidemiology, as a typically interdisciplinary research discipline, objectifies the socially induced or socialisation-based unequal distribution of diseases (Kawachi and Subramamian, 2018); or "the proof of connections between status markers and health indicators in population studies", as the social physician Siegrist (2005) expressed. On this basis, it is obvious that social epidemiology, from its traditionally transdisciplinary approach, primarily integrates medicine and sociology with each other; medicine because of the epidemiology that decisively constitutes it, sociology because of the traditional demand for ending social and health inequalities. Accordingly, the methodological integration of the social sciences with that of medical epidemiology is also carried out here. While it was developed significantly in the United States at the end of the nineteenth century, it has also been an integral part of the interdisciplinary health sciences established in the German-speaking world since the 1990s, and is an integral part of the efforts to achieve equal health opportunities in accordance with the Ottawa Charter for Health Promotion (1986). Whereas social epidemiology in general often refers back to bio-psycho-social modelling, the following section refers to the model of social and health inequalities (Mielck, 2000). This is based on vertical and horizontal social inequality: The social epidemiologist Mielck (2005) explained that the addition 'vertical' implicitly expresses that the characteristics listed here allow a division of the population into top, middle and bottom. Traditionally, income, occupational status and education are mentioned. The Robert Koch Institute, among others, frequently makes use of this approach of vertical socioeconomic status in its health reporting (RKI, 2015; Lampert et al., 2018). In addition, the following horizontal causes of social inequality are most frequently mentioned: Age, marital status, gender and nationality. On the one hand, the list is not complete, on the other hand, it has never been agreed upon as binding; it is therefore a more or less accepted construct, but one that is widely used in the social sciences. The fact that this construct has come in for—justified—criticism is to be understood solely on the basis of the following three arguments:

a) Regional differences are not taken into account. In anticipation of the results of this contribution, it should already be pointed out that there are considerable regional differences in Germany with regard to the distribution of wealth and poverty.
b) Occupational inconsistencies in the construct of the vertical socio-economic status: With the approach presented here, neither plumbers who have achieved considerable wealth, nor habilitated philosophers living on the edge of the poverty line, can be explained.
c) It is clear from this that people can ultimately be assigned to several strata in relation to the proposed characteristics and thus cannot be clearly allocated.

Taking these reservations into account, the construct of socio-economic status (SES) can and must be considered here as the basis of the model of social and health inequalities.

Burden such as hard physical and at the same time unergonomic work, the direct confrontation with fumes and toxic substances, shift work and last but not least also those of work aggravation already imply at the keyword level health burden that primarily affects the lower classes. Closely related to this are the coping resources: it is assumed that these are also less distinct in the lower socio-economic status strata. Central to this is the health-psychologically relevant construct of resilience with keywords such as appropriate self-assessment and information processing, the regulation of feelings and emotions, the conviction of being able to cope with demands, the ability to get support, to be able to take charge of oneself and solve conflicts, the ability to realise existing competences in the respective situation, and the general strategies for analysing and dealing with problems (Fröhlich-Gildhoff & Rönnau-Böse, 2011). The third area of social and health inequalities must be distinguished from these two areas: the different use of the healthcare and pension system. This is traditionally favoured in Germany by the worldwide unique differentiation into a box-like statutory health insurance system and a private health insurance system which is better off than the previous one. In addition to the established dichotomy, there are further factors differentiating the system socio-economically. On the one hand, this concerns, for example, recipients of transfer funds (so-called long-term unemployed) or migrants without a clarified residence status, who must receive counter-financing for health services on the basis of Social Code Book II in order to be able to counter-finance the additional financial resources required for the procurement of dental prostheses, spectacle frames or orthoses. On the other hand, above the socio-economically better-off groups of the upper class, there are those in a small elite who, in return for additional private payments, buy exclusive health or additional treatment of their choice. Thus, there are now at least four strata in the German health care system—and not three, as it is assumed in the traditional stratification of the vertical model—in concrete implementation of the inequality model shown in Fig. 9.2. In addition, there are

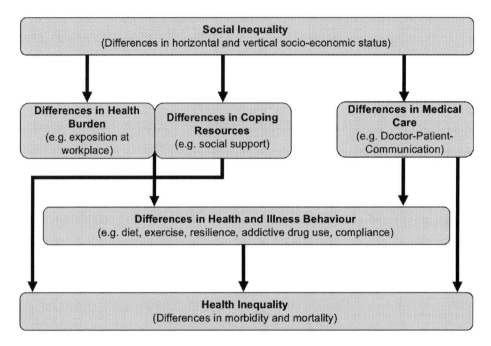

Fig. 9.2 Model to explain health inequalities (Mielck, 2005)

two relevant health-sociological working hypotheses in the present context, which are regarded as quasi fire accelerators on the way into the poverty trap, especially for the lower socio-economic classes:

- the causality hypothesis assuming that unemployment makes people ill, and
- the selection hypothesis implying that illness (chronic diseases, long-term illnesses, disabilities) makes people unemployed.

It is in the tradition of social epidemiological research to confirm established models, such as the model of social and health inequalities underlying this paper, by generating data. For this purpose, the use of routine health care data (Hjollund et al., 2019; Swart et al., 2014), which are available in abundance, is particularly suitable (see Fig. 9.3).

This type of data generation differs from the one established in social sciences, as it is neither based on a scientific question, nor is it hypothesis-based classically operationalized. Rather, as the introduction of the article already showed, in the present case, the core of the efforts was to bring together existing data sets of health insurance and accident insurance companies in order to make them usable afterwards.

Secondary data-oriented analyses offer a number of advantages. According to Zeidler and Braun (2012), the keywords here are cost-effectiveness, supra-regional

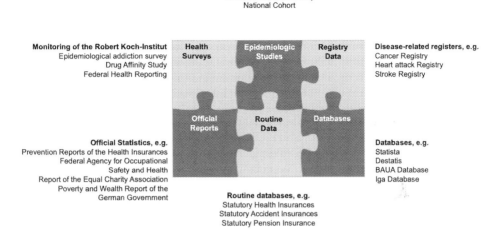

Fig. 9.3 The use of routine data in the field of social epidemiology

study populations and the elimination of study-related biases, which often affect smaller primary data source populations significantly. With regard to the evaluation of secondary data, the eleven guidelines and recommendations "Good Practice Secondary Data Analysis" of the "Working Group on the Collection and Use of Secondary Data (AGENS) of the German Society for Social Medicine and Prevention" (DGSMP) were taken into account. Specifically, the following data sets were subjected to a corresponding review and evaluation under the following question: To what extent does OHM guarantee a reduction of social and regional inequality in Germany In accordance with the model of social and health inequalities, the categories "differences in health burden", "differences in coping resources" and "differences in medical care" were used. The following data sets were subjected to a content analysis in the context of the secondary data analysis:

I. Prevention reports of the statutory health insurance companies: As already reported, the statutory health insurance funds in Germany are required by law (§ 20 of the German Social Security Code) not only to report annually on the health-promoting activities they have carried out as part of the Prevention Act, but also to include occupational health promotion as one of three areas. In addition, the annual document must also report on the expenditure used for this purpose. Currently (06/2020), only data from the reporting years 2015 to 2018 could be evaluated. These data are therefore only able to reflect a first trend. An additional problem for the analysis is the fact that the monetary resources used were increased annually from 2015 to 2018 in accordance with the law. The present guidelines were analysed with regard to the subcategories "company size combined with the number of enterprises reached" and "distribution of main target groups", which allow an indirect conclusion to the model of social and health inequalities.

II. DAK Health Reports: DAK is traditionally the health insurance company for employees, especially in the retail trade. Currently, (as of 01/03/2020, Euro-Information, 2020), there are 5,600,000 insured persons whose data is collected, documented, and analysed with annual focus topics.

III. BKK health reports: These are the reports of the umbrella organisation of a total of 72 individual company health insurance funds as well as four regional associations, where data on the health and illnesses of a total of 9,000,000 insured persons are available and can be analysed annually. For II and III, the sub-categories "data of incapacity-to-work", "duration of cases", "membership of economic groups" and "regional differences" were analysed and indirectly assigned to the model of this contribution.

IV. "Working World in Transition" by the Federal Institute for Occupational Safety and Health: These are compiled reports with data of different origins: Data from the Federal Statistical Office (Statistisches Bundesamt, 2020) are used to record employment and working hours; those on accidents and occupational diseases are evaluated by the umbrella organisation of the German statutory accident insurance. In 2012 and 2017/18, surveys were commissioned jointly with the Federal Institute for Vocational Education and Training (BiBB) on working conditions in the category of management responsibility; data from the statutory health insurance companies were used to record incapacity-to-work, and data from the German pension insurance funds was used to record pensions. Finally, data from the aforementioned initiative "Joint German Occupational Health and Safety Strategy" was used to record the occupational health and safety situation in Germany.

V. "DGB Index Gute Arbeit": The German Trade Union Confederation represents a total of 5,97 million members (Statistisches Bundesamt, 2020). The index continues the survey conducted by the "Initiative Neue Qualität der Arbeit" (INQA), which was also mentioned above. This is "a scientifically sound instrument for measuring the quality of work from the perspective of employees and represents an independent research achievement of the DGB, which is carried out in cooperation with various partners" (Institut DGB-Index Gute Arbeit, 2020).

In the overall context, the authors of this article initially considered including the so-called "iga.reporte" of the "Initiative Gesundheit und Arbeit" in the analysis because OHM-relevant data is also included in these documents. However, the thematic issues are highly diverse and cannot be related to each other in the context of the data analysis preferred here. Therefore, they were taken into account adequately in available positions, but not in relation to the time period, e.g., within the scope of a sociological qualitative content analysis.

9.3   Results: Current Effects of Occupational Health Management on Social and Regional Inequality in Germany

After almost 25 years of occupational health management in Germany, Fig. 9.4 illustrates the four main components of this business sector, which are bound by the respective legislation—completely independent of company size and economic sector.

However, even a superficial Internet-based comparison of large DAX-listed corporations with larger medium-sized companies reveals a clear difference, which cannot be explicitly discussed here. It is also obvious that correspondingly, the scope of action to small and micro enterprises differs from that of larger medium-sized enterprises in the number of full-time staff working in occupational health management. The next step is to find references from the above-mentioned secondary data sources and literature references to the dimensions mentioned in Fig. 9.4 in order to assign them to the three categories of the model of social and health inequalities in a second step.

9.3.1   Prevention Guideline

It should be noted at the outset that the Prevention Guideline classifies primary prevention and health promotion services together, in contrast to the theoretical construct of primary, secondary and tertiary prevention. In accordance with most recent explanations,

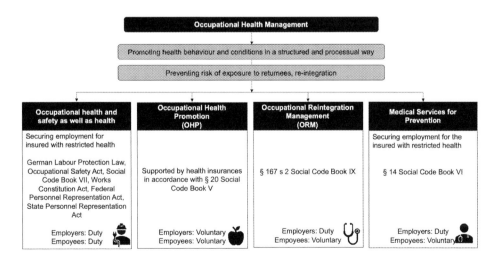

Fig. 9.4   Pillars of Occupational Health Management (following the GKV Spitzenverband / MDS, 2018)

a first tabular view of the company sizes reached with the measures according to § 20 of the Social Code Book V should be made (Table 9.1) possible.

From Table 9.1 it can be seen that, over the entire period, small (10–49) and micro (1–9) enterprises participate the least, although it can be assumed that larger companies (500–1499) and large enterprises have independently implemented an occupational health management system and are implementing it without using subsidies from the statutory health insurance funds.

As far as the sectors are concerned, there is a clear trend towards three areas: The category "Manufacturing industry" received the majority of subsidies, each with clearly more than 30%, followed by "Other services" (economic, other public / personal services, real estate / housing) and "Health and social services", each with approx. 16%. The number of employees reached increased from 1,302,383 to 2,152,547 between 2015 and 2018—this compared to the reference figure of approx. 44,300,000 employees in this period. In the reporting year 2018, the most recent for the time being, only just under 5% of the employees were reached with measures of occupational health promotion or support in the implementation of an OHM.

With regard to the model of social and health inequalities, another important parameter is the target groups of the occupational health promotion measures supported by the statutory health insurance (Table 9.2).

It is noticeable that the strategy shown in Table 9.2 is only directly addressed in the Prevention Guideline Report 2019 (retrospectively evaluating the reporting year 2018) with reference to the iga.report 29 and the multiplier strategy of the statutory health insurance funds (GKV & MDS, 2019). It is also clear, however, that the group of people affected by health inequalities, including employees without management responsibility and trainees, accounted for approximately two thirds of the people directly reached.

Table 9.1 Company sizes (columns) including number of companies reached in the evaluation period (lines). *,**

	1–9	10–49	50–99	100–499	500–1499	≥1500
2015	236	932	880	2495	851	380
2016	394	2101	2101	5647	1970	788
2017	707	2828	2651	7776	2651	1060
2018	977	3713	3713	5472	3713	977

*In the years 2016 (99%, −1) and 2018 (108%, +8), summative, implausible arithmetical errors were published in the report; these were adopted but must not remain unmentioned

**Absolute figures for 2015 were used, percentages from 2016 onwards. In Table 9.1, the absolute values from 2015 have been adopted in order to be able to relate them easier to the 3,483,961 companies in Germany mentioned above.

Table 9.2 Target groups of occupational health promotion (multiple answers possible, in percentage)

	2015	2016	2017	2018
Upper management level	30%	26%	23%	21%
Middle management level including master crafts-men / team leader	34%	33%	28%	28%
Employees without management responsibility	25%	21%	19%	16%
Trainees	15%	18%	20%	22%
Total groups exposed to health hazards, including…	28%	27%	25%	24%
…older workers	7%	7%	9%	9%
…employees with a migration background	2%	2%	4%	3%
… disabled people	not reported	not reported	2%	3%

9.3.2   DAK and BKK Health Reports

Due to its historical development as an employee health insurance fund, DAK-Gesundheit "insures in particular employees in typically female professions (e.g. in health care, trade, office jobs and administration; DAK-Gesundheit, 2019). The three occupational groups primarily insured in the company health insurance funds and thus forming a profile are "Medical health professions", "Non-medical health professions" and "Education, social and domestic professions, theology"; they belong to the economic groups "health care", "homes", and "social services" (BKK, 2015). A comparison leads to the following results (Table 9.3).

Both health insurance companies emphasize that "the extent of the cases of illness is of comparatively little importance for sickness rates due to their short duration" (DAK-Gesundheit, 2019) over the entire period. In addition, both insurance groups have in common that they deal with focus topics on an annual basis, which makes the further consideration of numerical parameters more difficult. For this reason, the focus topics are summarised in terms of the three main categories in the sense of a qualitative content analysis.

Table 9.3 Days / Average case duration in comparison (including rehabilitation and occupational accidents)

	BKK	DAK
2015	16.1	12.1
2016	18.1	12.9
2017	17.7	12.4
2018	18.5	12.6

It can be stated over the entire period, with regard to the DAK health reports, that musculoskeletal diseases (especially back problems according to ICD 10 - M54) dominated, followed by diseases of the respiratory system or infections of the respiratory tract and psychological and behavioural disorders. These are dominated by the ICD 10 diagnosis "Depressive episode" (F32). It is generally known that the diagnosis group of mental and behavioural disorders implies significantly longer absences compared to most other diseases. It is also assumed that women are more affected by the group of the so-called "F-diagnoses" (psychological and behavioural disorders) than men; in men, the diseases of the "musculoskeletal system and connective tissue" (M00-M99) dominate. Economic groups particularly affected by the burden of disease were the following in both insurance companies:

- Collection, treatment and waste disposal / cleaning professions
- Postal, courier, and express services / Transport and logistics professions
- Construction and civil engineering professions
- Nursing staff in care homes and homes for the disabled.

In relation to these particularly vulnerable economic groups, members of IT, information and communication technology professions, and financial services, as well as cross-economic group occupations in business management and organisation, are much less affected. In order to summarise the problem in depth: In addition to the data sets evaluated here, the Federal Health Reporting (2015) shows that the above-mentioned economic groups imply differences in occupational and qualification requirements. For the economic groups mentioned in the list above, (significantly) lower requirements are needed than for the professions in technology and management. With the study "German Health Update" (Gesundheit der Erwachsenen in Deutschland Aktuell-GEDA), the Robert Koch Institute was able to prove that the number of sick days is clearly related to the occupational status, which is one of the three pillars of the socio-economic status: For both women and men, people with low occupational status have a significantly higher number of sick days than those with a medium or higher occupational status. This is confirmed by the feeling of burden: This is felt more strongly by both women and men who have completed an apprenticeship than by those with a university degree (RKI, 2015).

The BKK was also able to prove an increased sickness burden of insured persons in connection with mental disorders and injury/poisoning in the context of temporary employment (BKK, 2019). As far as regional distribution is concerned, it is striking that the total number of occupational accidents in the Eastern federal states and Saarland is at a continuously higher level than in the West, with Baden-Württemberg always showing the lowest values overall; this is similar for health insurance funds, and is thus an important indicator of regional inequalities.

What is striking for both insurance groups during the observation period is that they both deal with the increased importance of mental health and work in the context of the epidemiological transition (BKK Health Report, 2019; DAK Psychoreport 2015 as a special report). This could reveal (delayed) reactions to the DGB-Index "Gute Arbeit 2015" (Institut DGB-Index Gute Arbeit, 2015), in which the increase in mental illness over the past three decades was addressed on the basis of the phenomenon of the so-called hectic work. It is striking that all the reports evaluated mention the topic of health promotion or support of occupational health management in the context of § 20 SGB V, if at all, then only on the margin.

9.3.3   Reports of the Federal Agency for Occupational Safety and Health "Working World in Transition"

In accordance with the profile of the Federal Agency (BAUA), the analysis of the annual reports focused on the development of risk assessment in the sense of the ArbSchG. In this part of its annual reports, the BAUA referred back to the actual client of the study, the National Occupational Safety and Health Conference. As one of the four pillars of OHM, the field of occupational health and safety is of great relevance. Each year, the BAUA's annual reports include additional focus topics, from which the 2017 report can also draw important conclusions for the OHM and the model of social and health inequalities. For the evaluated period (2015 to 2020), data of the NAK surveys from the years 2011 (for the reporting period 2014) and 2015 (2016 to 2020) serve as a basis. The 2015 survey focused here differed between company surveys (6500 companies; as in 2011) and employee surveys (5000 persons). The data in Table 1 reflect the stratified representative results of the company surveys.

Table 9.4 clearly shows that the tendency to carry out risk assessments increases with the number of employees: the smaller the company, the smaller the legal requirement to carry out risk assessments.

And as the table also shows, this applies particularly to micro and small enterprises, which account for most of the 43 million employees. In addition, there is a further problem, which is shown in Fig. 9.5.

In terms of an overall procedure aimed at continuous further improvements, only 12.9% of the companies implement the procedure stipulated by the ArbSchG. Particular importance is now attached to the risk assessment of mental stress, which still presents certain obstacles to implementation. A study used as an accompanying study in this regard comes to the conclusion that "lack of personnel" (38%), "lack of expertise"

Table 9.4 Realised risk assessment according to company size		
	1–9 employees	41%
	10–49 employees	70%
	50–249 employees	90%
	250 and more employees	98%
	Total	51%

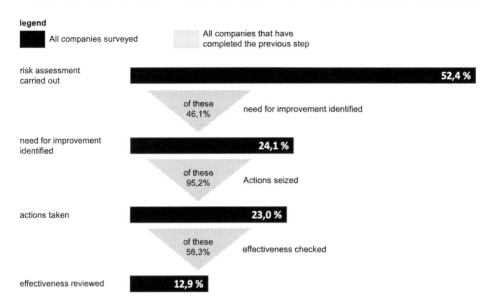

Fig. 9.5 Process steps of risk assessments with actual implementation (in percent)

(33.3%), "lack of information" (29.8%) and, alarmingly, even "lack of necessity" (26.3%) are the most frequently mentioned obstacles (Lenßen, 2015).

The reports "Working World in Transition" point out a social-health connection, particularly with regard to the suspected reports and acknowledgements of occupational diseases: "skin diseases", "noise-induced hearing loss" and "skin cancer due to UV radiation" occur above all in places which are characterised by strong noise or dirty air, and outdoor work. These are particularly jobs in road construction, industrial production and agriculture/forestry, where people with low socio-economic status are employed. These statements can be deepened with a supplementary survey of employees (2018) conducted by the BAUA. According to the report, it is mainly men who complain about working environments characterised by cold, heat, dampness, humidity, draughts and noise. In contrast, microbiological substances dominate the stressful working conditions of women. Social inequality has an impact on health, especially mental health. Accordingly, it is relevant that—similar to what was shown in the health insurance reports—there is a clear educational gradient in the categories "Planning and scheduling one's own work", "Influence on the amount of work" and "Own decision when to take breaks": The higher the last educational qualification, the higher the degrees of freedom in the dimensions mentioned (university degree before master craftsman/technician degree, in-company/school training, and completely unskilled workers without vocational qualification). Similar to the health insurance reports, the BAUA reports also come to the conclusion that "Public and other service providers, education, health", followed by "Manufacturing industry without construction" are the economic sectors with the most incidents of incapacity-to-work per 100 years of insurance membership. The number of days of inca-pacity-to-work per sick leave case supports an OHM, which is oriented to the increasing age demography: Whereas this is still six days in the age group of 20–24 years, it rises to 21 days in the age group between 60–64 years.

9.3.4 Focus Reports of the Confederation of German Trade Unions "DGB-Index Good Work"

Based on an employee survey conducted in 2006, the aforementioned "Initiative Neue Qualität der Arbeit" (founded in 2002), defined a construct of "good work", which was oriented to the demands of employees for the first time. The inquiry based on this was continued between 2007 and 2011 as a representative survey among the German work-force. Following an update resp. further development, the DGB-internal Institute DGB-Index Good Work (Institute DGB-Index Gute Arbeit), which was founded in the same year, has been functioning since 2013. The three categories of this construct analysing the quality of work are as follows:

Resources as extensive as possible (4 subcategories),

Minimum possible false loads/burden (4 subcategories) and

Job security and adequate income (3 subcategories).

The survey of dependent employees on the 42 fully standardised items was conducted as a telephone interview (Computer Assisted Telephone Interview, CATI). The number of respondents fluctuated during the survey period between a maximum of 9737 (2016) and a minimum of 4811 (2017). The scoring of the items leads to the creation of the four categories "Good Work" (100–80 points), "Upper Midfield" (79–65 points), "Lower Midfield" (64–50 points) and "Bad Work" (49 points or less). Multivariate, logis-tic regression analyses were used to verify the correlations (Institute DGB-Index Gute Arbeit, 2019). In addition to the extensive routine data of the prevention reports and the health insurances, the data generated by the DGB Institute have a relatively high general informative value in addition to the BAUA data; this applies both to OHM and the model of social and health inequalities. With the exception of the self-employed, freelancers, students and trainees, the data generated in this study were mainly from income groups, which are suitable for the purposes of corresponding data analysis and interpretation.

As Fig. 9.6 shows, the overall development during the reporting period was very con-stant. With the exception of 2015 (62 points in the overall score), the years from 2016 to 2019 each scored 63 points, which, according to the classification system, corresponds to the second highest value in the "lower middle field". Despite the great differences between the individual groups surveyed each year, the sub-scaled sub-indexes show a high degree of constancy too.

Unfortunately, only the Index 2019 has socio-demographic data from the total of 6574 respondents, which in turn is related to the overall index and the three sub-categories

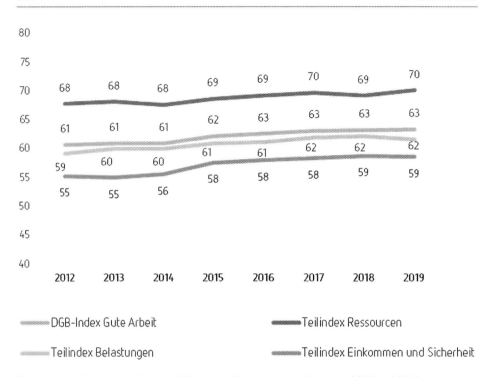

Fig. 9.6 Development of the overall index and its sub-indices between 2012 and 2019

(Table 9.5). In view of the constancy of the overall development, it is assumed in the present context that these values could be applied to the entire evaluation period.

The dimensions "Age Groups" and "Job Requirement Level" stand out particularly in the context of the present results. Overall and individual indices are rated much more positively in the youngest age group than in the age cohort between 56 and 65 years. A slight downward trend can also be observed for the intermediate old cohorts. The tendency that work rises with the increasing requirement level is apparent too. This can be confirmed by the high values in the dimension "leadership function" for those having a leadership position. As far as individual dimensions are concerned, it should also be mentioned that women feel less satisfied in terms of income and security. This reflects the long, sad and never-ending discussion about the equality of women, which is manifested in Article 3 of the Basic Law for the Federal Republic of Germany but is by no means practised nationwide. The DGB-Index confirms the BAUA reports with regard to the economic sectors in some areas. Out of a total of 18 sectors, "Trade", "Transport and storage", "Healthcare" and "Education", each scored 60 and 61 points, respectively, whereas "Information and communication" scored 70 points, placing it in the "Upper midfield" category; followed by "Public administration" and "Defense" with 69 points.

Table 9.5 Sociodemographic evaluation of the DGB-Index Good Work 2019

Index Points	DGB-Index Good Work	Partial Index Resources	Partial Index Burden	Partial Index Income & Safety
Average values	63	70	62	59
Sex				
Men	64	70	61	60
Woman	63	70	62	57
Full-time / Part-time by Sex				
Men in part-time < 35 h	61	68	62	63
Men in part-time in full time	64	71	71	61
Women in part-time < 35 h	62	70	63	55
Women in part-time in full time	63	70	60	59
Age Groups				
15 to 25 years	69	74	70	63
26 to 35 years	64	71	62	59
36 to 45 years	63	70	60	57
46 to 55 years	62	69	60	57
56 to 65 years	63	69	62	59
Job Requirement Level				
Helper / Trainees	62	68	69	51
Technical Restricted employees	62	69	61	57
Complex Trade Gate	64	71	62	60
High Complex Trade Gate	66	74	59	66
Leadership Function				
Leadership Function	65	74	59	62
No Leadership Function	63	68	62	57
Contractual time limitation				
Contractual Time Limitation	64	71	66	56
No Contractual Time Limitation	63	70	61	59
Customer Contact				
Very Often /Often	63	71	59	58
Rarely / Never	65	69	66	59

In addition to the highly comparable data of the routine questionnaire with 42 items, the DGB-Indices 2015 and 2019 should be mentioned in the context of the increase in mental and behavioural disorders, which has already been referred to in this article. In terms of the content, the focus topics "hustle and bustle" (2015) and "work intensity" revealed risk exposures, which would be easy to manage in the context of situation-based prevention through an adequate corporate culture, characterised by clear process chains and good interface management, among other things. In the DGB-Index 2015, 3195 of a total of 4916 people (65%) stated that they had to deal with too many processes and projects simultaneously. Just behind, 3097 people (63%) found that the personal assessment in their own working environment was too tight. With 61%, still above the 60% mark, 2999 respondents considered the set deadlines or time limits to be too tight, thus encouraging the phenomenon of "work rush". The results were essentially confirmed in the 2019 report. The Index 2016 mentions the effects of digitisation as a central source of the feeling of "work rush", which was proven and has a pathogenic effect during the evaluation period. Among other things, the report comes to the revealing conclusion that 5258 out of 9737 respondents believe that the amount of work has increased as a result of digitisation; this corresponds to 54% and was opposed by 682 persons (7%). This, still optional, connection should be given general importance in the future; this does not concern the GDB-Index only, but also the work epidemiology of every company. The reflection on the 2017 focus topic also revealed that employees in the "social services" sector, followed by "health care", "hotels and restaurants" and "education and training" rate the work-related exhaustion as a difficulty in reconciling work and private life. This could also imply additional references to identify group-specific risk exposures.

9.4 Discussion: Where Further Impulses Must Be Set

9.4.1 Discussion of the Prevention Guideline

First of all, the guidelines on prevention make clear the secret that is well-known in Germany, namely that health promotion / management and primary prevention are of very little importance despite the epidemiological transition. In the sense of the classic, deficit-oriented repair medicine, lifestyle-related illnesses/non-communicable diseases are given more than a clear subordination in the remuneration system of the statutory health insurance funds. This has been criticised particularly by public health circles, which have been academically established in Germany for more than 25 years ago but has had no nationwide consequences so far—apart from the dubious success of the Prevention Act. To make this clear: According to the data published by the "Verband der Ersatzkassen" (vdek, 2020), the statutory health insurances spent a total of 226,200,000,000 EUR on the medical care of their insured members in the last reporting year of 2018. The majority of this expenditure, almost 70%, was distributed to the hospital sector, and with a clear gap to outpatient care, which was almost equivalent to the supply of pharmaceuticals. In the same year, 172,165,808 EUR were invested in health promotion and primary prevention in the sense of § 20 Social Code Book V in the setting "Occupational Health Promotion" according to the prevention report of the statutory health insurance funds, thus not even 0.1%. This argumentation, which is often used from the perspective of public health and social medicine, is countered by the statutory health insurances saying that the genuine focus of such insurances lies in the nature of the matter, namely the care of sick people in their suffering. This is where the frequently embittered and polarised discussion in Germany often ends. According to the opinion represented here, the prevention reports lack the comparative figures provided in this article to relativise their modest actual investments in comparison to the need for action: The prevention reports of the statutory health insurers reveal much-more namely that, at most and in a figurative sense, regarding OHM only a kind of "emergency care" is being provided. In no way does this network follow a comprehensive prevention strategy that serves to provide adequate care for the above-mentioned risk groups in terms of health inequalities.

As a result of the scarce financial resources, it seems reasonable to invest the financial funds to convince small and micro-enterprises to develop their own OHM system. At the same time, this would mean a withdrawal from the direct occupational health promotion, which should not be in the interests of health insurance companies. After all, occupational health promotion is naturally also used as a popular marketing instrument in the sense of "Do good and talk about it". There is no doubt that the change of strategy would have an effect of "visibility-" or "loss of presence" in the companies, which would be otherwise present at health days or other major events. In the 2019 prevention report, there were 2,152,000 "reached employees" reported, but they could also be identified as potential insurance changers in the health insurance companies' marketing report. Compared to this, there are only 19,544 companies in the same year (2018). Even if the OHM of medium-sized enterprises with several persons appeared at consultation appointments, and the rate of small and micro enterprises receiving advice multiplied, the proportion of reached employees would be significantly smaller, and the advertising effects would be just as significantly reduced. Eventually, this discussion will inspire to consider the current strategy, which is certainly questionable from the point of view of small and micro-enterprises. This is because they are the losers at present, and the medium-sized companies, especially those with 100–249 employees, are the obvious winners of this policy.

9.4.2   Discussion of the DAK and BKK Health Reports

It must be emphasized, on the basis of the evaluated health reports (DAK Gesundheit 2015-2019, BKK Dachverband 2014-2019), that there are significant differences in health burden. This applies to both economic and professional groups. Since it can be demonstrated for the evaluated five-year period, this results in consequences for the OHM, which, if ignored, should lead to negative effects occurring much more quickly, but which, if strategically pursued, should nevertheless lead to moderate health-related consequences. This applies above all to the demographic ageing of companies, which is already noticeable in almost all sectors, with its epidemiologically measurable effects. The results of the reports lead to the conclusion that the OHM

- must be implemented above all in economic groups with low occupational status,
- must offer low-threshold education for people with low or no school qualifications,
- will have to focus on older people with age-adjusted burden of disease,
- must be strengthened in the Eastern federal states and in the Saarland, where greater efforts are required and
- should be focused on especially due to the changed workloads of the group of F-diagnoses.

Beyond that, it is noticeable that with the exception of the BKK Health Report 2018, the evaluated reports imply very similar results to the prevention reports of the German National Association of Statutory Health Insurance Funds discussed in the previous section: If so, then health promotion is mentioned in marginal notes at most. For example, the DAK Health Report 2017 states in the summary of a 192-page document that

> "Explanations for the level of sickness observed among DAK members, however, can also be sought at company level: If there is no increase in sickness levels here, this can be attributed, among other things, to activities of occupational health promotion and the consideration of employee health issues in organisational and personnel development in companies" (DAK Health, 2017).

When health expenditure in relation to the gross domestic product (GDP) is reflected in an EU-wide comparison, clear differences in the use of monetary resources become apparent. This can already be expressed in an exemplary manner by the relative density of doctors and nurses: Only Denmark shows similarly high values, with Germany being quite close to Sweden in terms of physician density, but having considerably more nurses; Denmark shows a higher number of professionals, but has considerably fewer physicians per 1000 inhabitants (OECD, 2019). The report "State of Health in the EU: Germany—Country Health Profile 2019" comes to the following conclusion in relation to the overall context, which is absolutely correct from the position taken here:

> "Resilience: Financial reserves accumulated by the health insurance system offset economic downturns, but future financial sustainability may become challenging as the population ages. There is potential for efficiency gains by centralising hospital activity, containing rising expenditures on pharmaceuticals and making better use of Health" (OECD, 2019).

This conclusion seems to be a noble goal in view of the far too large number of small hospitals distributed throughout the entire country without a "real" raison d'être, the unequal remuneration system of statutory and private health insurance companies, which is unique in the world, and the fact that drugs are considerably too expensive on the domestic reference market. Not to be underestimated in the urgently indicated paradigm shift on the part of the health insurance companies are their co-players, rather probably their opponents: the professional, the hospital representatives as well as often local or regional political prevention policies. If the necessary savings could be achieved successfully and sustainably, the statutory health insurance funds and their actors (statutory pension insurance, German Statutory Accident Insurance) could give considerable impetus to occupational health management, from which particularly micro and small enterprises could benefit much more than before.

9.4.3 Discussion of the Reports of the Federal Agency for Occupational Safety and Health "Working World in Transition"

Probably the most important findings of these reports are the ones, which reflect according to their own data, that only 52.4% of German companies carry out a risk assessment. Even more troublesome is the information that of these only 12.9% of all German companies actually go through the follow-up process to the proven effects. This raises further questions about the current state of OHM in Germany. This mainly affects micro (1–9 employees), and small enterprises (10–49 employees), which are located in both urban and especially rural areas and dominate these areas as employers. Because of its institutional links as a federal institution, the BAUA can certainly be accused of not being enough—with 20,000 companies visited each year. Therefore, the BAUA would demand more qualified personnel. However, the federal budget sets limits here, which are just as strict as they have been the hallmark of the public health service in Germany for many years. The health authorities are also unable to exercise an additional supervisory duty within the indexed framework. Thus, compliance issues regarding the minimum standards of OHM (only the conduct of risk assessments) should be dealt with by the companies themselves. Even if operation inspections are carried out to a minimal extent only, where missing risk assessments are identified as a malus, the risk of an actual restriction is comparatively low. This applies particularly to the mental health risk assessment. However, non-legally relevant consequences are already clearly visible in this regard. Young people are leaving, even fleeing from rural regions to urban centers, and looking for jobs in large companies using dazzling slogans such as "work-lif- balance" and having ergonomic workplace equipment in a preventive manner. In this context, the large automobile manufacturers should be mentioned, e.g., those introducing ergonomic production lines for the once "assembly line workers" as early as the end of the 1990's and having a proactive approach to the topic of corporate demography with an adequate work intensity and corresponding distribution of tasks. These companies have also had complex OHM institutions in the sense of Fig. 9.4 in order to implement such topics since the end of the last millennium. Thus, the BAUA reports and the surveys of 2011 and 2015, which serve as a basis for them, illustrate the need for action for micro and small companies, and for those which are also subject to the effects of failure to carry out risk assessments, together with further steps to be derived from them. Outstanding to well-qualified young people will simply no longer consider such companies to be lucrative in the future and will follow the mainstream into urban companies with good OHM.

In the canon of the National Occupational Safety and Health Commission (NAK), the Joint German Occupational Safety and Health Strategy (GDA), and the Initiative for Health and Work (iga), the biggest problem of the Federal Institute for Occupational Safety and Health (BAUA) appears to be its lack of public awareness. This is indicated by the high values of not conducted risk assessments (ca. 45–49%). It can also be said that these institutions and initiatives are completely unknown to large parts of the German population, sometimes even to public health experts. If one has hopefully learned about the institutions in the course of their studies, then they often diminish, if the graduates do not work in OHM. The institutions lack (media) presence and, in addition, monetary means to increase awareness. As far as the BAUA as a supervisory authority is concerned, it should not be underestimated that the deficiencies identified by its own staff could lead to restrictions. This makes the work more difficult, because usually only those companies which can afford a larger OHM staff have the knowledge of the network partners mentioned here.

9.4.4 Reflection of the Focus Reports "DGB-Index Good Work"

The survey of permanent employees reveals social inequalities too, and, in this case, only possibly health inequalities. The oldest age cohort (56 to 65 years) rates their job quality as worse than the age cohorts before them. If the level of requirements with its clear results were also considered, a clear need for action and requirements for OHM emerges regarding the DGB-Index: it is the older people without management skills and with low requirement profiles who consider their job quality to be the least good. The Index confirms the previously evaluated reports that there appear to be more sectors of the economy with more burden like "trade", "transport and location", "health" and "education" and sectors with less burden like "information and communication". This facilitates the development of a targeted action strategy by the agitators of a salutogenic and primary prevention-oriented overall strategy, which should lead to a more adequate allocation of resources. This strategic thinking, and above all action, should begin and end with the National Occupational Safety and Health Commission (NAC), the National Prevention Conference and the umbrella organisations of the health insurance companies, the German Pension Insurance and the German Statutory Accident Insurance.

The DGB-Indexes are not the only expression of the German Trade Union Confederation's proactive commitment to the health of their members and all other employees. Health belongs to the genuine core fields of employee representation. The findings evaluated here represent the position of the employees in the context of OHM. Frequently, the representatives of staff and works councils are not only members of the DGB, but also of those who co-decide or even carry out tasks of the OHM themselves. Therefore, the phenomena of work rush and work density, as well as the effects of digitisation will be discussed particularly in the future. The DGB-Indices will have the highest dissemination possibilities, and thus, works councils will have the opportunity to influence the reduction of social and health inequalities in companies within the framework of OHM.

9.5   Conclusion: The Setting Workplace Has Only Very Limited Chances of Intervention

With the core areas shown in Fig. 9.4

- Occupational health and safety
- Occupational health promotion
- Company integration management and
- Medical services for prevention

OHM has clearly delineated subject areas in terms of structure, which all are suitable for reducing health inequalities. However, it is mainly implemented in the above extent in large companies. Beyond that, the smaller the companies are, the less extensive are the relevant management services provided by the company. The large majority of companies in Germany are those which are worst off in terms of OHM, namely small and micro-enterprises.

Finally, Fig. 9.7 illustrates once again how large a network, which is necessary for a functioning OHM, is. Even for companies assigning only one person in full-time to

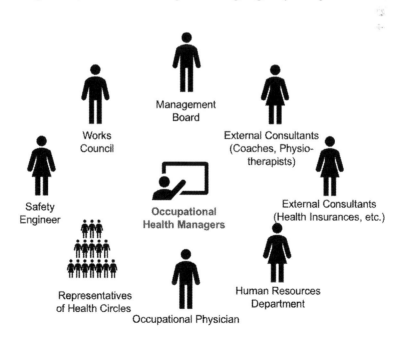

Fig. 9.7 Network of Occupational Health Managers

coordinate the four core tasks mentioned above, it will be impossible to implement all work packages at least in accordance with the legal requirements of the ArbSchG. In such cases, it is more important to obtain the support of the network partners analysed in this article. The main part of the network partners to be named in the context are the German Pension Insurance, the German Social Accident Insurance and the health insurance companies. However, very real limits remain on the whole.

9.5.1 Unfortunately, Health Insurance Remains Health Insurance—for the Time Being

It should not be overlooked that it is the historically grown genuine mission of the statutory and private health insurance companies to primarily finance the treatment of diseases and their consequences; in addition, there is the social security in case of illness, which also historically exists since 1881, and is closely connected to their core mission. The main focus of the statutory accident insurance funds is to prevent work-related accidents, to restore the ability of the insured persons in case of accidents, and to compensate them or their surviving dependents with cash benefits. In the present context, the main task of the pension insurance is and remains to provide monetary benefits in the event of a reduction in earning capacity, if employed persons are unable to work, or partially or completely disabled. This will also be the case on a permanent basis. A complete paradigm shift towards salutogenesis simply cannot be achieved due to these core tasks. However, the aspects developed in the discussion should be taken seriously—and health promotion and prevention services should not primarily be used as a synergetic marketing service. An orientation towards the socially disadvantaged regions and company sizes mentioned in the article should—finally!—be realised. In addition, the untenable differences in the remuneration system of private and statutory health insurance companies could be harmonised and the resulting savings could be invested in health promotion and primary prevention.

9.5.2 The Company and Ethics…

In addition to the general question of feasibility, OHM is ultimately also a responsibility towards employees—and thus towards corporate ethics. As already indicated in the introductory reflection on the term "health management", it can raise questions about the benefits or "usability". A provocative question can quickly arise in this context: Does OHM actually serve the employee and his work-life-balance, or is it established in order to achieve primarily profit-oriented goals? Thus, it concerns the ethical justifiability of health offers or, in addition, interventions. This begins far before questions of discharge management in the context of an addiction in terms of obligatory preliminary examinations or the likewise obligatory participation in event offers for movement, nutrition, and relaxation arise. The German legislation is very liberal in this respect, which in this context actually means that it is employee oriented.

9.5.3 The Patient Should Care: Starting to Take Responsibility for Themselves as Early as Possible

Then, in the end, is it up to the individual person to do something about social and health inequalities? Yes, indeed—at least for the most part and in terms of health promotion. Having a healthy diet, exercising moderately for thirty minutes five times a week, and spending their free time not only in front of the television or the games console; these are, first and foremost, activities over which the company should have no influence; much worse: it would be unimaginable, if it had. Schäffer et al. will be criticized again and again with regard to the random sample of their "Health Literacy Survey Germany" (HLS-GE). Nevertheless, the results, which reflect data of about 2000 people, should be appreciated with care and respect. The results show that 38.4% of Germans have sufficient, 44.6% problematic, and 9.7% inadequate health literacy, compared to only 7.3% having excellent ones. 54.3% of the German population have clear shortcomings in finding health information, then understanding, assessing, and ultimately implementing it. In addition, it should not be forgotten that the term "epidemiological transition" implies a change from the often hygiene- and ratio-related infectious diseases to behavioural lifestyle-related diseases. This is the main reason why the German federal government launched its "National Action Plan Health Literacy" in 2018. The fact that only one recommendation was listed for the setting "workplace" in this framework implies that health literacy, which is the main cause of social and health inequalities, must be dealt with in a much more complex and individualised way. In the overall context and its management possibilities, the setting workplace is only one of many possible approaches to individual health promotion and the epidemiological and demographic transition in German society as a whole. The central starting point remains the human being in their various settings and general behaviour—or also their individual interpretation of everyday life.

References

Arps, W., Lüerßen, H., Mikula, D., Naumann, F., Ohlsen, A., Stickling, E. (2019). BGM im Mittelstand 2019/2020 – Das Betrieb-liche Gesundheitsmanagement in Zeiten der digitalen Transformation. https://www.tk.de/resource/blob/2080176/d2a3ef84023b03bcbcb5248afd509aeb/bgm-im-mittelstand-2019-2020-digitale-transformation-data.pdf. Accessed 07 June 2020.

Bechmann, S. Jäckle, R., Lück, P., & Herdegen, R. (2011). Motive und Hemmnisse für Betriebliches Gesundheitsmanagement (BGM) – Umfragen und Empfehlungen. iga-Report 20. 2. Aufl. https://www.bgm-ag.ch/files/publich/literatur/pdf/motive-und-hemmnisse-fuer-betriebliches-gesundheitsmanagement.pdf. Accessed 8 June 2020.

BKK Dachverband. (2014). *BKK Gesundheitsreport 2014 – Gesundheit in Regionen: Zahlen, Daten, Fakten.* MWV.

BKK Dachverband. (2015). *BKK Gesundheitsatlas 2015 – Gesundheit in Regionen – Blickpunkt Psyche.* MWV.

BKK Dachverband. (2016). *BKK Gesundheitsreport 2016 – Gesundheit und Arbeit: Zahlen, Daten und Fakten.* MWV.

BKK Dachverband. (2017). *BKK Gesundheitsatlas 2017 – Gesundheit und Arbeit: Blickpunkt Gesundheitswesen.* MWV.

BKK Dachverband. (2018). *BKK Gesundheitsreport 2018 – Arbeit und Gesundheit Generation 50+: Zahlen, Daten, Fakten.* MWV.

BKK Dachverband. (2019). *BKK Gesundheitsreport 2019 – Psychische Gesundheit und Arbeit.* MWV.

Böhnke, E. (2005). *Standards für das Gesundheitsmanagement in der Praxis – Konsequenzen des gesetzlichen Präventionsauftrages für Unternehmen und den Arbeits- und Gesundheitsschutz* (S. 38–42). Diss, Wiesbaden, DUV.

Brüggemann, S., Niehues, C., Rose, A., & Schwöbel, B. (2015). *Pschyrembel der Arbeitsmedizin* (2nd ed., p. 123). De Gruyter.

Bundesagentur für Arbeitsschutz und Arbeitsmedizin. (2016). Arbeitswelt im Wandel – Jahresbericht 2016. https://www.baua.de/DE/Angebote/Publikationen/Praxis/A95.pdf?__blob=publicationFile&v=17. Accessed 5 June 2020.

Bundesagentur für Arbeitsschutz und Arbeitsmedizin. (2017). Arbeitswelt im Wandel – Jahresbericht 2017. https://www.baua.de/DE/Angebote/Publikationen/Praxis/A97.pdf?__blob=publicationFile&v=21. Accessed 5 June 2020.

Bundesagentur für Arbeitsschutz und Arbeitsmedizin. (2018). Arbeitswelt im Wandel – Jahresbericht 2018. https://www.baua.de/DE/Angebote/Publikationen/Praxis/A99.pdf?__blob=publicationFile. Accessed 5 June 2020.

Bundesagentur für Arbeitsschutz und Arbeitsmedizin. (2019). Arbeitswelt im Wandel – Jahresbericht 2019. https://www.baua.de/DE/Angebote/Publikationen/Praxis/A100.html. Accessed 5 June 2020.

Bundesagentur für Arbeitsschutz und Arbeitsmedizin. (2020). Arbeitswelt im Wandel – Jahresbericht 2020. https://www.baua.de/DE/Angebote/Publikationen/Praxis/A101.pdf?__blob=publicationFile&v=8. Accessed 5 June 2020.

DAK-Gesundheit. (2015a). DAK-Gesundheitsreport 2015. https://www.dak.de/dak/download/vollstaendiger-bundesweiter-gesundheitsreport-2015-2109030.pdf. Accessed 14 June 2020.

DAK-Gesundheit. (2015b). Psychoreport 2015 – Deutschland braucht Therapie; Herausforderungen für die Versorgung. https://www.dak.de/dak/download/DAK-Psychoreport_2015-1718180.pdf. Accessed 16 Nov 2019.

DAK-Gesundheit. (2016). DAK-Gesundheitsreport 2016. https://www.dak.de/dak/bundesthemen/gesundheitsreport-2016-2108986.html. Accessed 14 June 2020.

DAK-Gesundheit. (2017). DAK-Gesundheitsreport 2017. https://www.dak.de/dak/bundesthemen/muedes-deutschland-schlafstoerungen-steigen-deutlich-an-2108960.html. Accessed 14 June 2020.

DAK-Gesundheit. (2018). DAK-Gesundheitsreport 2018. https://www.dak.de/dak/download/gesundheitsreport-2018-pdf-2073702.pdf. Accessed 14 June 2020.

DAK-Gesundheit. (2019). DAK-Gesundheitsreport 2019. https://www.dak.de/dak/download/dak-gesundheitsreport-2019-sucht-pdf-2073718.pdf.Accessed 14 June 2020

Deutsche Gesetzliche Unfallversicherung (DGUV). (1999). Kooperationsprogramm Arbeit und Gesundheit. https://www.dguv.de/ifa/forschung/projektverzeichnis/bgz_0001.jsp. Accessed 10 June 2020.

Euro-Informationen. (2020). Die größten Krankenkassen: Versicherte 2020 – Der aktuelle Stand der Versichertenzahlen der gesetzlichen Krankenkassen. https://www.krankenkassen.de/krankenkassen-vergleich/statistik/versicherte/aktuell. Accessed 13 June 2020.

Faller, G. (2017). Was ist eigentlich Betriebliche Gesundheitsförderung? In G. Faller (Hrsg.), *Lehrbuch Betriebliche Gesundheitsförderung* (3. vollst. und erw. Aufl., S. 25–39). Hogrefe.

Fröhlich-Gildhoff, K., & Rönnau-Böse, M. (2011). *Resilienz* (2. Aufl.). Reinhardt.

Gemeinsame Deutsche Arbeitsschutzstrategie. (2019). Arbeitsprogramme. https://www.gda-portal.de/DE/GDA/Arbeitsprogramme/Arbeitsprogramme_node.html. Accessed 10 June 2020.

GKV-Spitzenverband. (Hrsg.). (2018). Leitfaden Prävention – Handlungsfelder und Kriterien nach § 20 Abs. 2 SGB V; Leitfaden Prävention in stationären Pflegeeinrichtungen nach § 5 SGB XI. https://www.gkv-spitzenverband.de/media/dokumente/presse/publikationen/Leitfaden_Pravention_2018_barrierefrei.pdf. Accessed 5 May 2020.

GKV-Spitzenverband, Medizinischer Dienst des Spitzenverbandes Bund der Krankenkassen. (Hrsg.). (2016). Präventionsbericht 2015 -Leistungen der gesetzlichen Krankenversicherung: Primärprävention und Gesundheitsförderung; Leistungen der Pflegeversicherung: Prävention in stationären Pflegeeinrichtungen – Berichtsjahr 2015. https://www.gkv-spitzenverband.de/media/dokumente/krankenversicherung_1/praevention__selbsthilfe__beratung/praevention/praeventionsbericht/2016_GKV_MDS_Praeventionsbericht.pdf. Accessed 13 June 2020.

GKV-Spitzenverband, Medizinischer Dienst des Spitzenverbandes Bund der Krankenkassen. (Hrsg.). (2017). Präventionsbericht 2016 -Leistungen der gesetzlichen Krankenversicherung: Primärprävention und Gesundheitsförderung; Leistungen der Pflegeversicherung: Prävention in stationären Pflegeeinrichtungen – Berichtsjahr 2016. https://www.gkv-spitzenverband.de/media/dokumente/krankenversicherung_1/praevention__selbsthilfe__beratung/praevention/praeventionsbericht/2017_GKV_MDS_Praeventionsbericht.pdf. Accessed 13 June 2020.

GKV-Spitzenverband, Medizinischer Dienst des Spitzenverbandes Bund der Krankenkassen. (Hrsg.). (2018). Präventionsbericht 2017 -Leistungen der gesetzlichen Krankenversicherung: Primärprävention und Gesundheitsförderung; Leistungen der Pflegeversicherung: Prävention in stationären Pflegeeinrichtungen – Berichtsjahr 2017. https://www.gkv-spitzenverband.de/media/dokumente/krankenversicherung_1/praevention__selbsthilfe__beratung/praevention/praeventionsbericht/2018_GKV_MDS_Praeventionsbericht.pdf. Accessed 13 June 2020.

GKV-Spitzenverband, Medizinischer Dienst des Spitzenverbandes Bund der Krankenkassen. (Hrsg.). (2019). Präventionsbericht 2018 -Leistungen der gesetzlichen Krankenversicherung: Primärprävention und Gesundheitsförderung; Leistungen der Pflegeversicherung: Prävention in stationären Pflegeeinrichtungen – Berichtsjahr 2018. https://www.gkv-spitzenverband.de/media/dokumente/krankenversicherung_1/praevention__selbsthilfe__beratung/praevention/praeventionsbericht/2019_GKV_MDS_Praventionsbericht_barrierefrei.pdf. Accessed 13 June 2020.

Hjollund, N., Valderas, J., Kyte, D., & Calvert, M. (2019). Health data processes: A framework for analyzing and discussing efficient use and reuse of health data with a focus on patient-reported outcome measures. *Journal of Medical Internet Research, 21(5),* e12412. https://doi.org/10.2196/12412.

Initiative Gesundheit & Arbeit. (2020). iga.Report 20 – Motive und Hemmnisse für Betriebliches Gesundheitsmanagement (BGM). https://de.statista.com/statistik/daten/studie/1929/umfrage/unternehmen-nach-beschaeftigtengroessenklassen/. Accessed 10 June 2020.

Initiative Neue Qualität der Arbeit. (2020). https://inqa.de/DE/startseite/startseite.html. Accessed 10 June 2020.

Institut DGB-Index Gute Arbeit. (2015). *DGB-Index Gute Arbeit – Der Report 2015: Mit dem Themenschwerpunkt Multitasking, unzureichende Personalausstattung, Arbeit ohne Pause*

– *Profilmerkmale der Arbeitshetze.* https://index-gute-arbeit.dgb.de/++co++83f44c88-9428-11e5-8b1e-52540023ef1a0. Accessed 13 June 2020.

Institut DGB-Index Gute Arbeit. (2016). *DGB-Index Gute Arbeit – Der Report 2016: Mit dem Themenschwerpunkt: Die Digitalisierung der Arbeitswelt – Eine Zwischenbilanz aus der Sicht der Beschäftigten.* https://index-gute-arbeit.dgb.de/++co++76276168-a0fb-11e6-8bb8-525400e5a74a. Accessed 13 June 2020.

Institut DGB-Index Gute Arbeit. (2017). *DGB-Index Gute Arbeit – Der Report 2017: Mit dem Themenschwerpunkt Arbeit, Familie, private Interessen – wodurch die Vereinbarkeit behindert wird und wie sie zu fördern ist.* https://index-gute-arbeit.dgb.de/++co++614dfaea-bee1-11e7-98bf-52540088cada. Accessed 13 June 2020.

Institut DGB-Index Gute Arbeit. (2018). *DGB-Index Gute Arbeit – Der Report 2018: Mit dem Themenschwerpunkt Arbeit mit Kunden, PatientInnen, Lernenden etc.* https://www.dgb.de/themen/++co++ebe87ffe-edc5-11e8-a379-52540088cada. Accessed 13 June 2020.

Institut DGB-Index Gute Arbeit (2019). *Jahresbericht 2019 – Ergebnisse der Beschäftigtenbefragung zum DGB-Index Gute Arbeit 2019 mit dem Themenschwerpunkt Arbeitsintensität.* https://www.dgb.de/presse/++co++e5a35cdc-1735-11ea-b183-52540088cada. Accessed 13 June 2020.

Institut DGB-Index Gute Arbeit (2020). *Jahresbericht 2020 – Ergebnisse der Beschäftigtenbefragung zum DGB-Index Gute Arbeit 2020 mit dem Schwerpunktthema Mobiles Arbeiten.* https://index-gute-arbeit.dgb.de/++co++b8f3f396-0c7f-11eb-91bf-001a4a160127. Accessed 21 Oct 2021.

Kawachi, I., & Subramanian, S. (2017). Social epidemiology for the 21st Century. *Social Sciences & Medicine, 196*, 240–245. https://doi.org/10.1016/j.socscimed.2017.10.034. Accessed 12 June 2020.

Lampert, T., Kroll, L. E., Kuntz, B., & Hoebel, J. (2018). Gesundheitliche Ungleichheit in Deutschland und im internationalen Vergleich: Zeitliche Entwicklungen und Trends. *JoHM, 3(S1)*, 2–26. https://doi.org/10.17886/RKI_GBE-2018-2019.

Lenßen, K. (2015). Gefährdungsbeurteilung psychischer Belastungen am Arbeitsplatz (GBpsych): Ein Präventionsansatz mit rechtlichem Rahmen und vielfältigem Nutzen. *Gesprächspsychotherapie Und Personenzentrierte Beratung, 4*(15), 198–205.

Mielck, A. (2000). *Soziale Ungleichheit und Gesundheit: Empirische Ergebnisse, Erklärungsansätze, Interventionsmöglichkeiten.* Huber.

Mielck, A. (2005). *Soziale Ungleichheit und Gesundheit – Einführung in die aktuelle Diskussion.* Huber.

OECD. (2019). Germany: Country health profile 2019, State of health in the EU. *OECD Publishing, 3.* https://doi.org/10.1787/36e21650-en.

Robert Koch-Institut. (2015). Gesundheit in Deutschland. https://www.rki.de/DE/Content/Gesundheitsmonitoring/Gesundheitsberichterstattung/GesInDtld/GesInDtld_inhalt.html. Accessed 23 Febr 2020.

Siegrist, J. (2005). *Medizinische Soziologie* (6., neu bearb. und erw. Aufl., S. 30–31) Urban & Fischer.

Singer, S. (2010). Entstehung des Betrieblichen Gesundheitsmanagements. In A. S. Esslinger, M. Emmert, & O. Schöffski (Eds.), *Betriebliches Gesundheitsmanagement – Mit gesunden Mitarbeitern zu unternehmerischem Erfolg* (1st ed., pp. 25–48). Gabler.

Spitzenverband der Gesetzlichen Krankenversicherungen, Spitzenverband der Medizinischen Dienste. (2019). Präventionsbericht 2019 – Berichtsjahr 2018. https://www.gkv-spitzenverband.de/media/dokumente/krankenversicherung_1/praevention__selbsthilfe__beratung/praevention/praeventionsbericht/2019_GKV_MDS_Praventionsbericht_barrierefrei.pdf. Accessed 30 May 2020.

Statista.com. (2010). Was hält davon ab, betriebliches Gesundheitsmanagement einzuführen? https://de.statista.com/statistik/daten/studie/164073/umfrage/gruende-zur-nicht-einfuehrung-von-gesundheitsmanagement-im-betrieb. Accessed 7 June 2020.

Statistisches Bundesamt. (2020). Statistiken zu Gewerkschaften in Deutschland. https://de.statista.com/themen/3099/gewerkschaften-in-deutschland/. Acessed 13 June 2020.

Swart, E., Ihle, P., Gothe, H., & Matusiewicz, D. (2014). *Routinedaten im Gesundheitswesen* (2. vollst. überarb. Aufl.) Huber.

Verband der Ersatzkassen. (2020). Daten zum Gesundheitswesen: Versorgung. https://www.vdek.com/presse/daten/d_ausgaben.html. Accessed 14 June 2020.

Wollschläger, D. (2015). Grundlagen der Datenanalyse mit R. Springer Spektrum (S. 287–323) Springer Nature.

Wright, M. T., v. Unger, H., & Block, M. (2010). Partizipation der Zielgruppe in der Gesundheitsförderung und Prävention. In M. T. Wright (Hrsg.), *Partizipative Qualitätsentwicklung in der Gesundheitsförderung und Prävention* (S. 35–52). Huber.

Wulf, I., Süß, S., & Diebig, M. (2017). Akteure der Gefährdungsbeurteilung psychischer Belastung – Perspektiven und Konflikte im betrieblichen Arbeits- und Gesundheitsschutz. *Zeitschrift Für Arbeitswissenschaften, 71*, 296–304.

Zeidler, J., & Braun, S. (2012). Sekundärdatenanalysen. In O. Schöffski, v.d. & Schulenburg, J. (Hrsg.), *Gesundheitsökonomische Evaluationen* (4., vollst. überarb. Aufl., S. 243–274) Springer.

Use and Significance of Expert Medical Advice on the Internet: Results of an Online Survey Among Users of German-Language Health Portals

10

Julian Wangler and Michael Jansky

Contents

10.1   Introduction 178
10.2   Current State of Research 179
10.3   Method. 180
10.4   Results 181
10.5   Discussion 184
         10.5.1   Strengths and Weaknesses of the Work 185
         10.5.2   Consequences for Clinics and Healthcare Practices 185
References. 186

Abstract

Introduction: Despite the continuing ban on the exclusive use of remote medical treatment in Germany, more and more patients are making use of expert medical advice on the internet. This study explores what motivates patients to seek online medical advice and the implications for the doctor-patient relationship. The focus is on general medical care. Method: The survey is an exploratory investigation that does not claim to be representative. 207 users of eleven German-language health and advice

J. Wangler (✉) · M. Jansky
Department of General and Geriatric Medicine, University Medical Center, Mainz, Germany
e-mail: Julian.Wangler@unimedizin-mainz.de

M. Jansky
e-mail: jansky@uni-mainz.de

portals were interviewed via online survey. In addition to descriptive analysis, a T-test for independent samples was used to identify significant differences between two groups. Where there were more than two groups, a simple variance analysis was performed. Two significance levels were tested (mean difference at level $p < .05$ and $p < .001$). Results: The majority of the surveyed users of health portals also make use of online advice. There is a surprisingly positive assessment of expert medical advice on the internet. Although there is often insufficient information on the identity and qualifications of medical experts, such experts are trusted. The findings show that online medical consultations can both support and weaken the doctor-patient relationship. It is significant that, for some of the respondents, there are signs of increasing uncertainty due to the use of these services (for example due to conflicting advice). Discussion: Based on the results of the survey, the authors argue that the issue of online research should be actively addressed during the patient consultation in order to prevent possible negative consequences for the doctor-patient relationship. In addition, it seems advisable to give more emphasis to this issue during training. Last but not least, improvements in the quality and transparency of online medical advice services should be considered.

10.1   Introduction

Websites that provide healthcare information are becoming increasingly popular (Krüger-Brand, 2015). Patients are also making increasing use of advice from s-called medical experts. Providers of such services advertise that their experts can quickly and easily remind health issues by, for example, naming a disease on the basis of symptoms described, or recommending specialists or medical services, or giving advice on dealing with chronic disease. This form of healthcare communication can have far-reaching consequences, as patients may not only disclose very intimate information about themselves, but may also prove to be highly receptive to the advice they are given (Rossmann & Karnowski, 2014).

For many portals, what exactly is meant by the term "expert" remains vague. Only some of the counselling services provide information on whether they use trained physicians. Other providers often answer queries using a pseudonym. The way in which experts can be contacted also differs. Thus there are expert forums integrated into heath information pages (e.g. Onmeda, Lifeline) or stand-alone forums (e.g. Cyberdoctor). There are also providers where communication is not via publicy accessible forums but via separate contact forms or chats (e.g. ThanksDoc).

From a legal point of view, online medical advice treads a fine line. Despite initial attempts to relax the code of conduct for doctors in the context of certain model projects, doctors are still forbidden from providing exclusively remote treatment (§ 7 (4)). Unless a personal assessment has been carried out beforehand, online consultation may provide only general information about a disease and its symptoms (Bundesärztekammer, 2015). In addition, § 9 of the Medicines Marketing Act (Heilmittelwerbegesetz) prohibits the advertising of remote diagnosis. In everyday life, the distinction between providing advice and an actual recommendation for treatment is often unclear. In 2012, legal action was taken against the service "Gesundheitsberatung.de" because it appeared to advertise medical advice that included treatment recommendations (Cologne Regional Court Judgement, 2012). Even today uncertainty remains as to whether online advice regarding general disorders counts as remote treatment.

10.2   Current State of Research

There have now been several systematic reviews of the use of online sources by patients (e.g. Cassidy & Baker, 2016), but only very few studies have addressed online medical advice services. This applies both to commercial services and to the online advisory services offered by certain health insurance companies.

One of the few German-language studies on the subject was conducted in 2015 by the North Rhine-Westphalia Consumer Centre and dealt with the quality assurance of such services. Using pre-prepared case vignettes, questions were asked on various expert sites and the answers were assessed against pre-defined transparency and quality criteria. Overall the results were not encouraging. Although a wealth of sometimes inappropriate data on users was collected, "transparency about the experts and their qualifications leaves much to be desired" (Verbraucherzentrale Nordrhein-Westfalen, 2015). The expert advice itself is often "inadequate", since the answer is usually limited to a short sentence "that provides the user with a recommendation on the subject but without further explanation" (ibid.). Moreover only a fraction of the services analyzed provided information on how they are financed.

In addition to the issues of quality and transparency, there is a lack of specific knowledge regarding the effects of online consultations. Previous studies have focused exclusively on consumers´ general online behavior when looking for health information. In addition to positive effects such as increased knowledge, patient empowerment and the potential for prevention, there are problems with, and limits to, the quality and source transparency of online health information (Baumann & Link, 2016). This can lead to confusion and even the wrong action being taken (Sethuram & Weerakkody, 2010). Also seen as a problem by many authors is the influence that the pharmaceutical industry may try to exert on health information on the internet, especially as product advertising is not always recognizable as such (Huh et al., 2005). Another possible negative consequence of researching health-related information on the internet can be an impairment of the doctor-patient relationship. Discrepancies between the treatment suggestions from a doctor and treatment suggestions on the internet can lead to a gradual loss of confidence (Hannawa & Rothenfluh, 2014; Schmidt-Kaehler, 2005). Studies show that between 10 and 16% of patients have rejected or modified treatment recommendations based on information from the internet (Baker et al., 2003; Weaver, 2008).

The Siemens Health Insurance fund recently commissioned a survey of its representatives. It does not deal specifically with advisory services but its results are nevertheless interesting (YouGov 2014). A quarter of all respondents who regularly use the internet to obtain information on health and illness do not visit a doctor at all. The study also deals with the phenomenon of "cyberchondria", a state of hyper-vigilance or anxiety in relation to one´s health and based on obtaining contradictory or incorrect information from the internet without the benefit of medical clarification (YouGov, 2014). It is assumed that high levels of internet use lead to existing personality traits (such as a tendency to hypochondria) being exacerbated (White & Horvitz, 2009, Eichenberg & Wolters, 2013). This phenomenon is addressed again in the presentation and discussion of the results.

It can be assumed that the potential effects of online medical advice correspond to the motives for seeking the advice in the first place. Powell et al., (2011) have compiled four categories of motives regarding the use of health information on the internet:

- The need for reinsurance, e.g. by obtaining a second opinion,
- the desire for additional information to deepen existing knowledge,
- the change of the patient role, in which the patient assumes responsibility by searching for information and the
- exchange of personal opinions and experiences with other persons.

In connection with the background information presented above, the following questions were at the centre of the investigation to be presented here:

- What motivates patients to seek medical advice on the internet?
- What advantages do patients associate with medical advice from the internet?
- What consequences does the use of medical advice from the internet have for the doctor-patient relationship?

10.3   Method

The survey is an exploratory investigation that does not claim to be representative. Research questions were put via an online questionnaire that was created mainly by the authors but that incorporated existing research results:

- The creation of the compact item battery for the identification of usage motives (cf. Tab. 10.1) was partly based on the motif bundles of Powell et al., (2011).
- For the derivation of the item battery for the consequences for the doctor-patient relationship (cf. Tab. 10.2), common impact assumptions for internet-based health communication were used, as listed by Rossmann and Karnowski (2014) and Baumann and Link (2016).
- Last but not least, the aforementioned quality analysis of medical consulting portals (Verbraucherzentrale Nordrhein-Westfalen, 2015) helped to add further distinct motives for use and effects in the two item batteries mentioned.

With regard to possible consequences for the doctor-patient relationship, the question-naire focused on GP care. The survey was conducted by means of the Lime Survey tool. Validation was carried out via pre-testing. The survey was then activated in the forums of eleven German-language health and advice portals with and without expert advice areas: "Net-Doktor Community", "Onmeda", "Frag-Dich-gesund", "Esando", "Sanego", "Med.de", "Med1.de", "Gesundheit.de", "Mein-Gesundheitsforum.de", "Platinnetz" and "Silversurfer". These portals were chosen because they cover a large, heterogeneous range of users, in particular "Net-Doktor Community" and "Onmeda". In order to guarantee anonymity, the portal through which the interviewees were recruited was not captured. The data was evaluated by using SPSS 23.0 for Windows. A T-test was used on independ-ent samples to detect significant differences between two groups. Where there were more than two grous, a simple analysis of variance was performed. Two significance levels were tested (mean value difference at the level $p < 0.05$ and $p < 0.001$). The survey ran from 10th October 2016 to 10th January 2017. In total 207 completed questionnaires were included in the evaluation. In sociodemographic terms, the sample can be described as follows:

- Gender: 50% male, 50% female
- Average age: 51 years (min.: 21, max.: 74 years)
- Level of education: secondary school 11%, junior secondary school (10–16 years) 27%, technical college or higher 38%, other 7%, not specified 17%
- Number of people in household: one person 22%, two persons 48%, more than two persons 24%, not specified &%
- Residential environment: (large or medium-sized town) 51%, rural (small town or rural community) 43%, not specified 6%

10.4   Results

At 80%, the majority of respondents ($n = 166$) use online medical expert advice at least from time to time (never: 20%). 41% seek occasional or frequent advice. Among woman, the proportion of those who frequently seek advice is 22%, almost three times as high as among men (8%, $p < 0.05$). Of those surveyed who make use of online medical advice, 70% use such services for research purposes in advance of a visit to the doctor. 56% state that they make use of medical expert advice after visiting a doctor in order to obtain further information or a second opinion. At 61%, a clear majority of respond-ents said that they trust the portal from which they usually receive expert medical advice either strongly or very strongly. Only one in five (22%) has little or no confidence (no data: 17%). Proof of this great popularity is the fact that less than one third (28%) of respondents state that they always or mostly look up the information received from the expert on an information portal such as "Wikipedia" (occasionally: 25%). A fifth (20% never does this (no information: 27%).

Respondents see various benefits in online medical advice services. Almost three-quarters (72%) appreciate the anonymity of the internet and believe that online advice is useful for a second opinion (73%, see Table 10.1). Two thirds (68%) consider this kind of information to be competent and therefore trustworthy. More than one in two (59%) assumes that the experts on most portals are real doctors. One third of all respondents (35%) believe that medical advice on the internet can replace a visit to the doctor. There are considerable gender differences: almost half of all men, but only a fifth of all women, sees such services as an adequate substitute. Despite this very positive assessment of online consulting, over 60% of respondents was in no doubt that the pharmaceutical industry is involved in the financing of medical advice sites and directly or indirectly advertises their products there.

Users were asked for an assessment of what has changed for them since they started using online medical consultations. As already stated, the questions focused on the patient´s relationship with their GP. A majority of respondents stated that, due to their use of medical experts on the internet, they understand doctors better (66%), are more critical (58%) and ask more questions (51%, see Table 10.2). On the other hand, 37% say that their GP´s advice is no longer as important as it used to be. As a result of using of these portals, almost one-third (32%) frequently do not visit their doctor or now change their doctor more frequently (31%). It is noticeable that, since using online advice, 44% of respondents admin to being occasionally more confused and less well informed. Faced with conflicting advice and information, these respondents frequently face decision dilemmas.

Table 10.1 Which statements do you agree with? (Response categories (Agree completely/Agree quite strongly) summarized), exact questionnaire wording not reproduced here

Statement	Total (N = 166)	Men (n₁ = 83)	Women (n₁ = 83)
The advantage of online medical advice is you can remain anonymous	72.4%	70.7%	74.1%
Online medical advice is useful when you need a second opinion	72.5%	62.5%*	882.4%*
Online medical advice is reliable	68.1%	65.5%	70.7%
Most of the experts who provide online medical advices are doctors	58.6%	55.2%	62.1%
Online medical advice can often be a substitute for a visit to the doctor	35.4%	**48.3%****	**22.4%****
Medical advice sites are financed by pharmaceutical companies	62.1%	63.8%	60.4%

*p<0.05., **p<0.001

Table 10.2 Using medical advice from the internet can have various consequences. Which statements do you agree with? (Response categories (Agree completely/Agree quite strongly) summarized), exact questionnaire wording not reproduced here

Statement	Total (N = 166)	Men (n₁ = 83)	Women (n₁ = 83)
I understand doctors better now	66.4%	63.8%	69.0%
I am now more willing to challenge doctors	57.7%	63.8%	51.7%
I can now deal better with ailments	55.1%	58.6%	51.8%
I now ask doctors more questions	50.8%	50.0%	51.7%
Since I´ve been getting medical advice, I sometimes find I am more confused	43.9%	41.4%	46.5%
My GP´s advice is now less important than it used to be	37.1%	41.4%	32.8%
I often no longer bother going to the doctor	31.9%	**39.6%***	**24.2%***
I+now change my doctor more frequently	31.1%	**37.9%***	**24.1%***

*p<0.05.

This finding can be examined in greater depth by linking it to specific self-characterization statements presented to interviewees at the start (cf. Table 10.3). Several statements on self-characterization were presented to all 207 respondents. Within the group of those seeking medical online advice (n = 166), 73 indicate that they have become more confused since using online advice. If one compares the overall sample with the group of those who claim to be more confused, one sees some indication of increasing health anxiety. So it can be seen that those persons who occasionally get confused since starting to use advice portals rate themselves as nervous, worried and introspective more than the average of all respondents.

Table 10.3 Which statements do you agree with? (Response categories (Agree completely/Agree quite strongly) summarized)

Statement	Total (N = 207)	More confused since using online advice (n = 73)
I am someone who easily gets nervous	39.4%	54.2%
Sometimes I worry I might have a serious illness	50.1%	62.8%
I often listen to my inner voice	70.4%	74.9%
I am not someone who gets worried easily	39.0%	28.5%

10.5   Discussion

Medical expert advice on the internet is no longer a niche phenomenon. Despite legal limitations it has established itself as part of the German healthcare system. These services are consulted by many patients both before and after a visit to the doctor. The results of the present survey of users of health and advice platforms show that online advice on health and illness is valued above all for its anonymity and used at least to obtain a second opinion.

Responses show that the features of online consultations are remarkably positive. In addition to the anonymity on the internet, what stands out is a profound and—in view of the poor transparency of many portals—largely unwarranted trust in the competence of the expert providing the advice. For a (primarily male) proportion of the respondents, this is so entrenched that they often regard online consultations as a substitute for visits to the doctor. It is noteworthy that a considerable number of patients assume that the experts on consultation portals are doctors.

In addition, the results of the survey indicate that the use of medical advice on the internet can have considerable effects not only on the health behavior of patients but also on the doctor-patient relationship. The consequences range from a more reflective and critical approach to doctors to disengagement from, and a more frequent change of one´s doctor.

In light of the results, online consultations appear to contribute in a significant number of patients to a weaking of their relationship with their GP. In this context, one can say that competition from the Internet has led to a loss of the doctor´s monopoly on information and influence (PwC, 2015; Baumann & Czerwinski, 2015). In view of the average age of well over 50 years, it can be seen that not only younger people are making more use of the online advice provided by experts, but also a large number of people in or approaching retirement. Studies have traditionally shown that older patients have a particularly strong attachment to their GP (Rieser, 2005). But in view of the now widespread adoption of the internet by the population as a whole, the results of the survey point to problems in this older age group as well.

Another finding is the considerable number of respondents who admit to being more confused after online consultation than before. This group is characterized by a high degree of uncertainty and latent fear of illness. It is true that the indicators collected are not sufficient to explain the extent to which expert medical advice on the internet influences and possibly reinforces hypochondriac behavior. They are however an indication that the online search for symptoms, clinical pictures and treatment recommendations poses challenges and risks for patients that should not be underestimated. The flood of information, as well as conflicting information and the opaque interests of the providers are some examples. Assessment of these offers is made even more difficult by low awareness of media and healthcare issues.

In view of the significantly increased influence of online information on the health behavior of patients, doctors in general and GPs in particular are facing new challenges.

Doctors today must assume that patients use the internet as a source of information and advice before and after their visit. The information gained in this way can have both positive and negative effects. Nonetheless surveys show that only some GPs and specialists take their patients´ online research into account or feel that they can disregard the advice offered by serious online healthcare sites (Bertelsmann Stiftung, 2016). Moreover, if, as current studies show, up to 16% of all GP practices in Germany do not yet have an internet connection, there is some catching up to do (Stiftung Gesundheit, 2015). Initiatives and surveys of medical students also show that they would like to see the internet playing a greater role in patient care in their future careers (Brinkmann & Nohl-Deryk, 2015, Jacob et al., 2014).

Previous analyses show that there is an enormous discrepancy between patient demand for online medical advisory services and the quality of such services (Verbraucherzentrale Nordrhein-Westfalen, 2015). Given the impact that online consultations can have on healthcare delivery, it is imperative that patients have a realistic picture of the possibilities and limitations of these services. The reliability of information and recommendations can be assessed only if the patient knows what qualifications online advisors have. There should also be a clear definition of the services an online consultation has to provide and where its limits lie. Minimum standards would need to be established, ideally by legislation.

10.5.1 Strengths and Weaknesses of the Work

The results of this survey are limited by the fact that they represent a snapshot of opinion among users of popular health platforms. Accordingly, it is an exploratory study. Due to the limited number of cases and the self-selection of the participants, the survey cannot claim to be broadly representative. The recipient should also take into account the fact that the interviewees are people who, judging by the time they spend on healthcare sites, have a pre-existing tendency to conduct healthcare research. In addition, the survey has only superficially determined to what extent the respondents are prone to health fears or show hypochondriacal tendencies. Nonetheless the fact that the survey is based on a broad sociodemographic sample underlines the significance of the findings.

10.5.2 Consequences for Clinics and Healthcare Practices

- It would appear sensible for doctors, during their consultations with patients, to actively address internet-based healthcare research, to discuss its potential and risk and to use it to improve the doctor-patient-relationship. It would be worth considering extending the anamnesis to include online research and, if necessary, granting more consultation time to patients who are anxious about their health or are unsettled by any contradictory information they have found online.

- To help GPs in particular to better respond to the online behavior of patients, this aspect should be given more emphasis during training.
- It would appear necessary to increase the quality and transparency of online medical consultations so that patients can better assess the possibilities and limitations of such services. Guidelines should be introduced to that end. Also worthy of consideration is a voluntary commitment on the part of the suppliers.

References

Baker, L., Wagner, T. H., Singer, S., & Bundorf, M. K. (2003). Use of the Internet and e-mail for health care information. *American Medical Association., 289,* 2400–2406.

Bertelsmann Stiftung. (2016). Ärzte sehen informierte Patienten kritisch. https://www.bertels-mann-stiftu ng.de/de/themen/aktuelle-meldungen/2016/juni/aerzte-sehen-informierte-patienten-kritisch. Accessed: 25 Nov. 2018.

Baumann, E., & Czerwinski, F. (2015). Erst mal Doktor Google fragen? Nutzung neuer Medien zur Information und zum Austausch über Gesundheitsthemen. In J. Böcken, B. Braun, & R. Meierjürgen (Eds.), *Gesundheitsmonitor 2015—Bürgerorientierung im Gesundheitswesen* (pp. 57–79). Bertelsmann Inhouse Print.

Baumann, E., & Link, E. (2016). Onlinebasierte Gesundheitskommunikation: Nutzung und Austausch von Gesundheitsinformationen über das Internet. In F. Fischer & A. Krämer (Eds.), *eHealth in Deutschland. Anforderungen und Potenziale innovativer Versorgungsstrukturen* (pp. 285–406). Springer.

Brinkmann, J., & Nohl-Deryk, P. 2015). Der Blick einer neuen Medizinergeneration auf Telemedizin und das Arztsein im Internetzeitalter. http://medizin-und-neue-medien.de/wp-con-tent/uploads/2015/03/Der BlickeinerneuenGeneration240215.pdf. Accessed 25 Nov. 2018.

Bundesärztekammer. (2015). (Muster-)Berufsordnung für die in Deutschland tätigen Ärztinnen und Ärzte. http://www.bundesaerztekammer.de/fileadmin/user_upload/downloads/pdf-Ordner/MBO/MBO_0 2.07.2015.pdf. Accessed 25 Nov. 2018.

Cassidy, J. T., & Baker, J. F. (2016). Orthopaedic patient information on the world wide web: An essential review. *The Journal of Bone and Joint Surgery., 98*(4), 325–328.

Cologne Regional Court judgement. (2012). Ref. 6 U 235/11. https://openjur.de/u/462481.html. Accessed 25 Nov. 2018.

Eichberg, C., & Wolters, C. (2013). Internetrecherche bei Gesundhietsfragen—Phänomen „Cyberchondrie". *Deutsches Ärzteblatt, 12*(2), 78–79.

Hannawa, A. F., & Rothenfluh, F. B. (2014). Arzt-Patient-Interaktion. In K. Hurrelmann & E. Baumann (Eds.), *Handbuch Gesundheitskommunikation* (pp. 110–128). Hans Huber.

Huh, J., DeLorme, D. E., & Reid, L. N. (2005). Factors affecting trust in online prescription drug information and impact of trust on behavior following exposure to DTC advertising. *Health Communication, 10,* 711–731.

Jacob, R., Kopp, J., & Schultz, S. (2014). Berufsmonitoring Medizinstudenten 2014— Ergebnisse einer bundesweiten Befragung. http://www.kbv.de/media/sp/2015_04_08_Berufsmonitoring_2014.web.pdf. Accessed 25 Nov. 2018.

Krüger-Brand, H. E. (2015). Internet als Quelle für Gesundheitsinfos. Deutsches Ärzteblatt, 108, Supplement PRAXIS 3/2015. 2.

Powell, J., Inglis, N., Ronnie, J., & Large S. (2011). The characteristics and motivations of online health information seekers: cross-sectional survey and qualitative interview Study. *Journal of Internet Medical Research, 13*(1), e20.

PricewaterhouseCoopers (PwC). (2015). Konkurrenz aus dem Internet: Informationsmonopol der Hausärzte geht verloren, Healthcare-Barometer. http://www.pwc.de/de/pressemitteilungen/de/konkurrenz-aus-dem-internet_informationsmonopol-der-hausaerzte-geht-verloren.html. Accessed 25 Nov. 2018.

Rieser, S. (2005). Arzt-Inanspruchnahme. *Deutsches Ärzteblatt, 102.* A 1096.

Rossmann, C., & Karnowski, V. (2014). eHealth und mHelath—Gesundheitskommunikation online und mobil. In K. Hurrelmann & E. Baumann (Eds.), *Handbuch Gesundheitskommunikation* (pp. 271–285). Hans Huber.

Schmidt-Kaehler, S. (2005). Patienteninformation und -beratung im Internet. Transfer medientheoretischer Überlegungen auf ein expandierendes Praxisfeld. *Medien & Kommunikattionswissenschaft, 53,* 471–485.

Sethuram, R., & Weerakkody, A. N. (2010). Health information on the Internet. *Journal of Obstetrics and Gynaecology, 30,* 119–121.

Stiftung Gesundheit. (2015). Ärzte im Zukunftsmarkt Gesundheit 2015: Die eHealth-Studie. Die Digitalisierung der ambulanten Medizin—eine deutschlandweite Befragung niedergelassener Ärztinnen und Ärzte. https://stiftung-gesundheit.de/pdf/studien/Aerzte_im_Zukunftsmarkt_Gesundheit-2015_eHealthStudie.pdf. Accessed 25 Nov. 2018.

Verbraucherzentrale Nordrhein-Westfalen. (2015). Was leistet medizinischer Rat im Internet? Ergebnisse einer empirischen Untersuchung des Onlineangebots „Medizinischer Expertenrat". http//www.verbraucherzentrale.nrw/publikationen/medizinischer-rat-im-internet. Accessed 25 Nov. 2018.

Weaver, J., Thompson, N., Weaver, S., & Hopkins G. L. (2008). Profiling characteristics of individual´s using Internet health information in healthcare adherence decision. Conference: 136st APHA Annual Meeting and Exposition, October 25–29, San Diego.

White, R. W., & Horvitz, E. (2009). Cyberchondria—Studies of the escalation of medical concerns in web search. *ACM Transactions on Information Systems, 27*(4), 1–37.

YouGov Deutschland AG. (2015). Dr. Internet: Online-Diagnose statt Arztbesuch? Patientenbefragung der YouGov Deutschland AG im Auftrag der Siemens Betriebskrankenkasse. https://www.sbk.org/uploads/media/pm-dr-internet-online-diagnose-statt-arztbesuch-sbk_150528.pdf. Accessed 25 Nov. 2018.

A Source Data Verification-Based Data Quality Analysis Within the Network of a German Comprehensive Cancer Center

11

Martina Borner, Diana Schweizer, Theres Fey, Daniel Nasseh and Robert Dengler

Contents

11.1   Introduction 190
11.2   Materials and Methods. 191
11.3   Results 193
11.4   Discussion 195
References. 199

T. Fey · D. Nasseh
Comprehensive Cancer Center of the Ludwig-Maximilians-University Munich, Munich, Germany

T. Fey
University Hospital of the Ludwig-Maximilians-University Munich, Munich, Germany

R. Dengler (✉)
FOM University of Applied Sciences, Munich, Germany
e-mail: robert.dengler@fom.de

D. Nasseh
Institute of Medical Information Processing, Biometry and Epidemiology of the Ludwig-Maximilians-University Munich, Munich, Germany

M. Borner
WMC Healthcare GmbH, Munich, Germany

D. Schweizer
HanseMerkur, Hamburg, Germany

M. Cassens et al. (eds.), *Transdisciplinary Perspectives on Public Health in Europe*, FOM-Edition, https://doi.org/10.1007/978-3-658-33740-7_11

189

Abstract

Routinely collected clinical data usually serve to support primary care. There are multiple patient related information sources including medical letters, laboratory reports or pathological findings. There is an ongoing trend to crosslink this information within data warehouses or other comprehensive datasets in order to utilize the data for secondary use. In case of unstructured information, e.g. medical letters, this process is often not fully automatable. Hence, the question has to be raised whether the manual interference, when transcribing and transforming data from the source systems into the joint system, has a harmful effect in terms of data quality and data analysis. This question has to be answered individually for different data sets but quantifying different aspects of data quality can support understanding the degree of these harmful effects. To quantify the manual transcription quality of tumor documentation data, the authors analyzed a representative sample of data in terms of the quality indicators correctness, completeness as well as timeliness. The methodological approach was based on a source data verification. Overall, correctness was quantified with 99.17%, completeness with 99.01% and timeliness with 65.61%. The authors conclude that in the given case the impact of manual transcription in terms of completeness, correctness as well as timeliness could be considered as a minor factor.

11.1   Introduction

The ongoing digitalization within the healthcare sector, and consequently within most modern hospitals leads to the accumulation of routinely collected data of most aspects of a patient´s local medical history (Kayyali et al., 2013). While the initial purpose of these data collections is to support the primary care of the patient, the data could potentially be utilized for secondary scenarios in terms of science and research. Large scale projects like the PCORNet in the US or the initiative of medical informatics in German – or more generally comprehensive medical registries aim at gathering this routinely collected data within data warehouses or comprehensive data bases, harmonizing data and finally making it available to research groups (Collings et al., 2014; Fleurence et al., 2014; Semler, 2016).

Unlike capturing structured data within a predefined setting, as it is the case within most clinical trials, it often seems hard to estimate whether data extracted from often unstructured routine data show a high enough data quality to be utilized within research projects (Hoffmann & Podgurski, 2013). Therefore the garbage-in-garbage-out principle poses a potential risk when working with routinely collected data (Rahm & Do, 2000). Thus, this paper aims to analyze and quantify some aspects of data quality of one large comprehensive tumor data set at a German university hospital (Medical Center of the University of Munich).

The given dataset presents the hospital´s local comprehensive cancer tumor documentation based on a installation of the software system CREDOS (Voigt et al., 2010). Current data about most aspects of a locally treated tumor case, meaning, decisions about the therapy, the actual treatments, details about the diagnosis, classification and histology as well as progression (e.g. progression or remission) are stored within the system. With Dec. 25th 2016 the system contained about approx. 80 data tables with circa 1000 attribute fields. Some of the information is retrieved automatically (e.g. OPS codes), while most of the data is manually collected by tumor documentation officers who converting and transcribing the often-unstructured data into the structured system.

The transcription from these letters and other unstructured sources into the documentation system is a potential error source, as tumor documentation officers have to understand where and how they can retrieve the data from the source systems and how they can correctly and completely fill in the information into the given structured documentation system (Inmon & Nesavich, 2007). Within this work, the authors were interested whether this manual transcription poses a potential risk in terms of data quality, and whether it significantly decreases the data quality. Furthermore, the work is meant to present a possible model for other – especially oncological – centers in terms of data quality control. Thus, the authors performed a source data verification, i.e. the comparison of a large sample of the data within the original source documents to the already entered information within the documentation system (Khosla et al., 2000). Consequently, completeness as well as correctness of the documentation quality can be measured and quantified. Additionally, the timeliness of the data was measured. Other quality indicators like concordance have not been considered within this work. Following the analysis phase, individual feedback was given to the tumor documentation officers in order to improve their documentation quality. Utilizing feedback in combination with a SDV (please introduce the abbreviation) has been shown to be one of the most effective ways to improve data quality (De Lusignan, 2005). The given feedback cycle is in accordance with the quality philosophy of Juran based on quality planning, improvement and control (Drescher et al., 2005).

11.2   Materials and Methods

The methodological approach is a SDV which aims at quantifying completeness, correctness as well as timeliness based on a sample of the documentation data. The practical part of this work was independently performed by two members of the comprehensive cancer center (CCC)-team who validated the inputs previously made by local tumor documentation officers. An error in terms of completeness was noted if present source data was wrongfully not transcribed into the system. Source data, which was transcribed, but not in a correct form, according to the center's standards and guidelines, resulted in correctness error. Timeliness was quantified by the time between the availability of the source documents and the moment when the data was entered into the CREDOS system. A timespan between these two dates larger than two moths resulted in a timeliness error. As it would be unfeasible to validate the whole data set, only a representative sample was chosen. Nonnemacher et al. (2014) give recommendations how to possibly restrict a data sample, though the authors based the selection of the sample on relevance of the given data fields (in terms of oncological documentation), as well as the given capacity of the SDV performing team. The authors will discuss some issues about the sample within the later parts of this work as improvements about the sample could be considered in upcoming quality checks. The local sample itself contains data concerning the following oncological entities:

A. eye
B. breast
C. colon
D. biliary tract
E. bladder
F. head and neck
G. liver
H. lung
I. stomach
J. brain or nervous system
K. kidney
L. oesophagus
M. prostate
N. pancreas
O. thyroid

Documentation officers are assigned to specific entities in the CCC. For data protection reasons, the authors anonymized both the entities (capital letters) as well as the names of the nine documentation officers (numbers). Some officers are responsible for more than one entity. Table 11.1 shows the detailed listing, which documentation officer is responsible for which organ entity.

It was decided that the sample should contain data of every major entity and every officer. Thus, individual errors of every officer could be spotted and discussed in a later feedback cycle which has been shown to be an effective way of improving data quality (De Lusignan, 2005). The sample itself was restricted to the years 2014 and 2015 (in terms of the date of first diagnosis of cancer). For each tumor documentation officer, 30

Table 11.1 Responsibility of documentation officer (pseudonymized to numbers) for organ entities (pseudonymized do capita letters)

Entity	Officer		Entity	Officer
A	1		I	5
B	2		J	8
C	5		K	3
D	4		L	5
E	3		M	9
F	6		N	4
G	4		O	5
H	7			

tumor cases were randomly chosen. As there were nine documentation officers, a total of 270 cases were validated throughout the SDV process. If a tumor documentation officer was e.g. responsible for three entities out of the 30 chosen cases, 10 were selected from each of their three entities. One case can consist of up to hundreds of individual data entries. Thus, the team decided to only validate only 24 of the seemingly most relevant data fields for each of the selected cases. Consequently, a total of 6480 data fields were validated for correctness, completeness and timeliness. The relevance of a data field was bilaterally decided by the researchers as well as the documentation team. Possible adaptions to this decision will be issued in the discussion section of this work. All selected data fields belong to one of the selected three main categories "diagnosis", "therapies" (for this analysis restricted to operations) and "progression" (Table 11.2).

The amount of errors (e) was set into relation with the total amount of tested cases (n) which allowed the quantification of correctness, completeness and timeliness (1-e/n). The generated results were confidentially presented as feedback to the individual tumor documentation officers. This feedback included their general performance as well as a discussion about systematic or more general common errors.

11.3   Results

The SDV was conducted for the whole sample. Thus, 6480 data fields had been validated in terms of the three categories. The data for one of the 16 organ entities showed a systematic data quality error. In this case, too many progression documents were created by the tumor documentation officer. According to the ADT (Arbeitsgemeinschaft Deutscher Tumorzentren – Work Association of German Tumor Centers), guidelines of the DKG (Deutsche Krebsgesellschaft – German cancer association) as well as the Bavarian Law of Cancer Registries (BayKRegG, art. 4, §5), structured progression information should only be collected if there is a notable status change within the case (e.g. remission) (Arbeitsgemeinschaft Deutscher Tumorzentren, 2017; Deutsche Krebsgesellschaft, 2016). Instead, the particular tumor documentation officer created a progression form for every visit of the patient whether or not significant changes occurred. This does neither threaten the correctness of the case nor the completeness but results in unnecessary volume problems. The authors therefore decided to exclude this entity from the section of results, concentrating on the remaining 15 organ entities including 5760 data fields. Table 11.3 shows the quantification of completeness, correctness as well as timeliness of the given data for the remaining organ entities. The overall correctness was measured with 99.17%, completeness with 99.01% and timeliness with 65.61%. While Table 11.3 shows the data quality of individual feedback, Table 11.4 shows the quality quantification within specific data fields.

Based on a heatmap Fig. 11.1 quantifies the quality within a data field for a specific organ entity.

Table 11.2 Description of selected fields within the given sample. Each field belongs to one of the three categories "diagnosis", "therapies" as well as "progression"

Diagnosis	
ICD-10	International Statistical Classification of Diseases and Related Health Problems
Histology	Indicates the tumor histology (morphology-code)
Date of diagnosis	Date, indicated in day, month and year, where the reportable diagnosis was first clinically or microscopically diagnosed
Localization	The exact location of the tumor (ICD-O format)
T-Classification	Size or direct extent of the primary tumor according to the TNM (tumor, nodes, metastases) classification
N-Classification	Degree of spread to regional lymph nodes according to the TNM classification
M-Classification	Presence of distant metastases
V-Classification	Tumor invasion into a vessel according to the TNM classification
L-Classification	Invasion into lymphatic vessels according to the TNM classification
Pn-Classification	Invasion from cancer cells into nerves according to the TNM classification
R-Classification	Overall assessment of the resection margin of the cancer, including possible distant metastases
Therapy (operation)	
Research operation	Local assessment of residual classification
OPS-Code	Description of all performed procedures or operations according to the OPS system
Date of therapy	Starting date of a therapy
Multimodal	A flag indicating a combination of at least two therapies, e.g. radio-chemotherapy or chemotherapy followed by surgery
Mortality after operation	Patient died within 30 days after surgery
Phase of therapy	Indicates whether the therapy is primary or secondary
Progression	
Progression: Overall assessment	Overall assessment of the disease (e.g. progression or remission)
Progression: Presence of metastases	Flag indicating whether a metastasis is present
Progression: Location of metastases	Location of a present metastasis
Progression: Status of metastases	Indication whether a metastasis is newly progressing
Progression: ECOG	Eastern Co-operative Oncology Group: Performance status: Describes the well-being of a patient

(continued)

Table 11.2 (continued)

Progression: Date of tumor conference	Date of any tumor conferences in terms of progression
Progression: Lymph nodes	Overall assessment of the regional lymph nodes

Table 11.3 Measurement of quality in terms of correctness, completeness and timeliness for every of the selected organ entities (A to O)

Entity	Documentation Officer	Correctness	Completeness	Timeliness
A	1	-	-	-
B	2	98.89	100	96.67
C	5	96.25	99.58	78.75
D	4	100	97.92	55.83
E	3	100	96.67	34.72
F	6	100	97.94	45.56
G	4	100	100	80
H	7	97.64	100	80.14
I	5	96.67	100	58.75
J	8	100	100	50.69
K	3	99.72	100	41.39
L	5	95.83	100	43.33
M	9	100	98.19	78.19
N	4	100	96.25	90
O	5	100	100	43.33
Total		**99.17**	**99.01**	**65.61**

In total the SDV was conducted by two individual researchers with a shared effort of about 48 workdays.

11.4   Discussion

The presented work provides insight into quantifying specific data quality indicators within the network of a large tumor documentation data set based on routinely collected data. It is primarily meant to give similar centers and networks an idea how to approach this issue and possibly quantify or improve their own data quality. As has been shown, secondary research projects can be based on routinely collected data (German Cancer Research Center, 2014; Semler, 2016). Hence, the question is whether the local data is

Table 11.4 Measurement of quality in terms of correctness, completeness and timeliness for every of the selected data fields

Data field	Correctness	Completeness	Timeliness
ICD-10	99.58	100	56.25
Histology	99.58	100	56.25
Date of tumor diagnosis	97.50	100	56.25
Localization	99.58	100	56.25
T-Classification	99.58	98.75	56.25
N-Classification	99.58	98.33	56.25
M-Classification	91.25	92.50	56.25
V-Classification	99.58	98.75	56.25
L-Classification	99.58	98.75	56.25
Pn-Classification	99.58	98.75	56.25
R-Classification	99.58	97.17	56.25
Research operation	99.17	100	56.25
OPS-Code	98.33	100	56.25
Date of therapy	99.58	100	56.25
Multimodal	99.58	99.58	56.25
Mortality after operation	99.17	92.08	56.25
Phase of therapy	99.58	99.58	56.25
Progression: Overall assessment	100	100	56.25
Progression: Presence of metastases	100	100	88.33
Progression: Location of metastases	100	100	88.33
Progression: Status of metastases	100	100	88.33
Progression: ECOG	100	100	88.33
Progression: Date of tumor conference	100	100	88.33
Progression: Lymph nodes	99.58	100	88.33
Total	**99.17**	**99.01**	**65.61**

suitable for secondary use and if it could be used for the purposes of research-oriented projects. Therefore, there should be efforts to minimize any problems within the data.

The authors study showed a correctness of 99.17%, a completeness of 99.01% and timeliness of 65.61% based on a SDV comparing a selected sample of a large tumor documentation system to the stored source information of the local hospital. As it is hard to find comparable and referenceable works, the authors of this contribution concluded that transcription errors within the given data set could be considered to be as a minor factor. Unfortunately, the question cannot be answered solely by the given analysis, however, the quantification as well as improvement of data quality should be seen as a gradual

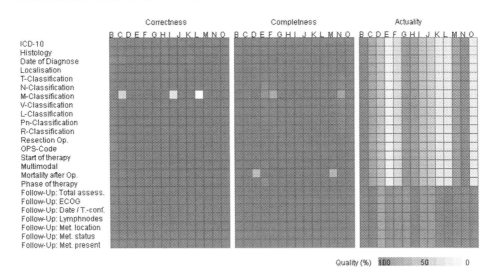

Fig. 11.1 Heatmap illustrating the quantified quality in terms of correctness, completeness as well as actuality for all organ entities (X-axis) and the individual validated data fields (y-axis)

process, and with this analysis focusing on the three given data quality indicators the authors were able to grasp an estimate of the general transcription quality of the local documentation of the given center.

Bray and Parkin (2009, 2009) give insight about maximum rates of missing data for specific data fields under which different organizations were willing to accept oncological data (reaching from 3 to 20%). Nevertheless, referenceable declarations or benchmarks about what should be considered as a good data quality in terms of the given three quality indicators in the field of oncology is hard to find (Bray & Parkin, 2009; Curado et al., 2007; Ferlay et al., 2005; Parkin & Bray, 2009). The authors of this work – in professional exchange with medical partners – believe that the overall transcription error of less than 1% in terms of correctness as well as completeness for the local analysis can be considered as a sufficiently good result to consider working with the data in other contexts. Thus, within the local setting the impact of transcription errors on research or other projects could most probably be considered as a minor factor. Still the work allowed to identify individual errors of the tumor documentary officers and to give them tailored feedback on how to improve. As Fig. 11.1 as well as Table 11.4 show there were some fields with a higher abundance of errors. In particular, in terms of correctness, this was the case for three entities within the field tracking the classification of the metastasis status (based on the TNM-classification system – Vol. 8). The reason for this error was that the stage M0 (meaning no metastasis in abundant) is viable for the clinical assessment of the TNM but not for the pathological assessment (Wittekind 2017). This issue was discussed with and given as feedback to the whole tumor documentation team and should be minimized within the future.

Another more prevalent error was the missing values within the field of postoperative mortality. The problem about this field is, that the date of death of a deceased patient is not automatically and immediately redirected to the tumor documentation team. Efforts have to be made to gain this information; hence, this field will remain problematic until the processes of accessing this information are optimized.

In general, this work also allowed gaining more information about a systematic error within the data of one entity, where too many progression information had been collected and stored. The systematic error was also noticed and criticized by external partners, thus could have been avoided if the SDV had been performed earlier. Nevertheless, the specific tumor documentation officer was trained on the given feedback and the occurrence of the error should be minimized within the future. The quality of the timeliness of the data set might appear to be low, but the authors have to place this in the context of the given timescale of only two months. The analysis shows that 65.61% of all routinely collected data was transcribed into the system within two months. The analysis of timeliness was conducted influenced by the introduction of a new German law, which entered into force in April 2017, which enforces clinical centers to send all information of a tumor patient towards the regional tumor registries within two months after their visits (BayKRegG, Art. 4§1). The fulfillment of the two months timeframe seems feasible by introducing monthly checks in terms of case completeness. Adherence to this demand won´t increase the workload, but requires continous documentation at every time. It excludes the possibility to accumulate large patient cohorts and document them in a large batch (e.g. once a year). Consequently, the authors/the community would expect much higher quality measurements in terms of timeliness for the upcoming years.

Following to this, the initial question – Can the data be used for research purposes? – still cannot entirely be answered. While, as mentioned before, one can quantify the transcription quality, based on this analysis and the fields selected within the sample, but cannot measure the input quality of the clinical physicians who write the medical letters and put the information into the source documents themselves. Therefore, if wrong information is entered into the source systems, this information will remain wrong, even if it is transcribed correctly (garbage-in-garbage-out-principle) (Rahm & Do, 2000). Methods of tackling this problem could be the implementation of structured or semi-structured medical letters with integrated plausibility checks. Though, medical letters should always leave enough freedom to document a patient´s detailed case. Therefore, besides the quality indicators of completeness, correctness and timeliness, there should be a future focus on consistency. Consistency describes implausibility based on defined rules within the data set as described in different other works (Bronnert et al., 2012; Sáez et al., 2012). Unfortunately, consistency is hard to measure as there can be countless of individual plausibility tests, especially within a set with a high data variety. In the end, even retrospective plausibility tests won´t guarantee that the initial information as supplied by the physicians is correct but spotted inconsistencies within the data can be reported to the physicians and help to train/change their documentation behavior or result in the formulation of new standard operation procedures (SOPs). Consequently, the center will also invest work based in this regard.

Nonetheless, the authors believe that the current data quality of the given local dataset should be sufficient for many (not all) retrospective research projects. As an example, as the American IRIS project has shown, it was possible to recreate the results of different clinical trials, based on large amounts of routinely collected data (Parke et al., 2017).

In the near future, in order to measure the impact of the feedback cycle, the center has decided to repeat the SDV for the coming years. Though, after the feedback from cooperation centers and registries, the authors will change the contents of the sample which will be used in the SDV. Within the current sample the authors only incorporate therapy related data of operations. Information about chemotherapies, or in general systemic therapies generally, could be of more interest as they have different starting and final times, as well as highly specific information about dosage and chemical agents. In general, all major categories of therapies should be regarded within a representative sample (operations, systemic therapies, radiation).

The required workload of 48 workdays for the analysis can appear extensive and might not be feasible for smaller centers. Even though, completeness and correctness within this analysis appeared to be acceptable within this work, this can be completely different at other sites and is highly dependent on the local documentation. Therefore, if centers are interested in supplying their data for e.g. research purposes, the authors highly recommend investing work at least to a certain degree (e.g. reducing the amount of samples) in order to control and quantify their own quality indicators.

References

Arbeitsgemeinschaft Deutscher Tumorzentren. (2014). Gemeinsamer einheitlicher onkologischer Basisdatensatz. BAnz AT 28.04.2014 B2

Bray, F., & Parkin, D. M. (2009). Evaluation of data quality in the cancer registry: principles and methods. Part I: comparability, validity and timeliness. *European Journal of Cancer, 45*(5), 747–755.

Bronnert, J., Clark, J. S., Cassidy, B. S., Fenton, S., Hyde, L., Kallem, C., & Watzlaf, V. (2012). Data quality management model (updated). *Journal of AHIMA., 83*(7), 721–725.

Collings, F. S., Hudson, K. L., Briggs, J. P., & Lauer, M. S. (2014). PCORnet, a national patient-centered clinical research network. *Journal of the American Medical Informatics Association., 21*(4), 576–577.

Curado, M. P., Edwards, B., Shin, H. R., Storm H., Ferlay J., Heanue M., & Boyle P. (2007). Cancer incidence in five continents. IARC scientific publication no. 160, Vol. IX. IARC.

De Lusignan, S. (2005). Using feedback to raise the quality of primary care computer data: A literature review. *Studies in Health Technology and Informatics., 116*, 593–598.
    Deutsche Krebsgesellschaft. (2016). *Erhebungsbogen für Onkologische Spitzenzentren und Onkologische Zentren.* DKG.

Drescher, W., Bergfort, I., & Lorenz, J. U. (2005). *Die bedeutendsten Management-Vordenker.* campus.

Ferlay, J., Burkhard, C., Whelan, S., & Parkin, D. M. (2005). Check and conversion programs for cancer registries (IARC/IACR tools for cancer registries). IARC technical report no. 42. IARC.

Fleurence, R. L., Curtis, L. H., Califf, R. M., Platt, R., Selby, J. V., & Brown, J. S. (2014). Launching PCORnet, a national patient-centered clinical research network. *Journal of the American Medical Informatics Association., 21*(4), 578–582.

Gabriel, R. A., Kuo, T. T., McAuley, J., & Hsu, C. N. (2018). Identifying and characterizing highly similar notes in big clinical note datasets. *Journal of Biomedical Informatics., 82*, 63–69.

German Cancer Research Center. (2014). CCP_IT des Deutschen Konsortiums für Translationale Krebsforschung. https://ccp-it.dktk.dkfz.de/. Accessed: 14 Jan. 2017.

Hoffman, S., & Podgurski, A. (2013). Big bad data: Law, public health and biomedical databases. . *The Journal of Law, Medicine & Ethics, 41*(1), 56–60.

Houston, L., Probst, Y., & Martin, A. (2018). Assessing data quality and the variability of source data verification auditing methods in clinical research settings. *Journal of Biomedical Informatics., 82*, 25–32.

Inmon, W. H., & Nesavich, A. (2007). Tapping into unstructured data: Integrating unstructured data and textual analytics into business intelligence. Pearson Education Inc., Boston. ISBN 9780132712910.

Kayyali, B., & van Kuiken, S. (2013). The big-data revolution in US health care: Accelerating value and innovation. https://digitalstrategy.nl/wp-content/uploads/E2-2013.04-The-big-data-revolution-in-US-health-care-Accelerating-value-and-innovation.pdf. Accessed 24 Apr. 2017.

Nonnemacher, M., Nasseh, D., & Stausberg, J. (2014). Datenqualität in der medizinischen Forschung – Leitlinie zum adaptiven Management von Datenquellen in Kohortenstudien und Registern. (Ed.) *Schriftenreihe zur der Telematikplattform für Medizinische Forschungsnetze.* 2., aktual. und erw. Aufl. Bd. 4.2. Berlin: Medizinisch Wissenschaftliche Verlagsgesellschaft.

Parke, D. W., Rich, W. L., Sommer, A., & Lum, F. (2017). The american academy of ophthalmology's IRIS® Registry (Intelligent research in sight clinical data): A look back and a look to the future. *Ophthalmology, 124*(11), 1572–1574.

Parkin, D. M., & Bray, F. (2009). Evaluation of data quality in the cancer registry: Principles and methods. Part II completeness. *European Journal of Cancer, 45*(5), 756–764.

Rahm, E., & Do, H. (2000). Data cleaning: Problems and current approaches. *Data Engineering, 23*, 3.

Sáez, C., Martínez-Miranda, J., Robles, M., & García-Gómez, J. M. (2012). Organizing data quality assessment of shifting biomedical data. *Studies in health technology and informatics, 180*, 721–725.

Semler, S. C. (2016). Medizininformatikerinitiative des BMBF – Vorstellung, aktueller Stand. „Deutsches Biobanken Symposium 2016." Parexel.

Voigt, W., Steinbock, R., & Scheffer, B. (2010). CREDOS 3.1 – a modular system for Tumor documentation for Epidemiological, Clinical, Tumor-Specific and Center-Register integrated into the HIS SAP/R3 IS-H. *Onkologie, 33*, 52–53.

Khosla, R., Vermna, D., Kaput, A., & Khosla, S. (2000). Efficient source data verification. *Indian Journal of Pharmacology., 32*(3), 180–186.

Wittekind, C. (2017). *TNM Klassifikation maligner Tumoren* (8th ed.). Wiley-VCH.

The National Decade Against Cancer 2019–2029: Contents of the Initiative and Some Critical Thoughts

12

Robert Dengler

Contents

12.1 Background 202
12.2 Contents of the Initiative 205
    12.2.1 Aims.. 206
    12.2.2 Action Fields 206
    12.2.3 Collaboration 207
    12.2.4 Contents of Funding Announcement 208
12.3 Some Critical Considerations 210
References... 212

Abstract

Due to the demographic development with ageing societies, certain lifestyle factors and a variety of other reasons, cancer incidence and prevalence will increase continuously, globally and in Germany. Therefore, under the lead of the Federal Ministry of Education and Research and the Federal Ministry of Health, the ten-year initiative "National Decade against Cancer" was launched in February 2019. In this initiative, in collaboration with various players in the health care system, it is intended to mobilize once again all forces in Germany in a targeted way to strengthen and purposefully advance cancer research in the fields of prevention, early detection, diagnostics and innovative therapies once again. The results of research should be quickly brought to

R. Dengler (✉)
FOM University of Applied Sciences, Munich, Germany
e-mail: robert.dengler@fom.de

© The Author(s), under exclusive license to Springer Fachmedien Wiesbaden GmbH, part of Springer Nature 2022
M. Cassens et al. (eds.), *Transdisciplinary Perspectives on Public Health in Europe*, FOM-Edition, https://doi.org/10.1007/978-3-658-33740-7_12

the people. The mission is to also use the experience and knowledge from the onco-logical care of cancer patients for research in order to improve quality and outcome parameters of their care. This article gives an overview of the scope, the aims, fields of action, project partners and collaborators as well as funding details of the project. In a critical outlook the probability is discussed whether this approach will better suc-ceed to overcome the barriers and problems of the German health care system with its different sectors, stakeholders and divergent scopes than the former programs like—e.g.—the National Cancer Plan.

12.1 Background

Cancer is still one of the biggest challenges facing modern medicine. Cancer is the sec-ond most common cause of death in our society and the most dreaded disease (Robert Koch-Institut, Gesellschaft der epidemiologischen Krebsregister in Deutschland e.V. 2017). Over the next 20 years, the number of cancer cases worldwide will double (Bray et al., 2018), and many people will live with their disease for many years to come. Global cancer data from the International Agency for Research on Cancer (IARC) sug-gests that the global cancer burden has risen to 18.1 million cases and 9.6 million can-cer deaths (ibid.). It is estimated that one-in-five men and one-in-six women worldwide will develop cancer over the course of their lifetime, and that one-in-eight men and one-in eleven woman will die from their disease. Several factors appear to be driving this increase, particularly a growing and ageing global population (ibid.) as well as an increase in exposure to cancer risk factors linked to social and economic development (Arndt et al., 2001). For rapidly-growing economies, the data suggests a shift from pov-erty- or infection related cancers to those associated with lifestyles more typical in indus-trialised countries (Fig. 12.1).

There are some indications that scaled-up prevention efforts are starting to reduce cancer incidence rates, e.g. lower lung cancer incidence in men in Northern Europe and North America, or in cervical cancer across most regions except Sub-Saharan Africa compared to 2012 data (Bray et al., 2018; Haberland et al., 2014).

Nevertheless, countries are facing an overall increase in the absolute number of can-cer cases. Asia accounts for nearly half of the new cancer cases and more than half of cancer deaths. Estimates suggest that Asia and Africa have a higher proportion of cancer deaths (7.3% and 57.3% respectively) compared with their incidence (5.8% and 48.4% respectively). IARC suggests this trend is likely due to higher frequency of cancer types associated with poorer prognosis, along with limited access to timely diagnosis and treat-ment. The 2018 data also suggests that countries with high Human Development Index (HDI) have 2–3 times higher cancer incidence than those with low or medium HDI. The

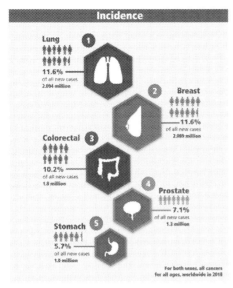 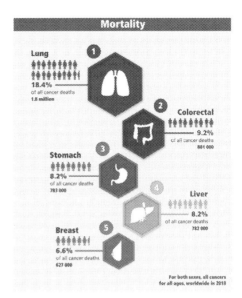

Fig. 12.1   Percentages of new cancer cases and cancer deaths worldwide in 2018 with the five most commonly diagnosed cancer types (IARC global cancer observatory database GLOBOCAN 2018)

leading cancers globally have also changed globally compared to 2012 data (Bray et al., 2018).

In Germany 43% of women and 51% of men will develop cancer during their life span (Robert Koch-Institut, Gesellschaft der Epidemiologischen Krebsregister in Deutschland e.V. 2017). This adds up to 230.000 woman and 260.000 men per year. The five cancer types with the highest yearly incidence rates are (Robert Koch-Institut 2019):

- breast cancer (72.000 women)
- prostate cancer (60.000 men)
- colorectal cancer (28.000 women and 34.000 men)
- lung cancer (19.000 women and 35.000 men)
- skin cancer/malignant melanoma (10.000 women and men each).

Median age of diagnosis is 67.2 years in women and 68.3 years in men. A continuous increase of cancer incidence (in total numbers) up to 2012 and still rising mortality can be seen. About 500,000 to 500,000 cancer cases are to be expected towards the end of the decade. Significant causes, besides others, are or ageing society, and—to a lesser extent –, exposure to risk factors (e.g. smoking in women) and a change in lifestyle (e.g. obesity) (Fig. 12.2 and Fig. 12.3).

In order to further improve the prospects of patients after a cancer diagnosis, new possibilities for early detection, diagnosis, therapy and follow up must be researched and benefit the affected person as quickly as possible. Effective ways of prevention need to be developed and implemented in order to reduce the incidence of new cancer cases in the long term. About 30–40% of all cancers are attributable to modifiable risk factors and are preventable by appropriate measures (Haberland et al., 2001, Robert Koch-Institut, 2016, OECD, 2013).

In addition to the National Cancer Plan (NKP) (Bundesministerium für Gesundheit, 2008), initiated in 2008, which focuses primarily on the further development of cancer care, Germany also needs a long-term research strategy in the fight against cancer. Greater awareness of all stakeholders for cancer research and prevention, strengthening of clinical trials, better collaboration of research and care, and faster transfer of new prevention are still needed, to bring diagnosis and treatment approaches with proven benefits into practice. A new openness in the field of the general population to talk about the

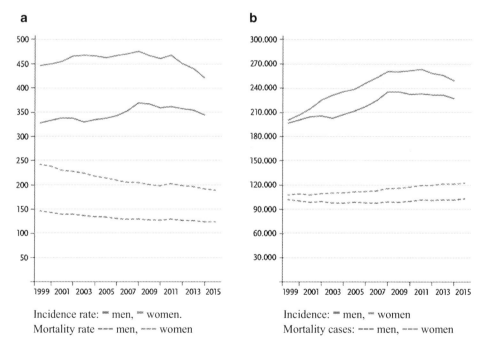

Fig. 12.2 Incidence- and mortality rates of cancer (ICD 10 C00-C97) in Germany 1999–2014. A: age-standardized data per 100.000 (EU-standard). B: Absolute numbers. (*Source* RKI, 2017)

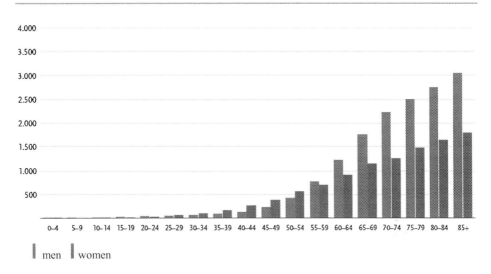

men ▌women

Fig. 12.3 Age specific incidence rate of cancer (ICD 10 C 00-C97), per 100.000, Germany 2013. (*Source* RKI 2017)

sensitive issue of cancer is necessary and also important. Therefore, under the lead of the Federal Ministry of Education and Research (BMBF) and the Federal Ministry of Health (BMG) together with a variety of partners, the ten-year initiative "National Decade against Cancer" was launched (Bundesministerium für Bildung und Forschung, 2019a). In the following chapters the contents, aims, fields of action and collaborating partners of the initiative are outlined.

12.2   Contents of the Initiative

This chapter outlines the details of the initiative as communicated by the German ministry (Bundesministerium für Bildung und Forschung, 2019a). The initiative intends a collaboration of representatives from politics, cancer research, research funding, health care, business and society is intended. It is the goal to mobilize all forces in Germany in a targeted way again to strengthen and purposefully advance cancer research in the fields of prevention, early detection, diagnostics and innovative therapies. The results of research should be quickly brought to the people and it should use the experience and knowledge from the oncological care of cancer patients for research in order to ultimately improve their care.

12.2.1 Aims

- Improving the lives of cancer patients through research and implementation of the results. At the end of the decade, early detection and treatment methods should cure cancer in three out of four patients or make it manageable in the long term—with a good quality of life for those affected.
- Cancer prevention should reduce the proportion of preventable cancers—today accounting for about 30–40% of total cancers—by 10% every 10 years; to about 36% in 10 years and 32% in 20 years. However, as it may take decades to develop cancer, this effect can be measured for the first time in 2040.
- Access to high-quality care: All people in Germany should have access to high-quality oncological care and innovation in cancer research, particularly via translational cancer research sites within reach and networking with regional and national care providers. The key to this is close collaboration between research institutions, university hospitals, qualified hospitals and specialized practices.
- Awareness: The population has become more aware of cancer prevention and confidence in cancer research; this should be strengthened by appropriate measures. Citizens actively participate in cancer prevention and research.
- Motivated and well-trained scientists and employees in the healthcare sector contribute to patient-oriented cancer research and oncological care.

12.2.2 Action Fields

- **Expand Cancer Research** Oncological research in Germany shall be strengthened and expand its position in international comparison. Through the development of personalized treatment methods and the further development of already existing therapies, both the quality of life and the survival of cancer patients after illness should be increased. The decisive basis is the comprehensive networking of actors involved and the conduct of clinical studies. Quality, medical precision, safety and efficiency of oncological care should be significantly increased through the use of digital technologies and processes in a multidisciplinary and cross-sectoral way. In addition to the further development of oncological diagnostics and therapy, this includes cancer follow up and the care of long-term survivors after cancer.
- **Actively Implementing Advances in Cancer Research** Cancer research structures should be strengthened in Germany—such as sites of the National Center for Tumor Diseases or the Comprehensive Cancer Centers (CCC)—to ensure nationwide accessibility for cancer patients and networking with regional and national care institutions. Promotion of modern structures and methods in order to provide the latest findings from current research to every specialist should take place. In addition, the experience and data from the clinical and medical practice should be incorporated into scientific

projects. It should also strengthen the applicability of innovative drugs and proven strategies in Germany and the networking of regional and supra-regional supply and research institutions.

- **Improve Prevention and Health** Developing research to further support health promotion, prevention and cancer screening activities in close collaboration with the NKP. This applies equally to prevention (e.g. lifestyle and vaccinations) as well as screening (e.g. screening programs and checkups, including methods of cancer screening for people at increased risk of cancer).
- **Promotion of Young Talents** Strengthening junior scientists in order to keep cancer research in Germany viable for the future.
- **Strengthening Participation** Patient advocacy groups and other patient organizations will be involved in oncological research topics. Thus, citizens should thus be reached and actively involved in the initiative and bring in additional perspectives and expertise.
- **Reinforce Mobilization / Communication** To raise awareness of the importance of cancer research among the general public as well as the immediate environment of those affected, break down existing taboos, bring progress and achievements to the public, and increase awareness of active prevention and screening. Different instruments of participatory decision-making, dialogue, subject information and public relations are intended.
- **Record Effectiveness** The National Decade against Cancer is designed as learning strategy. The strategy group develops the work program in dialogue with the partners and accompanies it. In addition, the strategy is continually adapted to current developments. This also means that it will be evaluated internally and externally.

12.2.3 Collaboration

Chaired by the parliamentary state secretary of the BMBF and the chairman of the German Cancer Research Center (DKFZ), the BMBF, the BMG, the involved collaborators, their institutions and other interest groups, are jointly shaping the National Decade Against Cancer. The strategy group and its working groups develop goals and milestones that are to be achieved within the decade. Other social groups can join the initiative and participate. Close cooperation with the actors and bodies of the NKP is planned.

Partner organizations:

- The task of the BMG is to ensure that cancer research and the treatment of cancer patients are more closely interlinked than before. It brings together all substantial actors of the cancer care together, which are already united in the NKP.
- Cancer patient advocacy / self-help groups bring the patient´s perspective into the initiative. It may draw on experience gained through involvement in clinical trials and participation in patient advocacy panels.

- The confederation of Statutory Health Insurances (GKV Spitzenverband) is committed to ensure that innovations with proven benefits for patients are included in the list of statutory health insurance benefits.
- The industrial health economy with its associations, companies, service providers and partners should contribute its expertise in biotechnology, medical technology, telemedicine and diagnostics. In particular, they are asked to work towards data-driven innovations for health services research and oncology health services.
- The university medical institutions in universities in Germany and the DKFZ are contributing their research structures and expertise to the initiative in order to generate critical mass and synergies in cancer research through close cooperation. The university clinics offer patients access to clinical studies, also for complex or rare tumor diseases.
- DKFZ and the German Cancer Aid (DKH) will enter into a new strategic partnership and establish a future oriented "National Cancer Prevention Center", in order to systematically expand prevention research and applied prevention in Germany and to establish it comprehensively with other partners.
- The medical societies and professional associations are contributing their networks and expertise, e.g., establish new methods of care and to reflect the results of day-to-day care in research. Through the certification of centers nationwide, the German Cancer Society (DKG) brings its experience in the quality analysis and development of cancer care.
- The professional organization of office-based hematologists and oncologists (BNHO) is also one of the collaborative partners of the project. The BNHO with its CEO is part of the strategic circle and the working group communication. BNHO´s practices bring their care networks to treatment to ensure rapid knowledge transfer. They work closely with other service providers. Data from oncological care help to test the effectiveness and practicability of innovative concepts under everyday conditions. Oncologists in private practice care for an increasing number of cancer patients (Fig. 12.4) of approximately 600.000 annually, who become continuously older over time (Fig. 12.5). BNHO and the Scientific Institute of Office-Based Hematologists and Oncologists in private practices (WINHO) intend to apply for the first wave of funding of the initiative.

12.2.4 Contents of Funding Announcement

In addition to the initiated collaboration and the defined fields of action, the BMBF has issued a first funding announcement in February 2019 (Bundesministerium für Bildung und Forschung 2019b) which aims to review and compare established preventive measures, diagnostics and therapeutic procedures. in potentially practice-changing studies. It allocates up to 62 million Euros of funding support in the framework of the national Decade. Funding is divided into two phases:

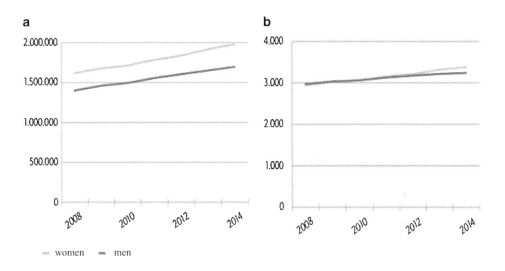

a

b

⸺ women ⸺ men

Fig. 12.4 German cancer patients within the statutory health system (GKV) treated by office-based physicians 2008–2014. A) Treated GKV insured patients. B) Patients per 100.000 insured individuals (age adjusted)

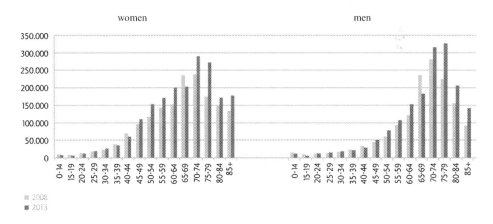

Fig. 12.5 GKV-insured patients as of age-groups and gender. (*Source:* Kassenärztliche Bundesvereinigung (KBV))

- **Concept Development Phase** In the first phase, scientific planning work will be carried out, which will provide the necessary basis for the implementation of the subsequent realization phase. This phase serves the scientific development of the study concept with the active involvement of relevant interest groups, especially of patients or their representatives. The development of the study concept also includes a scientifically sound, comprehensive and systematic evaluation of the literature and relevant study registers for the purpose of recording the current state of research, which goes beyond the scope of the research necessary for the application. The establishment and expansion of the study group, the verification of the recruitment potential and the development of study design and methodology are further aspects of this planning work. At the end of the first phase, based on the scientific findings of the planning work, a detailed application for the realization of the study has to be submitted.

- **Implementation Phase** In the subsequent phase, the implementation and exploitation of the results of the confirmatory, multicentric clinical study takes place. If necessary and expedient, the realization study can be preceded by a feasibility study, which serves the further preparation of this study. Possible goals of the feasibility study can be the operationalization of patient relevant endpoints, the testing of patient relevant treatment regimens, taking into account their feasibility and acceptance, a benefit assessment of the new therapy, a dose determination and / or an estimate of the benefit-risk ratio. All relevant interest groups or their representatives should be involved. Towards the end of the feasibility study, a report and, if appropriate, a modified application for further implementation of the study must be submitted.

In addition, a further funding initiative will be launched on the major unresolved issues of cancer research and the interface between research and care is planned by the establishment of new locations of the National Center for Tumor Diseases (DKFZ) (Bundesministerium für Bildung und Forschung, 2019a, Bundesministerium für Bildung und Forschung 2019b).

12.3   Some Critical Considerations

Whether the National Decade Against Cancer will be successful as far as its goals and intentions are concerned, will not only depend on the amount of funding resources and the efforts of the involved stakeholders to generate innovative programs and clinical studies. It will be at least as important whether the involved participants and their institutions will be able to overcome the historically grown sectoral and institutional borders of care with their implications (different scopes and reimbursement systems, uneven economic and competition situations, etc.), which were and still are barriers of an efficient, intersectoral, patient- and outcome-oriented care in Germany (Sachverständigenrat, 2012). A successful movement towards better care cooperation would require the support of all parties involved. Up to now, however, these parties have agreed—due to intrinsically conflicting interests—only on a mini-consensus. As a consequence, only intersectoral care programs or contracts with little or no care relevance have been established up to this point.

In addition, from the author´s point of view, the National Decade still resembles an "old school" definition of scientific institutions and research. The impact of Public Health (PH), concerning contents and institutions, is not really incorporated. Many of the

"Action Fields" tasks belong to the classical fields of PH; this is not reflected, but merely specified for cancer research. In the field of cancer, there are also more effective and efficient PH concepts in global and even European comparison. Also, PH has not only a surveillance function, but also a policy advisory function. In the sense of this function, would a clearer and more offensive positioning against excessive alcohol consumption, nicotine and sugar not be demanded? And what about "health literacy", for example in the light of the results of the HLS-GER, showing significant deficiencies in the German population (Schaeffer et al., 2017).

Concerning "Collaboration", the current concrete research trends in cancer research should be integrated: For the past "Horizon 2020", for the future "Horizon Europe" (Kelly, 2019). Who has cooperated with whom in the past years? What trends are emerging, e.g. childhood cancer (Wallenfels, 2019)?

In this context, it can be asked whether lessons were learned from another joint collaboration project of the same Ministries and with nearly identical stakeholders, with a history of more than 10 years: The National Cancer Plan (NKP). Therein, centers of oncology care are defined as "a network of qualified and jointly certified, interdisciplinary and intersectoral institutions" (Bundesministerium für Gesundheit, 2008) which encompasses the entire supply chain for those affected. This includes inpatient and outpatient facilities. Hence, there is already a plan how this cooperative network can provide cancer patient care. However, the development so far has rather led to more centralization. Yet we need a network coverage of all regions.

Other shortcomings were evident too. First, an inventory of the existing evidence was missing. All stakeholder organizations were asked for input, the different groups and the emerging corporatism were moderated by the Ministry of Health. As a consequence, the relevant experts presented themselves and their institutions stressing their group interests in a rather isolated manner. In addition, the experiences of other EU or OECD countries in developing and implementing their National Cancer Control Plans (NCCP) haven´t been integrated (Schlingensiepen, 2017).

Implementation was also difficult because of the lack of integration between self-government institutions of the health system (Selbstverwaltung) on the one hand and science and the professional sector on the other. This break in the system affected the NKP negatively (Schlingensiepen, 2017). While the self-administration developed directives for the care of cancer patients, the medical societies developed medical guidelines; the processes were not coordinated, leading to a high level of heterogeneity.

In addition, from the author´s point of view, a lack of cooperation between the ministries was evident and the discrepancies therefore were not surprising. The BMBF was not even involved, interdisciplinary action at the level of ministries was therefore missing, at least to some extent. When the NKP was published by the Ministry of Health (BMG), the Ministry of Education and Sciences (BMBF) issued an Action Plan on Individualized Medicine. This was an example of ministerial competition, even though the leaders of them belong to the same political party. The lack of cooperation between the two ministries has contributed to the fact that researchers and clinicians did not feel to be adequately represented in the work on the NKP. In essence, results of the NKP mostly consist of implementation recommendations to the ministry and expert reports (Bundesministerium für Gesundheit, 2017). The Cancer Early Detection and Registration Act, implemented in 2013, may serve as one of the rare positive achievements of the NKP.

In summary, the BMG, the BMBF and all other contributors should now develop a real common strategy and learn from the drawbacks of the NKP. We urgently need a variety of oncology networks covering the country as a whole, as it was outlined in the NKP in 2008. We need adequate framework conditions, so that regional and supra-regional networks can be established and care provider can join them. When talking about how to organize oncology care, it´s not about stakeholders, it´s about the cancer patient. Therefore, the future lies not in a few solitary CCCs, but in innovative network structures which bring competence to the areas where cancer patients live. Otherwise, an overall concept for the improvement of care of people suffering from cancer will not be implemented again. In conclusion, it is hoped that the current initiative will overcome the described problems of the past and that it inaugurates an efficient cooperative network for the sake of a better care of cancer patients. However, what will be achieved ultimately, can only be evaluated at the end of the National Decade.

Acknowledgements   I would like to thank Dr. W. Baumann and A. Weeke for a critical review of the manuscript.

References

Arndt, V., Stürmer, T., Stegmaier, C., Ziegler, H., Dhom, G., & Brenner, H. (2001). Socio-demographic factors, health behavior and late-stage diagnosis of breast cancer in Germany. *Clinical Epidemiology, 54*(7), 719–727. https://doi.org/10.1016/S0895-4356(00)00351-6

Bray, F., Ferlay, J., Soerjomataram, I., Siegel, R. L., Torre, L. A., & Jemal, A. (2018). Global cancer statistics 2018: GLOBOCAN estimates of incidence and mortality worldwide for 36 cancers in 185 countries. *Cancer Journal for Clinicans, 68*, 394–424.

Bundesministerium für Bildung und Forschung (Hg.) (2019a). Startschuss der nationalen Dekade gegen Krebs. Pressemitteilung 004/2019. https://www.bmbf.de/startschuss-der-nationalen-dekade-gegen-krebs-7755.html. Accessed: 19. Febr. 2019.

Bundesministerium für Bildung und Forschung (Hg.) (2019b). Richtlinie zur Förderung praxisverändernder klinischer Studien zur Prävention, Diagnose und Therapie von Krebserkrankungen—Nationale Dekade gegen Krebs. *Bundesanzeiger.* https://www.bmbf.de/foerderungen/bekanntmachu ngen-2256.html. Accessed: 19. Febr. 2019.

Bundesministerium für Gesundheit (Hg.) (2008). Nationaler Krebsplan. Übersicht und Ziele. https://ww w.bundesministerium.de/fileadmin/Dateien/3_Downloads/N/Nationaler_Krebsplan/181120_Download_UEbersicht_Ziele_des_Nationalen_Krebsplans.pdf. Accessed: 22. Febr. 2019.

Bundesministerium für Gesundheit. (ed.) (2017). Nationaler Krebsplan. Handlungsfelder, Ziele, Ergebnisse 2017. https://www.bundesgesundheitsministerium.de/fileadmin/Dateien/3_Downloads/N/N ationaler_Krebsplan/Informationspapier_Nationaler_Krebsplan.pdf. Accessed: 22. Febr. 2019.

Haberland, J., Wolf, U., Baras, N., Dahm, S., Wienecke, A., & Kraywinkel, K. (2014). Entwicklung früherkennungsrelevanter Krebserkrankungen seit den 1970er Jahren in Deutschland. *UMID, 1*, 21–26.

Haberland, J., Bertz, J., Görsch, B., & Schön, D. (2001). Krebsinzidenzschätzungen für Deutschland mittels logliniarer Modelle [Cancer incidence estimates for Germany via log-linear models]. *Gesundheitswesen, 63*(8–9), 556–560. https://doi.org/10.1055/s-2001-16687

Kelly, E. (2019). Experts debate the merits of €1B EU cancer moonshot, and how it could work. https://sciencebusiness.net/framework-programmes/news/experts-debate-merits-eu1b-eu-cancer-moonshot-and-how-it-could-work-0.21.3.2019. Science Business. Brussels. Accessed: 1. Oct. 2019.

Nagel, E., Neukirch, B., Schmid, A., & Schulte, G. (2017). *Wege zu einer effektiven und effizienten Zusammenarbeit in der ambulanten und stationären Versorgung in Deutschland*. Gutachten im Auftrag des Zentralinstituts für die Kassenärztliche Vereinigung (Zi).

OECD, European Commission (Ed.) (2013). Focus on health. Cancer care: assuring quality to improve survival. https://doi.org/10.1787/9789264194564-en.

Robert Koch-Institut, Gesellschaft der epidemiologischen Krebsregister in Deutschland e.V. (ed.) (2019). Krebs in Deutschland 2013/2014. 11. Ausg. https://www.brebsdaten.de/Krebs/DE/Content/Publikationen/Krebs_in_Deutschland/kid_2017/krebs_in_deutschland_2017.pdf_blob=publicationFile. Accessed: 19. Febr. 2019.

Robert Koch-Institut (ed.) (2016). Bericht zum Krebsgeschehen in Deutschland 2016. Berlin November 2016. https://krebsdaten.de/Krebs/DE/Content/Publikationen/Krebsgeschehen/Krebsgesch ehen_node.html. Accessed: 19. Febr. 2019.

Sachverständigenrat (SVR) zur Begutachtung der Entwicklung im Gesundheitswesen. (2012). Wettbewerb an der Schnittstelle zwischen ambulanter und stationärer Gesundheitsversorgung. Sondergutachten 2012. Deutscher Bundestag. Drucksache 17/102323.

Schaeffer, D., Vogt, D., Berens, E. M., Messer, M., Quenzel, G., & Hurrelmann, K. (2017). Health literacy in Deutschland—Eine repräsentative Erhebung in der Allgemeinbevölkerung (HLS_GER). In D. Schaeffer & J. M. Pelikan (Eds.), *Health literacy: Forschungsstand und Perspektiven* (pp. 129–143). Hogrefe.

Schlingensiepen, I. (2017). Gemeinsame Strategie beim Krebsplan nötig. *ÄrzteZeitung online*. 7.6.2017. https://www.aerztezeitung.de/politik_gesellschaft/versorgungsforschung/article/937343/kritik-deutschen-krebsgesellschaft-gemeinsame-strategie-krebsplan-noetig. html?sh=72&h=-12908522. Accessed: 1. Oct. 2019.

Wallenfels, M. (2019). „Horizon Europe". Europa im Kampf gegen Krebs im Kindesalter. https://www.aerztezeitung.de/politik_gesellschaft/gesundheitspolitik_international/article/985255/horizon-europe-europa-kampf-krebs-kindesalter.html). Springer Medizin Verlag GmbH, Neu-Isenburg. Accessed: 1. Oct. 2019.

A Comprehensive Method for Multi-Criteria Evaluation of Health Regions

13

Aleksandar Tsenov, Velko Iltchev and Hristomir Yordanov

Contents

13.1   Introduction 218
      13.1.1   Health-Related Quality of Lfe 218
      13.1.2   Regional Quality of Care 219
      13.1.3   Regional Infrastructure Features 219
13.2   The Method 220
      13.2.1   The Health Region Properties 220
      13.2.2   The Fuzzy Evaluation Method 220
13.3   A Practical Example 222
13.4   Conclusion 225
References 225

Abstract

In this work, a comprehensive method for complex evaluation of analytically defined Health regions is proposed. The main objective of the work is to create a suitable processing concept, based on the recently proposed model for situating "Health

A. Tsenov · V. Iltchev · H. Yordanov (✉)
Faculty of German Engineering and Economics Education, Technical University, Sofia, Bulgaria
e-mail: hristomir.yordanov@fdiba.tu-sofia.bg

A. Tsenov
e-mail: aleksandar.tsenov@fdiba.tu-sofia.bg

V. Iltchev
e-mail: velko.iltchev@fdiba.tu-sofia.bg

M. Cassens et al. (eds.), *Transdisciplinary Perspectives on Public Health in Europe*, FOM-Edition, https://doi.org/10.1007/978-3-658-33740-7_13

Regions", which fully encompasses properties, that form and describe one health region. These properties are defined as key indicators and quantized according to the aim of the work, in order to verify a comprehensive, abstract fuzzy method for multic-riteria evaluation of Health regions.

13.1 Introduction

In a recent work, based on several investigations within the competition "Health Regions of the Future", initiated by the German Federal Ministry of Education and Research (BMBF), the authors used a simple model of the structure and connections between the main components of a health region as shown in Fig. 13.1, (George, 2009). Definition of regional health care (RHC): RHC is understood as meaning all joint activities of a region (or city), which are subject to the aim to organize the health care quality (a), the quality of life of those affected (b) and the attractiveness of a region (c). In doing so, a practice is selected which is also based on the criterion of economic superiority over centrally presented care strategies (d).

13.1.1 Health-Related Quality of Lfe

Among the most important health-related quality of life factors one can count among all:

- health and age;
- health and gender;
- health and marital status (including the number of children);
- health and educational level;
- health and income;
- health and employment;

Fig. 13.1 The four guiding criteria of a regionally presented health care: quality of life, quality of medical results, character of the regional infrastructure (location characteristic), and economic efficiency (George, 2009)

- health and sports;
- health and unhealthy habits (alcohol, smoking) (Vankova D. et al., 2012).

All these factors can be quantified (e.g., as a percentage) and the data can be collected relatively easily and regularly – e.g. at population number. This allows the creation of a collection of data of the same kind, which can be implemented as a suitable data structure. Each factor can be further decomposed to achieve higher accuracy and extensibility.

13.1.2 Regional Quality of Care

Regional care is provided through several strategies for prevention, treatment and rehabilitation: the development of these strategies is ensured by the analysis of several data on the spread of diseases, hospitals, rehabilitation centers, objects of healing tourism, etc.:

- number of populations in the administrative regions of the country;
- number of patients with different diseases;
- proportion of mortality and incidence of various diseases;
- degree of prevention, treatment and rehabilitation;
- availability of health facilities.

This might include current projects in the field of health care. The high success rate of these projects is mainly due to the good results in social welfare, and not so much through the health care system.

13.1.3 Regional Infrastructure Features

In order to be able to introduce suitable features for the modeling of the health regions and to identify these as key indicators, the proposed method adheres to the following points:

- Easy accessibility: this is ensured by giving patients the opportunity to present their complaints in a suitable form and with a choice of entitlements.
- Fast processing: timely processing is important. The receipt is confirmed, in the case of complex facts an interim report is given.
- Protection of personal data: removing personal data of patients when providing information for statistical analysis or to third parties.
- Independence: in addition to a clear process, this means independent and qualified processing by suitable and trained employees.

- Transparency: the transparent ways of complaint management for third parties, from the acceptance of a complaint to the recommendation for intervention, as well as an annual report.
- Responsibility: by securing a final processing, in which the obligations of the parties are defined.

Finally, the legitimacy of regional healthcare is explained by its potentially close relationship with the integrated healthcare contracts.

The economical superiority requires other approaches to be analyzed, evaluated and estimated. Therefore, it will be not a part of this investigation.

13.2   The Method

13.2.1 The Health Region Properties

The metrics of the Health region properties are captured in the form of Critical Success Factors (CSFs), Key Performance Indicators (KPIs) and activity metrics for the health regions management processes (George, 2009; Hilbert, 2008). CSF would use these metrics as input in identifying improvement opportunities for each region. Some important metrics used for the evaluation process proposed in this work, are shown in Table 13.1. In the following analysis, we simplify the description of the formula of the metrics – in most cases each characteristic includes several subcharacteristics. This simplification will not affect the method and conclusions of fuzzy evaluation method.

13.2.2 The Fuzzy Evaluation Method

In an element set $U = \{u_1, u_2, u_3, \cdots, u_n\}$ each element denotes one of the characteristics in evaluation metrics of the Health region definition. Here n is the number of characteristics in evaluation metrics. Suppose that the evaluation set is $V = \{v_1, v_2, v_3, \cdots, v_m\}$, where m is the number of the evaluation levels. The value of evaluation is the degree of u_i to v_j.

We define a fuzzy matrix $R = (r_{ij})_{m \times n}$, where the element r_{ij} denotes the membership degree of the i-th element in the set U to the j-th element in the set V.

Suppose that the set $A = \{a_1, a_2, a_3, \ldots, a_n\}$ is the fuzzy matrix set of the weights of each characteristics—ai denotes the weight of the element u_i in the set U. The set A is the calculation of the membership degree. In this work we choose the Pairwise Comparison method (Tsenov et al., 2011) to calculate the set A. The elements in the set A satisfy normalization condition:

$$\sum_{i=1}^{n} a_i = 1. \tag{13.1}$$

Table 13.1 Basic Steps of the proposed fuzzy evaluation approach (Tsenov, 2012; Tsenov et al., 2011)

No	Component	Property	Description	Code
1	Health bound life quality	Health and age	HA = healthy population /population in age range × 100%	HR1
2	Health bound life quality	Health and sex	HS = healthy population / males (females) × 100%	HR2
3	Health bound life quality	Health and income	HI = healthy population / population with incomes in range × 100%	HR3
4	Regional infrastructure features	Easy accessibility	EA = appropriate care supply objects / all care supply objects × 100%	HR4
5	Regional infrastructure features	Independency	IN = qualified care staff / all care staff × 100%	HR5
6	Regional infrastructure features	Transparency	TR = number of published approaches in care in a year	HR6
7	Regional health quality	Population of the region	PR = Number	HR7
8	Regional health quality	Number of people under care	PC = Number	HR8
9	Regional health quality	Mortality	MI = Share of death/ PR	HR9

Suppose that the effect degree of the evaluation set V element—a fuzzy matrix set is $B = \{b_1, b_2, b_3, \ldots, b_m\}$. Here b_i means the weight of the evaluation decision in the set V. The calculation of the set B is performed using the equation $B = A \circ R = \{b_1, b_2, b_3, \ldots, b_m\}$. The operator "$\circ$" denotes compound algorithm operator (Adamar multiplication (Kuo-Ming Chao et al., 2005)).

The evaluation result of S is calculated in the following steps: In order to get the accurate calculation, the weight of each evaluation is calculated first using the following equation:

$$\delta_j = \frac{b_j}{\sum_{i=1}^{m} b_i}, j = 1, 2, \ldots, m. \tag{13.2}$$

Then we compute the total evaluation S for each evaluation level v_j using the following equation:

$$S = \sum_{j=1}^{m} \delta_j v_j. \tag{13.3}$$

13.3   A Practical Example

The characteristics in Table 13.1 are evaluated according to the fuzzy evaluation method described above. The key is how to get the membership degree set A. There are several known methods to calculate A (Tsenov et al., 2011). The proposed approach applies to a very new problem and therefore the Pairwise Comparison method is chosen. That means that every two characteristic's membership degree is being compared to create the membership sequence with which fuzzy set A is abstracted.

The sequence relation in Table 13.2 is obtained from element set $U = u_1, u_2, u_3, u_4, u_5, u_6, u_7, u_8, u_9$. The result of the comparison of every two characteristics is shown. Because the most characteristics have different values for different services, Table 13.2 gives just an instance of relationships. The same method may be used for different situations as well.

In Table 13.2 the symbol "$=$" means that the membership degrees to A of the two characteristics are the same; "$\geq$" means that the membership of HR_i to A is higher than that of HR_j; and "$\leq$" means that the membership degree of HR_i to A is lower than that of HR_j.

The set A is calculated from Table 13.2: $\forall u_i, u_i \in U$ let p_{ij} denote the membership degree of u_i/A to u_j/A. The rules to compute p_{ij} are

$$0 \leq p_{ij} \leq 1; \quad i,j = 1, 2, \cdots, n \tag{13.4}$$

$$p_{ij} + p_{ji} = 1; \quad \forall i \neq j. \tag{13.5}$$

The fuzzy relation matrix $\mathbf{P} = (p_{ij})$ is calculated according to Table 13.2 and Eqs. (13.4) and (13.5):

Table 13.2 Membership degree of health region evaluation metrics

Item	HR1	HR2	HR3	HR4	HR5	HR6	HR7	HR8	HR9
HR1	$=$	$\geq$	$\geq$	$\leq$	$\geq$	$\geq$	$\leq$	$\leq$	$\leq$
HR2	$\leq$	$=$	$\leq$	$\leq$	$\geq$	$\geq$	$\leq$	$\leq$	$\leq$
HR3	$\leq$	$\geq$	$=$	$\leq$	$\geq$	$\geq$	$\leq$	$\leq$	$\leq$
HR4	$\geq$	$\geq$	$\geq$	$=$	$\geq$	$\geq$	$\leq$	$\leq$	$\leq$
HR5	$\leq$	$\leq$	$\leq$	$\leq$	$=$	$\leq$	$\leq$	$\leq$	$\leq$
HR6	$\leq$	$\leq$	$\leq$	$\leq$	$\geq$	$=$	$\leq$	$\leq$	$\leq$
HR7	$\geq$	$\geq$	$\geq$	$\geq$	$\geq$	$\geq$	$=$	$\geq$	$\geq$
HR8	$\geq$	$\geq$	$\geq$	$\geq$	$\geq$	$\geq$	$\leq$	$=$	$=$
HR9	$\geq$	$\geq$	$\geq$	$\geq$	$\geq$	$\geq$	$\leq$	$=$	$=$

$$\mathbf{P} = \begin{bmatrix} 1 & 0.6 & 0.6 & 0.4 & 0.6 & 0.6 & 0.4 & 0.4 & 0.4 \\ 0.4 & 1 & 0.4 & 0.4 & 0.6 & 0.6 & 0.4 & 0.4 & 0.4 \\ 0.4 & 0.6 & 1 & 0.4 & 0.6 & 0.6 & 0.4 & 0.4 & 0.4 \\ 0.6 & 0.6 & 0.6 & 1 & 0.6 & 0.6 & 0.4 & 0.4 & 0.4 \\ 0.4 & 0.4 & 0.4 & 0.4 & 1 & 0.4 & 0.4 & 0.4 & 0.4 \\ 0.4 & 0.4 & 0.4 & 0.4 & 0.6 & 1 & 0.4 & 0.4 & 0.4 \\ 0.6 & 0.6 & 0.6 & 0.6 & 0.6 & 0.6 & 1 & 0.6 & 0.6 \\ 0.6 & 0.6 & 0.6 & 0.6 & 0.6 & 0.6 & 0.4 & 1 & 1 \\ 0.6 & 0.6 & 0.6 & 0.6 & 0.6 & 0.6 & 0.4 & 1 & 1 \end{bmatrix} \quad (13.6)$$

The fuzzy set A is calculated by the averaging method and for the given values for the p_{ij} the following values are obtained:

$$A = \{0.556, 0.511, 0.533, 0.578, 0.467, 0.489, 0.644, 0.667, 0.667\} \quad (13.7)$$

After normalisation we obtain the modified set A':

$$A' = \{0.108, 0.099, 0.105, 0.114, 0.091, 0.096, 0.125, 0.131, 0.131\} \quad (13.8)$$

According to the steps (1)–(3) of Sect. 13.2.2 and to the above calculations.
for the fuzzy set A, the following three HR metric sets are obtained:

$$U_1 = \{98, 97, 97, 98, 97, 97, 100, 99, 99\}; \quad (13.9)$$

$$U_1 = \{98, 98, 98, 98, 98, 98, 98, 98, 98\}; \quad (13.10)$$

$$U_1 = \{97, 96, 97, 98, 95, 96, 99, 98, 98\}. \quad (13.11)$$

The evaluation set is $V = \{\text{Excellent, Very good, Good, Poor}\} = \{100, 80, 60, 40\}$. In Eqs. (13.12), (13.13), and (13.14) below, the **R** matrices of the three systems, defined above by their *HR* metrics, are described. Each matrix **R** is computed by expert evaluation. We suppose that 100 experts give scores for each system. The number of experts for each evaluation level can be used as the elements of the matrix **R**. For instance, 0.99 in the first column means that 99 of the 100 experts gave "Excellent" to the corresponding metric.

$$\mathbf{R}_1 = \begin{bmatrix} 0.98 & 0.01 & 0.01 & 0 \\ 0.97 & 0.01 & 0.01 & 0.01 \\ 0.97 & 0.02 & 0.01 & 0 \\ 0.98 & 0.01 & 0.01 & 0 \\ 0.97 & 0.01 & 0.01 & 0.01 \\ 0.97 & 0.01 & 0.01 & 0.01 \\ 1 & 0 & 0 & 0 \\ 0.99 & 0.01 & 0 & 0 \\ 0.99 & 0 & 0.01 & 0 \end{bmatrix} \quad (13.12)$$

$$\mathbf{R_2} = \begin{bmatrix} 0.98 & 0.01 & 0.01 & 0 \\ 0.98 & 0.01 & 0.01 & 0 \\ 0.98 & 0.01 & 0.01 & 0 \\ 0.98 & 0.01 & 0.01 & 0 \\ 0.98 & 0.01 & 0.01 & 0 \\ 0.98 & 0.02 & 0 & 0 \\ 0.98 & 0.01 & 0.01 & 0 \\ 0.98 & 0.01 & 0.01 & 0 \\ 0.98 & 0.01 & 0.01 & 0 \end{bmatrix} \tag{13.13}$$

$$\mathbf{R_3} = \begin{bmatrix} 0.97 & 0.01 & 0.01 & 0.01 \\ 0.96 & 0.02 & 0.01 & 0.01 \\ 0.97 & 0.02 & 0.01 & 0 \\ 0.98 & 0.02 & 0 & 0 \\ 0.95 & 0.02 & 0.02 & 0.01 \\ 0.96 & 0.01 & 0.02 & 0.01 \\ 0.99 & 0 & 0.01 & 0 \\ 0.98 & 0.01 & 0.01 & 0 \\ 0.98 & 0.01 & 0.01 & 0 \end{bmatrix} \tag{13.14}$$

The calculation results of the corresponding sets B are as follows:

$$B_1 = \{0.98121,\ 0.00849,\ 0.00744,\ 0.00286\}; \tag{13.15}$$

$$B_2 = \{0.98000,\ 0.01096,\ 0.00904,\ 0.00000\}; \tag{13.16}$$

$$B_3 = \{0.97429,\ 0.01284,\ 0.01073,\ 0.00394\}; \tag{13.17}$$

The three systems evaluation genes δ are calculated from the sets B using (13.2), then the total evaluation score S is calculated according to (13.3):

$$S_1 = 99.361; \tag{13.18}$$

$$S_2 = 99.4192; \tag{13.19}$$

$$S_3 = 99.0776. \tag{13.20}$$

The conclusion from evaluation result of S is {System-2, System-1, System-3} in the sequence of service management quality from the best to the worst.

The same conclusion may be obtained through a visual analysis, but only if the score of metrics is not very complex. In this example we show that when the score of metrics is more complex, it is easier to get the evaluation result of service management quality using fuzzy evaluation algorithm than using direct analysis. In addition, in this example we have used only nine Service Level Management metrics. The number of the HR metrics is much higher.

In this work we didn't made any classification of the metrics being evaluated. The fuzzy based approaches allow clustering of the metrics according common characteristics of the metrics on a given level of abstraction (for example: unit of measurement). Such clustering will improve the complexity of the evaluation and, therefore, the use of fuzzy based handling is almost obligatory.

The proposed approach is open for future enhancement: firstly, there is no limitation of the number of the metrics to be evaluated; and secondly, it is possible to implement other methods for producing the relation matrices, such as cosine distance, Euclidean distance etc.

13.4 Conclusion

Service management is very important for service provision in correct, effective and economic ways. This paper analyzes the increasing service management requirement and points out that the evaluation metrics of service management quality is valuable and useful to improve and evaluate service management.

Based on the analysis and reference of HR care management content, the evaluation metrics of HR-oriented care management quality is presented. Then fuzzy evaluation method is used to evaluate care management quality. The process of fuzzy relation matrix A' calculation based on Pairwise Comparison and the calculation of evaluation results is also presented. A simple example is explained to illustrate the validity and correctness of the fuzzy evaluation method. The metrics evaluation is a foundation to extend and to improve for different requirements and the evaluation algorithm can be amended to adapt multiple complexities.

References

George, W. (2009). "Gesundheitsregionen" und "Regionale Gesundheitsversorgung". In S. Eble, W. H.?, (Hg.), *Gesundheitsnetzwerke initiieren: Kooperationen erfolgreich planen,* (pp. 293–307). Med. Wiss. Verlagsges.

Hilbert, J. (2008). Das Gesundheitswesen als Jobmaschine? Vor den Erfolg haben die Götter den Schweiß gesetzt! In Berlin: Wegweiser, *Jahrbuch Gesundheitswirtschaft 2008: Prozessoptimierung, eHealth und Vernetzung*, pp. 144–145.

Iltchev, V., & Tsenov, A. (2018). Informational aspects of modelling the health regions in Bulgaria. *FDIBA Conference Proceedings, 2*, pp. 13–16.

Kuo-Ming C., Younas, M., Chi-Chun, L., & Tao-Hsin T. (2005). Fuzzy matchmaking for web services. In *19th International Conference on Advanced Information Networking and Applications (AINA'05)*, Volume 1 (AINA papers), vol. 2, pp. 721–726.

Tsenov, A. (2012). Customer satisfaction based demand analysis of mobile services. In *Proceedings of the XLVII International Scientific Conference ICEST 2012*, vol. 1, pp. 67–70.

Tsenov, A., Ivanov, I., Poparova, T., Neykov, S., Ivanova, L., & Gadjeva, M. (2011). Fuzzy evaluation of customer satisfaction with mobile services. In *2011 10th International Conference on Telecommunication in Modern Satellite Cable and Broadcasting Services (TELSIKS)*, vol. 2, pp. 665–668.

Vankova D., Usheva, N., & Feschieva, N. (2012). Quality of life related to health in the community, *Social Medicine, 2/3 2012*, ISSN 1310–1757, pp. 26–29

The Commercial Value of Health-Related Data—An Empirical Study

14

Klemens Waldhör

Contents

14.1   Introduction 228
14.2   Research Questions 229
14.3   Models for Health Related Data 229
14.4   Methods 231
           14.4.1   Waldhör's Survey 232
           14.4.2   Horn-Survey 232
14.5   Results of the Waldhör and Horn Surveys 235
           14.5.1   Results of Waldhör's Survey 235
           14.5.2   Results of the Horn Survey 237
14.6   Answers to the Research Questions 238
14.7   Summary and Conclusions 241
References 243

Abstract

Currently, users supply health data to platform providers for free. The provider of the data – the user, the patient – has no control over how organizations monetize their data. In most cases, they do not even know where the data go. This contribution explores the view of the user – what their perception is of the value of their health data and how they can be remunerated by platforms which want to use the data. The conducted surveys show that the user expects different payments depending on the

K. Waldhör (✉)
FOM University of Applied Sciences, Nuremberg, Germany
e-mail: klemens.waldhoer@fom.de

usage: Up to 50€ for noncommercial research and up to 500€ for commercial purposes; and the user fully neglects the usage of their data for social media.

14.1   Introduction

Somewhere in July 2028: You are sitting in front of your doctor in the local medical
center. He looks at his screen and simultaneously shows you the results of your latest
medical examination on an extreme high-resolution display. He seems a little bit worried, his brows are furrowed when he points to a specific part of an image of your brain.
"This doesn't look very good; our Med AI has classified this cell cluster as a class A
malignant tumor!" Shocked as you are, you do not even understand his next words.
"There is a very slim chance that you survive the next six months." "Oh my God, is there
no treatment available? My family, my children!" you stutter. "No, unfortunately not,
the tumor is very rare, not really in the research focus and people die so fast that data
are not really available," he states. "But, sorry," his face starts shining, "I just received
a message from our medical trust center xHealth, that you have participated in our lifelong medical health data study. And, good luck, our partner xGenThep which uses this
data has just developed a specific gene-based drug combination which could help in your
case and looks very promising. It is in its first trial stage. You could participate in this
trial program if you want to." You remember now that about 10 years ago, you signed
a paper where you gave your permission to share all your health-related data with the
newly formed data trust center xHealth. Part of this data sharing deal was that you get
preferential access to new medical treatments and drugs. And now it really pays off, it
seems to save your life now.

Although this sounds futuristic, data and esp. medical heath data, form the core of
the new data and the AI driven approach in the development of medical treatments. This
could come true in the next decade based on massive new data streams arising from a
combination of collected personal data from sensors, health records, genetic databases,
and even what you say to Alexa, what you buy on Amazon or how you type on your PC.
Mathematical models based on blood related data can even estimate the probability of
developing Alzheimer's or how it will develop (Preische et. al., 2019) or how your state
of health degrades (Lutze & Waldhör, 2017). The data currently collected of the user by
a vast number of different health platform providers are the key success factor.

That data are generated on different occasions, by several stakeholders and are stored
in different places: At stakeholders like patients, doctors, hospitals, social insurances,
public health system-practitioners, and -institutions, but also privately by using fitness
trackers, smartwatches, or cell phones with specialized apps (e.g. drug intake etc.).
Nowadays, all this data is stored in various not interconnected information systems. They
contain interesting and important information which could be used for different purposes
in research, big data analytics, pharmaceutical studies, health studies, etc.

This book contribution sets the focus on the financial value of health-related data. So far, big players like Apple, Google, Microsoft, or Fitbit try to get this type of data into their health repositories, promising the platform's users advantages like supplying health related information, fitness information, training plans, etc. They never really inform the user what they do or how the data will be utilized – essentially monetizing it. Most literature in this area investigates the view of the (cloud based) service providers and speculates or derives a model about the value of the data provided by users. Literature rarely discusses what the user thinks about the value of their data given away basically for free – except the problems associated with the relatively new General Data Protection Regulation (GDPR) impact.

This paper also discusses a different approach: When and to which extent are people willing to share their health data, what is the perceived value of this data from the perspective of users, how much money should service or platform providers pay for collecting the data. This could radically change the view on the ownership and usage of personnel health data. In the following "user" is mainly used for the data source. This can be patients, sports enthusiasts, persons tracking their vital data – basically everyone collecting health-related data as a private entity.

14.2   Research Questions

The main research questions to be answered in this study are as follows:

1. What is the user's willingness to share health data with research and commercial institutions and social platforms?
2. Which renumeration or rewards are expected in Euros for sharing data?

The study does not investigate in detail why people want to share or do not want to share their data, despite this being a very interesting aspect. Its main goal is to provide a descriptive and qualitative approach from which further investigations could arise. It only describes the implication of the results for business models and platform operators briefly. An in-depth discussion on these topics can be found at Horn (2018).

14.3   Models for Health Related Data

Nowadays, health data are kept in different data silos. Each organization collecting or producing health-related data stores it in their proprietary information systems with limited access for the original provider of the data, in most cases those what the user defined before. Data is produced from various sources: From data originating from individual activities (fitness trackers, cellphones, entering nutrition data in web portals) to data produced when participating in the healthcare industry (medical examination and diagnosis, medication, surgery, vaccinations, X-Rays, healthcare insurances, nursing services etc.). Although all this data has the same origin, namely the patient/user, the access, the exploitation and the usage of data – beyond their first main usage for diagnosis or similar purposes, is out of the original data provider's control.

Economic advantages have been realized by the platform operators like Facebook, Apple, Amazon, Microsoft, and Google (Alphabet) – the famous dominating FAAMG gang (Kenton, 2019). They collect and aggregate data at enormous rates without involving the user. Although the platforms provide in most cases storage of data at no cost for the user, the utilization and the profits are based on that data. The 60 biggest platform providers stand for about 7,000 billion USD exceeding all classical companies with their value (Schmidt, 2018). Data is power, and even more powerful if it can be transformed into information. A key aspect in their business models is the more or less legal usage of the data. Health-related data are just one aspect of the global data game, nevertheless an extremely important one, both from the side of the user and for the platform providers. On the one hand, health data are inherently private and specifically protected by laws. On the other hand, they form a mighty sword in the hand of organizations which can use them successfully (research, marketing, etc.). For a discussion on chances and challenges confer Spiekermann (2019) or von Kalle et al. (2017). This article will not focus on the aspect of patient orientation in the course of the health digitalization, which is a significant topic and obviously related to the data collection game and which can bring advantages to the patient (Müller, 2017).

If data and here esp. personal data form the core of the data (information) economy, how can those assets be administered and controlled? Schneider (2019) distinguishes between four approaches or views for administering the data:

a) Data as private good: Humans produce data which form the source of the data economy, although the owner of the value, i.e. the user, is currently only perceived as a passive consumer, not as an actor. Users must be explicitly involved in the value chain and paid. GDPR mainly focus on this aspect of the data as a private good and aims to protect the rights of the user. But as written above, this view is contradicted by the big platform providers which consider data as their business property protected by specific terms of use and transfer of rights.

b) Data as public good: Data will be considered as a public asset. The private data silos must be socialized. Data should be controlled and used by public authorities. Private usage is possible but must be paid for.

c) Data as commons (in German: "Allmende"): Ownership and usage is regulated by commonly negotiated rules and agreements between individuals and the society. This approach shares some common ideas with open source software or creative common licenses. One can use data basically for free but must make their own data accessible for all participating individuals and organizations. And the results are shared as well.

d) Data as trusteeship: Data are handed over to a trustee who organizes the usage principles on a fair basis for all involved parties. The trustee operates independently of any organization. Data are organized in data trusts and administered by the trustee.

Further on, the aspect of private good-view will be considered. It is obvious that the user is discriminated compared to the platforms which have the organization, hardware, software and money to enforce their view of the data world. Real information about the financial aspects of the health data from the user's view can be found sparcely in the literature. Customers have a "value" for the platforms, but which value is brought by the platform to the customer (user)? The author doesn't mean the value of knowing how many steps a user made during a day but the profit the user can make if the platform provider creates money from the user data. As an example, Microsoft paid 260$ per month to active users when it acquired LinkedIn in 2016 (Short & Todd, 2017). N'Guessan et al. (2019) determine the value of an insurance customer at about 52 USD, for the pharmaceutical industry about 11 USD, and gives an overall estimation for insurances in 26.000 USD, and 2.156 USD for the pharmaceutical industry if one would make the data work. In an experiment Zannier (Bloor, 2018) sold his data via Kickstarter for 2 USD a day, receiving overall about 2,000 USD. This experiment shows that customers can get a remuneration for their data and companies are willing to pay for it. The opposite approach is to determine the value of user data on the basis of some economical models (Kannan et al., 2018). In the following, the article will focus on the value of health data and examine the expectations of the users.

14.4   Methods

Two surveys were conducted on this topic in 2017 and 2018.

Waldhör's Survey: The first survey titled "Der Wert von Gesundheitsdaten" (The value of health data) started in 2017 and is an ongoing project. The web address is as follows: https://www.socisurvey.de/meddatawert/. The survey is internet-based, no paper-based surveys were undertaken. As the idea of the project was to get the estimates of persons about the value of their health data, esp. data generated by fitness trackers, etc. The assumption is that the topic is mainly of interest for internet affine persons. The questionnaire is available in German and English (Waldhör, 2018). The Waldhör data presented in this contribution were collected from June 7th, 2017 till June 23rd, 2019 (N = 207).

Horn's Survey: The other survey was conducted as part of a bachelor thesis (Horn, 2018) supervised by the author. The focus of the Horn-Survey was to explore chances and risks for health data sharing platforms. The Horn data presented in this contribution were collected from March 6th, 2018 till May 25th, 2018 (N = 527).

Both surveys asked users different questions about their perceptions on health data, e.g. if they would share their data, and if yes which data, for which purpose (research, commerce) and which renumeration they would expect for it. Based on this, the idea of an electronic commerce platform for health data was investigated.

14.4.1 Waldhör's Survey

The data and results presented in this paper were collected based on the above-mentioned questionnaire. The results represent the current state of data. The participants could choose between the German and the English version, although the overall number of participants decided for German. The recruitment of the participants was carried out through FOM contacts (mainly students), Facebook and Twitter. The questionnaire consisted of three main parts: the first part (MDxxx) deals with health-value-related remuneration questions, the second with health-related sharing willingness, and the third part (PExxx) with demographic items. Table 14.1 gives an overview of the collected variables that have been collected.

Sociodemographic Aspects of the Waldhör-Survey
During the period of this paper, overall 207 persons participated in the survey. For the analysis, only the responses of persons were included who at least answered 80% of the questions which resulted in 194 valid interviews (Table 14.2).

The presentation of the following results is based on the full 194 valid questionnaires. No significant relevant differences based on independent variables like gender etc. could be identified (Table 14.3).

14.4.2 Horn-Survey

The Horn-Survey (Horn, 2018) was available through the questionnaire web portal "Umfrageonline" (www.umfrageonline.com) at www.umfrageonline.com/s/95ffd92. The questions were in German only. It was active from 7th June 2017 until 31st August 2018. Overall, 527 persons participated, 293 females and 234 males. The survey consisted of 16 items. An overview is given in Table 14.4. Only the items in bold were taken into account in this paper.

Table 14.1   Overview questionnaire items Waldhör-Survey

Variable	Item	Type: Values
Remuneration related items		
MD01_01	Overall willingness to share health data	METRIC: percentage, 1–100
MD02	Estimated value of health data	ORDINAL: 0€, 20€, 30€, 40€, 50€, 70€, 100€, 200€, 500€, >500€, priceless
MD05	Remuneration for non-commercial research	ORDINAL: 0€, 20€, 30€, 40€, 50€, 70€, 100€, 200€, 500€, >500€, priceless
MD06	Remuneration for commercial research	ORDINAL: 0€, 20€, 30€, 40€, 50€, 70€, 100€, 200€, 500€, >500€, priceless
MD07	Remuneration for commerce	ORDINAL: 0€, 20€, 30€, 40€, 50€, 70€, 100€, 200€, 500€, >500€, priceless
MD08	Remuneration for social networks	ORDINAL: 0€, 20€, 30€, 40€, 50€, 70€, 100€, 200€, 500€, >500€, priceless
Sharing data related items		
MD03_01	Non-commercial medical research	BINOMINAL: yes/no
MD03_02	Commercial medical research (pharmaceutical industry, etc.)	BINOMINAL: yes/no
MD03_03	Saving lives	BINOMINAL: yes/no
MD03_04	Benefit for mankind	BINOMINAL: yes/no
MD03_05	Receiving preferential treatment in the course of the disease	BINOMINAL: yes/no
MD03_06	Getting new drugs in case of illness	BINOMINAL: yes/no
MD03_07	Health insurance cheaper	BINOMINAL: yes/no
MD03_08	Do not care	BINOMINAL: yes/no
MD03_09	If data protection requirements (anonymity) are met	BINOMINAL: yes/no
Sociodemographic Items		
PE01	Gender	BINOMINAL: male / female
PE02_01	Age	METRIC: Number 0–100

(continued)

Table 14.1 (continued)

Variable	Item	Type: Values
PE03	Family status	NOMINAL: Single, Married / Partnership, Divorced / Separated / Widow
P304	Education	NOMINAL: Mandatory School, Training, Technical College, Any other Graduation Degree, Graduation Degree, University / College
PE05	Job	NOMINAL: Self-employed / Freelancer, Employee / Private, Officer / Public Service, Worker, Farm / Forest, Retired, Housewife / -man (exclusive), Currently without paid employment, Pupil, Military / Civilian Service, Student
PE08	Social networks	BINOMINAL: yes/no
PE09	Medicine Portals	BINOMINAL: yes/no
PE10_01	Comments	TEXT

Table 14.2 Various sociodemographic data

Gender	#	Family status	#
Male	102	Single	74
Female	74	Married / Partnership	96
Job	**#**	Divorced / Separated / Widow	6
Self-employed/independent professions	20	**Education**	**#**
Employee / Private	99	Mandatory School	2
Officer/Public Service	22	Training	14
Worker	10	Technical College	12
Farm/Forest	1	Any other Graduation degree	25
Retired	2	Graduation Degree	24
Housewife/-man (exclusive)	0	University, College	99
Currently without paid employment	0	Overall numbers may differ	
Pupil	1	due to missing values in various categories	
Military/Civilian Service	0	Overall Questionnaires	207
Student	21	Valid Questionnaires	194

Table 14.3 Cross Tabulation of Use of Social Media (Facebook, etc.) and medicine portals

Use of Social Media	Medical Portals		
	No	Yes	Sum
No	45	85	130
Yes	8	38	46
Sum	53	85	176
Chi-squared = 4.7897, df = 1, p-value = 0.0283			

14.5 Results of the Waldhör and Horn Surveys

14.5.1 Results of Waldhör's Survey

Overall Willingness to Share Data

First, the overall willingness to share data and their associated value was checked (Fig. 14.1 and 14.2). 10% intervals were used and as it can be seen, the willingness to share is relatively equally distributed. If the overall sharing willingness into two distinct clusters (0–50%) and (51–500%) will be divided, the distribution is nearly equal (95 vs. 99 cases). This shows that without further differentiation on sharing reasons, it can only be concluded that about half of the participants are more or less ready to share their data. Figure 14.3 shows a closer look into the willingness to share health data depending on the purpose or usage of sharing. As it can be seen, people are ready to share data if they see some overall positive outcome, e.g. when sharing benefits mankind, saves lives of other, gives access to privileged treatment or new types of drugs. Data protection must be guaranteed. Interestingly, saving money in health insurance is not a key motivator for sharing data. Looking at the research-related side, people would support non-commercial research (university, hospital) but dislike sharing data for commercial research reasons (pharmaceutical industry).

Perceived Value of Health Data

Now, a first look will be taken into the question what the perceived value of health data is (Fig. 14.3). The median is in the 200€ class with a strong tendency of about 20% participants, stating that their health date are priceless, no money can price their data. From that, it can be concluded that people are aware that their health data have a relatively high value and that they would expect a remuneration of at least 200€. It is important to note that the values are based on monthly estimates.

Figure 14.4 presents how the perceived remuneration is related with the type of usage. As it can be seen in Fig. 14.5, people prefer sharing data for non-commercial research for a modest remuneration (median $6 \leq 50$€) while they expect a much higher remuneration for commercial research (median $10 = 500$€) which is in line with their overall sharing preference for research. This is supported by a χ^2 test resulting in χ^2 of 238.5934, df = 121, p-value = 1.029e-09. Thus, people definitively would support non-commercial

Table 14.4 Overview questionnaire items Horn-Survey

Item#	German Item	English Item	Type /Values
1	**Wie hoch ist Ihre allgemeine Bereitschaft, Gesundheitsdaten auf einer elektronischen Handelsplattform zu teilen?**	**To which extent are you willing to share your health data on a platform generally?**	**NOMINAL: 1–6**
2	**Welche Gesundheitsdaten wären Sie bereit zu teilen?**	**Which health data were you to share?**	**NOMINAL**
3	**Mit wem wären Sie bereit Ihre Gesundheitsdaten uneingeschränkt zu teilen?**	**With whom would you share your data without limitations?**	**NOMINAL**
4	Wie wichtig ist Ihnen der Datenschutz in Bezug auf Ihre Gesundheitsdaten?	Importance of data protection?	NOMINAL: 1–6
5	Welche Geräte benutzen Sie mindestens einmal die Woche?	Which devices do you use at least once a week?	NOMINAL
6	Welche Arten von Apps benutzen Sie mindestens einmal die Woche?	Which type of applications do you use at least once a week?	NOMINAL
7	Nehmen Sie an einem Bonusprogramm (z.B. Payback) teil?	Do you take part in a payback program?	BINOMINAL: yes / no
8	An welchem Bonusprogramm nehmen Sie teil?	In which bonus program do you participate?	NOMINAL
9	Welches Bonusprogramm ziehen Sie persönlich vor?	Which bonus program do you prefer?	NOMINAL
10	Würden Sie für eine bestimmte Anzahl von Punkten Ihre Gesundheitsdaten teilen?	Were you willing to share your health data for bonus points?	BINOMINAL: yes / no
11	Wie viele Punkte würden Sie gerne im Monat für Ihre Gesundheitsdaten erhalten?	How many bonus points would you like to have for your health data?	NOMINAL
12	**Würden Sie für Geld Ihre Gesundheitsdaten teilen?**	**Would you share your health data for money?**	**BINOMINAL: yes / no**
13	**Wie viel Geld (in Euro) würden Sie gerne im Monat für Ihre Gesundheitsdaten erhalten?**	**How much would you like to become for your health data per month?**	**METRIC: €**
14	Tragen Sie bitte im unteren Textfeld Ihr Alter ein	How old are you?	BINOMINAL: Male / female

(continued)

Table 14.4 (continued)

Item#	German Item	English Item	Type /Values
15	Wählen Sie bitte Ihr Geschlecht aus	Gender	METRIC
16	Wie haben Sie von dieser Umfrage erfahren?	How did you get this survey?	NOMINAL

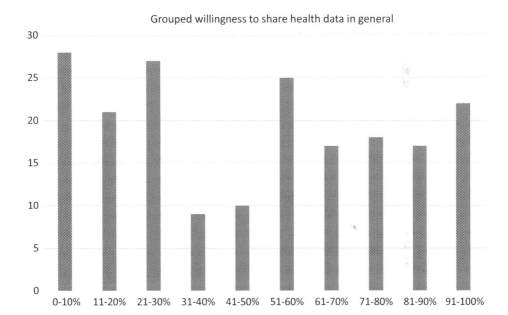

Fig. 14.1   Grouped willingness to share health data in general

research with their data while being much more skeptical about commercial research. People are even more skeptical about commercial usage of health data, e.g. for advertisement purposes (median $11 \geq 500€$). and disregard using it in social networks (median 12: priceless).

14.5.2 Results of the Horn Survey

In order to compare the results of Waldhör's and Horn's Surveys, only those items from Horn's Survey were used which have a counterpart in the Waldhör Survey.

Horn asked the willingness to share health data. The results are in line with the Waldhör Survey, although the Horn-Survey shows a slight tendency not to share compared to the Waldhör Survey (Fig. 14.5). Horn used different categories for the remuneration of €-classes; in Fig. 14.7, the Horn-€-classes have been mapped to the Waldhör

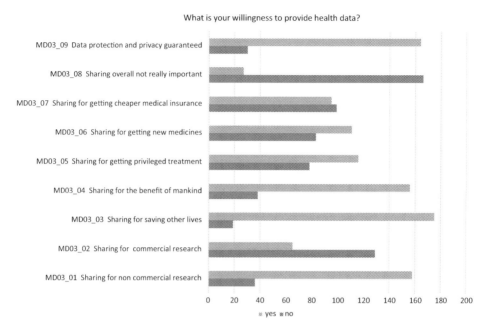

Fig. 14.2 What is your willingness to provide health data?

classes. The Horn-Survey results in a median of 9: 200€ which is similar to the Waldhör Survey (ibid.). Horn also examined a different kind of remuneration, e.g. some kind of bonus programs like "BahnCard points" (Deutsche Bahn) or Miles and More (Lufthansa). The results are difficult to interpret because such bonus points are difficult to transfer into real value and differ from provider to provider heavily.

In addition, Horn asked which type of health data people would prefer sharing:Personal information like size, weight, sport activities and medical information like doctor visits, illnesses, X-ray data, etc. (Horn, 2018). A clear direction towards non-hard-medical-related information was shown. Horn asked – and that is partially different from the Waldhör Survey – with which type of organization people would share their data (Fig. 14.6). The results of the Waldhör Survey show that people prefer sharing data for non-commercial research in contrast to commercial research and social medial.

14.6   Answers to the Research Questions

People have a minor tendency not to share data if they do not know what will be done with the data. Both surveys show that people assign a median value of about 200€ in general to share their health data. The results also show that people prefer non-commercial use of their data compared to commercial use. The Waldhör Survey also shows that

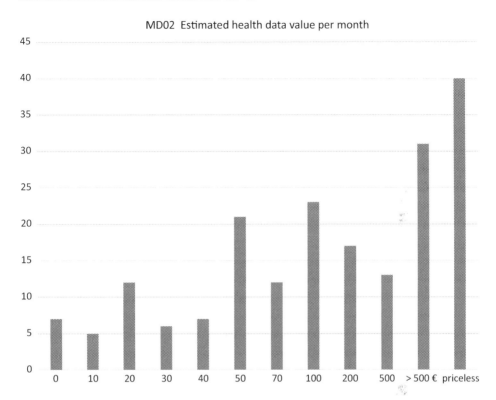

Fig. 14.3 Estimated health data value per month

social use ("help mankind") or individual benefits ("get new medicine") are preferred reasons for sharing data. The Waldhör Survey reflects that people expect about 50€ or less if data are used for non-commercial research while they expect at least 500€ for commercial research. People neglect sharing of data with social media platforms. Thus, the two research questions can be answered as follows:

1. What is the user's Willingness to Share Health Data with Research and Commercial Institutions and Social Platforms?
   People prefer sharing data with non-commercial research institutions, they do not want to share them with social platforms. People want to know what happens to their data.
2. Which Remuneration or Rewards Are Expected in Euros for Sharing Data?

In general, 200€ are expected, differentiating from 50€ for non-commercial and 500€ for commercial research.

Besides the main results, people require a GDPR conformant handling of their data.

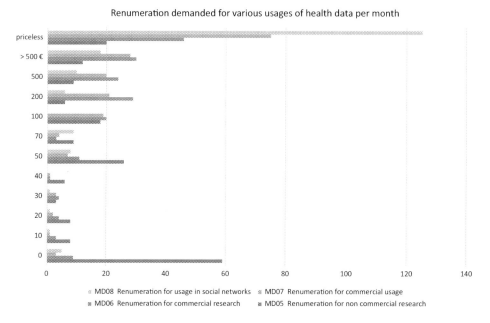

Fig. 14.4 Renumeration demanded for various usages of health data per month

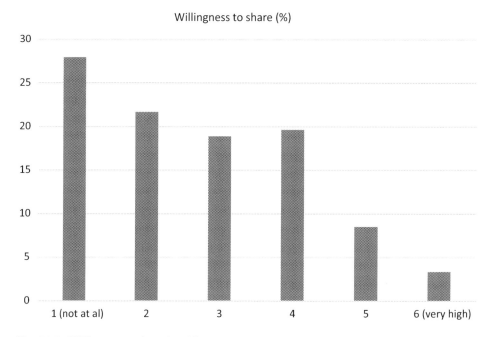

Fig. 14.5 Willingness to share data (%)

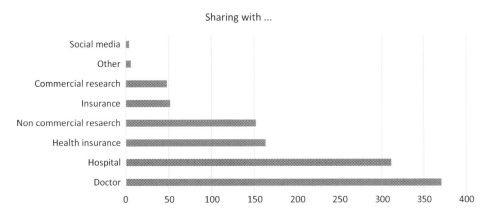

Fig. 14.6 Willingnesss sharing data with …

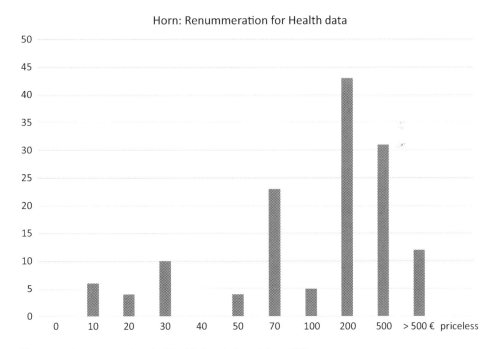

Fig. 14.7 Renummeration for Health data (adapted from [2]);

14.7   Summary and Conclusions

It can be seen on the basis of the results presented that most people are willing to share their health data but their willingness differentiates heavily as to with whom and how much they would anticipate for the data in cash or equivalents. Most people have no problem with sharing their data for medical (university) based research. They would offer their data for free or a very small amount of money for that. In case of industrial research, they expect being paid in the range of 500€ per month (whether this is realistic or not) or receiving some special benefits in the future if treatment is needed (e.g. getting privileged access to new drugs). Users are very skeptical about providers like Google, Apple or Facebook. Either they do not want to share their data at all or will be paid at a very high level (> 500€ per month).

What can be learned from that? Establishing an electronic health data platform with paid access for the health industry providers would bring additional income for participating users, raising the amount of health data available, broadening the access to data for researches and industry on a fair basis and essentially helping to provide a balanced relationship between users providing health data and interested parties using this data.

Building a platform which is trusted by the user will not be a trivial task. Currently, users provide their data for free, mainly because they have no real alternatives. Most platforms are cloud based and therefore immediately transfer data collected on smart-watches or mobile devices to the platform provider who is in most cases also the provider of the hardware. Users have no real control over who else will gain access to their data apart from their primary providers. There are rare exceptions, like Samsung, which keeps the data on the user hardware. As a result of the platform diversity, i.e. moving from one platform to another, is challenging for the user, and often involves losing all or part of their data. A common platform, e.g. built on a common business model, could solve this problem. Hardware and software providers would automatically integrate collected data in a GDPR conform way into the platform.

It is more problematic and difficult to integrate data produced in the core of the health system, visits by doctors, treatments, etc. This data would create real benefit both for the user and the research. Users could get access to their health records and provide those to interested parties. Unfortunately, this topic is not solved in Germany currently. Each involved party is sitting on its data silos and does not want to share them or is not allowed to do so – even with the patient's (user's) consent. This is up to the legislator to provide a satisfying solution.

The user could decide how their data can be used. They move from the consumer to the actor side. They could be rewarded in cash if an organization wants to use their data or could get preferential access to new treatments or drugs if participating in a longitudinal study. They could also neglect the participation, just keeping the data for themselves, safely stored in the platform. On the contrary, it could mean that they must pay to the commercial providers if they store the data on the platform.

Ultimately, a platform with a fair "exchange rate for health data" will help in the creation of a fully enriched digital health twin (Lutze, 2019), where all health-related data is stored in the life of the user. It will be open for new types of health services and health players (startups) as well as allow the application of advances in AI and Machine Learning (ML) based analysis.

In any case, a model like that could bring a new balance into the current market of health data which at least now is heavily centered towards commercial organizations. Both the user and organization side could benefit once realizing the value of data. Platforms would be forced to pay for data or offer a real value for it in exchange.

References

Bloor, R. (2018). How much is your $$$data worth – PermissionIO – Medium. https://medium.com/pe rmissionio/how-much-is-your-data-worth-c28488a5812e. Accessed: 7 July 2019.

Horn, W. (2018). *Untersuchung zu Chancen und Risiken einer elektronischen Handelsplattform für Gesundheitsdaten. Unpublished qualification work.* FOM Hochschule.

Kannan, K., Anathanarayanan, R., & Mehta, S. (2018). What is my data worth? From data properties to data value. http://arxiv.org/pdf/1811.04665v1. Accessed: 7 July 2019.

Kenton, W. (2019). FAAMG Stocks. https://www.investopedia.com/terms/f//faamg-stocks.asp. Accessed: 8 July 2019.

Lutze, R., & Waldhör, K. (2017). Personal Health Assistance For Elderly People Via Smartwatch Based Motion Analysis. In C. Giraud-Carrier (Ed.), 2017 IEEE International Conference on Healthcare Informatics: 23–26 August 2017, Park City, Utah: Proceedings (pp. 124–133), IEEE.

Lutze, R. (2019). Digital Twins in eHealth - Prospects and Challenges Focussing on Information Management. In IEEE (Ed.), *IEEE International Conference on Engineering, Technology and Innovation (ICE/ITMC).*

Müller, K. (2017). Mehr Patientenorientierung durch Digitalisierung im Gesundheitswesen. In B Bergh, A. Brandner, R. Eils, U.M. Gassner, B. Haferkamp, D. Heckmann, O. Heinze, C. Kalle, & C. Klose (Eds.), *Big Data und E-Health, DatenDebatten* (1st ed., pp. 109–121). Erich Schmidt.

N´Guessan, W., Svärd, J., Norman S. (2019). How Much Is Your Data Worth? http://stenor.github.io. Accessed 7 July 2019.

Preische, O., Schultz, S. A., Apel, A., Kuhle, J., Kaeser, S. A., Barro, C., Gräber, S., Kuder-Buletta, E., LaFourgere, C., Laske, C., Vöglein, J., Levin, J., Masters, C. L., Martins, R., Schofield, P. R., Rossor, M. N., Graff-Radford, N. R., Salloway, S., Ghetti, B., … Jucker, M. (2019). Serum neurofilament dynamics predicts neurodegeneration and clinical progression in presymtomatic Alzheimer´s disease. *Nature Medicine, 25*(2), 277–283.

Schmidt, H. (2018). Wert der Plattform-Ökonomie steigt im ersten Halbjahr um 1 Billion Dollar". https:// www.netzoekonom.de/2018/06/24/wert-der-plattform-oekonomie-steigt-im-ersten-halbjahr-um-1-billion-dollar. Accessed: 7 July 2019.

Schneider, I. (2019). Regulierungsansätze in der Datenökonomie. *Aus Politik Und Zeitgeschichte, 69*(24–26), 35–41.

Short, J. E., & Todd, S. (2017). What´s your data worth? *MIT Sloan Management Review, 58*(3), 17–19.

Spiekermann, M. (2019). Chancen und Herausforderungen in der Datenökonomie. *Aus Politik Und Zeitgeschichte, 69*(24–26), 16–21.

v. Kalle, C., Ücker, F. Eils, & R. Schickhardt, C. (2017). Chancen von Big Data für den Gesundheitsbereich und die medizinische Forschung. In B Bergh, A. Brandner, R. Eils, U.M. Gassner, B. Haferkamp, D. Heckmann, O. Heinze, C. Kalle, & C. Klose (Eds.), *Big Data und E-Health, DatenDebatten* (1st ed., pp. 85–96). Erich Schmidt.

Waldhör, K. (2018). Selftracking mit Wearables: nützliche Informationen oder sinnlose Datensammelleidenschaft?: 6. Bayerischen Tag der Telemedizin - Forum 9 "mHealth – AAL – Smart Home". 6. Bayerischen Tag der Telemedizin - Forum 9 "mHealth – AAL – Smart Home".

Health Apps in the Area of Conflict Between State Regulation and IT Architectures

15

Dominik Schrahe and Thomas Städter

Contents

15.1	Introduction		247
15.2	State of the Art		248
	15.2.1	The Digital Care Act (DVG)	248
	15.2.2	Market Situation Health Apps	248
	15.2.3	Health Apps and the New Medical Device Regulation (MPG)	250
	15.2.4	IT Security and Data Protection in Medical Practices and Hospitals	251
15.3	Technical and Regulatory Requirements in Connection with the DVG		252
	15.3.1	Data Protection and IT Security Requirements Regarding Health Apps	252
	15.3.2	Connection of Apps to the IT Infrastructure of Doctors and Hospitals	253
15.4	Discussion of the Question "What´s in it for Me?"		254
	15.4.1	…From the Patient´s Perspective	254
	15.4.2	…From the Perspective of the App Provider	256
	15.4.3	…From the Perspective of the Doctor/Hospital	261
	15.4.4	…From the Perspective of Society	262
15.5	Conclusion		264
References			265

D. Schrahe (✉) · T. Städter
FOM University of Applied Sciences, Munich, Germany
e-mail: Dominik.Schrahe@fom-net.de

T. Städter
e-mail: thomas.staedter@fom.de

245

Abstract

"Data protection is for healthy people" (Original quote translated from German) (Rohrer, B. (2016). „Datenschutz ist was für Gesunde". https://www.deutsche-apotheker-zeitung.de/news/artikel/2016/09/13/jens-spahn-philosophiert-ueber-die-zukunft-der-versorgung. Accessed 21 April 2020.)—with this statement, Health Minister Jens Spahn has already attracted attention several times, but also identified data security as the "achilles heel for acceptance in the digitization of the healthcare system" (Beerheide 2019a). Reconciling the two statements is likely to be just as difficult as making health apps secure and data protection friendly while at the same time ensuring that they are accepted as a means of treatment by all the players involved.

Based on the current developments in Germany—Digital Supply Act, (Digitale Versorgung Gesetz (DVG) in German) Medical Device Regulation, (Medizinproduktegesetz (MPG) in German) health apps on prescription—the involvement of the player app provider, patient, doctor or hospital and social health insurance in the medical consultation process and obstacles in the implementation are shown. The question arises whether more digitization in this context (e.g. Big Data, AI) means that data protection is weakened.

The aim is to model the cause and effect chain for motivating the players. Critical factors for the successful introduction and implementation of health apps are identified.

The goal was achieved by carrying out a qualitative content analysis for current scientific articles and online sources from 2018 until today. This resulted in the following priority categories:

- IT security in medical practices and hospitals
- IT security and data protection in health apps
- Regulatory requirements and test methods for health apps
- Interoperability of existing IT infrastructures at medical practices and hospitals

The following conclusions can be drawn from this:

The use of health apps should optimize healthcare from the point of view of quality and efficiency as well as legal requirements. This is currently taking place under conditions that casts doubt on the consistent implementation on the one hand and the acceptance by doctors, hospitals and app providers on the other. Support measures are needed to bring about harmonization and standardization.

15.1   Introduction

Compared to other sectors, the German healthcare system is far behind regarding the degree of digitization. In the ranking of the German Federal Ministry of Economics (BMWi) monitoring report of Digital Economy (BMWi, 2018), the healthcare system in Germany is with 37 points on the last place compared to all industries considered. That means only half as many points as the ICT[1] industry. Even the realization that digitization could be important for their own company is only shared by 15 percent of companies in the healthcare sector, and just as few companies in this sector give digitization a strategic priority. In contrast, 70 percent of companies in healthcare, more than in any other sector, assume that digitization plays a minor role in corporate success (BMWi, 2018). With the DVG, Health Minister Jens Spahn is not only trying to push the digitization of the German healthcare system but is also driving it forward very quickly according to experts (Krempl, 2019a; Gieselmann, 2019). According to the health minister, the aim is not necessarily to find the best solution regarding patient safety or data protection, but to pass laws that create a short-term benefit and thus acceptance for the digitization of the healthcare system (Beerheide, 2019a). Health data have so far been subject to a double protection, since in addition to the requirements of data protection law, medical confidentiality also protects against disclosure. In contrast to the GDPR, the latter has an effect beyond the death of the patient (Lucas et al., 2019). The DVG provides two changes which, according to critics, could lead to a weakening of data protection: Healthcare data should be used for research purposes. In addition, health apps are to be integrated into the healthcare system by being paid by social health insurance in case of prescription by doctors. The latter is the focus of this article because such apps have so far become known rather for the non-compliant handling of health data (Gieselmann et al., 2019; Weiß, 2019a). Furthermore, neither an interoperable EHR[2] (BMG, 2020a) nor health information systems (HIS) that offer interfaces to health apps, are existing in Germany (Caumanns, 2019; Albrecht, 2016). The aim of this article is therefore to model the cause and effect chain for motivating actors to provide or use health apps and to identify critical success factors for the introduction and implementation of health apps. For this purpose, after the State of the Art chapter describing the legal basis as well as the current situation regarding digitization, health apps, IT security and data protection in healthcare system, the new technical and regulatory requirements of the DVG and MDR are addressed. The focus is on IT security, data protection and technical interoperability aspects of health apps. Based on this, the discussion will address the question "What´s in it for me?" out of the perspective of the most important players - patients, app providers, doctors and hospitals. Finally, a cause and effect chain for motivating the players is modelled and critical success factors for successful integration are identified.

---

[1] Information and communications technology.

[2] Electronic health record.

15.2   State of the Art

15.2.1 The Digital Care Act (DVG)

The Act for Improved Care through Digitization and Innovation, or Digital Care Act (DVG) for short, was passed by the German Bundestag in November 2019 and contains a number of new regulations on the use of digital technologies in the healthcare system and the handling of the data generated in this area. The Digital Health Applications Regulation (DiGAV) and the Patient Data Protection Act (PDSG), which have been available as drafts since January and February 2020, are intended to provide further specification. The draft bill of the PDSG was adopted by the cabinet in April 2020. In the public discussion, one innovation of the DVG is particularly highlighted. Doctors can prescribe health apps from 2021 on and social health insurance must pay for it under certain circumstances. However, there are still unanswered questions from both a medical and a data protection point of view. The precondition for prescribability in case of health apps is the completion of a certification procedure at the Federal Institute for Drugs and Medical Devices (BfArM) and inclusion in the central directory for health apps. In addition to medical functionality, quality and safety, the requirements for approval also include compliance with data protection regulations and state-of-the-art IT security. Contrasting this, the proof of positive effects on healthcare, which is also required, can be submitted within 12 months after inclusion in the directory and thus after the start of prescribability (§139e para. 1, 2, 4 SGB V). The BfArM, which has so far been less technically or digitally focused, has hired four new employees to carry out the examination procedure (Beerheide, 2020a). They are tasked to examine health apps of lower risk classes according to the Medical Device Regulation (MPG), under which the Act combines the risk-classes I and IIa (§33a para. 1, 2 SGB V).

In addition, the DVG contains further changes that are intended to advance the digitization of the German healthcare system. For example, interoperability is to be promoted using IT systems in hospitals that have been approved by the Society for Telematics (Krempl, 2019b). App providers will also be obliged to allow the export of data collected within the app in interoperable formats. From July 2021, it should be possible to export the data to the EHR (BMG, 2020a). This is to be made available to the patients by the social health insurance from 2021 (§342 para. 1 SGB V).

15.2.2 Market Situation Health Apps

The terms health apps or the keyword mHealth are used in many ways, but not always standardized (Evers-Wölk et al., 2018). Different sources also count different numbers of health apps available in the common app stores. It can be assumed that the number is a low six-figure sum (HVB, 2018; Research2Guidance, 2018; Evers-Wölk et al., 2018). When looking at the download counts it is noticeable that apps for supporting or tracking training sessions, so-called fitness apps, are particularly popular (Priori Data, 2020). This popularity has already been observed for several years on most international markets (Murnane et al., 2015; Statista, 2018a). Apps of this kind, which can also be assigned to the lifestyle and fitness category, are aimed to support a healthy lifestyle and are therefore used preventively (Kramer et al., 2019). With a share of more than 20 percent, such apps are most popular in the app stores (Lucht et al., 2015).

The literature differentiates medical apps, which support patients in dealing with their chronic or acute illnesses. This group includes apps for medical decision support, dosage calculators or reminder apps for taking medication (Kramer et al., 2019). With a share of 18 percent, this group is also widespread in the app stores (Lucht et al., 2015). However, a clear differentiation to the first group mentioned is sometimes difficult, as for example diet apps or sleep trackers can be assigned to both categories. An international comparison shows that the German population is more critical of medical apps than people in other countries. For example, apps for reminding people to take medication are used by 22 percent of respondents in USA, while the same category of apps was used by only 11 percent of respondents in Germany. A similar picture emerges for apps for the detection of disease symptoms, which were used by 19 percent of respondents in USA, but only by 6 percent in Germany (Statista, 2018b). Medical apps that belong to the diagnosis and treatment group account for a share of 13 percent in the popular app stores (Lucht et al., 2015). This article will use health apps as a generic term for both groups like the DVG does.

The market for health apps is mostly unregulated, testing systems are missing and most apps are not produced in Germany or Europe (Hibbeler, 2019). The unauthorized data sharing of sensitive health data, such as that became known with the app Ada, (Gieselmann, 2019) has been no exception up to now. A study examining the 100 most downloaded health apps found out that almost 80 percent of the apps share user data in an unauthorized way with third parties and 13 percent of the apps communicate not fully encrypted, so that further unauthorized access to the data can occur (Grundy et al., 2019). Login data, which in turn can be used to access health data, can be intercepted in 80 percent of the apps examined (ePrivacy GmbH, 2015). Many apps also require potentially dangerous, but above all not necessary for the purpose, permissions during installation, such as reading the telephone status or exact positioning - in each case more than 25 percent (Grundy et al., 2019). This behavior is clearly prohibited by the minimum standards of the German Federal Office for Information Security (BSI) (BSI, 2020). Technical vulnerabilities in the implementation are no exceptions (Hibbeler, 2019). It was also found that around two-thirds of providers, sharing user data to third parties as part of their business model. The usage and forwarding behavior of these third parties is uncertain. However, an analysis of their data protection regulations leads to the assumption that the data could be shared again especially with companies such as Alphabet or Facebook (Grundy et al., 2019). Another survey concludes that more than half of the apps examined do not provide a privacy policy (ePrivacy GmbH, 2015). Questions of data protection, e.g. for what purpose exact location data or telephone logs are collected, how long they are stored, for what purpose they are shared with whom, have apparently not been considered by app providers. Technical measures like pseudonymization or anonymization or asking for informed and explicit consent from users are not common as well (BSI, 2020).

If patients are nevertheless willing to expose themselves to potential data protection risks, the question of the medical benefits of the usage of available health apps arises, since efficacy studies are hardly available until today. It is therefore not surprising that studies have also found out that the quality of medical content of health apps is rather mediocre (Chuchu et al., 2018; Terhorst et al., 2018).

However, the status quo also includes the fact that health apps are normally offered free of charge. According to a US study, the proportion of free health apps is 86 percent (Tabi et al., 2019). For the Google Play Store an even lower share of paid apps of around 6 percent is assumed. But even paid apps are as cheap as two euros or less in 60 percent of cases (Evers-Wölk et al., 2018). As already described, app providers are thus earning money from other business models such as advertising or the sharing of data. In case of apps selected by the patient in combination with an informed consent to data processing, this behavior may be legally compliant, but is not acceptable if apps are prescribed by doctors as therapy. According to surveys, 60 to 75 percent of Germans have data protection and data security concerns regarding health apps, yet about one-third of them uses them (Eggert et al., 2018; KKH, 2019). Due to the large number of applications available in the app stores with considerable qualitative differences, the selection process of a suitable application is very complex from the patients' point of view. In addition, there is a dynamic process of development triggered by regular updates, which was previously unknown in the medical environment.

Basically, it must also be considered that the idea of using apps in therapy is not entirely new, in contrast to the current depiction of the German Ministry of Health. As early as 2015, the CHARISMHA study summarized that the integration of applications into the standard healthcare usually requires the approval procedure as a medical device for proof of functionality, safety, quality and medical benefit (Albrecht, 2016). Also, a few CE certified apps can be prescribed and reimbursed as medical devices already now (Ehlers et al., 2020; Evers-Wölk et al., 2018; Lucht et al., 2015).

15.2.3 Health Apps and the New Medical Device Regulation (MPG)

Health apps that are prescribable in the sense of the DVG are defined as medical devices of low risk class whose main functionality is based on digital technologies (§33a para. 1 SGB V). This implies that health apps must first meet the requirements of the MPG and go through the corresponding approval procedure. The result of this is a CE certification of the apps, which proves that they meet the requirements of the MPG (Art. 2 No. 43 MPG). Only very few of the health apps available in the common app stores have been CE certified to date (Albrecht, 2016; Buschner, 2019). Surveys assume a market share of less than half a percent (Gießelmann, 2018). However, whether an app is a medical device according to the MPG is largely decided by the app provider throughout the definition of the purpose of the app. This procedure has been considered problematic for a long time, as exact criteria for the classification as a medical device seem to be missing due to the lack of a clear definition of the term medical purpose in the MPG. This is particularly alarming, as apps of this kind can involve serious risks. For example, if illnesses are not detected by so-called "symptom checker apps", therapy may not take place at all or only with a time delay, which can cause lasting damage to the health of patients. Inappropriate therapy as a result of an incorrect diagnosis also prevents the success of treatment and could lead to additional strain on the patient. It is therefore extraordinarily important that only health apps which medical effectiveness has been scientifically proven in a testing procedure are used. (Albrecht, 2016) The new MPG transposes the EU Medical Devices Regulation of 2017 and therefore had to be tightened in parts by 26th of May 2020 (Gieselmann, 2019). In particular the risk classes, which are the basis for necessary safety measures have to be taken by the app providers, are often higher than in the old version of MPG (Albrecht, 2019; Kraus-Füreder, 2018; Schüz et al., 2020). Some health apps are likely belonging to risk class I as non-invasive products. However, active products used for diagnostic and monitoring purposes are excepted from this, these are to be classified in class IIa. This classification also applies to software that provides information that is subsequently used for therapeutic or diagnostic purposes (BfArM, 2020b). Since the DVG intends using health apps for purposes of detection, treatment, relief of symptoms and to support medical diagnosis, many of them will also have to be assigned to risk class IIa (BMG, 2020a).

15.2.4 IT Security and Data Protection in Medical Practices and Hospitals

According to the European Organization for Cyber Security, two-thirds of hospitals in Europe were affected by IT security or data protection incidents in 2019 (Krempl, 2020a). The IT security company Kaspersky also comes to similarly high figures with infection attempts on 19 percent of all computers and other devices in the healthcare system (Hillienhof, 2019). The same applies to Germany, where deficits in IT security are often explained with low financial and personnel resources in the IT departments of hospitals (Kannenberg, 2020). While large hospitals are already part of critical infrastructures within the meaning of the BSI and thus have to meet special requirements in IT security, medical practices are not bound to the BSI specifications usually due to the significantly lower case numbers. The sensitivity of the processed data however shows that there is also a considerable threat potential (Krüger-Brand, 2019a). Today security and data protection incidents in practices occur on a regular basis (Eikenberg, 2019).

Considering the specialization of medical practices, IT service providers take a special position for the safeguarding of IT security in medical practices. However, the procedures of these service providers sometimes have a considerable negative impact on security. There are known cases in which nobody else, but the service provider had the passwords to access administration accounts and thus had full access to patient data (Hoppenstedt, 2020). In addition, it can currently be assumed that more than 90 percent of practices are less securely connected to the telematics infrastructure by their IT service providers than required. More detailed investigations revealed that about one-third of the practices had specific security lacks (Berndt et al., 2019). A significant problem is the so-called parallel operation of the connector to the telematics infrastructure, whereby the connector is not in the position between the internet router and the IT devices but next to them. This results in computers being able to access internet services more easily and are therefore more vulnerable to attacks from the internet (Hoppenstedt, 2020). In addition, weaknesses in the authentication procedure have been criticized so far (Krempl, 2020b). Nevertheless, the practices' owner is liable for potential data protection violations caused by an unsecure connection to the telematics infrastructure (Krüger-Brand 2019b). As a result, the legislator has attempted to make improvements with the DVG. For example, IT service providers must prove their qualification for the installation and maintenance of components of the telematics infrastructure to doctors on request. (§332 para. 1, 2 SGB V) This obligation is likely to be of particular benefit to resident doctors, even if the demand of the Association of Statutory Health Insurance Physicians wanted to get a certification obligation for IT service providers at first (Schmedt, 2019).

15.3   Technical and Regulatory Requirements in Connection with the DVG

15.3.1 Data Protection and IT Security Requirements Regarding Health Apps

In case of health apps, it must generally be assumed that special categories of personal data are processed in accordance with Art. 9 GDPR. This results in particularly strict requirements for technical security and data protection requirements such as informed consent. A fundamental challenge also results from the generally international target market of smartphone apps. The location of data processing is therefore rarely limited to Germany or Europe, and processing is often carried out by cloud providers (Albrecht, 2016). A processing location outside of Europe is permitted in the DiGAV, if there is an adequacy decision.

In the context of the DVG, app providers are obliged to implement extensive data protection and data security mechanisms. For the exact implementation, an appendix of the DiGAV with 84 measures is handed out, based on which app providers can prove that the measures have been fulfilled. Among others, aspects such as consent, storage limitation, confidentiality and integrity, correctness, authentication, logging and hardening are covered (BMG, 2020a).

Health apps are often used for controlling medical devices. This results in further potential attack scenarios, against which security measures must be set up. For example, data can be read or even manipulated at the usually wireless interface between the medical device and the app (e.g. Bluetooth or NFC). Therefore, not only privacy could be compromised, but also patients' health could be significantly harmed, for example by manipulating the data transmission on insulin pumps. It should also be noted that other apps installed on the patient's smartphone may be technically capable of accessing or manipulating data health apps (Albrecht, 2016). Technical measures such as encryption and signature procedures are necessary here too.

15.3.2 Connection of Apps to the IT Infrastructure of Doctors and Hospitals

Even without considering the security aspects, which increases the complexity of the connection dramatically, challenges are evident when exchanging data between different practices and hospital information systems. The German healthcare system does not seem to have overcome this challenge to date, which means that it has a lower degree of digitization in an international comparison as well as compared to other sectors in Germany. The connection between the above-mentioned systems often fails already because of their architecture and development status, since HIS are usually individually grown systems with proprietary interfaces. In addition to a high degree of dependency, low IT budgets in the healthcare sector are again an obstacle to modernization (Albrecht, 2016; Caumanns, 2019). In contrast to a new conception of these systems—called the greenfield approach—there are considerable additional costs and possibly limitations to the reachable security level through updates due to the underlying conditions of the existing HIS including connected systems (brownfield approach) (Hopkins et al., 2008). Especially in case of health apps, which are installed on the mobile devices of patients to collect data decentrally, improvements of healthcare can only be fully exhausted if they can be connected to existing systems (Albrecht, 2016; Kraus-Füreder, 2018). Although the E-Health Act, which came into force in 2015, already aimed at this (Vosshoff et al., 2015), the standardization of machine-readable data exchange formats is only now being addressed in Germany (§355 para. 2 SGB V, BMG, 2020b). While neighbouring European countries use electronic exchange procedures in combination with nomenclatures like SNOMED CT, (Caumanns, 2019), the transmission of doctors' letters, laboratory results or ECGs in Germany is still frequently done via fax (Faxendicke, n.d.). In comparison to supposed Third World countries such as Tanzania, surprisingly similar challenges arise regarding data exchange (Freye et al., 2020). By 2021, 15 years after the first demands for introduction, SNOMED CT is now to be made available free of charge by the BfArM to the players in the German healthcare system, initial trials are currently underway. The universal nomenclature will not only standardize descriptions, but also avoid confusion of terms. In addition, free texts such as doctors' letters can also be digitally processed more easily, which is particularly important for research purposes but also for translation into other languages (Krüger Brand, 2020; BMG, 2020b).

However, many health apps are still seen as "isolated solutions" that are not interoperable with HIS or EHRs. If health data collected through apps should be exchanged with the doctor responsible for treatment, transcription by hand or printing is still common practice today (König, 2019), and is recommended even by BfArM (2020a). Apps that offer an interface for data export to send them by e-mail to the doctor can be seen as comparatively interoperable (Terhorst et al., 2018). However, the non-encrypted transmission of patient data via e-mail violates the integrity and confidentiality principle of the GDPR (Petri, 2018) and should therefore not be used by patients. Internationally, the HL7 FHIR standard is emerging as an exchange format between health apps and the IT infrastructures in the healthcare sector (Caumanns, 2019). Previous pilot tests for linking health apps to hospital IT in Germany, comparing to that, require dedicated gateway servers to prepare the app data syntactically and semantically. Direct and standardized communication between apps and HIS interfaces are for the moment impossible in Germany. (König, 2019) This shows that the reasons for the complexity of linking health apps with central IT infrastructures in the healthcare sector are not only to syntactic and semantic specifications for data exchange, but also to regulatory and technical requirements that ensure secure and legally compliant data exchange (Albrecht, 2016). This challenge has also been addressed with the DiGAV, which, in addition to the data protection and IT security requirements described above, also requests the implementation of measures with the goal of interoperability and compatibility (BMG, 2020a).

15.4   Discussion of the Question "What´s in it for Me?"

15.4.1 …From the Patient´s Perspective

The fundamental openness of some patients towards health apps is obvious regarding the number of users of individual apps and the growing demand (Paulsen et al., 2017). Almost three quarters of Germans also support the DVG regulations in terms of health apps on prescription. Just as many are afraid of private companies using their sensitive health data. However, about half assume that the new regulations will result in additional costs for the healthcare system, but only a small benefit (PwC, 2020). Nevertheless, apps that can be assigned to the area of tracking and self-management already contribute to increasing health awareness. There are comparatively few apps in the areas of diagnosis and therapy at present (HVB, 2018). Considering the focus of the German healthcare system, and the social health insurance system, it is clear however that only preventive, self-management measures are not the center of the services prescribed by doctors (Evers-Wölk et al., 2018). Accordingly, the DVG will not contribute to the "distribution" of apps to patient groups that want to use them out of lifestyle reasons. Instead, the use of health apps according to the DVG should always support existing medical therapy and be integrated into the healthcare context (BMG, 2020a, BfArM, 2020a). As a result, doctors do not expect patients to show great demand for health apps within the meaning of the DVG (Bünte, 2020).

However, even apps which functionality is aimed to support medical therapy have not proven their medical effectiveness yet (Albrecht, 2016). At the same time, side effects are poorly researched (Schüz et al., 2020). This is expected to change as a result of the approval procedure from CE certification to approval by the BfArM, so that from the patient's point of view the trustworthiness is increased. Although the significance of CE certification for quality and benefit as well as data protection and technical safety remains limited (Ehlers et al., 2020), the approval of the BfArM will extend the scope of this certification to explicitly cover these aspects in future. This will result in a considerable added value for patients when selecting medically and technically safe apps. Previous individual certifications with a limited scope tended to lead to a false sense of security, as in case of Ada Health, which was advertising with a valid ISO 27001 certificate, that was obviously not effective to data protection (Heidrich et. al., 2019).

If health apps are founded on an empirical basis and are technically well implemented, positive healthcare effects and thus a positive medical effect for patients can be achieved, as a study on chronically ill patients shows, which examined hospital stays. The use of health apps to support medication and motivation reduced the frequency of hospital admissions. In contrast, positive effects on the length of in-hospital-stays was not found to be significant (Knoch, 2019). Nevertheless, restrictions in medical efficacy and patient safety may occur due to the provisional approval of health apps by the DVG without a proof of positive effects on healthcare. In the first year after approval of an app, patients could be exposed to new risks in the worst case (Beerheide, 2019b). In addition, positive healthcare effects require that apps are used regularly—analogous to drug treatment. So far this does not seem to be the case on the user side, as interest is usually high only at the beginning of health app usage and most users uninstall them after a short time. An essential criterion for the duration and intensity of use is likely to be the individual perception of use by patients, which currently varies greatly between different health app categories. For example, calorie counter apps are perceived as useful twice as often (40 percent) than apps that monitor patients' mood and well-being. The ability to share health data to the treating doctor also increases the perceived usefulness (Evers-Wölk et al., 2018, Lucht et al., 2015).

However, even if positive medical effects occur in individual cases in using health apps, benefits must be weighed against potential risks. Previous digital health applications have often become known through data breaches (Gieselmann et al., 2019, Weiß, 2019a). Even though they can be economically very harmful for app providers, the actual damage is caused on the side of the patients, whose health data has been published or shared without permission, for example. The criticism that data protection cannot be sufficiently guaranteed even for health apps according to the DVG was expressed just as often (Krempl, 2019c) as the lack of patient safety when using health apps (Weiß, 2019b).

Therefore, from the patient's point of view no clear benefit can be derived from the new regulations that exceeds the already discussed risks from technical vulnerabilities and data protection as well as not proven medical efficacy in first year. This is also reflected by the patients in Germany, 93 percent of whom do not want data to be shared without their consent, but three quarters of them fear that personal data could be shared with companies outside Germany and the European Union (PwC, 2020). Most patients reject health apps due to this criterion (Evers-Wölk et al., 2018), the DVG, which also allows data processing by non-European cloud providers, only addresses this issue in part.

15.4.2 …From the Perspective of the App Provider

The MPG results in several requirements for health apps and their manufacturers that must be fulfilled before the start of an approval procedure as defined by the DVG. Health apps, for example, have lower error tolerances and must have a different approach to product risks in comparison to other apps (Ehlers et al., 2020). Manufacturers are therefore obliged to establish an internal risk and quality management system and to maintain technical product documentation (Art. 10 para. 2, 4 MPG). This includes, besides further obligations, the control of suppliers and subcontractors, which in case of apps could affect cloud providers or software developers which programming libraries are integrated into the health app. For the former, the BSI recommends a certification according to the "cloud computing compliance criteria catalogue" (BSI-C5), which only very few cloud service providers meet so far. For the latter, the BSI requires tight monitoring and in case of vulnerabilities fast updates. The use of app versions with vulnerable libraries should be deactivated by the app provider (BSI, 2020). In addition to these technical requirements, the establishment of the above-mentioned risk management systems also leads to a considerable effort, especially as these are continuous processes over the entire life cycle (Albrecht, 2016). In addition, medical devices must be accompanied by instructions for use with pictorial representations of purpose and safety of the app, beyond that the patient must be informed about the risks of usage (Art. 7 MPG). Should the medical device nevertheless cause damage, the app provider may be liable for that (Art. 10 para. 16 MPG). In order to comply with these regulations and to contribute to medical expertise, the manufacturer is obliged to appoint at least one person who proves his expertise in the field of the medical device by appropriate certificates and at least four years of work experience. For small businesses, recourse to a person that fulfills these requirements is sufficient (Art. 15 para. 1, 2 MPG). Further measures are determined depending on the risk class of the medical device. For example, safety reports including any preventive or corrective measures taken must be generated on a regular basis for apps in the class IIa (Art. 86 para. 1 MPG).

From the point of view of app providers, especially small and medium-sized ones, the requirements of the MPG described above cause a resource expenditure that can reduce the interest in approving apps as medical devices (Kraus-Füreder, 2018), as the low number of CE certified health apps today shows. MPG approval procedures most often fail due to inadequately reduced risks and insufficient clinical data (Gießelmann, 2018), which in case of apps in risk class I can also be taken from the literature (Lucht et al., 2015). Nevertheless, a corresponding certification is the requirements for the BfArM approval procedure (Weckerling, 2019). Here, the CE mark is seen as an indication of the app's functional capability, which means that some features do not need to be tested again. Nevertheless, the BfArM's test procedure requires, in addition to many others, the submission of a user manual, a description of the patient target group and functions, a statement of compatibility for both smartphone platforms and, if applicable, other devices, and an evidence of the positive medical effects of the app. If a study has not yet been conducted to proof the positive healthcare effects, a plausible justification for that effects is sufficient for the period of one year. At the latest afterwards, these must be proven by comparative medical studies (BMG, 2020a). Just in very rare cases it is possible to extend that period to a maximum of two years (BfArM, 2020a).

In the process of approval, including the proof of positive healthcare effects, the BfArM gives app providers advice since mid-May 2020 (Beerheide, 2020b), for which the app provider is charged between 250 and 5,000 euros depending on the effort. In addition, 3,000 to 9,900 euros will be charged for inclusion in the central directory after approval of the app. Changes that have a significant impact on security, functionality, quality, data protection or data security must be reported to the BfArM. The notification is to be made 3 months before the change is implemented (BMG, 2020a), which seems to be a lot when looking at development cycles of smartphone apps but corresponds to the processing time calculated by the BfArM for all app approvals (Rychlik, 2019), even if the BfArM calls it "Fast-Track" (BfArM, 2020a). Excluded from the obligation to report changes are minor adjustments in the layout of the app or the correction of software errors that are not relevant for patients. The review resulting out of a change notification is charged between 1,500 euros and 4,900 euros. However, these fees can be reduced by up to 75 percent if the change does not result in a corresponding economic benefit for the app provider, for example, because the target group for the app is very small. Further costs can be derived from the requirements of the DiGAV. As a requirement for app providers that do not allow any deviation, the DiGAV requests, the conduction of a data protection impact assessment (DPIA) and the introduction of a procedure for regularly checking the effectiveness of the technical and organizational measures (TOMs) that have been set up. A penetration test or security audit might be useful for verification purposes, even if such a test or audit is explicitly required only for apps with a very high protection requirement. At the same time, the DiGAV assumes that "special protection requirement" [3]is generally identified for health apps. Starting in 2022, app providers will also be required to have a certified information security management system that meets the requirements of ISO 27001 or BSI Basic Protection, which will again require considerable organizational effort by the providers. The obligatory complete listing of all software

---

[3]Original quote translated from German.

libraries used and not developed in-house as well as the procedure to be set up for the recognition and elimination of resulting risks (BMG, 2020a; Albrecht, 2016) also contributes to another considerable effort in the app development processes. Not less effort in the development and testing process is caused through the obligatory requirement for intuitive and barrier-free usability, which must be confirmed by tests with focus groups. Further increases in complexity in the area of development can be expected from the requirements for an offline functionality of the app as well as plausibility checks, also in the medical sense, of all data entered or received through interfaces from other devices (BMG, 2020a). Data protection legislation and the IT security requirements based on the sensitivity of the processed data must also be explicitly considered from the beginning of the design phase and in the architecture of the applications. This includes, for example, two-factor authentication as well as mechanisms that detect and prevent unusual access attempts based on place or time. In addition, the principles of security and privacy by default must be applied, according to which the default settings must always provide maximum data protection and maximum security (BSI, 2020; DSK, 2016).

Usually one year after the initial registration, proof of positive healthcare effects must be provided. For this purpose, comparative studies must be conducted according to generally accepted scientific standards (BMG, 2020a). The costs therefore arising for the app provider are highly dependent on the content of the app, the Ministry of Health assumes costs up to a maximum of the low six-digit range (Krempl, 2020c). The design of corresponding studies will have to be shown, as study designs for testing health apps have not yet been established (Gregor-Haack, 2018). The Office of Technology Assessment of the German Bundestag also points out that studies for testing health apps can be used for a limited period due to the high innovation and update speed (Evers-Wölk et al., 2018). This point is also acknowledged and critically reviewed in the literature (Jake-Schoffman et al., 2017). The DiGAV makes no explicit statements on the necessity of repeating corresponding studies. In any case, the app provider should plan them exactly, since positive effects of care are always proven for a defined patient group, for other groups the app will not be prescribable.

After development app providers will have to deal with recurring expenses not only because of the deployment of mentioned management systems. Further costs will be caused through the mandatory requirement for continuously available free German-language support to assist users in operating the digital health applications. In addition, it must be ensured that app content always corresponds to the state of medical research (BMG, 2020a). Considering the know-how of health app providers today, this requirement is more than challenging. Depending on studies, the share of pure software developers without any healthcare-background among them is estimated to be between 51 percent (Research2Guidance, 2018) and 73 percent (Tabi et al., 2019). App providers from the healthcare sector are rather rare, that´s why a lack of specialist knowledge in health apps is often criticized (Evers-Wölk et al., 2018). For example, a US study examining more than 300 apps from the field of medication management concludes that only 15 percent of the apps were developed with participation of healthcare experts (Tabi et al., 2019). Health app providers are therefore often new players in the healthcare sector with rather limited financial resources (Gregor-Haack, 2018). For established players in the healthcare sector, limited skills in digital technologies causes a significant barrier for entry (Evers-Wölk et al., 2018, Lucht et al., 2015), whereas app providers from the software industry are challenged to fulfil the new regulations in healthcare. For example, previous monetization strategies of app providers based on personal data (Albrecht, 2016) are now legally excluded. Apart from the actual use of the app, personal data may only be used to prove positive healthcare effects, for billing purposes or to guarantee the functionality of the app. The processing for showing relevant advertisement is explicitly excluded (BMG, 2020a; Schluckebier, 2020). In addition, health apps that should be paid by social health insurance must be completely free of advertisement (BMG, 2020a).

It can be summarized that the careful development and approval procedure of apps is not only complex, but also expensive from the perspective of app providers, making many previous projects impossible to realize (Müller et al., 2019). This is because up to now, almost 80 percent of health app providers revenue is less than 100,000 USD per year (Research2Guidance, 2018). At the same time less than 5 percent of all Android health apps have been installed more than 50,000 times (Lucht et al., 2015), so that a higher pricing per app would not lead to large earnings in most cases. A comparison between these number and the development and operating expenses described above shows that the majority of the current app providers are financially far from being able to strive after approval according to the BfArM procedure. It can be assumed that the economic risks associated with the approval procedure will in future be accepted mainly by established manufacturers of medical devices (Albrecht, 2019). The exact costs for the development, approval and maintenance of a health app are difficult to quantify in general. Table 15.1 therefore shows two scenarios, that are based on the minimum respectively the maximum cost rates from the relevant fee schedules. The cost items that do not originate from the fee schedules are approximate values that can be exceeded or fallen below in individual cases.

This leads to the conclusion that the requirements for health apps to increase patient safety and medical use can be justified (Albrecht, 2016), but these requirements can hardly be met economically by the app providers that have been active on the market up to now. Even the large providers have to accept high investments in order to obtain approval from the BfArM for a health app, but for the majority of the current health app providers the approval costs for an app alone will exceed the total annual revenue that is currently generated with several apps. A larger scope of the app portfolio, so that investments and running costs such as the introduction of an ISMS or operation and support can be spread over several apps, should thus become a critical success factor for app providers. In addition, interfaces for interoperability with devices and centralized IT infrastructures in the healthcare sector will be critical to the success of healthcare app providers (Lucht et al., 2015, Evers-Wölk et al., 2018). An innovative culture through the participation of many start-ups is not to be expected due to the high regulatory barriers for entry and is not necessarily appropriate due to the level of professionalism expected. The costs for the studies to prove positive healthcare effects are likely to be the highest

Table 15.1 List of costs for health app development and the approval process from the perspective of an app provider

Activity	Costs Minimum Scenario (in euro)	Costs Maximum Scenario (in euro)
App development, testing and documentation (cf. Turner-McGrievy et al., 2017)	50,000*	500,000*
MPG approval procedure for CE certification (cf. Gießelmann, 2018)	5,000*	20,000*
Penetration test	1,000 *	10,000 *
Study to prove positive healthcare effects	10,000*	100,000*
Advice for inclusion in the central directory of health apps	250	5,000
DVG approval procedure for inclusion in the central directory of health apps	3,000	9,900
If no study was carried out before approval procedure: Check of the evidence of positive healthcare effects after trial	1,500	6,600
Proportionate: Costs for implementation and operation of management systems (risk management, ISMS from 2022 on) (cf. BDR, 2018)	50,000**	100,000**
SUBTOTAL Development and first approval	**>80,000**	**>660,000**
Change to the initial approval according to MPG	100***	1,100***
Change to the initial approval according to DVG	1,500*** (with cost reduction at least 375)***	4,900*** (with cost reduction at least 1,225)***

*)This cost item cannot be taken from the relevant legislation/fee regulations and is therefore based on regular market prices.

**)Concrete figures are not available, except for energy suppliers. Based on the authors experience, costs of 50,000 to 100,000 euros can be expected. It should be noted that these costs are not incurred per app. The effort for the management systems increases only slightly when several apps are created.

***)These costs will be charged regularly for each significant change or further development of the app.

cost factors in the approval process for health apps. However, these only have to be submitted one or even two years after the app has been launched on the market. Due to the dynamic development of digital products, especially apps, the high costs of medical studies and the additional costs for approval due to significant changes, the question of the motivation of app providers to deliver proof of positive healthcare effects arises. The criticism that the possibility of submitting proof of positive healthcare effects one year after approval would create a false incentive for app providers to create new apps every year and thus circumvent the proof in the long term has been expressed several times (Krempl, 2019c; Beerheide, 2019b). From the perspective of the app providers, there are several reasons for the described procedure, particularly because of app prices must be negotiated only from the second year on (BfArM, 2020a). The costs for the German healthcare system are estimated by the social health insurance to be 2.5 billion euros annually (May, 2019). These costs would have to be paid without any verifiable medical benefit if the above-mentioned strategy would be adopted. In the worst-case scenario, negative health effects would result from approved but not medically tested health apps that could lead to further costs in the healthcare system.

15.4.3 …From the Perspective of the Doctor/Hospital

The previous attractiveness of recommending health apps to support therapy from the perspective of doctors is shown by a Forsa survey on the use of health apps from 2019, which found that only four percent of health app uses were based on doctors' recommendations (KKH, 2019). Here, the DVG is trying to create a more positive setting starting in 2021 and will meet the challenge of selecting suitable apps (Albrecht, 2016). However, doctors will have advantages if they have direct access to vital parameters of, for example, chronically ill patients or if they are informed as soon as patients exceed a critical threshold. Experts therefore assume that the integration of health apps into the care system requires standardized technical interfaces (Evers-Wölk et al., 2018; BfArM, 2020a). Studies with health apps for diagnosis or monitoring also conclude that added value can be achieved primarily through automatic interfaces to doctors and hospitals (Fruhwirth et al., 2019; Skolarus et al., 2017). These also have a positive effect on the perceived usefulness of health apps by patients (Evers-Wölk et al., 2018). As already mentioned, the basis for such interfaces as well as the EHR is just being created in Germany so that their widespread availability could not be expected in the short to medium term.

Nevertheless, doctors can consider health apps for therapy as part of their free choice of the correct treatment method. If, however, it subsequently turns out that they had been inappropriate for the treatment, for example, because they were ineffective, and the patient's state of health got worse as a result, claims for compensation by patients are possible. Considering delayed evidence of positive healthcare effects, there should be at least a strong tendency for doctors not to use health apps without corresponding evidence in the treatment process. However, doctors will be less able to assess the implementation of health apps in terms of data protection and IT security, which could also result in harm to patients (Albrecht, 2016).

This means that the limited medical potential of health apps must also be weighed against medical and theoretical liability risks. Due to the limited medical benefit to date, it is hardly conceivable that doctors will prescribe health apps on a significant scale from 2021 onwards.

15.4.4 …From the Perspective of Society

For all three addressed healthcare players, the opportunities created by the DVG and especially health apps seem to bring rather small benefits. When weighing up potential risks, neither patients nor doctors and hospitals can be expected to be highly motivated to prescribe and use health apps. The high standards applied in the development of health apps are appropriate due to both medical and data protection damages. App providers, however, have to take a considerable economic risk due to high investments. This business model only becomes profitable if many doctors prescribe the health apps of the provider. The strategy of reducing costs by avoiding expensive studies to prove positive healthcare effects, which seems to be attractive at first glance, would lead to considerable negative effects on the quality of health apps, which could ultimately harm patients. In addition, the lack of evidence of positive effects is a further motivation not to prescribe health apps for doctors. The cause and effect chain resulting from this can be seen in Fig. 15.1 and only allows the conclusion that the positive effects on healthcare resulting from health apps will remain very low in the short to medium term.

Although data protection concerns regarding health apps are addressed by the BfArM approval procedure, the effective protection of special categories of personal data during processing and storage, both on mobile devices and in cloud providers data centers, possibly in non-European countries, is questionable. The BSI assumes that the special

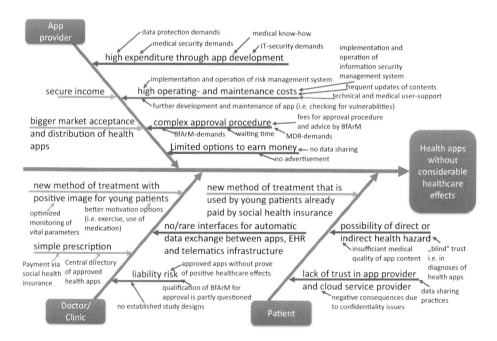

Fig. 15.1 Cause and effect chain for health apps on prescription within the DVG

requirements for the operation of digital health applications can be covered neither by existing mobile devices nor by existing cloud services, leaving residual risks (BSI, 2020). This topic is only partially taken up by the governing parties. Despite all assertions of the importance of data protection, such as the statement by the Federal Minister of Health, Mr. Spahn, that data security is critical for acceptance in the digitization of the healthcare system (Beerheide, 2019a), various government politicians argue in cases of doubt for a weakening of data protection (Beerheide, 2018; Voss, 2020). Even the Minister of Health in person, became known for the statement that data protection is mainly for healthy people before his term of office (Rohrer, 2016).

This article shows, that in addition to data protection issues, further support measures are required to integrate health apps into healthcare successfully. Therefor critical success factors, as well as the requirements necessary to achieve them, are shown in Fig. 15.2.

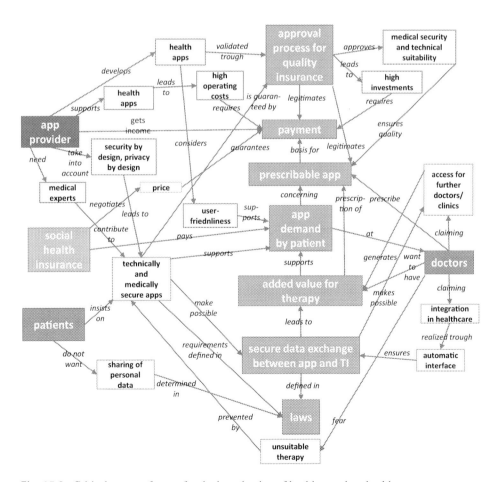

Fig. 15.2   Critical success factors for the introduction of health apps into healthcare system

15.5   Conclusion

The DVG and the laws based on it, start with the digitization of the German health-care system at a point, where there is a considerable need to catch up. Digitization will undoubtedly be driven forward by the measures of the law, the dimension of further development and the degree to which Health Minister Spahn's goal of creating short-term benefits through digitization of the healthcare system will be reached, remains to be seen. This article has shown that both technical and regulatory hurdles for the implementation of the measures in the DVG regarding health apps are challenging. Especially in Germany, technical prerequisites are still largely lacking. The comprehensive use of standardized data exchange formats is addressed with the DVG. But the telematics infrastructure as a central data exchange and communication infrastructure between health-care service providers does not yet seem to have reached the desired degree of stability and reliability that would be necessary for sustainable digitization (Borchers, 2020). In many cases IT security and data protection compliance in hospitals and medical practices is still far away from the appropriate level of protection for the data categories processed there. Despite this unpromising basis, the DVG will tackle projects such as the integration of health apps into the German healthcare system, that would even be ambitious for countries with a higher degree of digitization in the healthcare sector. This raises the question of the right priorities and a sense of proportion when investing urgently needed financial resources in the social healthcare system.

The discussion shows that the motivation of all major players to create, prescribe and use health apps is rather low. Despite a complex approval procedure, which is financially hardly feasible for the majority of the current health app providers, data protection concerns remain. The cause and effect chain showed above can only lead to the conclusion that health apps will continue to have little impact on healthcare. Nevertheless, the critical success factors that have been identified show that the DVG, for example by forcing increased technical interoperability between IT systems in healthcare, is providing important incentives. However, the interoperability next to many other basic conditions still need to be created before apps can be successfully and comprehensively integrated into the healthcare system. An important quality criterion in this context is likely to be the future penetration of health apps through all age groups. Up to now, health apps have been used mainly by younger patients, the usage behavior of patients over 60 years is declining dramatically (Eggert et al., 2018). Considering the symptoms and frequencies of sickness as well as the functions of the DVG-sponsored health apps, this ratio would have to be reversed. Whether such effects will occur remains to be seen.

The German healthcare system is thus only at the beginning of its digitization. This makes it comparatively easy to implement the legally required principles of security and privacy by design. Nevertheless, in the long term, permanent further development of security measures will be necessary both on the side of health apps and on central IT infrastructures in healthcare system. This is because the security measures that have been implemented are constantly confronted with new attack scenarios (Gießelmann, 2019). The political goal of creating short-term benefits that can be experienced as quickly as possible, even if the regulations are not perfect in terms of IT security and data protection, does not seem very far-sighted in this context and does not fit in with the sensitivity of the data concerned and the possible consequences for patients if something goes wrong. Thus, it is not yet clear whether patients will have to pay triple for health apps, with their social health insurance contributions, their data and their health.

References

Albrecht, U. V. (2019). Verordnung und Erstattung von Gesundheits-Apps: Guter Start, viele Herausforderungen. *Deutsches Ärzteblatt*, *116*(33–34), A-1470.

Albrecht, U. V. (Ed.) (2016). Chancen und Risiken von Gesundheits-Apps (CHARISMHA). Hannover: Medizinische Hochschule.

BDR. (2018). *Einführung eines InformationssicherheitsManagement-Systems (ISMS) bei Energieversorgern*. Bundesdruckerei.

Beerheide, R. (2018). CDU-Politiker wirbt für Datenspende. https://www.aerzteblatt.de/nachrichten/99767/CDU-Politiker-wirbt-fuer-Datenspende. Accessed: 19. Jan. 2020.

Beerheide, R. (2019a). Spahn ruft nach Ehrlichkeit bei der Debatte um Datensicherheit. https://www.aerzteblatt.de/nachrichten/107696/Spahn-ruft-nach-Ehrlichkeit-bei-Debatte-um-Datensicherheit. Accessed: 10. Jan. 2020.

Beerheide, R. (2019b). Gesetz zur digitalen Versorgung auf dem Weg. https://www.aerzteblatt.de/nachrichten/sw/Datenschutz?nid=104529. Accessed: 19. Jan. 2020.

Beerheide, R. (2020a). Digitale Gesundheitsanwendungen: Transparenz bei Herstellern. *Deutsches Ärzteblatt*, *117*(5), A-185.

Beerheide, R. (2020b). Anträge für Apps ab Mitte Mai möglich. https://www.aerzteblatt.de/nachrichten/112193/Antraege-fuer-Apps-ab-Mitte-Mai-moeglich. Accessed: 11. May 2020.

Berndt, C., Kampling, K., & Klofta, J. (2019). Patientendaten sind meist schlecht geschützt. https://www.sueddeutsche.de/politik/patientendaten-hacker-sicherheit-1.4678689. Accessed: 16. Apr. 2020.

BfArM. (2020a). Das Fast-Track-Verfahren für digitale Gesundheitsanwendungen (DiGA) nach § 139e SGB V - Ein Leitfaden für Hersteller, Leistungserbringer und Anwender. Bonn: Bundesinstitut für Arzneimittel und Medizinprodukte.

BfArM. (2020b). Orientierungshilfe Medical Apps. https://www.bfarm.de/DE/Medizinprodukte/Abgrenzung/MedicalApps/_artikel.html. Accessed: 28. March 2020.

BMG (2020a). Verordnung über das Verfahren und die Anforderungen der Prüfung der Erstattungsfähigkeit digitaler Gesundheitsanwendungen in der gesetzlichen Krankenversicherung (Digitale-Gesundheitsanwendungen-Verordnung –DiGAV) Referentenentwurf 09.04.2020. https://www.bundesgesundheitsministerium.de/fileadmin/Dateien/3_Downloads/Gesetze_und_Verordnungen/GuV/D/DiGAV_RefE.pdf. Accessed: 12. Apr. 2020.

BMG. (2020b). Entwurf eines Gesetzes zum Schutz elektronischer Patientendaten in der Telematikinfrastruktur (Patientendaten-Schutz-Gesetz –PDSG) Gesetzentwurf 31.03.2020. https://www.bundesgesundheitsministerium.de/fileadmin/Dateien/3_Downloads/Gesetze_und_Verordnungen/GuV/P/Gesetzentwurf_Patientendaten-Schutz-Gesetz_-_PDSG.pdf. Accessed: 12. Apr. 2020.

BMWi. (2018). Monitoring-Report Wirtschaft DIGITAL 2018. Berlin: Bundesministerium für Wirtschaft und Energie.

Borchers, D. (2020). Elektronische Gesundheitskarte: Versichertenstammdatendienst gestört. https://heise.de/-4769840. Accessed: 30. May 2020.

BSI (2020). Sicherheitsanforderungen an digitale Gesundheitsanwendungen – Technische Richtlinie BSI TR-03161. Bonn: Bundesamt für Sicherheit in der Informationstechnik.

Bünte, O. (2020). Kassenärzte: Vorerst kein Hype bei Gesundheits-Apps. https://heise.de/-4627419. Accessed: 9. Febr. 2020.

Buschner, S. (2019). Informatik von Gesundheitsapps. In S. Rietmann, M. Sawatzki, & M. Berg (Eds.), *Beratung und Digitalisierung* (pp. 325–340). Springer.

Caumanns, J. (2019). Zur Diskussion: Stand der Digitalisierung im deutschen Gesundheitswesen. *Zeitschrift Für Evidenz, Fortbildung Und Qualität Im Gesundheitswesen, 143*, 22–29.

Chuchu, N., Takwoingi, Y., Dinnes, J., Matin, R. N., Bassett, O., et al. (2018). Smartphone applications for triaging adults with skin lesions that are suspicious for melanoma. *Cochrane Database of Systematic Reviews*. https://doi.org/10.1002/14651858.CD013192

DSK. (2016). Entschließungen der 91. DSK am 06. und 07. April 2016 in Schwerin. *Datenschutz Und Datensicherheit, 40*, 391–393.

Eggert, S., Sulmann, D., & Teubner, C. (2018). *Einstellung der Bevölkerung zu digitaler Unterstützung in der Pflege.* Zentrum für Qualität in der Pflege.

Ehlers, A. P., & Bartholomä, J. (2020). Medizin 4.0 (Digital Health) – Chancen und Risiken. In M. A. Pfannstiel, R. Jaeckel, & P. Da-Cruz (Eds.), *Market Access im Gesundheitswesen* (pp. 343–362). Springer Gabler.

Eikenberg, R. (2019). Nachholbedarf bei der IT-Sicherheit deutscher Arztpraxen. https://heise.de/-4602788. Accessed: 19. Jan. 2020.

ePrivacy GmbH. (2015). Datensicherheit und Datenschutz von Medical Apps. Hamburg: EPrivacy GmbH.

Evers-Wölk, M. Oertel, B., & Sonk, M. (2018). Gesundheits-Apps Innovationsanalyse. Wienands Print.

Faxendicke. (n.d.). Fax in der Medizin ist unsicher. https://faxendicke.org. Accessed: 27. Febr. 2020.

Freye, M., Kipker, D. K., Ezekiel, R. B., & Mwamlangala, D. F. (2020). Strengthening protection of personal data in the health sector: A comparative analysis of the Tanzanian and German eHealth system. *Datenschutz Und Datensicherheit, 44*, 393–397.

Fruhwirth, V., Enzinger, C., Weiss, E., Schwerdtfeger, A., Gattringer, T., et al. (2019). Use of smartphone apps in secondary stroke prevention. *Wiener Medizinische Wochenschrift, 170*, 41–54.

Gieselmann, H. (2019). Warum Sie bei Medizin-Apps unbedingt das Kleingedruckte lesen sollten. https://heise.de/-4483550. Accessed: 8. Febr. 2020.

Gieselmann, H., Eikenberg, R., & Tremmel, S. (2019). Massive Datenschutzmängel in der Gesundheits-App Ada. https://heise.de/-4549354. Accessed: 8. Febr. 2020.

Gießelmann, K. (2018). Medizinprodukte: Risikoklasse für Apps steigt. *Deutsches Ärzteblatt International, 115*(12), A-538.

Gießelmann, K. (2019). „Neuen Sicherheitsmaßnahmen stehen stets auch neue Angriffsmöglichkeiten gegenüber". https://www.aerzteblatt.de/nachrichten/100202/Neuen-Sicherheitsmassnahmen-stehen-stets-auch-neue-Angriffsmoeglichkeiten-gegenueber. Accessed: 19. Jan. 2020.

Gregor-Haack, J. (2018). Erstattung von Health-Apps durch die gesetzliche Krankenversicherung. *Bundesgesundheitsblatt-Gesundheitsforschung-Gesundheitsschutz, 61*(3), 328–333.

Grundy, Q., Chiu, K., Held, F., Continella, A., Bero, L., et al. (2019). Data sharing practices of medicines related apps and the mobile ecosystem: Traffic, content, and network analysis. *British Medical Journal.* https://doi.org/10.1136/bmj.l1920

Heidrich, J., Tremmel, S. (2019). Datenschutzprobleme: Ada bessert nach. https://heise.de/-4602775. Accessed: 9. Febr. 2020.

Hibbeler, B. (2019). Gesundheits-Apps: Mehr Sicherheit und Nutzerkompetenz notwendig. https://www.aerzteblatt.de/nachrichten/101827/Gesundheits-Apps-Mehr-Sicherheit-und-Nutzerkompetenz-notwendig. Accessed: 19. Jan. 2020.

Hillienhof, A. (2019). IT-Geräte in medizinischen Einrichtungen stehen im Fokus von Cyberangriffen. https://www.aerzteblatt.de/nachrichten/108264/IT-Geraete-in-medizinischen-Einrichtungen-stehen-im-Fokus-von-Cyberangriffen. Accessed: 19. Jan. 2020.

Hopkins, R., & Jenkins, K. (2008). *Eating the IT elephant: Moving from greenfield development to brownfield*. IBM Press.

Hoppenstedt, M. (2020). Feuerfest trotz TI. *Der Freie Zahnarzt, 64*, 12–23.

HVB. (2018). *Fakten zum Thema Gesundheits-Apps*. Hauptverband der österreichischen Sozialversicherungsträger.

Jake-Schoffman, D. E., Silfee, V. J., Waring, M. E., Boudreaux, E. D., Sadasivam, R. S., et al. (2017). Methods for evaluating the content, usability, and efficacy of commercial mobile health apps. *JMIR mHealth and uHealth*. https://doi.org/10.2196/mhealth.8758

Kannenberg, A. (2020). Bayern: Datenschützer warnen vor Datenlecks auch in einzelnen Kliniken. https://heise.de/-4660088. Accessed: 1. March 2020.

KKH. (2019). App auf Rezept: Einfluss von Ärzten ist bislang gering - KKH forsa-Umfrage: Zahl der Nutzer von Fitnesstrackern hat sich verdoppelt. https://www.kkh.de/presse/pressemeldungen/app-auf-rezept-einfluss-von-aerzten-ist-bislang-gering. Accessed: 13. Apr. 2020.

Knoch, J. (2019). Der Nutzen von smartphonebasierten Gesundheits-Apps beim Selbstmanagement von COPD-Patienten. *Karger Kompass Pneumologie, 7*(2), 81–82.

König, R. (2019). Patient journey: Der Patient als Informationsbroker. *kma-Klinik Management aktuell, 24*(12), 44–45.

Kramer, U., Borges, U., Fischer, F., Hoffmann, W., Pobiruchin, M., et al. (2019). DNVF-Memorandum-Health and Medical Apps. *Das. Gesundheitswesen, 81*(10), 850–854.

Kraus-Füreder, H. (2018). *Gesundheits-Apps. Grundlagenpapier unter besonderer Berücksichtigung des Aspekts Gesundheitskompetenz*. Institut für Gesundheitsförderung und Prävention.

Krempl, S. (2019a). "Frontalangriff auf Grundrecht": Digitalreform des Gesundheitswesens kommt voran. https://heise.de/-4579916. Accessed: 9. Febr. 2020.

Krempl, S. (2019b). Gesundheitswesen: Bundestag für Apps auf Rezept und zentrale Datenauswertung. https://heise.de/-4582028. Accessed: 9. Febr. 2020.

Krempl, S. (2019c). Bundestagsanhörung: Starke Bedenken gegen Gesundheits-Apps auf Rezept. https://heise.de/-4558480. Accessed: 9. Febr. 2020.

Krempl, S. (2020a). Cybersicherheitsbehörde: Kliniken sollen Notfallplan für Malwarebefall entwerfen. https://heise.de/-4668130. Accessed: 10. March 2020.

Krempl, S. (2020b). Datenschützer droht mit Stopp der elektronischen Patientenakte. https://heise.de/-4698992. Accessed: 19. June 2020.

Krempl, S. (2020c). Apps auf Rezept: Datensammeln soll erlaubt sein, "umfassendes Tracking" nicht. https://heise.de/-4644993. Accessed: 9. Febr. 2020.

Krüger-Brand, H. E. (2019a). Datensicherheit: Mehr Rechtssicherheit für Praxen. *Deutsches Ärzteblatt, 116*(45), A-2057.

Krüger-Brand, H. E. (2019b). IT-Sicherheit: Konnektor ist nicht das Problem. *Deutsches Ärzteblatt*, 116(18), A-875.

Krüger-Brand, H. E. (2020). SNOMED CT: Meilenstein für die Standardisierung. *Deutsches Ärzteblatt, 117*(15), A-766.

Lucas, B., Jahn, O., Walcher F., Piatek, S., & Röhrig, R., et al. (2019). Nutzung von Routinedaten in der Lehre. *Deutsches Ärzteblatt, 116*(3), A-72.

Lucht, M., Bredenkamp, R., Boeker, M., & Kramer, U. (2015). *Gesundheits- und Versorgungs-Apps. Hintergründe zu deren Entwicklung und Einsatz*. Universitätsklinikum Freiburg.

May, W. (2019). AOK rechnet mit Milliardenkosten durch verordnete Gesundheits-Apps. https://www.aerzteblatt.de/nachrichten/103781/AOK-rechnet-mit-Milliardenkosten-durch-verordnete-Gesundheits-Apps. Accessed: 19. Jan. 2020.

Müller, P. F., Dressler, F. F., & Miernik, A. (2019). Uro mHealth: Gesundheits-Apps in der Urologie. *Aktuelle Urologie, 50*(01), 94–99.

Murnane, E. L., Huffaker, D., & Kossinets, G. (2015). Mobile health apps: adoption, adherence, and abandonment. *Adjunct Proceedings of the 2015 ACM International Joint Conference on Pervasive and Ubiquitous Computing and Proceedings of the 2015 ACM International Symposium on Wearable Computers*, 2015, 261–264.

Paulsen, N., & Schenk, A. (2017). Fast jeder Zweite nutzt Gesundheits-Apps. https://www.bitkom.org/Presse/Presseinformation/Fast-jeder-Zweite-nutzt-Gesundheits-Apps.html. Accessed: 28. Apr. 2020.

Petri, T. (2018). Kliniken melden Datenschutzverstöße nach Art. 33 DSGVO—Erste Erfahrungen einer Aufsichtsbehörde. *Datenschutz und Datensicherheit, 42*(12), 753–757.

Priori Data. (2020). Ranking der beliebtesten Gesundheits- und Fitness-Apps im Google Play Store nach der Anzahl der Downloads weltweit im April 2020 (in Millionen). https://de.statista.com/statistik/daten/studie/688733/umfrage/beliebteste-gesundheits-und-fitness-apps-im-google-play-store-nach-downloads-in-deutschland/. Accessed: 12. May 2020.

PwC. (2020). Healthcare Barometer. Düsseldorf: PricewaterhouseCoopers GmbH Wirtschaftsprüfungsgesellschaft.

Research2Guidance. (2018). mHealth Developer Economics – Connectivity in Digital Health. 6th Edition, Berlin: Research2Guidance.

Rohrer, B. (2016). „Datenschutz ist was für Gesunde". https://www.deutsche-apotheker-zeitung.de/news/artikel/2016/09/13/jens-spahn-philosophiert-ueber-die-zukunft-der-versorgung. Accessed: 21. Apr. 2020.

Rychlik, R. (2019). Den Arzt ersetzen können und sollen die Gesundheits-Apps nicht. *Gesundheitsökonomie & Qualitätsmanagement, 24*(06), 275–276.

Schluckebier, K. (2020). Apps auf Rezept – Werbung verboten. https://www.datenschutz-beauftragter-info.de/apps-auf-rezept-werbung-verboten/. Accessed: 28. March 2020.

Schmedt, M. (2019). Digitalisierung: Verteufeln hilft nicht. *Deutsches Ärzteblatt, 116*(47), A-2159.

Schüz, B., & Urban, M. (2020). Unerwünschte Effekte digitaler Gesundheitstechnologien: Eine Public-Health-Perspektive. *Bundesgesundheitsblatt-Gesundheitsforschung-Gesundheitsschutz, 63*, 192–198.

Skolarus, L. E., Piette, J. D., Pfeiffer, P. N., Williams, L. S., Mackey, J., et al. (2017). Interactive voice response—An innovative approach to post-stroke depression self-management support. *Translational Stroke Research, 8*(1), 77–82.

Statista Global Consumer Survey. (2018a). Welche dieser Gesundheits-Apps und smarten Gesundheits-Geräte (mit dem Internet vernetzt) haben Sie in den letzten 12 Monaten genutzt?. https://de.statista.com/prognosen/810056/umfrage-in-deutschland-zu-health-apps-und-smarten-gesundheitsgeraeten. Accessed: 24. Jan. 2020.

Statista Global Consumer Survey. (2018b). Anteil der Nutzer von Apps zur Erinnerung der Medikamenteneinnahme nach Ländern weltweit im Jahr 2017. https://de.statista.com/statistik/daten/studie/1029115/umfrage/anteil-der-nutzer-von-apps-zur-erinnerung-an-medikamente-nach-laendern/. Accessed: 24. Jan. 2020.

Tabi, K., Randhawa, A. S., Choi, F., Mithani, Z., Albers, F., et al. (2019). Mobile apps for medication management: Review and analysis. *JMIR mHealth and uHealth*. https://doi.org/10.2196/13608

Terhorst, Y., Rathner, E. M., Baumeister, H., & Sander, L. (2018). Help from the app store?: A systematic review of depression apps in German app stores. *Verhaltenstherapie, 28*(2), 101–112.

Turner-McGrievy, G. M., Hales, S. B., Schoffman, D. E., Valafar, H., Brazendale, K., et al. (2017). Choosing between responsive-design websites versus mobile apps for your mobile behavioral intervention: Presenting four case studies. *Translational Behavioral Medicine, 7*(2), 224–232.

Voss, A. (2020). Ein Manifest für die digitale Souveränität und geopolitische Wettbewerbsfähigkeit Europas. https://www.axel-voss-europa.de/wp-content/uploads/2020/01/AVoss-Digital-Manifesto-2020-deutsch-1.pdf. Accessed: 25. Jan. 2020.

Vosshoff, A., Raum, B., & Ernestus, W. (2015). Telematics in the public health sector. Where is the protection of health data?. *Bundesgesundheitsblatt, Gesundheitsforschung, Gesundheitsschutz, 58*(10), 1094–1100.

Weckerling, S. (2019). Gesundheits-Apps jetzt auf der Überholspur?. *Gynäkologie + Geburtshilfe, 24*(1), 55–55.

Weiß, E.-M. (2019a). Zyklus-Apps senden sensible Daten an Facebook. https://heise.de/-4518705. Accessed: 9. Febr. 2020.

Weiß, E.-M. (2019b). Bayerischer Ärztetag gegen Gesundheits-Apps. https://heise.de/-4554314. Accessed: 8. Febr. 2020.

Acceptance Analysis and ELSI-Aspects of Sensor-Based Care-Management: Certain Results from a Qualitative Study Addressing Dehydration Management

16

Christian Heidl, Sebastian Müller and Jürgen Zerth

Contents

16.1 Introduction 272
16.2 Background and Questions 272
    16.2.1 Dehydration as an Use-Case 273
    16.2.2 Questions Towards a Methodological Based Framework of Acceptability 274
16.3 Methodology 275
    16.3.1 Theoretical Aspects 275
16.4 Empirical Approach 278
16.5 Discussion 280
References 281

Abstract

Healthcare Interventions are often based on a variety of components, e.g different products, processes and adaption of organizational rules that have to be considered.

C. Heidl · S. Müller · J. Zerth (✉)
SRH Wilhelm Löhe Hochschule, Fürth, Germany
e-mail: Juergen.Zerth@wlh-fuerth.de

C. Heidl
e-mail: Christian.Heidl@wlh-fuerth.de

S. Müller
e-mail: Sebastian.Mueller@wlh-fuerth.de

M. Cassens et al. (eds.), *Transdisciplinary Perspectives on Public Health in Europe*, FOM-Edition, https://doi.org/10.1007/978-3-658-33740-7_16

Dehydration can be one example for such a hybrid multi perspective innovation that has to be effectively implemented in a service workflow. A newly developed sensor-based dehydration system is aimed to enforce the monitoring of dehydration and concomitantly the associated care-management process. Hence, technology directly tackles the organizational skill mix of caregivers. A study employing mixed-methods shows that a dehydration sensor could enhance interface management for all stake-holders involved. In consequence, such an enhanced dehydration management could have fewer "revolving door" effects between nursing homes and clinics. However, the perceived impact of sensorics upon interpersonal relationship between caring and cared person seems to be relevant for acceptance of professional caregivers. The view on care-givers' acceptance and their attitudes towards implementation of technologies into a typical personalized care-relationship raise further questions on personal, organizational as all as societal aspects of acceptability.

16.1   Introduction

Dehydration is one of the 10 most common reasons for older people to be admitted to hospital and a potential risk factor for further serious health consequences. Dehydration is based on multi-factorial reasons, i.e. personal as well as setting factors are relevant for explaining risks of dehydration for elderly people. However, validated methods for detecting dehydration in medicine which can be directly used for developing a sensor-based management strategy are not yet available. Hence, a two-part strategy, developing an adequate sensor module that can be implemented in different analogue workflows was the main focus of the research project "SeLe - Sensors for an Improved Quality of Life".[1] A service-based technology solution is intended to remedy care problems connected with dehydration. In order to address different stakeholder aspects some main questions for acceptability have been elaborated in the project, especially categories describing care-givers' acceptance and ethical tensions towards an altered way of care. In consequence, some patterns of a more comprehensive ELSI-focus have been addressed.

16.2   Background and Questions

Healthcare interventions are based on a variety of interconnected components which comprise products, processes and organizations. Therefore, the evaluation of this intervention strategy involving product-organisational interaction is a specific form of

[1] The project was funded by the Federal Ministry of Education and Research (BMBF), funding code: 16SV7479. We would also like to thank Ms. Regina Prenzel for her outstanding editorial work.

complex intervention (Craig et. al. 2008). Considering dehydration management in that way, it has to be discussed how digitalization can change nursing care, especially with regard to the dimensions of skill and grade mix (Berliner Bündnis für Altenpflege, 2016). What are the main benefits of a digitalized nursing strategy and what are the challenges and opportunities for the different stakeholders involved in the process?

Although there is some distrust among care-givers regarding technical aids and digitalized care, for example the fear that everyday life will be made more difficult and that human attention will be lost as a result of technology (Health & Care Management, 2015). Some market forecasts for the digital health market predict a continuous increase for the next years (Al-Razouki, 2018). Strategies towards monitoring one's own health status are also driving aspects of scaling up the digitalized healthcare market (Duttweiler, 2016). The number of people who are able and want to monitor their health status is increasing (Zhang & Ho, 2017). Despite these developments and forecasts for gains in effectiveness and efficiency, the influence of digitization on older people and especially on old age has hardly been investigated in the scientific community to date (Schmidt & Wahl, 2016). Therefore the project at hand represents typical questions for an expanded technology assessment in a sense of ELSI (ethical, legal, social implications)-Measurements.[2]

16.2.1   Dehydration as an Use-Case

The project "SeLe" has set itself the task of developing a dehydration early warning system based on innovative sensor technologies. This system should be able to indicate the dehydration status via a traffic light on a wristband and a Bluetooth connection. The sensor is to be attached to the skin with the help of a plaster. The recorded data should also be transferred to nursing documentation software (or to the so-called digital patient files) of an old people's or nursing home, or to the tablet of the outpatient nursing service. There is plausibility of getting an effective change in caregivers' time management and time constraints which could be beneficial for sides, cared person as well as care-givers.

Older people are more affected by the problem that they often no longer feel sufficiently thirsty. Due to diseases such as high blood pressure, diabetes mellitus, urinary incontinence and heart disease as well as the intake of medication (e.g. diuretics), it is more difficult for the elderly body to maintain an adequate state of hydrogenation

---

[2] In Europe, the consideration of aspects such as ELSA (ethical, legal, social aspects) and RRI (Responsible Research and Innovation, increasingly used in Europe) as responsible research is increasingly being analyzed and implemented in research projects (Zwart et al., 2014). In the United States of America, in the context of the Human Genome Project (HGP) (1990–2003), the developers investigated that information obtained by mapping and sequencing the human genome would have a significant effect on individuals, families, and society (NIH, 2012).

(source). Seniors suffering from dementia, in particular, are at great risk of being dehydrated with impacts for different serious illnesses (states of confusion, dizziness, circulatory failure) (Thomas et al., 2003; Xiao et al., 2004). Dehydration, along with pneumonia and malnutrition, is one of the most frequent causes of death in people with dementia. In addition, people in need of care who live in inpatient facilities (e.g. nursing homes) have a ten times higher risk of dehydration (Wolff et al., 2015).

Up to now, no scientifically-based validated method has been developed to measure a person's dehydration status directly and reliably (Schaefer, 2017). All clinical tests used to date to measure dehydration are not sufficient for getting an accurate assessment of dehydration status of older people. Often, standardized tests used to measure dehydration are not accurate enough or produce false results (DNQP, 2017). Several tests must therefore be combined, as otherwise a demonstrably well-founded dehydration condition is often not precisely analyzed (Hooper et al., 2015).

Currently, the dehydration assessment takes place over a period of several days (approx. three days), with the drinking and excretion quantity being recorded in writing by a nurse approx. every two hours.[3] In consequence, a sensor-based approach in the sense of "Sele" would alter the overall interaction of nursing. Sensor-based technology innovation comprises three parts that have to be considered. First of all it is the impact of ICT-enhanced monitoring of dehydration. However in consequence the adjusted monitoring framework has secondly a direct impact upon the teamworking-process in care, especially the work organization. At least, changes between technology, nurses and organizational factors have to be considered as well as some regulatory and cultural aspects for the way of nursing (cf. Pascal, 2017).

16.2.2 Questions Towards a Methodological Based Framework of Acceptability

Dealing with a sustainable prediction for successful implementation of sensor-based technology for dehydration management, different multi-faceted aspects of various stakeholders have to be addressed. With regard to social and ethical issues in the Sele-project, some references to ELSI (ethical, legal, social implications) were employed. The focus of ELSI-research within the Sele-Project was to identify relevant personal-based restraints in accepting sensor-based technology and elaborating care-givers' tension towards an altered form of care-giving process based on monitoring-based cues for care-giving needs.

Acceptance as a multi-faceted strategy reflects the extent to which various interest groups need to implement technologies in healthcare markets (Sekhon, 2017). Using the technology acceptance model by Davis et al. (1989), the analysis will examine

---

[3] According to a qualitative interview conducted within a Nursery Manager.

the acceptance of benefits and usability in greater depth. Especially among stakeholders involved in typical workflow scenarios for dehydration management in long-term care units (nurses, physicians, care-givers, etc.), there is an important aspect underlying the acceptance of assistive technology and its profitable application for continuous use in everyday work. We employed a specific way of addressing "ELSI-aspects" called "SIEB"-approach used by IDC-Research Institute (Jaensch et. al., 2019).

Within that ELSI-orientated SIEB-method, micro-level aspects of acceptance and ethical confirmations should be focused as well as overall aspect of macro-level acceptability according to Sekhon et. al. (2017). In addition to an examination of processes related to the implementation of the system in everyday care provision (workflow analysis) and an acceptance analysis of the stakeholders involved, this study pays particular attention to the ethical, legal and social implications (ELSI aspects). The following research questions were derived from this project:

1. What effects does the use of a sensor for monitoring the dehydration status have on the workflow in the care sector?
2. What acceptance settings are based on among relevant stakeholders with regard to the use of a technical system for monitoring dehydration?
3. Are there some first impacts for an expanded ELSI-discussion that could be triggered by implementing a market-ready version of a "Sele"-Management-System?

16.3 Methodology

16.3.1 Theoretical Aspects

According to SIEB-Framework we first analyzed the micro-level perspectives of projected settings for implementing a "Sele-System". Here, individual aspects of tension towards technology as well as acceptance factors of professional nurses are worth to elaborate. A full picture of a comprehensive view of interaction process is depicted in fig. 16.1.

For the first step within the funded project we employ a qualitative approach for preparing a broader view of individual receptions of new technology. Applying to Linstone (1999)[4] we only focus on the personal perspective of a complex organizational change that will probably occur by the implementation of a sensor-based organizational model in dehydration management. In the context of this paper, the aspects acceptance, personal ethical aspects and partly some insights of corporate culture on meso and micro

---

[4] Linstone addresses in a multiple approach three perspectives as heuristic for complex changes: Technical, organizational and personal.

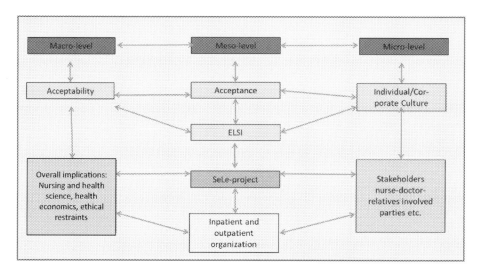

Fig. 16.1 Impact of ELSI on the example of the BMBF project SeLe

level of nursing staff (stakeholders) will be examined. In order to answer the aforementioned research questions, we employed a qualitative study design (Table 16.1).

Fourteen guideline-based expert interviews were conducted. The data evaluation was based on the qualitative content analysis according to Mayring (2008). The interviewed experts were stakeholders in inpatient nursing facilities and outpatient nursing services. These included facility managers and managing directors as well as quality management officers and nursing services and nursing staff (including geriatric nurses and coma nurses) of two nursing homes in Nuremberg, one nursing home in Düsseldorf and one outpatient service in Nuremberg. The age group of the interviews was between 30 and 55 years. Four men and 10 women were interviewed.

The questionnaire was developed on the basis of the technology acceptance model TAM (Davis et al. 1989) and the expert standard for nutrition (German Network for Quality Development in Nursing 2017). The technology acceptance model by Davis et al. (1989) was extended by some aspects of socioeconomic factors that would calibrate the individual stakeholders' decisions for acceptance.

Table 16.1 Study design

Type of study	Qualitative study design, interpretative approach
Sampling	14 experts from different nursing settings
Data collection	Guideline based expert interview
Data evaluation	Qualitative content analysis according to Mayring

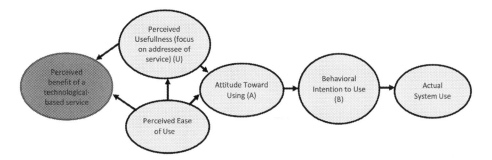

Fig. 16.2 Model of acceptance (following Davis et al. 1989)

We decomposed the TAM-model applying to two main focuses for individual reception. First of all the perceived usability is the stakeholder's assessment how the sensor-based technology is capable of fulfilling the minimum technical requirements,
for example taking into account and referring to the EU Data Protection Ordinance
(EU-DSGVO) (EU Data Protection Ordinance, EU-DSGVO, 2018). Moreover, the perceived usability refers to the subjective assessment of the acting user in what the minimum effort is involved in learning how to use the system. Structural properties and
usability aspects are also relevant here.

From the presented acceptance model (Fig. 16.2), the subjective assessment of the stakeholder with regard to the perceived benefit resembles a mirror to a prediction of using the
systems. However, we cannot infer a strict causality from intention to use because of prin-
cipal-agent relationships in organized long-term care units a principal can enforce agents—
here nurses to use a system—but with the risk of hidden less efforts of them. Finally the
grade of **perceived usefulness** represents the expectation towards the service-level impact
of a technology, considering nursing care-giving process impacts the outcome for the care-
process and the expected outcome that the person receiving care is likely to notice.

Additional to perceived usefulness The perceived ease of use (perceived usability) is
the stakeholder's assessment of the systems impact upon the workflow, which is strongly
connected with aspects like care-giver burden or disutility when doing work. Especially,
whether a system is capable of meeting the minimum technical requirements or which
structural and technical properties are needed, the sensor seems to be relevant here.
Thus, the perceived usability represents the product level of the system. Indicators for
structural and technical properties are, for example, the shape of the sensor, the measuring point or the ways in which the data should be transmitted and how safe these ways
should be.

In the course of the survey, the key questions were adapted in the sense of an iterative
approach on the basis of the previous interviews.

Table 16.2 Exemplary excerpts of the interviews

Category	Perceived Usability	Perceived Usefulness
Dimension	Structural property	Treatment quality
Indikator	Hazards when measuring	Reduced documentation effort
Examples from interviews	"Yes, so with the box is already hard and disturbing pressure sores, decubitus and so on I find that can/ would now also be such a thing that occurs to me" (I9, paragraph 27)	"In the case if you then, how shall one say, perhaps drinking protocol or fluid balance then not need, which is sometimes difficult to conduct. That one says, one has there evenly measured values which one can enter and that is then made faster, read off, compared than likewise the other measures. Therefore it can be a time saving and bring a certain efficiency with it." (Interview 1, paragraph 43)

16.4   Empirical Approach

The qualitative content analysis resulted in seven evaluation dimensions: Structural and technical properties of the sensor (perceived usability); treatment quality, process costs/ speed, patient documentation, ELSI aspects (perceived usefulness). Exemplary excerpts are shown in Table 16.2.

The evaluation categories are listed in Table 16.2 (Results—exemplary excerpts). (However, for a comprehensive presentation of the entire subcategories, it was not possible to list them comprehensively in this article for reasons of space).

In the qualitative content analysis, five main categories emerged from the interviews conducted. These categories are acceptance - perceived benefits, acceptance - perceived usability, assessment of acceptance by respondents, personal moral concerns and patient documentation.

Acceptance - perceived personal benefit

The participants who were interviewed assigned significant importance to the aspects of higher quality of care and time savings with regard to nursing care

"Yes, I mean if it's good now, if it's good for the resident to improve the quality of life, why not? That's how I see it personally." (Interview 3 - PDL, paragraph 112)

"I think we could use the staff then for the care, for the real resource-oriented care, which we simply do not have temporally" (Interview 3 - PDL, paragraph 66)

The use of SeLe is intended to make everyday care easier:

"Make work easier in any case." (Interview 8 - Nurse [Intensive vegetative state], paragraph 10)

"But I guess that would be a support for us. For us certainly one thing, partly to make things easier." (Interview 3 -PDL, paragraph 78)

Reduction of documentation effort:

"If one saves the paperwork thereby (interview 12 - nurse, paragraph 19)

Legal costs:

"So I can't imagine personnel planning right now." (Interview 4 - management, paragraph 82)

"[…] do not imagine that it has an impact on the resource" (Interview 9 - QM/PDL, paragraph 42)

Acceptance - perceived usability

Objective data:
"To give nurses a sense of security. So would produce security to say so. Is their assessment which they actually only perceive from visual perception, drinking quantity perception, changes in skin or eyes and so on" (Interview 4 - Management, Paragraph 57)
"Sure, because the problem is, how do I know an exsiccosis. When is someone exsikiert?" (Interview 3 - PDL, paragraph 40)
"Yeah, I think so, we have a lot of residents who have never drunk a liter and a half a day in their lives. So simply also biographically seen," (Interview 11 - PDL paragraph 28)
Design/technical properties:
"What else could it/yes/ be in a watch or the like. In terms of things to install quasi/ or build things that look similar to the equipment that is already there." (Interview 12 - nurse, paragraph 30)
"resistant to washing and so on" (Interview 9 - QM/PDL, paragraph 42)
"then it should be really flat" (Interview 9 - QM/PDL, Paragraph 52
Measuring points:
2x back, 2x between the shoulder blades, 2x legs, 1x foot sole, 1x arm

Expectation on the beneficiaries acceptance

Acceptance by residents/patients:
"That's the case with our dementias in particular, so that every foreign body or everyone is not accustomed to first disturbs". (Interview 12 - nurse, paragraph 22)
"Yeah, because if you do it somewhere where they see it, they do it, they rip it all out. They also rip out the infusion and everything. They defend themselves against everything" (Interview 3 - PDL, paragraph 37)
Acceptance by relatives:
"Then I would say if I were relative rightly, my mother, my father is here in a facility where 24 h someone is and I also assume that care is taken that he drinks enough" (Interview 11 - PDL, paragraph 60)
Acceptance by nursing staff:
"does it perhaps even take the professionalism? If the nursing staff then rely on this device saying to me when the resident is dehydrated and don't really look any more //mhm// and that would probably be exactly the opposite of what one wants to achieve with SISS, for example, to strengthen the professionalism, perhaps that takes the professionalism" (Interview 9 - QM/PDL, Paragraph 29)

Personal moral aspects (representation of overall ethical concerns)

Ethical Implications	"On the other hand, there is now less room for manoeuvre in recognizing a palliative phase or something like that" (Interview 4 - Management, Paragraph 76) "is just like with other things when do we decide to stop? Because otherwise I already have an extension of the dying phase if I constantly add liquid" (Interview 3—PDL, paragraph 112)

Social Implications	"So they would also have to consider there is to say also still a socio-political differentiation. That means if someone can afford it and the other one can't afford it. Do I have unequal treatment? Is it then only a question of money, the use of technology now, that someone does not come to harm? (Interview 4—Management, paragraph 84) "[…] it would be bad if we could get somewhere, that we only react to one person or one care, if an instrument tells us it's time now." (Interview 5 - PDL, paragraph 64) "I don't know if I want to rely on it, because I think drinking the whole thing is personal contact again, where I learn a lot about people again." (Interview 11—PDL paragraph 77)
Legal Implications	"What legal consequences will it have if this thing is red? And nobody reacts to it. Does that have legal consequences? For the one who doesn't react or?" (Interview 4—management, paragraph 77) "Can anyone still say no I don't like it, I don't like technique." (Interview 4 - line, paragraph 73)
Data protection implications	"a legal thing, it is always/of course depends on what kind of data is still passed on, or stored" (Interview 8 - nurse [Intensiv-Wachkoma], paragraph 26) "[…] the transmission paths are secure." (Interview 7 - nurse, paragraph 20)

16.5   Discussion

The implementation of sensor-based dehydration management deals with various aspects of organizational change. The view on the acceptance of care-givers and their attitude towards implementation of technologies in a typical personalized care relationship raises further questions about personal, organizational and all social aspects of acceptance. Especially in the context of implementation of technical innovations, an analysis of a broader view of acceptability is required. However, it should also be critically noted that in course of participatory technology development of an "acceptance orientation" takes place within a certain framework and beyond technology development distortions (bias types);acceptance bias, source bias, pro-innovation bias etc. are identified which can occur during technology implementation and diffusion in order to successfully shape participation (Hagen et al., 2018).

For future research projects, ideally ELSI aspects should be collected at the beginning of a project and continuously (in longitudinal section) analyzed and adapted until the end of the project (Manzeschke et al., 2013). If ELSI aspects are identified at the beginning of the development of the technical assistance system by all project participants and disciplines and if work is continuously carried out on them, the communicative exchange within the project consortium improves and the acceptance of the technical innovation strenghens the effectiveness of project translation and bias species that occur can be clearly identified and solved.

Implementing of a sensor-based measurement without any organizational and personal change strategy involving all stakeholders from the early beginning could probably induce negative impacts on the competencies of care-givers and on the relationship between different care-givers (Benner, 2017). Furthermore, Lindemann et al. (2019) emphasizes that automated monitoring of health values could also lead to a loss of importance of the practical experience of nursing staff.

The results so far prove the topicality and the need for an adjustment of the dehydration management in outpatient and inpatient sector, since on the one hand there were no indications of an acute dehydration problem in institutions surveyed, but on the other hand there was a problem with regard to the interface between inpatient institutions and hospitals.

Our result is only a first spotlight to multiple perspectives of organizational complexity corresponding with a sensor-based technology. From the individual perspective of care-givers we have to sum up some concerns about the risk of losing competence within the care-giving process, because the actual competence that the nurse formerly possessed (assessment of the patient's dehydration state) can no longer be adequately assessed if the technology fails. Furthermore, the SeLe system may also have some potential for a better effectiveness and efficiency that helps to recalibrate the organizational workflow and the staffing of nurses.

Here, the relation between automation and staffing has to be discussed in a more detailed manner. Referring to recent literature on efficiency measurements in implementing technology in nursing frameworks we can infer potential substitutive or complementary effects on the nursing care-mix the technology can induce (Lu et. al., 2019). Finally, the expected time gains for nurses in consequence of a monitored-based Sele System have to be evaluated by more detailed studies. Those should encompass different patient categories, different skill and grade mixes and a more detailed view on reimbursement as well organizational implementation factors.

References

Al-Razouki, M. (2018). Who will pay for digital health? The investor point of view, In Rivas, H., Wac, E. (Eds.). *Digital health. Scaling healthcare to the world* (pp. 289–328). Springer.

Benner, P. (2017). *Stufen zur Pflegekompetenz. From Novice to Expert* (3., unv. Aufl.). Bern: Hogrefe.

Berliner Bündnis für Altenpflege. (2016). Pflege 4.0. Verändern Digitalisierung und intelligente Technik die Dienstleistung Pflege? Tagungsband des Berliner Bündnisses für Altenpflege am 25. Mai 2016, Berlin. S. 6.

Craig, P., Cieppe, P., Macintyre, S. et. al. (2008). Developing and evaluating complex interventions: the new Medical Research Council guidance. *BMJ, 337*, 319–340 (2000). https://doi.org/10.1136/bjj.a1655

Deutsches Netzwerk für Qualitätsentwicklung in der Pflege. (2017). Expertenstandard Ernährungsmanagement zur Sicherstellung und Förderung der oralen Ernährung in der Pflege. *Schriftenreihe des Deutschen Netzwerks für Qualitätsentwicklung in der Pflege*. Osnabrück.

Davis, F. D. (1989). Perceived usefulness, perceived ease of use, and user acceptance of information technology. *MIS Quarterly, 13*, 319–340.

Duttweiler, S., et al. (Eds.). (2016). *Leben nach Zahlen* (p. 205). Self-Tracking als Optimierungsprojekt.

EU Datenschutzgrundverordnung. (2018). Inhalte der EU Datenschutzgrundverordnung (EU-DSGVO). https://www.datenschutz-grundverordnung.eu. Accessed: 25 June 2019.

Hagen, H., Nitschke, M., Schlindwein, D., & Goll, S. (2018). Akzeptanz als Problem, Partizipation als Lösung? Zu Prämissen und Bias in der partizipativen Forschung. In R. Weidner, A. Karafillidis (Hg.), Dritte Transdisziplinäre Konferenz „Technische Unterstützungssysteme, die die Menschen wirklich wollen (pp. 127–138). Konferenzband 2018. http://www.humanhybridrobot.info/wp-content/uploads/2015/01/TCST-2018-Konferenzband-Technische-Unterstützungssysteme-die-die-Menschen-wirklich-wollen_komprimiert.pdf. Accessed: 7 June 2020.

Health & Care Management. (2015). Die Pflege der Zukunft. http://www.hcm-magazin.de/die-pflege-der-zukunft/150/10739/292423. Accessed: 13 February 2017.

Hooper, L., Abdelhamid, A., Attreed, N. J., Campbell, W. W., Channell, A. M., et al. (2015). Clinical symptoms, signs and tests for identification of impending and current water-loss dehydration in older people. *Cochrane Database of Systematic Reviews*. https://doi.org/10.1002/14651858.CD009647

Jaensch, P., Schneider, M., Heidl, C., Müller, S., & Zerth, J. (2019). Bewertung technischer Innovationen im Gesundheitswesen am Beispiel der Pflege als multiperspektivische Herausforderung: der SIEB-Ansatz. In J. Zerth, J. Schildmann, & E. Nass (Hrsg.), *Versorgung gestalten. Interdisziplinäre Perspektiven für eine personenbezogene Gesundheitsversorgung* (pp. 181–197). Kohlhammer.

Lindemann, G., Fritz-Hoffmann, C., Matzusaki, H., & Barth, J. (2019). Zwischen Technikentwicklung und Techniknutzung: Paradoxien und ihre Handhabung in der ELSI-Forschung. In B. Gransche & A. Manzeschke (Hrsg.), Das geteilte Ganze—Horizonte Integrierter Forschung für künftige Mensch-Technik-Verhältnisse (pp. 133–151). Springer.

Linstone, H. A. (1999). *Decision making for technology executives: Using multiple perspectives to improved performance*. Artech House.

Lu, S., Huaxia, R., & Seidmann, A. (2019). Does technology substitute for nurses? Staffing decisions in nursing homes. *Management Science, 64*(4), 1842–1859.

Manzeschke, A., Weber, K., Rother, E., & Fangerau, H. (2013). Ergebnisse der Studie »Ethische Fragen im Bereich Altersgerechter Assistenzsysteme«. https://www.technik-zum-menschen-bringen.de/service/publikationen/ethische-fragen-im-bereich-altersgerechter-assistenzsysteme. Accessed: 24 June 2019.

National Human Genome Research Institute (NIH). (2012). ELSI Planning and Evaluation History. https://www.genome.gov/10001754/elsi-planning-and-evaluation-history/. Accessed: 26 June 2019.

Pascal, C. (2017). Tapping the full potential of ehealth: Business models need economic assessment frameworks. In L. Menvielle, A.-F. Audrain-Pontevia W. Menvielle (Eds.), The digitalization of healthcare. New challenges and opportunities (pp. 39–58). Palgrave Macmillan.

Schaefer, R. (2017). Diagnostik und Therapie der Dehydratation beim älteren Menschen. *Deutsche Medizinische Wochenschrift, 142*, 481–484.

Schmidt, L., & Wahl, H. W. (2016). Wie verändert Technik das Alter(n) und die Gerontologie. http://econtent.hogrefe.com/doi/abs/https://doi.org/10.1024/2297-5160/a000003.

Sekhon, M., et al. (2017). Acceptability of healthcare interventions: An overview of reviews and development of a theoretical framework. *BMC Health Service Research, 17*, 88.

Thomas, D. R., Tariq, S. H., Makhdomm, S., Haddad, R., & Moinuddin, A. (2003). Physician misdiagnosis of dehydration in older adults. *Journal of the American Medical Directors Association, 4*(5), 251–254.

Wolff, A., Stuckler, D., & McKee, M. (2015). Are patients admitted to hospitals from care homes dehydrated? A retrospective analysis of hypernatraemia and in-hospital mortality. *Journal of the Royal Society of Medicine, 108*(7), 259–265.

Xiao, H., Barber, J., & Campbell, E. S. (2004). Economic burden of dehydration among hospitalized elderly patients. *American Journal of Health-System Pharmacy: AJHP: Official Journal of the American Society of Health-System Pharmacists, 61*(23), 2534–2540.

Zhang, M., & Ho, R. (2017). M-health and smartphone technologies and their impact on patient care and empowerment. In L. Menvielle, A.-F. Audrain-Pontevia, & W. Menvielle, W. (Eds.), The digitalization of healthcare. New challenges and opportunities (pp. 277–291). Palgrave Macmillan.

Zwart, H., Landeweerd, L., & van Rooij, A. (2014). Adapt or perish? Assessing the recent shift in the European research funding arena from 'ELSA' to 'RRI'. *Life Sciences, Society and Policy.* https://link.springer.com/article/https://doi.org/10.1186/s40504-014-0011-x. Accessed: 29 May 2020.